BIOPSYCHOLOGY

Rob McIlveen and
Richard Gross

Hodder & Stoughton

A MEMBER OF THE HODDER HEADLINE GROUP

DEDICATION

To Gill, William, and Katie. R.M.
To Jan, Tanya, and Jo, with my love. R.G.

Order: Please contact Bookpoint Ltd, 39 Milton Park, Abingdon, Oxon OX14 4TD.
Telephone: (44) 01235 400414. Fax: (44) 01235 400454. Lines are open from 9 am - 6 pm
Monday to Saturday, with a 24-hour message answering service.
Email address: orders@bookpoint.co.uk

British Library Cataloguing in Publication Data
McIlveen, Rob
  Biopsychology
  1. Psychobiology
  I.Title   II. Gross, Richard
  152

ISBN 0 340 67379 6

First published 1996
Impression number 10 9 8 7 6 5 4 3 2
Year   2004 2003 2002 2001 2000 1999 1998

Typeset by Wearset, Boldon, Tyne and Wear.
Printed in Great Britain for Hodder & Stoughton Educational, a division of Hodder Headline Plc, 338, Euston Road, London NW1 3BH by Redwood Books, Trowbridge, Wiltshire BA14 8RN.

BIOPSYCHOLOGY

Rob McIlveen and
Richard Gross

CONTENTS

INTRODUCTION   **1**

Part 1: Basic neural and hormonal processes and their influences on behaviour

CHAPTER **1**   THE NERVOUS SYSTEM AND NEURONAL ACTIVITY   **5**

Introduction and overview; glial cells and neurons; the structure of neurons; the function of neurons; neurotransmitters and neuromodulators; conclusions; summary

CHAPTER **2**   THE CENTRAL NERVOUS SYSTEM   **15**

Introduction and overview; the spinal cord; the brain; conclusions; summary

CHAPTER **3**   THE PERIPHERAL NERVOUS SYSTEM AND THE ENDOCRINE SYSTEM   **24**

Introduction and overview; the peripheral nervous system; the endocrine system; conclusions; summary

Part 2: Cortical functions

CHAPTER **4**   SOME METHODS AND TECHNIQUES USED TO INVESTIGATE CORTICAL FUNCTIONS   **33**

Introduction and overview; clinical and anatomical methods; invasive methods; non-invasive methods; conclusions; summary

CHAPTER **5**   THE CEREBRAL CORTEX   **44**

Introduction and overview; the theory of localisation; the primary motor area; the primary sensory areas; association areas in the cortex; association areas not involved in motor or sensory functions; holism as an alternative to localisation; conclusions; summary

CHAPTER **6**   LANGUAGE AND THE BRAIN   **54**

Introduction and overview; cortical areas, language, and language disorders; the relationship between cortical areas and language; language: localisation, lateralisation and holism; conclusions; summary

CHAPTER **7**   ASYMMETRIES IN THE CEREBRAL HEMISPHERES AND THE 'SPLIT-BRAIN'   **61**

Introduction and overview; cerebral asymmetries and the 'split-brain'; cerebral asymmetries and the intact brain; an answer to Fechner's question?; conclusions; summary

CHAPTER **8**   THE NEUROPHYSIOLOGICAL BASIS OF VISUAL PERCEPTION   **70**

Introduction and overview; light; the eye; from the eye to the brain; colour vision; theories of colour vision; colour constancy; conclusions; summary.

Part 3: Awareness

CHAPTER **9**   BODILY RHYTHMS   **82**

Introduction and overview; circadian rhythms; infradian rhythms; ultradian rhythms; diurnal rhythms; circannual rhythms; conclusions; summary

CHAPTER **10**   THE FUNCTIONS OF SLEEP   **93**

Introduction and overview; studies of total sleep deprivation; evolutionary theories of sleep function; restoration theories of sleep function; studies of REM sleep deprivation; restoration theories of REM sleep function; memory consolidation theory of REM sleep function; the sentinel theory of REM sleep function; the oculomotor system maintenance theory; the physiology of sleep; conclusions; summary

CHAPTER **11**   THE FUNCTIONS OF DREAMING   **103**

Introduction and overview; dreams: some basic research findings; Sigmund Freud's theory of dream function; a 'problem-solving' theory of dreaming; 'reprogramming' theories of dreaming; Hobson and McCarley's 'activation synthesis' theory of dreams; Crick and Mitchison's 'reverse learning' theory of dreams; conclusions; summary

CHAPTER **12**   HYPNOSIS AND HYPNOTIC PHENOMENA   **111**

Introduction and overview; a brief history of hypnosis; inducing a hypnotic state; characteristics of the hypnotic state; individual differences in hypnotic susceptibility; the genuineness of hypnosis; a 'state' or 'special processes' theory of hypnosis; a 'non-state' theory of hypnosis; some practical applications of hypnotic phenomena; hypnosis and behaviour control; conclusions; summary

CHAPTER **13**   SOME DRUGS AND THEIR EFFECTS ON BEHAVIOUR   **120**

Introduction and overview; tolerance, dependence, addiction and withdrawal; types of psychoactive drug; the depressants; the stimulants; the opiates; the hallucinogens; cannabis; conclusions; summary

Part 4: Motivation, emotion and stress

CHAPTER **14**   MOTIVATION AND THE BRAIN   **131**

Introduction and overview; hunger; external stimuli for hunger; the hypothalamus and eating; drinking; the hypothalamus and drinking; primary and secondary drinking; conclusions; summary

Contents

CHAPTER **15** THEORIES OF MOTIVATION   **140**

Introduction and overview; types of motive; instinct theories of motivation; drive theories of motivation; optimum level of arousal theory of motivation; incentive theory of motivation; opponent-process theory of motivation; Maslow's theory of motivation; Freud's theory of motivation; conclusions; summary

CHAPTER **16** EMOTION AND THE BRAIN   **150**

Introduction and overview; the hypothalamus and emotion; the limbic system and emotion; the cerebral hemispheres and emotion; sex differences, emotion, and the hemispheres; conclusions; summary

CHAPTER **17** THEORIES OF EMOTION   **158**

Introduction and overview; the James-Lange theory of emotion; the Cannon-Bard thalamic theory of emotion; Schachter and Singer's theory of emotion; Lazarus' theory of emotion; conclusions; summary

CHAPTER **18** STRESS   **169**

Introduction and overview; what is stress?; the effects of stress on the body; stress and illness; reducing stress; conclusions; summary

REFERENCES   **181**

INDEX   **190**

PICTURE CREDITS   **199**

ACKNOWLEDGEMENTS

It is a pleasure to acknowledge the following for their encouragement, support and help in reviewing and commenting on the material contained in this book: Hugh Coolican, Roger Lindsay, and Julie Lord. Any errors that remain in the book are, of course, solely the responsibility of the authors. Thanks too to Tim Gregson-Williams and Julie Hill at Hodder for their continued support throughout the book's production.

INTRODUCTION

Psychologists approach the problem of understanding behaviour and mental processes from a variety of perspectives. Biopsychology, as Green (1994) has observed, is just one of many names given to that area of science which studies the relationship between biology, behaviour, and mental processes. In particular, biopsychologists concentrate on the role played in our behaviour and mental processes by the nervous system (of which the *brain* is a major component).

As both teachers and examiners, we know that biopsychology is one of the least popular areas of the syllabus. At least one reason for this is what one of our colleagues has termed its *latinate nomenclature*. You may have heard the song in which the singer tells us that 'the hip bone's connected to the thigh bone, and the thigh bone's connected to the knee bone'. Whilst probably not singing about it, biopsychologists do talk about the hypothalamus being connected to the pituitary gland by means of the infundibulum. It would take an ingenious composer to get rhythm-and-rhyme out of that, and whilst most of us could hazard a reasonable guess as to where a hip, thigh and knee bone could be found, words like *hypothalamus*, *pituitary gland*, and *infundibulum* offer us very few clues! Indeed, as words go, they are pretty daunting!

In a way, starting the study of biopsychology is a little like finding yourself at a party and trying to follow a conversation between hi-fi enthusiasts whose speech is peppered with 'woofers', 'tweeters', 'slave amplifiers' and so on. Moving to another room you might encounter the motor cyclists and their 'twin overhead cam shafts' coupled with 'torque injection'. At the drinks table might be the soccer enthusiasts debating the merits of the '4-4-2 system' as compared with '4-3-3', and how useful a 'sweeper' is in a 'christmas tree formation'.

The fact is that all specialisms have their terminology and biopsychology is no exception. What we think is probably off-putting for students is that biopsychology seems to have much more terminology than other areas of psychology and, because of its relationship with biology, is perceived as being more 'scientific' in some way.

But just as anyone who becomes interested in hi-fi systems gradually comes to use terms like 'woofer' and 'tweeter' with knowledge and confidence, anyone who becomes interested in biopsychology will eventually be able to tell their *arcuate fasciculus* from their *electro-encephalogram* and use the terms appropriately and with confidence.

We have tried to make our coverage both accessible and informative to students new to biopsychology, whether they are studying it at A/AS level, undergraduate level, or as part of some other course. While there will always be different views as to exactly what should be included in a book such as this, we feel that we have opted for those topics which the large majority of readers would expect to find, plus one or two that may be less 'mainstream', such as hypnosis.

The book is divided into four parts which correspond to the titles of the sub-sections identified in the AEB syllabuses, and each of the chapters in the four parts deals with the subject content the syllabuses require students to be familiar with. In the following, we will describe what we intend to cover in each of the book's four parts.

The first part, *Basic neural and hormonal processes and their influences on behaviour*, consists of three chapters which cover the 'nuts and bolts' of biopsychology. We begin Chapter 1 by briefly outlining the way in which the human nervous system is organised and distinguish between the *central* and *peripheral nervous systems*. We continue the chapter by looking at the composition of the nervous system and the two main types of *cell* that can be found within it. Since one of these cells, the *neuron*, is the basic structural unit or 'building block' of the nervous system and is involved in all aspects of our behaviour, we pay particular attention to it. After describing the structure of a typical neuron, we then take an in-depth look at the way in which neurons work, that is, how informaton is transmitted within a single neuron and between different neurons.

As we point out in Chapter 1, the central nervous system consists of the *brain* and *spinal cord*. In Chapter 2, we describe the organisation, structure and functioning of this system and we pay particular attention to the brain (which is of considerably more interest to a biopsychologist than the spinal cord!) We identify a number of brain structures and, on the basis of biopsychological research findings, describe the roles these structures are believed to play.

The peripheral nervous system consists of the nerves that connect the central nervous system with the sense organs, muscles, and glands. In Chapter 3, we describe the two essential functions of the peripheral nervous system. These are the sending of information from the outside world to the central nervous system (which occurs via the sense organs) and the transmission of information from the central nervous system to produce a particular behaviour (which is achieved through the peripheral nerves to our muscles). Chapter 3 also considers the way in which the peripheral nervous system interacts with the *endocrine system,* a system of glands that secrete substances called *hormones* directly into the bloodstream. Although the endocrine system is not technically a part of the nervous system at all, it is the interaction between it and the peripheral nervous system which causes adjustments to our internal physiological processes and influences our behaviour.

The second part of this book is entitled *Cortical functions* and consists of five chapters. The *cerebral cortex* is the surface layer of the brain and is the most recently evolved and important part of it. In Chapter 4, we describe some of the methods and techniques that have been used to investigate cortical functioning, some of the findings that have been obtained, and some of the limitations concerning the interpretation of these findings. We consider the methods and techniques under three separate headings. First, we look at what we term *clinical and anatomical methods.* By this, we mean those methods and techniques that investigate the effects of accidental damage to, or disease of, the brain. Then, we look at what we term *invasive methods,* that is, methods which involve deliberate intervention such as chemically or electrically stimulating the brain or deliberately damaging it.

Invasive methods for purely experimental purposes are conducted exclusively on non-human animals. It has been pointed out to us that we present these methods without making any comment on their *ethical acceptability.* Let us be clear that these methods offend our own sensibilities as much as they are likely to offend

those of perhaps the majority of readers. Limitations of space prevent us from debating the ethics of using non-human animals in the ways we describe and the purposes to which they are put. Perhaps you will see this as a weak defence and, possibly, as no defence at all. Despite our objective presentation of the methods, we can only repeat the serious reservations we have about some types of research involving non-human animals. It is an issue to which we will return in a forthcoming publication, and which we have dealt with in other publications. We finish Chapter 4 by looking at what we term *non-invasive methods,* which we define as those which involve recording cortical activity in ways that do not require deliberate intervention.

We begin Chapter 5 by noting that the cerebral cortex is most developed in human beings and that this is without doubt what separates us from other animals. As well as being the last part of the brain to stop growing and differentiating, it undergoes greater structural change and transformation than any other part of the brain. In the first part of Chapter 5 we take a detailed look at the role played by the cerebral cortex in *motor* and *sensory* aspects of behaviour. After this, we examine other areas of the cortex (so-called *association* areas) which do not seem to be involved in motor or sensory aspects of behaviour, but do play a role in the more complex psychological functions of learning, thinking, memory, and so on. Chapter 5 also introduces the view that psychological functions are *localised* in particular areas of the cortex and the alternative view (termed *holism*) which proposes that psychological functions are controlled by neurons throughout the brain.

The remaining three chapters of this part of the book build on the material covered in Chapter 5. Chapter 6 identifies the parts of the cortex that play a role in the production and comprehension of *language,* and examines the behavioural consequences of damage to those parts. We also use Chapter 6 as the opportunity to further discuss the localisation and holism perspectives that we introduced in Chapter 5.

Although the *cerebral hemispheres* (that is, the two halves of the brain) look to be mirror images of one another, there has been considerable interest in whether they are functionally similar or if each is specialised for particular mental processes and behaviour (a phenomenon known as *lateralisation*). In Chapter 7, we examine the evidence relating to *asymmetries* in the cerebral hemispheres. Much of the data relating to cerebral asymmetries comes from studies of people whose cerebral hemispheres have been surgically divided. As well as being a rich source of data concerning the specialisms of the two hemispheres, such *split-brain studies* also pose interesting philosophical questions concerning the nature of consciousness which we attempt to address at the end of Chapter 7. In addition to split-brain studies, we also consider data relating to hemispheric specialisation obtained from people with intact cerebral hemispheres.

Chapter 8, the final chapter in this part of the book, examines the neurophysiological basis of *visual perception*, that is, the structures and processes involved in visual perception. We begin by briefly looking at *light*, the 'messenger' that tells us about the colour, size, shape, location and texture of objects and surfaces. Then we discuss the *eye*, the organ responsible for vision. The main part of Chapter 8, however, looks at the way in which light information is transformed by the brain and the theories that have been advanced to explain the phenomena of *colour vision* and *colour constancy*.

Part three of this book is entitled *Awareness* and consists of five chapters. The first part of Chapter 9 describes research findings relating to some of the physiological and psychological factors associated with five types of *bodily rhythm*. One of the bodily rhythms we pay particular attention to is the *ultradian rhythm*. The most researched ultradian rhythm is *sleep*, and we spend some time examining what is known about the rhythms that occur during that altered state of consciousness.

In Chapter 10, we continue our examination of sleep and discuss the various theories that have been offered to explain the functions that sleep serves. Much of this research involves depriving animals of sleep and observing the consequences of this deprivation. Chapter 10 describes what such studies have found and how these relate to the various theories that have been proposed. We also briefly consider some of the physiological processes that occur during sleep.

For some researchers, the question of why we sleep has a very simple answer: we sleep because we need to *dream*. If this is the case, then dreaming presumably serves some sort of useful function. We turn our attention to the functions of dreaming in Chapter 11. We begin by outlining some of the basic research findings concerning dreams. After this, we examine some of the theories that have been proposed to explain the function of dreaming. Whilst biopsychological theories are our main concern, we also examine theories from other areas of psychology in order to compare and contrast them.

Chapter 12 considers *hypnosis* which, like dreaming, has long been of interest to both the layperson and professional psychologist. We begin by briefly looking at the history of hypnosis and at some of the now discredited attempts to explain the phenomenon in physiological terms. After describing the induction of a hypnotic 'trance', we consider the major characteristics of hypnosis and some of the theories that have been advanced to explain it. We conclude Chapter 12 by looking at some of the potential practical applications of hypnosis and the issue of hypnosis and behaviour control.

Chapter 13, the final chapter in part three, examines the effects that some types of *drug* have on our behaviour. In a forthcoming publication we will look at the ways in which drugs have been used in the treatment of psychological disorders. In Chapter 13, however, we confine our consideration to some of the drugs which are used to alter consciousness for the purposes of pleasure. Although such drugs might be termed 'recreational', some of the effects they produce hardly constitute most people's idea of having fun. As well as describing the psychological effects produced by these drugs, Chapter 13 also explores what is known about the way in which they influence aspects of our physiology.

The final part of this book is entitled *Motivation, emotion and stress* and consists of four chapters. In Chapter 14, we look at research into the relationship between brain systems and *motivation*, paying particular attention to the role played by the brain in the motivational states of *hunger* and *thirst* (which we make brief reference to in Chapter 2 when we introduce the concept of *homeostasis*). Although we show that there is considerable evidence to suggest that one particular brain structure is strongly implicated in eating and drinking, we also consider the role played by external factors in these behaviours.

In Chapter 15, we look at both physiological and psychological theories of motivation. After describing the various types of motive, we examine theories of motivation in terms of the extent to which they are supported by the evidence. We also explore the similarities and differences between various theories in terms of the ways in which they try to explain motivated behaviour.

Chapter 16 explores the relationship between brain systems and *emotion*. Two brain structures have been of particular interest in connection with the experience and expression of emotion, and in Chapter 16 we examine research findings relating to them. We also consider more recent research which has concentrated on the differences between the cerebral hemispheres with respect to the experience of emotion, and on findings related to sex differences, emotion and the cerebral hemispheres.

In Chapter 17, we look at attempts to explain the sequence of events that occurs when we experience an emotion. We outline several theories of emotion, some of which are primarily physiological in their orientation and some of which acknowledge the role played by cognitive factors. We also discuss the evidence for and against these theories in an attempt to reach a conclusion as to which most adequately explains the experience of emotion.

The final chapter in this book, Chapter 18, investigates *stress*. We look in detail at the theories and research findings concerning the effects of stress on the body, and explore some of the illnesses that have been linked with stress. These include infectious diseases, cancer, cardiovascular disorders, and hypertension. We conclude our consideration of stress by looking at some of the methods by which stress can be reduced.

We hope that this rather lengthy introduction has given you a strong flavour of the material we cover in this book. For each chapter, we offer an *Introduction and overview* in an attempt to identify the main areas the chapter deals with. At the end of each chapter we offer brief *Conclusions* and a detailed *Summary* of the points that have been made. These, we feel, will be particularly helpful to students in terms of allowing them to review particular chapters, and in terms of organising the material for revision purposes.

Although we have not chosen to include a glossary of terms, the *Index* to this book identifies in bold type where in the text a definition of a particular word or phrase can be found.

As writers who are aware of the ever-increasing demands placed on teachers and students, we appreciate that there are bound to be parts of this book that will receive more attention than others. We have tried to write it so that it is possible to 'dip into' particular chapters. If you feel that we can improve on this, please do not hesitate to contact us at the publisher's address.

Rob McIlveen and Richard Gross

PART 1

Basic neural and hormonal processes and their influences on behaviour

THE NERVOUS SYSTEM AND NEURONAL ACTIVITY

Introduction and overview

The nervous system (NS) is the network of all the nerve cells in the human body. The NS enables us to receive, process, and transmit information originating both within and outside the body. The NS is, therefore, our primary communication system. We can divide the NS into two major components, the *central nervous system* (CNS) and the *peripheral nervous system* (PNS). The CNS consists of the neural material in the *brain* and *spinal cord*, and is the point of origin of all complex commands, decisions, and evaluations. In the following chapter we will examine the CNS in detail, paying particular attention to the brain.

The PNS has two functions. First, it sends information *to* the CNS from the outside world, muscles, and organs. Second, it sends messages *from* the CNS to all the muscles and glands of the body. We will look at the PNS in detail in Chapter 3, and will also consider the way in which it interacts with the *endocrine system*, the system that secretes hormones into the body's bloodstream.

The NS is a complicated network of electrical and chemical events. Our first aim in this chapter is to examine the composition of the nervous system and two of the main types of cell that can be found in it.

These are called *glial cells* and *neurons*. Since neurons are the basic structural units or 'building blocks' of the NS, and are involved in all aspects of an organism's behaviour, we shall pay particular attention to them. After describing the *structure* of a typical neuron, we will then look in depth at the way in which neurons work, that is, how they *function* within the NS.

As we will see, the communication of information between neurons is a biochemical process involving substances called *neurotransmitters* and *neuromodulators*. In the final part of this chapter, we will consider the role played by some of these in our behaviour.

Glial cells and neurons

A neuron can be defined as a cell that processes and transmits information. In the human NS there are around 10 to 12 billion neurons (or nerve cells) of which around 80% are found in the *brain*, and in particular the topmost outer layer of the brain which is called the *cerebral cortex* (see Chapter 5). The NS also contains many more smaller cells called *glial cells*. One of the functions of glial cells is to supply nutrients and provide structural support to neurons, thereby directing their growth.

Another function of glial cells is to insulate neurons by

forming *myelin sheath* (see below). Glial cells also remove the debris left over following the death of a cell and provide the brain with a barrier to certain substances from the bloodstream. They do this by attaching themselves to the small blood vessels in the brain. Because glial cells are highly selective in terms of what they allow to pass in or out of blood vessels, the brain is protected from the harmful effects of substances that are sometimes carried in the blood. Recently, it has been suggested that glial cells carry information between the various parts of the nervous system (Cornell-Bell, et al. 1990). However, exactly what information is conveyed is unclear at present.

We can identify three main types of neuron. *Sensory* (or *afferent*) neurons respond directly to external stimuli such as light, sound and touch, and transmit this sensory information to the CNS. *Motor* (or *efferent*) neurons carry messages from the CNS to the muscles and glands of the body. The activities of these two types of neuron are integrated by a third type called *association* (or *connector*) neurons. Any neuron which is not classified as a sensory or motor neuron and which transmits messages to other neurons is called an association neuron. These constitute about 97% of the neurons in the CNS, and the CNS is the only part of the NS in which they are found.

The role played by the different types of neuron can be illustrated by considering the *reflex*. Accidentally touching a hot stove is painful, and our reaction is quick – we withdraw our hand. The change in temperature is detected by sensory neurons which pass this information on to association neurons. These then pass the information to motor neurons which instruct the muscles to remove the hand. This so-called *reflex arc* occurs quickly because of the speed at which information is passed. Some sorts of neural impulse travel very slowly, at around two to three miles per hour. The impulses involved in a reflex action, however, travel at speeds of over 200 miles per hour. As a result, a message will take about $\frac{1}{50}$th of a second to reach the brain from the toe.

The reflex is made even quicker by the fact that its production actually bypasses the brain. Of course, information about painful stimuli does reach the brain, but because it takes longer to arrive there than it does for the reflex arc to be completed, we have withdrawn our hand before we begin to feel pain. In evolutionary terms this is very useful: the hand has been removed before too much damage has been sustained, but the fact that we have experienced some pain enables us to learn that certain stimuli (such as hot stoves) should not be touched in the future.

Suppose, however, that you are carrying a very hot plate using worn-out oven gloves. Given what we have said above, we would expect that the motor neurons controlling the hands would cause us to drop the plate. This does, of course, sometimes happen, but on at least some occasions we are able to carry the plate to a suitable surface before we remove our hands. The way in which we achieve this will be explained on pages 9–10!

We can apply the principle we used to describe a simple reflex to much more complicated behaviours. Consider, for example, the neuronal activity involved in responding correctly to a question you have been asked, about, say neurons. Sensory neurons record the sound waves and the information is interpreted in the part of the brain that deals with auditory information. In order to recall the answer, association neurons associated with memory must be activated. Neurons associated with language must formulate the answer and motor neurons in the tongue and mouth must excite the correct muscle groups to produce your response.

THE STRUCTURE OF NEURONS

Although no two neurons are identical, most share the same basic structure and work in essentially the same way. A typical neuron is shown in Figure 1.1.

The *cell body* (or *cell soma*) houses the nucleus of the cell (with the genetic code) and contains the mechanisms that control the metabolism and maintenance of the cell. Branching out from the cell body are *dendrites*, so called because they resemble tree branches (dendrite is the Greek for 'tree'). These receive information from other neurons and carry that information *towards* the cell body. The *axon* transmits messages *away* from the cell body to other neurons, muscles or gland cells. Axons vary in size. Those that run from the brain to the base of the spinal cord, for example, or from the spinal cord to the tip of the thumb may be as long as three feet. By contrast, axons which are typically found in the cerebral cortex of the brain are often less than $\frac{1}{10000}$th of an inch in length.

Note that a group of axons bundled together is called a *nerve* if it occurs in the PNS and a *tract* if it occurs in the CNS. Humans have 43 pairs of peripheral nerves,

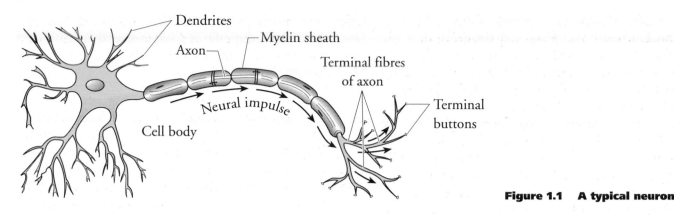

Figure 1.1   A typical neuron

one nerve from each pair on the left side of the body and one on the right. We shall discuss these, which constitute the nerves of the PNS, in Chapter 3.

Some nerves are coated with *myelin sheath*. This is part protein and part fat and consists of the membranes of a type of glial cell called the *Schwann cell*. These expand and wrap repeatedly around the axon. The principal function of myelin sheath is to insulate axons from one another and from electrically charged atoms (or ions) found in the fluids that encase the NS. By insulating axons from one another, myelin sheath helps to prevent neurons from 'scrambling' messages. Myelin sheath also helps the neuron act with greater efficiency, since Schwann cells speed up the rate of information transmission. In some people, the myelin sheath that surrounds the axon breaks down. This produces the condition called *multiple sclerosis* which is characterised by severe disorders of movement and sensory functions, which eventually leads to death.

The myelin sheath surrounding an axon is not continuous, but is segmented such that at the *Nodes of Ranvier* the axon is actually exposed rather than insulated. As we will see below, this also enables information to be transmitted faster than would be the case if the myelin sheath was continuous. At the end of a typical axon are *terminal buttons*. The role played by these is described in detail on page 8.

THE FUNCTION OF NEURONS

Neurons have three major functions. These are receiving messages, responding to those messages, and sending messages. In order to understand these functions, we need to know how information is able to travel *within* a single neuron and how information can be transmitted *between* neurons or from neurons to other cells of the body.

The transmission of information within a neuron

An inactive neuron, that is, one which is not transmitting information, contains positively charged potassium ions and large, negatively charged protein molecules. The fluid that surrounds a neuron, however, is richly concentrated in positively charged sodium ions and negatively charged chloride ions. The cell membrane keeps the positively charged sodium ions out by the action of what are called *sodium-potassium pumps* and the membrane is said to be *impermeable* to sodium ions. However, potassium and chloride ions are allowed to move in and out of the cell membrane fairly freely and the membrane is said to be *semi-permeable* to these ions. The net result of this is that when it is inactive (or in its *resting state*) the neuron is *polarised* and the inside of the cell is negatively charged relative to the outside by about 70 millivolts (70 thousandths of a volt).

When a neuron is activated by a stimulus, the sodium channels open for about one millisecond and the neuron becomes *permeable* to sodium ions which flood into it. This causes the neuron to become *depolarised* and the charge inside it momentarily changes from its resting state value of −70 millivolts to an active state of about +40 millivolts. This is called the *action potential* and it has a value of 110 millivolts (that is, the difference between −70 and +40 millivolts). A chain reaction is then set off in which the sodium channels open at adjacent sites all the way down the axon. However, almost as soon as these channels open they close again, and potassium channels open instead. This allows potassium to move *out* through the membrane and restores the resting state potential of −70 millivolts.

The sequence of events described above applies to neurons that are *unmyelinated*. As we saw earlier, however, with myelinated neurons the sheath surrounding the axon is segmented with uninsulated Nodes of Ranvier. What happens with myelinated neurons is that the electrochemical action potential 'jumps' from one node to another. This process is called *saltatory conduction* (saltatory means 'leaping'), and allows information to be conducted faster than if the myelin sheath was continuous or if the fibre was unmyelinated. The speed of an impulse, then, is in part determined by the presence or absence of myelin sheath. It is also determined by the diameter of an axon. Impulses travel faster down thick axons than down thin axons.

In order to cause a response in a neuron, a stimulus must be of a certain intensity. A stimulus which is not strong enough might cause a shift in the electrical charge in a small area of the neuron, a phenomenon known as a *graded potential*. After a very brief time, the neuron will return to its normal resting state. However, when a stimulus is sufficiently strong to exceed the neuron's *threshold of response*, an action potential will occur. The sequence of events occurring in the 'firing' of a neuron is shown in Figure 1.2.

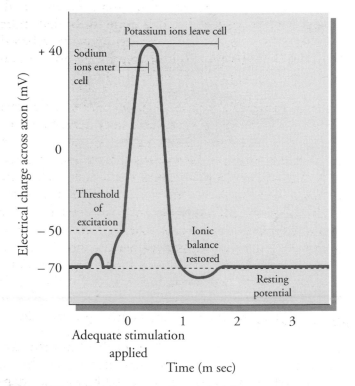

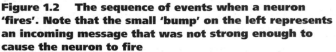

Figure 1.2   The sequence of events when a neuron 'fires'. Note that the small 'bump' on the left represents an incoming message that was not strong enough to cause the neuron to fire

Neurons either 'fire' or do not 'fire' in response to a

stimulus. This is known as the *all-or-none rule*. A useful way to think of the rule is to compare the firing of a neuron with the firing of a gun. If the trigger is pulled the gun either fires or does not fire; there is no middle ground. Thus, it doesn't matter how strong a stimulus is, it will either cause a neuron to fire (if the stimulus is above the threshold of response) or it will not (if it is below the threshold of response). However, we should note that the stronger a stimulus is, the more *often* a neuron will fire, and a very strong stimulus will produce a volley of responses from the neuron.

There is always a brief period of around one or two milliseconds during which a neuron that has just 'fired' will not 'fire' again irrespective of the size of the stimulus. This is known as the *absolute refractory period* (ARP). After the ARP there is another brief period of a few milliseconds called the *relative refractory period* (RRP). The RRP is a 'time of recovery' for the neuron during which sodium is prevented from passing through the neuronal membrane. A neuron will fire during the RRP, but only if the stimulus applied to it is considerably stronger than the threshold of response. Some neurons are capable of firing as many as 1,000 times a second whereas others can only fire a few times a second.

The transmission of information between neurons

The way in which neurons communicate between one another can be explained by looking at what happens to the action potential once it has passed down the axon. For a small number of neurons, the axon transmits information *directly* to the cell body of another neuron. However, for most neurons an action potential's journey along the axon is ended by its arrival at a terminal button. These house a number of tiny sacs which are called *synaptic vesicles*. Synaptic vesicles contain between 10 and 100,000 molecules of a chemical messenger called a *neurotransmitter*.

Terminal buttons approach, but do not touch, the other cells of the body (that is, other neurons, muscles or glands). The electrochemical message sent down the axon stimulates the synaptic vesicles to discharge their neurotransmitters into the $\frac{1}{25000}$th of an inch gap between the terminal button and the dendrite of a receiving neuron. The gap between the two is called the *synaptic cleft* or *synapse* (from the Greek meaning 'point of contact'). For the Spanish neuroanatomist Santiago Ramon y Cajal (1832–1934), the synapse was one of

8

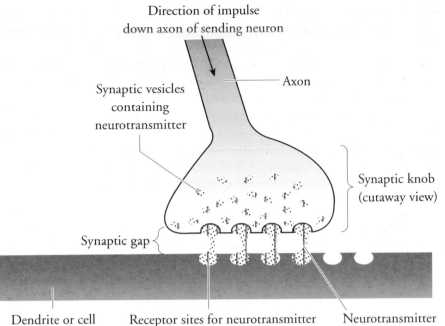

Direction of impulse
down axon of sending neuron

Axon

Synaptic vesicles
containing
neurotransmitter

Synaptic knob
(cutaway view)

Synaptic gap

Dendrite or cell
body of receiving neuron

Receptor sites for neurotransmitter
coming across synaptic gap

Neurotransmitter
crossing synaptic gap

**Figure 1.3   The processes involved
in synaptic transmission**

nature's marvels which he called the 'protoplasmic kiss'.

The end of the terminal button releasing the neuro-transmitter molecules is called the *pre-synaptic mem-brane*, whereas the dendrite of the neuron which receives the molecules is called the *post-synaptic mem-brane*. The post-synaptic membrane contains special *receptor sites* made of complex protein molecules. The receptor sites act as 'locks' and are precisely tailored to match the shape of the neurotransmitter molecules which act as 'keys'. This is shown in Figure 1.3 above.

It takes a neurotransmitter molecule a mere $\frac{1}{10000}$th of a second to make the trip from the pre- to the post-synaptic membrane. In an ingenious study, Heuser and his colleagues (1979) literally 'froze' this process in action. The researchers stimulated neurons from a frog's leg by means of a small electric current. The neu-rons were then dropped against a super-cooled block of copper. This 'froze' the biochemical reactions taking place and with the aid of an electron microscope Heuser and his colleagues were able to observe the pre- to post-synaptic membrane journey of neurotransmit-ter molecules.

Several dozen neurotransmitters have been identified. According to Iversen (1979), neurotransmitters are not randomly distributed throughout the brain but are located in specific groups of neurons. Lloyd, et al. (1984) have suggested that it is quite likely that more than one kind of neurotransmitter may be released from the same terminal button depending on the *pat-tern* of the action potential which reaches it.

Neurotransmitters have an *excitatory* and/or *inhibitory* effect on a receiving neuron. Excitatory neurotransmit-ters cause a 'local breakdown' in the cell membrane of the receiving neuron. This allows sodium ions to flood in and potassium ions to flood out which makes the receiving neuron more positively charged and more likely to 'fire'. Inhibitory neurotransmitters have the opposite effect with the result that the receiving neuron becomes even more negatively charged and much less likely to 'fire'. The excitatory or inhibitory effects of a neurotransmitter depend on how much of it there is. If no more of a neurotransmitter crosses the synaptic cleft, its effects on the receiving neuron quickly fade.

Each neuron may have hundreds of dendrites and ter-minal buttons. As a result, a single neuron can be 'in touch' with many other neurons at both its input (den-dritic) end and its output (terminal button) end. Indeed, it has been estimated that if one million neu-rons were connected two at a time in every possible way, the number of possible combinations would be 10 to the power of 2,783,000! Some of the neurons that form synapses with a receiving neuron will be excitatory and some inhibitory. The 'decision' to 'fire' or not depends on the *combined* effects of all the neurons with which a receiving neuron forms synapses.

If the number of excitatory neurons is the same as the number of inhibitory neurons, they cancel each other out and the neuron does not fire. If enough excitatory synapses are active, their combined effect may be sufficient to exceed the threshold of response, a process called *summation*. Inhibitory synapses are important because they help to control the spread of excitation through the highly interconnected NS. This keeps activity channelled in appropriate networks of 'circuits'. It is believed, for example, that epileptic seizures might be caused by the excitation of many different brain circuits at the same time. The process of inhibition may actually prevent all of us from having seizures much of the time. As another (more mundane) example, consider the action of flexing the arm. This could not be achieved if the neurons controlling the triceps were inhibited and those controlling the biceps excited.

Although many neurons communicate exclusively with other neurons, some, as we noted earlier on in this chapter, form synapses with glands and muscles. All of the muscle fibres with which a motor neuron forms synapses, for example, contract with a brief twitch when an axon transmits a message. The strength of a muscular contraction therefore depends on the number of motor neurons whose action potentials are causing the release of neurotransmitters. Of course, whether a muscle contracts or not, or glandular activity is initiated or inhibited, depends on what neurotransmitters are released.

Excitation and inhibition allow us to explain why we are able to carry a very hot plate to a convenient surface rather than reflexively dropping it (see page 6). Hot objects increase the activity of excitatory neurotransmitters that communicate with motor neurons controlling the muscles of the hands. However, this excitation is counteracted by neurons in the brain which release inhibitory neurotransmitters. The activity of the inhibitory neurons is greater than that of the excitatory neurons with the result that the brain prevents the withdrawal reflex from occurring and hence we do not drop the plate.

The effect of a neurotransmitter is brought to an end either by *de-activation*, in which it is destroyed by special enzymes, or by *re-uptake*. Re-uptake, which is by far the more common process of the two, occurs very quickly and neurotransmitters have only a very brief time in which to stimulate the post-synaptic receptor sites. The rate at which the terminal button takes back the neurotransmitter determines how long its effects will last for. As we will see in Chapter 13, psychoactive drugs affect the nervous system by altering the rate of neurotransmitter re-uptake. If a drug inhibits the process of re-uptake then the neurotransmitter remains in the synaptic cleft for a longer period of time and continues to stimulate the post-synaptic receptor sites. The inhibition of re-uptake, then, *increases* the effect of the neurotransmitter.

Neurotransmitters and neuromodulators

Earlier on we noted that several dozen neurotransmitters have been identified. The vast majority of these play an important role in the communication between neurons in the brain. Neurotransmitters are not, however, found exclusively in the brain. Some, for example, can be found in the spinal cord, the peripheral nerves and certain glands.

One neurotransmitter that has been extensively investigated is *Acetylcholine* (ACh). This neurotransmitter is excitatory at synapses between nerves and muscles that control voluntary movement and inhibitory at the heart and other locations. ACh occurs at every junction between a motor neuron and a muscle. When it is released to muscle cells, the muscle contracts.

Curare, a poison used in hunting by South American Indians, prevents ACh from lodging in receptor sites. The result of this is paralysis, and since the victim cannot contract the muscles used in breathing, death occurs from suffocation. Certain nerve gases and insecticides also affect ACh and cause fatal muscular paralysis. They achieve this by destroying the enzyme *Acetylcholinesterase* (AChE) which ordinarily deactivates ACh. As a result of ACh build-up, further synaptic transmissions are prevented. The *Botulinum toxin*, a poison present in improperly canned food, blocks the release of ACh. Less than one millionth of a gram can paralyse and kill a human. By contrast, the venom of the Black Widow spider causes large amounts of ACh to be released, which induces violent muscle contractions in the victim.

ACh is particularly concentrated in a part of the brain called the *hippocampus* (see Chapter 2), a brain structure which plays a role in memory. ACh has been implicated in *Alzheimer's disease*, which is characterised by a gradual impairment in memory and other cognitive functions. It seems that in Alzheimer's disease there is a progressive deterioration of ACh-producing neurons. According to Bartus, et al. (1982) drugs that increase the amount of brain ACh (such as *Choline*, a chemical found in our diet) facilitate learning and memory. Drugs that block the post-synaptic ACh receptors, however, and prevent ACh from having any action, appear to disrupt learning and memory.

Dopamine is primarily an inhibitory neurotransmitter and is involved in voluntary movements, learning, memory and arousal. Deficiencies have been linked to *Parkinson's disease*, a disorder in which the sufferer progressively loses muscle control and which is characterised by muscle tremors and jerky, uncoordinated movements. It would seem that in Parkinson's disease, dopamine-producing neurons degenerate. Parkinson's disease cannot be treated using dopamine itself since the molecule is incapable of crossing the bloodstream-brain barrier. However, its progress can be slowed by the drug *L-Dopa* which is converted to Dopamine by the brain.

Dopamine has also been linked to the psychological disorder *schizophrenia*. It has been suggested that schizophrenics have more receptor sites for dopamine in an area of the brain involved in emotion and thought. Quite possibly, dopamine is over-utilised in the schizophrenic brain and it is this which causes the characteristic symptoms of hallucinations, thought disorder and emotional disturbances. Interestingly, the *phenothiazines* (a group of drugs used to treat schizophrenia) are believed to block the action of dopamine by locking it out of the receptor sites it tries to occupy (Snyder, 1984).

Serotonin is primarily an inhibitory neurotransmitter that seems to play a role in emotional arousal and sleep (see Chapter 10). Deficiencies have been linked to anxiety, mood disorders, and insomnia. Elevated levels have also been linked to disturbances in mood and other psychological disorders such as childhood autism. Exactly what role serotonin plays, and whether it acts independently or with other neurotransmitters, is not yet clear.

Norepinephrine (or *noradrenaline*) is produced mainly by neurons in the brain stem. It acts as both a neurotransmitter and a *hormone* (see Chapter 3). Norepinephrine speeds up heart rate and other bodily processes involved in general arousal. It has also been implicated in learning, memory, and the stimulation of eating. Both excesses and deficiencies of norepinephrine have been linked to mood disorders. The drug *Reserpine*, which reduces the amount of norepinephrine by preventing it from being stored in vesicles, has a potent tranquillising effect. *Amphetamine* (see Chapter 13), by contrast, increases the amount of norepinephrine that is released and has a stimulating effect.

The most common inhibitory neurotransmitter in the NS is *Gamma-Amino-Butyric Acid* (*GABA*). Although it is found in all parts of the NS, it is particularly concentrated in the brain, where it can be found in up to one third of the terminal buttons. GABA plays a role in motor behaviour and in the inherited disease *Huntingdon's Chorea* in which involuntary movements are accompanied by a progressive deterioration in cognitive functions. Quite possibly, Huntingdon's Chorea is caused by the degeneration of GABA-producing neurons in the part of the brain involved in motor control. GABA may also be involved in the modulation of *anxiety*, since drugs which are used to relieve anxiety (such as *Valium*) increase the activity of GABA (Tallman & Gallagher, 1985).

The term *neuromodulator* has been used to describe any chemical substance which 'primes' neurons so that they will respond by either increasing or decreasing the action of specific neurotransmitters. The most intensely researched of these are known as *endogenous opioid peptides* or *endorphins*. Pert & Snyder's (1973) discovery of these occurred during research into the effects of the pain-killing chemical *morphine* (see Chapter 13). The research findings suggested that morphine exerted its effects by binding to certain receptor sites in the brain. Pert and Snyder reasoned that it was unlikely that the brain had evolved specific receptor sites to accommodate molecules from the opium poppy (where morphine comes from). They believed that the body must produce its own internal (or endogenous) morphine-like substance, hence the term endorphins.

Endorphins are inhibitory and once they have locked into a receptor site, neurotransmitters are prevented from occupying the same receptor site. Like morphine, endorphins relieve pain. One of them, *B-endorphin*, has been found to be 48 times more potent than morphine when injected into the brain, and three times more potent when injected into the bloodstream. Another, *encephalin*, inhibits receptors in the spinal cord and neurons that transmit pain messages. However, whilst encephalin shares the pain-relieving effect of other endorphins, it is somewhat weaker and shorter-acting.

It has been suggested that the release of endorphins occurs as a response to painful stimuli. Endorphin levels have, for example, been shown to increase during pregnancy and further increase during labour (Cahill & Akil, 1982). As well as their pain-relieving role, endorphins have also been suggested to play a role in hunger, sexual behaviour, mood regulation, and body temperature.

Endorphins may also explain the *placebo effect*. It has long been known that inactive substances can relieve pain if a person is led to believe that a pain-relieving drug has been taken. In one investigation, Levine, Gordon & Fields (1979) studied dental patients shortly after they had been a given a placebo and undergone oral surgery. The patients were then given a chemical called *naloxone* which is an opium antagonist, that is, it blocks the pain-relieving effects of morphine. The results showed that naloxone increased the reported pain of those who had responded to the placebo,

suggesting that the placebo had somehow caused the brain to release endorphins and the naloxone had reversed their effect.

The role of neurotransmitters, the endorphins and other neuromodulators, such as the *prostoglandins*, is currently the subject of much research. However, the recent finding that endorphins are sometimes found in the same neurons as other neurotransmitters has complicated our understanding of the way in which neurotransmitters work. We still have a long way to go towards understanding the relationship between neurotransmitters, neuromodulators, mental processes and behaviour.

Conclusions

In this chapter we have looked in some detail at basic neural processes. We now know something about the structure of the neuron and the way in which it transmits and receives information to and from a variety of sources. We have also looked at the some of the chemical substances involved in the transmission and reception of information, and the ways in which they affect our behaviour.

SUMMARY

- The nervous system (NS) is our primary communication system, enabling us to receive, process, and transmit information arising from both within and outside the body.
- The NS is divided into the **central nervous system** (CNS), comprising the brain and spinal cord, and the **peripheral nervous system** (PNS). The PNS sends information to the CNS from the outside world, muscles, and organs, and sends messages from the CNS to all the body's muscles and glands; it also interacts with the **endocrine system**.
- The human NS consist of 10–12 billion **neurons** (or nerve cells), which are the 'building blocks' of the NS, 80% of which are found in the brain, concentrated mainly in the **cerebral cortex**.
- **Glial cells** supply nutrients to the neurons, direct-

ing their growth, and insulating them by forming **myelin sheaths**. They also clean up the remains of dead cells and protect the brain from potentially harmful substances in the bloodstream.
- **Sensory** (or **afferent**) **neurons** respond directly to external stimuli, such as light and sound, **motor** (or **efferent**) **neurons** carry messages from the CNS to the muscles and glands, and **association** (or **connector**) **neurons**, which are only found in the CNS, integrate the activities of the first two.
- In a **reflex arc**, information about the stimulus is passed quickly (about 200 mph) from sensory neurons, to association neurons, and then to motor neurons, which instruct the muscles to act; the brain is by-passed, which speeds up the process and prevents excessive harm being done.

- The same principle can be applied to more complex behaviour, such as answering a verbal question; here, various sensory, association, and motor neurons in the brain involved with hearing, memory, and language, are activated.
- All neurons share the same basic structure. This includes the **cell body** (or **soma**), which contains the nucleus, **dendrites**, which branch out from the cell body and receive information from other neurons, and the **axon**, which carries information to other neurons, muscles, or glands. Axons can vary considerably in length. Bundles of axons in the PNS are called **nerves**, while in the CNS they are called **tracts**.
- **Myelin sheaths** are made from **Schwann cells** (a type of glial cell), which insulate axons from each other and from ions in the surrounding fluid. This speeds up the process of information transmission, increasing efficiency of the neuron. Multiple sclerosis involves breakdown of the myelin sheaths.
- The myelin sheath is segmented, with the axon exposed at the **Nodes of Ranvier**; this speeds up the transmission of information.
- An inactive neuron (in its **resting state)** contains positively charged potassium ions and negatively charged protein molecules. The fluid surrounding the neuron has many positively charged sodium ions and negatively charged chloride ions. The sodium ions are kept out of the neuron (making it **impermeable**) by **sodium-potassium pumps**; but it is **semi-permeable** to potassium and chloride. The inactive neuron is **polarised**.
- When an (unmyelinated) neuron is activated by a stimulus, it becomes **permeable** to sodium ions, which flood into it, i.e. it becomes **depolarised**. The charge inside changes from -70 millivolts to 40 millivolts (the **action potential**) all the way down the axon, but the resting state is restored almost immediately.
- In myelinated neurons, the action potential travels down the axon by **saltatory conduction**, jumping from one node to another.
- An action potential will only occur if the stimulus exceeds the neuron's **threshold of response**. Neurons either fire or don't (the **all-or-none rule**); the stronger the stimulus, the more **often** a neuron will fire.
- For about 1–2 milliseconds after firing, a neuron will not fire again (the **absolute refractory period**); this is followed by the **relative refractory period**, during which the neuron may fire again depending on the strength of the stimulus.
- For most neurons, the action potential travels to a terminal button, which contains **synaptic vesicles**, which contain **neurotransmitters** ('keys'). These are released from the **pre-synaptic membrane** into the **synaptic cleft/synapse** and are received by the **post-synaptic membrane**, which contains special **receptor sites** ('locks').
- There are several dozen neurotransmitters, located in specific groups of neurons. They have an **excitatory** and/or **inhibitory** effect on the receiving neuron, making it more or less likely to fire respectively.
- A single neuron can have contact with large numbers of other neurons, some of which will be excitatory, some inhibitory. If there is an equal number of both kinds, the neuron will not fire, but if enough excitatory synapses are active, their combined effect (**summation**) may be sufficient to exceed the threshold of response.
- Inhibitory synapses help to control the spread of excitation through the NS (as in epileptic seizures), channelling activity in appropriate circuits.
- The effect of a neurotransmitter is ended either by **de-activation** or, more commonly, by **re-uptake**. Psychoactive drugs affect the NS by changing the rate of re-uptake; inhibition of re-uptake **prolongs** the effect of the neurotransmitter.
- **Acetylcholine** (ACh) is excitatory at synapses between nerves and muscles that control voluntary movement, but inhibitory at the heart and elsewhere. Curare, nerve gases, and insecticides produce paralysis by destroying **acetylcholinesterase**, which normally deactivates ACh.
- ACh is concentrated in the hippocampus and Alzheimer's disease may involve a progressive deterioration of ACh-producing neurons. Drugs that increase the amount of brain ACh facilitate learning and memory.
- **Dopamine** is primarily an inhibitory neurotransmitter involved in voluntary movements, learning, memory, and arousal. Parkinson's disease seems to involve a degeneration of dopamine-producing neurons. **L-Dopa** is converted to dopamine by the brain. Patients suffering from schizophrenia may have an excess of receptor sites for dopamine; the phenothiazines block the action of dopamine.
- **Serotonin** is primarily inhibitory and is involved in emotional arousal and sleep. **Norepinephrine/noradrenaline** acts as both a neurotransmitter and a **hormone**; it speeds up the heart and other bodily processes involved in arousal. Amphetamines increase release of norepinephrine and have a stimulating effect.

- **Gamma-Amino-Butyric Acid** (GABA) is concentrated in the brain and is the most common inhibitor in the NS. Degeneration of GABA-producing neurons involved in motor control may be the cause of Huntingdon's Chorea.
- **Neuromodulators** prepare neurons to respond to the action of specific neurotransmitters. The most intensely researched neuromodulators are **endogenous opioid peptides** (or **endorphins**), the body's own internal, morphine-like, painkillers. Endorphin levels increase in response to painful stimuli and are probably involved in the **placebo effect**.

THE CENTRAL NERVOUS SYSTEM

Introduction and overview

As we noted in Chapter 1, the central nervous system consists of two major parts, the brain and the spinal cord, whose primary function is to integrate and coordinate all body functions and behaviour. Knowledge of the existence of a relationship between the brain and behaviour is not new. In a surgical guide written 3,000 years before the birth of Christ, an Egyptian physician described a patient who had fractured his skull and later displayed difficulty in walking. However, it is only in the last 100 years or so that our knowledge about the brain has advanced significantly.

Our aim in this chapter is to look at the organisation, structure and functioning of the central nervous system. We will begin by looking briefly at the spinal cord but will devote the majority of this chapter to describing what is known about the brain.

The spinal cord

The spinal cord is a thick column of nerve fibres that emerges from the bottom of the brain and runs down the whole length of the back. It is encased by the *spinal vertebrae*, bony structures which protect the spinal cord from injury. There is no precise point at which the spinal cord ends and the brain begins. As we will see, the spinal cord widens as it enters the skull and becomes the brain stem.

The spinal cord acts as the main 'communication cable' between the central and peripheral nervous systems (see Chapter 3). Messages from neurons enter and leave the spinal cord by means of 31 pairs of *spinal nerves*, each pair of which innervates a different and fairly specific part of the body. For the most part, these nerve fibres contain both sensory neurons (in order to transmit information to the brain) and motor neurons (in order to convey the brain's response to the muscles and glands). At the junction with the spinal cord itself, however, the nerves divide into two *roots*. The *dorsal root*, which is towards the back of the body, contains sensory neurons, whereas the *ventral root*, which is towards the front of the body, contains motor neurons.

Although the spinal cord is not as interesting as the brain, at least from a psychological perspective, its importance to our normal functioning cannot be underestimated. If the spinal cord is severed, paralysis occurs. The further up the spinal cord the damage occurs the more extensive is the paralysis. The spinal cord also plays a key role in certain reflex actions (see Chapter 1). *Spinal reflexes* do not involve the brain and are mainly protective in that they enable the body to avoid serious damage and maintain muscle tone and posture. Some spinal reflexes involve only sensory and motor neurons. Most, however, are more complex than this. The example we used in Chapter 1 of touching a hot stove involves association neurons as well as sensory and motor neurons. Figure 2.1 overleaf illustrates the spinal cord and spinal nerves.

The brain

THE DEVELOPMENT OF THE BRAIN

There are two main ways in which we could 'divide' up the brain in order to examine its structures. Some researchers prefer to adopt the *triune model* of the brain advanced by the neurophysiologist Paul MacLean (1973, 1982). As its name suggests, the triune model identifies three main parts. The *central core* is the oldest part of the brain. MacLean has called it the *reptilian brain* because the structures it contains in humans are virtually identical to the structures found in the brains of existing reptiles. The *limbic system* is more recent than the central core, and developed in early mammals about 100 million years ago. MacLean refers to it as the *old mammalian brain*. The third component of MacLean's triune model is the most recently evolved. The *cerebral cortex* developed in the last 2 million years, but only in some mammals. For that reason, MacLean terms it the *new mammalian brain*.

A second way of 'dividing' up the brain is to base the division on what happens during the foetal stage of life. In this stage, the structure of the nervous system

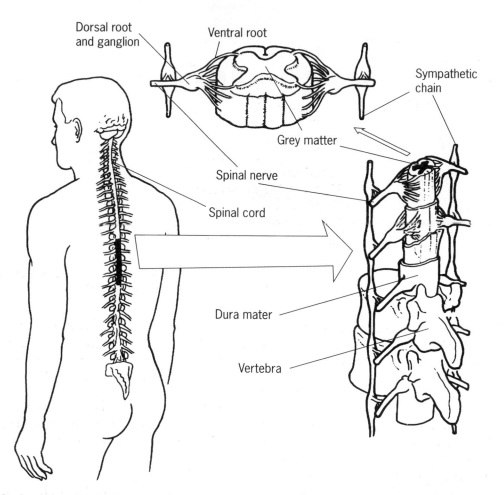

Figure 2.1   The spinal cord and spinal nerves. (From Rosenzweig and Leiman, 1989). The left diagram shows a general view of the spinal column with a pair of nerves emerging from each level. The right diagram shows how the spinal cord is surrounded by bony vertebra and enclosed in a membrane, the dura mater. Each vertebra has an opening on each side through which the spinal nerves pass. The top diagram shows the location of the spinal cord grey matter and the white matter that surrounds it. In the grey matter are interneurons and the motorneurons that send axons to the muscles. The white matter consists of myelinated axons that run up and down the spinal column.

emerges from a single tube of neural tissue (the *neural tube*). The lower part of the neural tube will become the spinal cord. As the foetus develops, the lower part also puts out 'streaks' of neural tissue which will eventually become the *peripheral nervous system* (see Chapter 3). The top of the tube swells into an enlargement that will become the brain. Growth occurs quickly, and in the developing foetus it is possible for us to identify three separate sections, although we should note that in the adult brain these sections are not so easy to distinguish. The lowest section of the upper end of the neural tube is called the *hindbrain*. The second, immediately above it, is the *midbrain*. The section at the very top of the neural tube is the *forebrain*.

In this chapter, we will use the second way of 'dividing' up the brain as the basis for our consideration of its

structures. All of the structures we will shortly be describing are present at birth, but they require time to develop fully. Figure 2.2 opposite shows the human brain at four stages of development.

At birth, the brain has almost all of its full complement of neurons and is closer at birth to its adult size than any other organ. Neurons continue to grow after birth and grow in terms of size and complexity rather than number. At six months, the development of synaptic connections between neurons, coupled with the development of the glial cells and myelin sheath we described in Chapter 1, results in the brain already being half its eventual adult weight. At one year, the brain is about 60% of its eventual adult weight and by the age of ten this figure has risen to 95%. The brain reaches its maximum weight (between 1200 and 1500

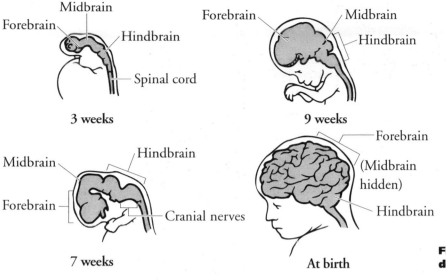

3 weeks

9 weeks

7 weeks

At birth

Figure 2.2   The brain at four stages of development

grams) by the age of 20. Once it is fully grown, it loses weight by about one gram per year. This is the result of its neurons dying without being replaced.

It is not the size of the human brain that is its most remarkable feature, since there are many animals which have brains both larger and heavier than our own. What is remarkable is the vast complexity of interconnections between neurons in the brain. As we saw in Chapter 1, the number of possible ways in which neurons can be interconnected is, literally, astronomical, since the potential number of interconnections is larger than the number of atoms in the universe!

The human brain is extremely soft and fragile. It is encased by three different sets of membranes called *meninges*. The outer one is thick and unstretchable whereas the two inner ones are thinner and more fragile. Between the two inner meninges is *cerebrospinal fluid* (CSF). This is similar to blood plasma, the clear liquid that remains when white and red blood cells are removed from the blood. CSF is produced continuously by specialised blood vessels in the *ventricles* or hollow chambers of the brain. As a result of CSF flowing out of the ventricles and into the meninges, the brain is provided with a 'liquid cushion' in which it floats instead of resting against the skull. Without CSF, the brain would be bruised and injured by any movement of the head.

Essentially, the brain has three main functions. These are to take in information from the senses, to interpret this information, and to act on it. In the remainder of this chapter, and in part two of this book, we will examine how these functions are achieved and the structures that are involved in achieving them. We will begin with the hindbrain, continue with the midbrain, and conclude with the forebrain.

Figure 2.3 overleaf shows a front-to-back cross section of the brain and identifies the principal structures we will talk about in this chapter.

The hindbrain

Three structures constitute the hindbrain. These are the *medulla oblongata* (or, for short, the *medulla*), the *pons*, and the *cerebellum*. Since the hindbrain is found in even the most primitive vertebrates, we can consider it to be the earliest part of the brain to have evolved (cf. MacLean, 1982).

The *medulla* is the first structure that emerges from the spinal cord as it widens on entering the skull. It contains all the nerve fibres that connect the spinal cord to the brain. Most of these fibres cross the medulla in such a way that, generally, the left half of the body is connected to the right half of the brain. This sort of arrangement is called a *contralateral connection* in contrast to an *ipsilateral connection* in which the nerve fibres from one half of the body go to the *same* half of the brain.

Although it is only one and a half inches long, the medulla regulates vital functions such as heart rate, blood pressure, respiration, and body temperature via its connections with the *autonomic nervous system* (see Chapter 3). The medulla receives sensory information directly from receptors in the body and exerts its effects through

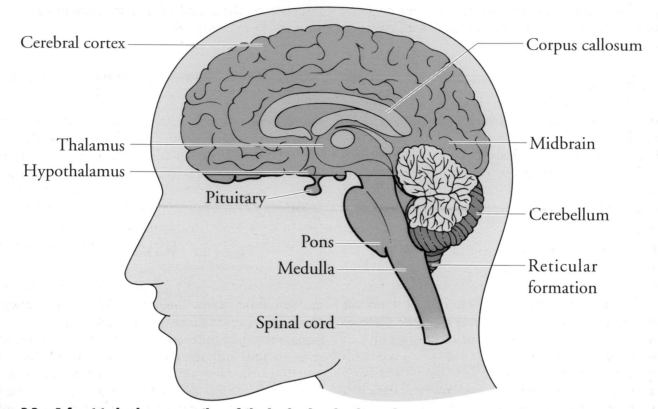

Cerebral cortex

Corpus callosum

Thalamus

Hypothalamus

Midbrain

Pituitary

Cerebellum

Pons

Medulla

Reticular formation

Spinal cord

Figure 2.3   A front-to-back cross-section of the brain showing its major structures. Note that the limbic system and basal ganglia surround the areas of the hypothalamus and thalamus, but are difficult to depict in a two-dimensional illustration

the nerve fibres that constitute the *peripheral nervous system* (see Chapter 3). As well as its role in the functions described above, the medulla also plays a role in other physiological activities such as vomiting, coughing, and sneezing. Overdoses of certain drugs depress the functions of the medulla and *can* lead to death. A very small lesion in a critical location *does* cause immediate death.

The *pons* is a bulge of white matter that lies forward of the medulla oblongata. Its name comes from the Latin word meaning 'bridge', and it is so called because of the bundle of hump-backed nerves that pass through it. The pons is an important connection between the midbrain and the medulla, and is vital in integrating the movements of the two halves of the body. The pons also plays a role in functions related to attention, respiration, alertness and sleep (see Chapter 10).

The *cerebellum* lies behind the pons. It consists of two 'creased' or *convoluted* hemispheres which extend outward to the back of the skull on either side of the pons. The cerebellum is involved in maintaining balance and, although it does not initiate movement, it is responsible for 'smoothing' muscular movements so that they occur in an integrated fashion.

The cerebellum also handles certain reflexes, especially those to do with breathing and balance. The classic signs of drunkenness (poor co-ordination and balance) are at least in part due to the alcohol-induced depression of neural activity in the cerebellum. If the cerebellum is damaged, a lack of muscular co-ordination, stumbling, and muscle tone may occur. The cerebellum is also important in learning and programming motor responses, that is, it acts as a kind of *muscular memory*. The sequence of movements involved in learning to ride a bike, for example, are programmed into the cerebellum so that we never forget them and engage in them 'automatically'.

For Eccles (1973), the cerebellum is a computer which controls complex motor behaviour and leaves the rest of the brain free for conscious activity. It accounts for about 11% of the brain's entire weight and only the *cerebrum* (see page 21) is heavier. The cerebellum also contains *Purkinje cells*, which are capable of forming synapses with up to 100,000 other neurons. This is more than any other kind of neuron found in the brain and, given the sequence of movements involved in playing a complex piece of music such as Rimsky

Korsakoff's *Flight of the Bumble Bee*, we can begin to appreciate why there is the need for such rich potential interconnections between neurons.

The midbrain

The relatively small division of the brain known as the midbrain is not really a separate structure that can be easily isolated, since it is essentially an extension of the hindbrain and connects the forebrain to the spinal cord. The principal structure of the midbrain is the *reticular formation*. This is a tangle of nerve cells and fibres (the word 'reticulum' means 'net' and refers to this tangle).

The fibres of the reticular formation ascend from the spinal cord to the forebrain carrying mainly motor information. This is important in maintaining muscle tone and controlling various reflexes. One of these, the *orienting reflex*, is a general response to a novel stimulus as in the case of a dog pricking up its ears in response to a noise. Animals which use sound as their major sensory system, such as bats, have a very prominent auditory area in the midbrain. In humans, the reticular formation includes the area that controls eye reflexes such as the dilation of the pupils, and eye movements. It is also important in hearing as well as being one of several places in the brain where pain is registered.

The reticular formation is vitally important in maintaining our general level of arousal or alertness. Because it is also involved in sleep and waking (see Chapter 10), it is sometimes referred to as the *reticular activating system* and has been called the 'consciousness system'. Stimulation of the reticular formation causes messages to be sent to the *cerebral cortex* (see Chapter 5) which make us more alert to sensory information. Drugs which lower its activity cause us to lose consciousness, and damage to the reticular formation can produce a comatose state.

The reticular formation also plays a role in screening incoming information, that is, filtering out irrelevant information whilst allowing important information to be sent to other areas of the brain. Through the reticular formation, we *habituate* to constant sources of uninformative information such as the ticking of a clock in a room in which we are reading a book. However, sudden changes in stimulation will cause the reticular formation to respond even if we happen to be asleep at the time. A good example of this is the response of sleeping parents to the cries of their baby and their lack of response to the sound of a lorry thundering past the window (see Chapter 9).

The forebrain

The forebrain consists of the *thalamus, hypothalamus, basal ganglia, limbic system*, and *cerebrum*.

We possess not one thalamus but two *thalami*. These are joined egg-shaped structures located near the centre of the brain. Each of the thalami acts as a 'sensory relay station' for all sensory information except *olfaction*, the sense of smell. This has its own sensory relay station, the *olfactory bulb*, which is located in the limbic system (see below). Many of the messages that travel from one part of the brain to another also pass through the thalami.

Nerve fibres from our various sensory systems enter the thalami from below and the information carried by them is transmitted to the cerebral cortex by nerve fibres exiting from above. For example, sensory information from the ears travels to the part of the cortex involved in hearing via a part of the thalami called the *medial geniculate body*. Other parts of the thalami include the *ventrobasal complex*, which transmits information about the sense of touch and body position which is fed in from the body via the spinal cord, and the *lateral geniculate body*. The lateral geniculate body is involved in vision, and we will have more to say about its role in Chapter 8.

The thalami also receive information from the cortex, mainly dealing with complex limb movements, that is directed to the cerebellum. In coordination with other brain activities occurring in the reticular formation and other structures, the thalami have also been suggested to play a role in sleep and attention.

The *hypothalamus* consists of a tiny collection of nuclei located beneath the thalami. The hypothalamus weighs about four grams and occupies less than one cubic centimetre of tissue. For its size, however, the hypothalamus is a remarkable and extremely important part of the brain which is involved in a wide variety of complex behaviours. These include helping to regulate the sympathetic branch of the autonomic nervous system (see Chapter 3) and the control of the *pituitary gland*, the gland which controls the rest of the body's *endocrine glands* (see Chapter 3). We will discuss the interaction between the hypothalamus and pituitary gland further in Chapter 18 when we look at the way in which the body reacts to stress.

The hypothalamus also plays a central role in *species-typical behaviour* and *homeostasis*. Species-typical behaviours are those which are exhibited by most members of a species and which are important to survival. Physiological psychologists sometimes refer to these as the four Fs: feeding, fighting, fleeing and 'reproduction'. However, there are other species-typical behaviours that are controlled by the hypothalamus. These include drinking, nest-building, and caring for offspring. The role of the hypothalamus in some of these behaviours will be explored in more detail in Chapter 14.

Homeostasis comes from the Greek 'himos' meaning 'same' and 'stasis' meaning 'stand-still'. Homeostasis refers to the maintenance of a proper balance of physiological variables such as body temperature, concentration of fluids, and the amount of nutrients stored in the body. The hypothalamus receives information from sensory receptors inside the body and is therefore well-informed about changes in physiological status. It also contains specialised receptors that monitor the various characteristics of the blood that flows through the brain such as its temperature, nutrients, and the amount of dissolved salts. As we will see in Chapter 14, the functions of the hypothalamus can involve either non-behavioural physiological changes (such as the regulation of temperature by sweating or by increasing metabolic rate) or actual behaviours (such as taking off or putting on a coat).

If the hypothalamus is damaged, then various behavioural impairments can occur. These include changes in food intake, sterility, or the stunting of growth (see Chapter 3). The major areas of the hypothalamus and their specialised functions are: the *anterior*, *supraoptic* (both are involved in water balance), *presupraoptic* (heat control), *ventromedial* (hunger), *posterior* (sex drive) and *dorsal* ('pleasure').

The *basal ganglia* are embedded in the mass of white matter of each cerebral hemisphere and lie beneath the cerebral cortex and in front of the thalami. The basal ganglia are involved in the control of muscular movement and the coordination of the limbs. Whilst the cerebellum controls rapid movements, it seems that the basal ganglia control slower movements and mediate the beginning and end of a movement. If the basal ganglia are damaged, changes in posture and muscle tone occur, leading to jerks, tremors, and twitches.

Much of the brain's *dopamine* (see Chapter 1) is produced in the basal ganglia and degeneration of neurons in this area have been implicated in *Parkinson's disease*, a disorder characterised by tremor, rigidity, and a poverty of spontaneous movements. (It is also worth noting that the basal ganglia should really be called the basal nuclei. 'Ganglia' is a word usually used to describe collections of cell bodies *outside* the nervous system, whereas the same collection *inside* the nervous system is usually referred to as a 'nuclei'.)

The *limbic system* is a series of structures located near the border between the *cerebrum* and parts of the hindbrain (its name comes from the Latin 'limbicus' meaning 'bordering'). The limbic system is only fully evolved in mammals, and as we ascend the *phylogenetic scale* the proportion of limbic system decreases and the proportion of *cerebral cortex* increases.

Included as limbic system structures are the *olfactory bulbs, hippocampus, amygdala, septum pellucidum, cingulate gyrus, mamillary body, fornix*, and *anterior commissure*. The thalami and hypothalamus are also sometimes included as limbic system structures. At one time, the limbic system was called the 'nose brain' because it contains the olfactory bulb. However, many of the limbic system structures play little or no direct role in olfaction, and as a result the term is no longer used.

The largest structure in the limbic system is the hippocampus, which lies between the thalami and the cortex. Its name comes from the Greek meaning 'sea horse' after its appearance. The hippocampus plays an important role in memory, and people who suffer damage to it seem to be unable to form new memories although some memories for events occurring prior to the damage are unaffected.

The limbic system is particularly involved in behaviours which satisfy motivational and emotional needs. Destruction of the *amygdala*, for example, has been shown to cause monkeys and other mammals to behave in a docile way. Electrical stimulation of the same area can, however, sometimes elicit rage and violent attacks from a previously tame or placid animal. Damage to the septum pellucidum leads some mammals to respond aggressively to the slightest provocation. In humans, stimulating the septum results in a person experiencing pleasant and positive sensations, and septum stimulation has been used therapeutically to bring relief from the physical pain of advanced cancer. In Chapters 14 and 16, we will consider further the role of the limbic system and other structures (such as the hypothalamus) in relation to motivation and emotion.

The *cerebrum* is virtually non-existent in the lower vertebrates. Fish, for example, have no tissue that would be recognised as cerebrum. As we move from the lower vertebrates to humans, we find that the growth of the cerebrum accounts for the change in brain weight compared to body weight. Pound for pound, humans have more brain in comparison to body weight than any other animal. In humans, the cerebrum is the most prominent brain structure which enfolds, and therefore conceals from view, most other brain structures. Over 75% of neurons are located in the cerebrum, and it accounts for about 80% of the brain's weight. The axons that fill the cerebrum interconnect with the neurons of the cortex and with those of other brain regions.

The cerebrum is divided into two *cerebral hemispheres* which are connected by the *corpus callosum*, a dense mass of commisural (or 'joining') fibres, which conveys information back and forth from one hemisphere to another. As long as the hemispheres are connected, each receives information about the other's activities almost simultaneously. Severing the nerve fibres of the corpus callosum is not life-threatening, although it does produce some extremely interesting psychological effects. We shall discuss some of these in Chapter 7.

The surface layer of the cerebrum is called the *cerebral cortex*, a layer which is only one and a half to three millimetres thick but at its deepest extends to about 10 millimetres. The cortex is the most recently evolved and important part of the cerebrum. Indeed, for many researchers the cerebrum is but a 'support system' for the cortex. In appearance, the cortex is pinkish-grey in colour, hence the term 'grey matter'. This is because it consists of cell bodies whereas the other parts of the brain and nervous system are white in appearance and consist of myelinated axons.

The cortex is folded into a pattern of 'hills' and 'valleys' called *convolutions* which are produced during the brain's development when the cortex folds back on itself. The total surface area of the cortex is around 2,400 square centimetres, and convolutions are nature's way of confining the cortex to a skull that has to be narrow enough to pass through the birth canal. The convolutions also facilitate the interconnections between different parts of the cortex that are needed to control complex behaviours.

Whilst some species other than humans possess a cortex, it is much smaller in surface area, shallower, and less complex than ours. As a general rule, the greater the proportion of brain devoted to the cortex, the more complex and flexible is an animal's possible range of behaviours. The cortex, then, accounts for our fantastic information processing capabilities. If the cortex ceases to function, a person vegetates without sensory experiences, voluntary movement, and consciousness.

The larger 'hills' (or 'bulges') are called *gyri* (the singular being *gyrus*) whilst the deeper 'valleys' are called *fissures* or *sulci* (the singular being *sulcus*). One of these, the *longitudinal fissure*, runs down the middle of the cerebrum and divides it into the two cerebral hemispheres. Two other natural fissures occur in each hemisphere. These are the *lateral fissure* (or *fissure of Sylvius*) and the *central fissure* (or *fissure of Rolando*).

Using the lateral and central fissure, we can divide each of the hemispheres into four distinct areas or *lobes* which are named after the bones beneath which they lie. These are the *frontal lobe*, *parietal lobe*, *occipital lobe*, and *temporal lobe*. Figure 2.4 illustrates these.

This division is a convenient 'geographical' one but, as we will see, each lobe carries out many functions at least some of which involve interactions with other lobes. A much better way of 'mapping' the cortex is in terms of areas of it that, during the course of evolution, have become specialised to perform certain tasks. Three areas of cortex can be identified in terms of the general functions they have. These are the *motor areas*, *sensory areas* and *association areas*. Because of their importance, we will devote all of Chapter 5 to them.

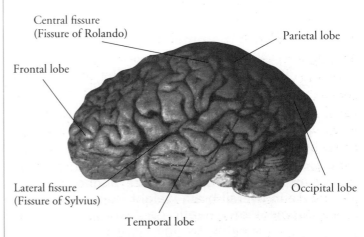

Central fissure
(Fissure of Rolando)

Parietal lobe

Frontal lobe

Lateral fissure
(Fissure of Sylvius)

Occipital lobe

Temporal lobe

Figure 2.4   The lobes of the brain

Conclusions

In this chapter we have looked at the organisation, structure and functioning of the central nervous system, and paid particular attention to the brain. As we have seen, it is possible to identify a number of different structures in the brain and, with some degree of confidence, describe the roles these different structures play.

SUMMARY

- The central nervous system (CNS) consists of the brain and the spinal cord, whose primary function is to integrate and co-ordinate all body functions and behaviour.
- The **spinal cord**, encased by the **spinal vertebrae**, is a thick column of nerve fibres running from the base of the brain down the entire length of the back. It is the main communication cable between the CNS and the peripheral nervous system (PNS).
- Messages from neurons enter and leave the spinal cord via 31 pairs of **spinal nerves**, each pair innervating a different part of the body, and containing both sensory and motor neurons. At the junction with the spinal cord itself, the nerves divide into the **dorsal root** (containing sensory neurons) and the **ventral root** (containing motor neurons).
- Damage to the spinal cord causes paralysis, which increases the further up the damage occurs. **Spinal reflexes** enable the body to avoid serious damage and maintain muscle tone and position.
- The **triune model** divides the brain into the **central core** (or **reptilian brain**), the **limbic system** (or **old mammalian brain**), and the **cerebral cortex** (or **new mammalian brain**).
- The brain can also be divided up in terms of foetal development. The lower part of the **neural tube** becomes the spinal cord and the PNS. The top swells into what will become the brain, with three identifiable sections, the **hindbrain, midbrain**, and **forebrain**.
- All the major brain structures are present at birth. It has almost its full complement of neurons, but they continue to grow in size and complexity. Increase in overall brain weight is also due to the development of synaptic connections, glial cells, and myelin sheaths; by age 20, it has reached its maximum weight.
- The brain's most remarkable feature is the vast complexity of the interconnections between neurons.
- The soft and fragile brain is encased by three sets of membranes called **meninges**; between the two inner meninges is **cerebrospinal fluid** (CSF), produced by specialised blood vessels in the **ventricles**. CSF helps to cushion the brain, so that it does not rest against the skull.
- The **hindbrain**, the earliest part of the brain to develop, consists of the **medulla oblongata**, the **pons**, and the **cerebellum**.
- The **medulla** contains all the nerve fibres connecting the spinal cord to the brain, arranged in the form of a **contralateral connection**. It regulates vital, **autonomic** functions, such as heart rate, and reflexes, such as vomiting, exerting its effects through its connection with the PNS.
- The **pons** is an important link between the midbrain and the medulla and is vital in integrating the movements of the two sides of the body. It is also involved in attention, respiration, alertness, and sleep.
- The **cerebellum** consists of two **convoluted** hemispheres towards the back of the skull. It is involved in maintaining balance and helps to smooth muscular movements so that they occur in an integrated manner. Alcohol depresses neural activity in the cerebellum and damage can produce loss of co-ordination and muscle tone.
- The cerebellum also enables us to perform sequences of movements, such as those involved in learning to ride a bike, in an automatic way, leaving the rest of the brain free for conscious activity. It contains **Purkinje cells**, which can form synapses with up to 100,000 other neurons, more than any other kind of neuron in the brain.
- The **midbrain** is not a separate structure, but is an extension of the hindbrain and connects the forebrain to the spinal cord. The main structure is the **reticular formation** (or **reticular activating**

system), which helps maintain muscle tone and controls reflexes, such as the **orienting reflex** and pupil dilation, and controls our general level of arousal/alertness. Reduced activity or damage can cause loss of consciousness or coma, and it also controls **habituation** and response to sudden changes in stimulation while we are asleep.

- The **forebrain** consists of the **thalamus, hypothalamus, basal ganglia, limbic system**, and **cerebrum**.

- Each of the two **thalami** acts as a sensory relay station for incoming sensory information (except **olfaction**, for which the **olfactory bulb** in the limbic system serves the same function). The **medial geniculate body** transmits auditory information, the **ventrobasal complex** transmits information about touch and body position, and the **lateral geniculate body** is involved in vision.

- The **hypothalamus** regulates the sympathetic branch of the ANS, controls the **pituitary gland** (which controls the rest of the **endocrine system**), and plays a central role in **species-specific behaviour** and **homeostasis**. It receives information from sensory receptors inside the body, as well as containing specialised receptors which monitor the blood that flows through the brain.

- Damage to the hypothalamus can result in behavioural impairments, depending on the area involved and its specialised functions: the **anterior** and **supraoptic** (both involved in water balance), **presupraoptic** (heat control), **ventromedial** (hunger), **posterior** (sex drive), **dorsal** (pleasure).

- The **basal ganglia** are involved in the control of slow muscular movements and control the beginning and end of a movement. They produce much of the brain's **dopamine** and degeneration of neurons in this region may be involved in **Parkinson's disease**.

- The **limbic system**, the proportion of which decreases relative to the proportion of the **cerebrum** as we ascend the **phylogenetic scale,** is a series of structures, including the **olfactory bulb, hippocampus, amygdala, septum pellucidum, cingulate gyrus, mamillary body, fornix,** and **anterior commissure**. The thalami and hypothalamus are sometimes included.

- The **hippocampus** plays a crucial role in the formation of new memories, while the limbic system as a whole is involved in motivational and emotional behaviours. The **amygdala** and **septum** are both involved in the control of aggression.

- The **cerebrum** enfolds most other brain structures and contains over 75% of neurons. It divides into two **cerebral hemispheres**, joined by the **corpus callosum**, which transmits information between them. The surface layer is the highly convoluted **cerebral cortex**, the most recently evolved and most important part of the cerebrum.

- The cortex is naturally divided by **gyri** and **fissures** (or **sulci**). The **longitudinal fissure** divides it into the two hemispheres, while the **lateral fissure** (or **fissure of Sylvius**) and the **central fissure** (or **fissure of Rolando**) demarcate the **frontal, parietal, occipital,** and **temporal lobes** of each hemisphere. An alternative division relates to the specialised functions of different areas, namely the **motor, sensory,** and **association areas**.

THE PERIPHERAL NERVOUS SYSTEM AND THE ENDOCRINE SYSTEM

Introduction and overview

As we mentioned in Chapter 1, the peripheral nervous system (PNS) consists of the nerves that connect the central nervous system (CNS) with the sense organs, muscles and glands. We also noted that the PNS has two essential functions. The first is to send information to the CNS from the outside world (which it does via the sense organs). The second is to transmit information from the CNS to produce a particular behaviour (which it does through the peripheral nerves to the muscles). Clearly, then, without the PNS, information about the outside world would not reach the brain and the brain would be unable to send instructions to the muscles and glands.

Our first aim in this chapter is to look at the way in which the PNS operates. Following this, we will look at the way in which it interacts with the *endocrine system*. Although the endocrine system is not technically a part of the nervous system at all, it is the interaction between it and the PNS which causes adjustments to our internal physiological processes, and influences our *behaviour*.

The peripheral nervous system

Some of the nerves that constitute the peripheral nervous system are attached to the spinal cord and serve all of the body below the neck. Humans have 31 pairs of what are called *spinal nerves*. Other nerves are directly attached to the brain and serve sensory receptors and muscles in the neck and head. We have 12 pairs of these *cranial nerves*. The PNS is divided into two parts called the *somatic nervous system* and the *autonomic nervous system*. The former is concerned with the external world, whilst the latter is concerned with the internal world, that is, the function of our internal organs.

THE SOMATIC NERVOUS SYSTEM

Sometimes called the skeletal nervous system, the somatic nervous system (SNS) connects the CNS to sensory receptors and the skeletal muscles. This allows us to move voluntarily. Messages to the CNS travel by means of sensory (or afferent) neurons. The instructions from the CNS to the muscles travel by means of motor (or efferent) neurons (see Chapter 1). Although sensory and motor neurons send information in different directions, they are bound together in the same nerves for most of their length. Thus, the sensory neurons tell the brain what is 'out there' and the brain acts on this information by sending instructions to the skeletal muscles.

If sensory neurons are damaged, we can lose sensation in the part of the body which is served by those neurons. If motor neurons are damaged, paralysis of the muscles in the part of the body served by the neurons can occur. Because damaged neurons are not replaced, the loss of sensation and paralysis can be permanent.

THE AUTONOMIC NERVOUS SYSTEM

In contrast to the SNS, the nerves of the autonomic nervous system (ANS) connects the CNS to the internal organs (or *viscera*), glands, and 'smooth' muscles (those which are not striped like the skeletal muscles are) over which we do not seem to have direct control. Included here, for example, are the muscles involved in the digestive system. As we will see, the primary function of the ANS is to regulate internal bodily processes. However, the ANS does this mainly by sending information to and from the CNS. As important as the ANS is, we should remember that it is the CNS which ultimately controls things.

The ANS is so called because it appears to operate as an independent or *autonomous* system of control. Although we learn to control some autonomic functions, such as urination and defecation, these functions would be carried out in the absence of our control of them. Thus, many of our bodily processes are con-

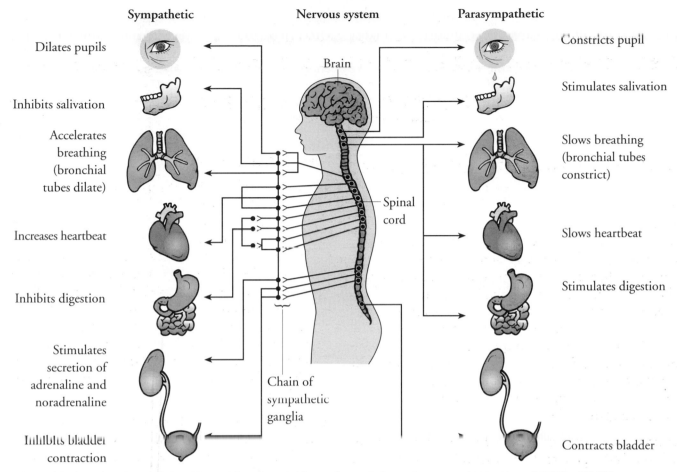

Figure 3.1   Some of the organs affected by the two branches of the ANS. From Hassett and White (1989)

trolled by the ANS without requiring our own conscious effort. The ANS is divided into two branches which are structurally different and which operate in different ways. The two divisions are called the *sympathetic* and *parasympathetic* branches of the ANS. Some of the organs affected by the two branches of the ANS are shown in Figure 3.1.

The bundles (or *ganglia*) of neurons that comprise the sympathetic branch are interconnected so that they form a long vertical chain on each side of the spinal cord. The sympathetic division originates in the two middle portions (the thoracic and lumbar regions) of the spinal cord. The interconnections between the neurons allow the sympathetic branch to act as a *unit*. The fact that this branch seemed to make the organs work 'in sympathy' led to its name, although we now know that the sympathetic branch can also act selectively on a single organ.

Essentially, the sympathetic branch prepares the body to expend energy. In addition to those effects shown in

Figure 3.1, the sympathetic branch also increases blood pressure, releases sugar from the liver into the blood (for energy) and increases blood flow to the muscles used in physical action. As we shall see shortly, the sympathetic branch also tells the *endocrine system* to begin releasing *hormones* into the bloodstream in order to further strengthen these responses.

Walter Cannon (1927) suggested that the major function of the sympathetic branch was to mobilise the body for an emergency, and he called its activation the *fight-or-flight response* since the physiological changes that occur are designed to help us defend ourselves or flee from a threatening situation. It has been shown, for example, that when animals are given chemicals that de-activate the neurotransmitters of the sympathetic branch, they find it difficult to learn to escape from an electric shock (Lord, King & Pfister, 1976). The role played by the sympathetic branch of the ANS in response to stressors is discussed in detail in Chapter 18.

Parasympathetic ganglia are much more widely distributed than those of the sympathetic branch. As Figure 3.1 shows, the nerve fibres originate at either end of the spinal cord, and as a general rule we can say that nerve fibres are near the organs they affect. However, because the nerve fibres are less interconnected than is the case with the sympathetic branch, the parasympathetic branch tends to act less as a unit and more on individual organs.

Figure 3.1 indicates that the parasympathetic branch operates in the opposite way to the sympathetic branch and stimulates processes that serve to restore or conserve the body's energy. The system also carries out the body's 'maintenance needs'. As well as promoting digestion, the parasympathetic branch provides for the elimination of waste products and directs tissue repair. Parasympathetic activity predominates when we are relaxed or inactive, or when an emergency necessitating sympathetic branch activity has passed.

Many of our internal organs are connected to both branches of the ANS. The fact that the ANS can influence our internal organs in two directions means that our internal environment can be kept in a balanced state. As we noted in Chapter 2, we use the term *homeostasis* to describe the processes by which the internal systems of the body are maintained at equilibrium despite variations in the external conditions.

The fact that the sympathetic and parasympathetic branches often oppose each other in order to maintain the balance of the internal organs has led to them being described as *antagonistic*. Whilst this is generally true, there are some behaviours which are controlled exclusively by one branch or the other. For example, sweating is controlled by the sympathetic branch whereas crying is controlled by the parasympathetic branch. We should also note that although the two branches of the ANS operate in opposite ways, they do function cooperatively. The sexual response in males is a good example of this. In order for an erection to occur, parasympathetic activity is necessary. In order for ejaculation to take place, sympathetic activity is necessary.

Traditionally, psychologists have regarded the ANS as the 'automatic' part of the body's response mechanism. Thus, it was generally believed that we could not tell our ANS when to speed up or when to slow down. However, there is some evidence which challenges this view. In a famous study, Dicara & Miller (1968) reported that rats could be taught to alter their heart rates using operant conditioning techniques. The same effect has also been reported in humans. *Yogis*, for example, can apparently slow their heart rate and energy consumption to such a degree that they can survive in a sealed box for periods of time which would ordinarily kill a human.

Miller pioneered the application of this ANS control with *biofeedback*, the use of monitoring equipment to record a particular bodily process (such as heart rate) and which signals (or 'feeds back') when the process has changed in the desired direction. Whilst there seems little doubt that biofeedback can be effective, it is not clear exactly how its effectiveness is achieved. Some psychologists, for example, believe that a reduction in heart rate, say, occurs *indirectly* as a result of the skeletal muscles in the chest being used to slow down breathing and hence heart rate. In support of their claim, these psychologists point to the fact that the results originally reported by Dicara and Miller have never been replicated (Walker, 1984).

The ANS exerts its effects by direct neural stimulation of body organs and by stimulating the release of *hormones* from the *endocrine glands*. It is to the endocrine system that we now turn our attention.

The endocrine system

Our bodies contain two types of gland, those with ducts and those without. A duct is a passageway that carries substances to specific locations and secretes these substances directly onto the surface of the body or into body cavities. Glands with ducts are called *exocrine glands*. Tears, sweat and saliva, for example, all reach their destination by means of ducts. From a psychological perspective, exocrine glands are not particularly interesting. Much more interesting are the glands which are ductless, that is, secrete their products directly into the bloodstream. These *endocrine glands* are of much greater interest to psychologists because of the role they play in behaviour. Figure 3.2 opposite shows some of the major glands of the endocrine system.

The products secreted by the endocrine glands are called *hormones* (from the Greek word 'horman' meaning 'to stimulate' or 'to excite'). These are powerful chemical messengers that affect our physical state and behaviour in a variety of ways. To a degree, hormones are similar to the other messengers we talked about in

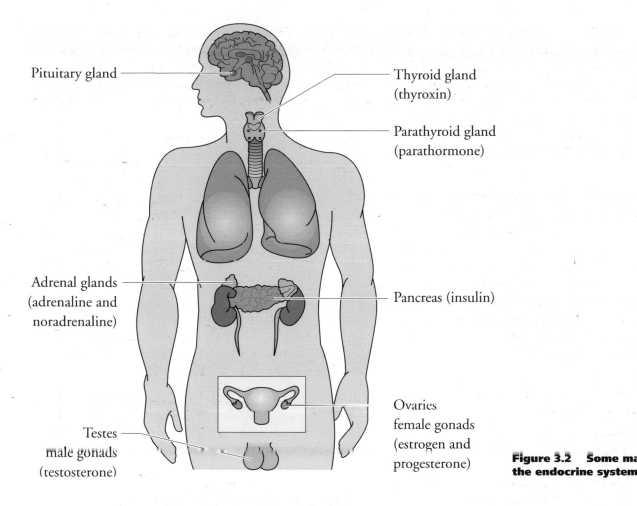

Pituitary gland

Thyroid gland
(thyroxin)

Parathyroid gland
(parathormone)

Adrenal glands
(adrenaline and
noradrenaline)

Pancreas (insulin)

Ovaries
female gonads
(estrogen and
progesterone)

Testes
male gonads
(testosterone)

**Figure 3.2   Some major glands of
the endocrine system**

Chapter 1, *neurotransmitters*. As we will see, hormones are poured into the bloodstream and circulate throughout the body. However, like neurotransmitters, hormones act only on receptors in particular locations of the body. Indeed, at least one chemical (*norepinephrine* – see below) can be classified as both a neurotransmitter and a hormone depending on the task it is performing and where it is located.

In other ways, hormones are very different to neurotransmitters. One difference is in terms of the speed at which they exert their influence. As we saw in Chapter 1, neurotransmitters can convey a message in a few fractions of a second. Because hormones are discharged into the blood, the endocrine system influences behaviour in a broader but slower way than the nervous system. Consequently, when an immediate behavioural reaction is required (such as a reflexive action), the nervous system plays the major role.

Many of the hormonal activities we will shortly describe enable our bodies to maintain steady states.

They achieve this by means of mechanisms that measure current levels and signal glands to release appropriate regulatory chemicals whenever the steady state is disturbed. To maintain the steady state, information must then be fed back to the glands. This type of system is called a *negative feedback loop*. Thus, whenever the required amount of a hormone has been secreted, the gland is instructed to stop.

The endocrine and nervous system interact in complex ways, and the endocrine system plays a major role in regulating development and helping to coordinate and integrate complex psychological reactions (we will explore this interaction in detail in Chapter 14 when we look at the physiological mechanisms involved in motivation). In essence, though, the endocrine system is regulated by the *hypothalamus* (see pages 19–20) which exerts its influence through its effect on the *pituitary gland*. The pituitary is sometimes referred to as the 'master gland' because the hormones it releases control the secretion of the other endocrine glands.

THE PITUITARY GLAND

The pituitary gland is located deep within the brain, slightly below the hypothalamus to which it is connected by means of a network of blood vessels called the *infundibulum* or *pituitary stalk*. The pituitary gland consists of two parts each of which functions separately from the other. The *anterior pituitary* (towards the *front* of the gland) is controlled by *releasing hormones* or *factors* produced by the hypothalamus and transmitted via the pituitary stalk.

At least eight hormones are produced by the anterior pituitary. One of these is *somatotrophin* or *growth hormone*. This affects the metabolic functions that determine the growth of muscles, bones and glands. Overproduction of this hormone can lead to *acromegaly*, a condition in which a person grows two or three feet taller than would be the case if the hormone was produced normally. Underproduction of somatotrophin results in arrested growth development and the affected child becomes a *midget*.

Another hormone produced by the anterior pituitary is *prolactin* or *lactogenic hormone*. This regulates maternal behaviour in mammals such as rats. It has been shown, for example, that when blood from a new mother rat is transfused into another female rat, the recipient displays typical maternal behaviour. In humans, prolactin stimulates the production of milk during pregnancy.

The anterior pituitary provides us with an excellent example of the interaction between the endocrine and nervous system we mentioned earlier. As we know, the anterior pituitary is controlled by the hypothalamus. One of the hormones released by the anterior pituitary causes another gland, the *gonads* (see below), to produce yet other hormones. These affect the hypothalamus causing changes in behaviour or feeling. The hypothalamus, then, not only influences the anterior pituitary, but is influenced by it.

The *posterior pituitary* (towards the *back* of the gland) is controlled by the nervous system. One hormone it secretes is *oxytocin* which instructs the uterus to contract during childbirth. Shortly after a woman has given birth, the stimulation of the nerve endings in and around the nipples sends messages to the brain that cause oxytocin to be released. Oxytocin then causes contractile cells in the breast to eject milk, an example of what is called a *neuroendocrine reflex*. Both prolactin and oxytocin are also secreted in males although their function, if indeed there is one, is not known.

Antidiuretic hormone (ADH) is manufactured in the hypothalamus but is stored in the posterior lobe of the pituitary. This hormone acts on the kidneys, causing them to decrease the amount of water that is drawn from the body tissues and passed to the bladder. When we are dehydrated, ADH is released as a way of conserving fluid. When we are hydrated, that is, our intake of liquid is excessive, ADH is not released at all and the amount of urine we pass is dramatically increased. The role of ADH in the regulation of drinking is further discussed in Chapter 14.

THE ADRENAL GLANDS

The adrenal glands are located above the kidneys. They have an outer layer (or *cortex*) and an inner core (or *medulla*). The action of the adrenal cortex is regulated by *adrenocorticotrophic hormone* (ACTH) which is another hormone produced by the anterior pituitary (and is itself released in response to *corticotrophin-releasing hormone* which is produced by the hypothalamus). The adrenal cortex secretes as many as 20 different hormones which are called *corticosteroids* or *cortical steroids*. In general, steroids promote muscle development, increase resistance to stress (by fighting inflammation and allergic reactions; see Chapter 18), and stimulate the liver to release stored sugar which influences the body's ability to produce energy quickly. Not surprisingly, it is steroids which are taken by bodybuilders and athletes in order to enhance their performance, although such use is not without its dangers.

The adrenal medulla is stimulated by the autonomic nervous system to produce *epinephrine* and *norepinephrine* (which, as we mentioned earlier on in this chapter, also acts as a neurotransmitter). Epinephrine is manufactured exclusively by the adrenal glands and activates the sympathetic branch of the automatic nervous system to produce the characteristic pattern of physiological activity we described on page 25. Norepinephrine is produced by the adrenal glands and at other sites in the body. It raises the blood pressure by causing the blood vessels to become constricted. Norepinephrine is also carried by the bloodstream to the anterior pituitary, where it triggers the release of yet more ACTH (see above). This prolongs the response to stress and has the effect of preparing the body to deal efficiently with threat (see Chapter 18).

THE THYROID GLAND

The thyroid gland is located just below the larynx or 'voice box'. As a result of production of *thyrotrophic hormones* by the anterior pituitary, the thyroid gland produces one primary hormone, *thyroxin,* which plays an important role in controlling the rate at which the body burns food to provide energy. Primarily, thyroxin raises the body's metabolism by increasing the use of oxygen and the level of heat production. When this hormone is overproduced, it leads to a condition called *hyperthyroidism* which is characterised by excitability, insomnia, and weight loss (even though the appetite for food is huge). Underproduction of thyroxin produces a condition called *hypothyroidism* which is characterised by the opposite effects to those of hyperthyroidism. Because thyroxin affects metabolism, untreated hypothyroidism in infants can lead to *cretinism,* a condition which is characterised by stunted growth and mental retardation.

THE PARATHYROID GLANDS

The parathyroid glands are embedded in the thyroid gland. There are four small organs which secrete *parathormone.* This controls the levels of calcium and phosphate in the blood and tissue fluids. How much calcium there is in our blood directly affects the excitability of our nervous system. People with too little parathormone tend to be hypersensitive and suffer from muscle spasms. By contrast, people with too much parathormone tend to be lethargic and have poor muscle coordination.

THE PANCREAS

The pancreas, which is located in a curve between the stomach and small intestine, plays a major role in controlling the level of sugar in the blood and urine by secreting the regulating hormones *insulin* and *glucagon.* These two hormones work against each other in order to keep the blood-sugar level properly balanced. When insulin is oversecreted, the result is too little sugar in the blood. This produces a condition called *hypoglycaemia* which is characterised by chronic fatigue, shakiness, and dizziness. These symptoms are often confused with *anxiety* and when people seek help for anxiety they sometimes find, through blood tests, that they are hypoglycaemic. Dietary restrictions are usually used to control the condition.

When insulin is inadequately secreted or underutilised, *hyperglycaemia* occurs. This is characterised by an excess amount of sugar in the blood which the kidneys attempt to remove by secreting more water than usual. As a result, the body's tissues become dehydrated and poisonous wastes accumulate in the blood. This condition is known as *diabetes mellitus* and can lead to coma and death. Fortunately, it can be treated by means of insulin injections and a special diet which keeps the blood-sugar level normal.

THE GONADS

The gonads are the sexual glands – *ovaries* in women and *testes* in men. Both the ovaries and testes are stimulated by *luteinising hormone* which is produced by the anterior pituitary. In addition, *follicle stimulating hormone,* which is also produced by the anterior pituitary, causes egg cells in the follicles in the ovaries to ripen.

There are three main types of sex hormone secreted by the tissue located within the gonads. All three occur in both men and women, but in different amounts. These hormones control the development of *primary sex characteristics,* that is, those which are directly involved in reproduction such as the growth of the penis and the ability of the testes to produce sperm. They also control the development of *secondary sex characteristics,* that is, those characteristics which differentiate the sexes but which are not directly involved in reproduction. These include things like the distribution of body hair and the deepening of the voice.

The most potent of the masculinising hormones, which are called *androgens,* is *testosterone.* Primarily, androgens are produced in the testes but they are also produced in the ovaries and the adrenal cortex. If testosterone was not secreted about six weeks after conception, then all of us would be females since testosterone stimulates the prenatal differentiation of the male sex organs.

The ovaries produce *estrogen* and *progesterone.* Estrogen is, in fact, a generic term which encompasses several female sex hormones that are also produced in the testes and adrenal cortex. Estrogen leads to the development of female reproductive capacity and secondary sex characteristics such as the accumulation of fat in the breasts. Progesterone stimulates the growth of the female reproductive organs and maintains pregnancy.

Both estrogen and progesterone regulate the menstrual cycle. Estrogen levels rise after menstruation, the monthly sloughing off of the inner lining of the uterus, leading to the development of an egg cell and the growth of the inner lining of the uterus. When estrogen reaches peak blood level, the egg cell is released by the ovary. Then, the inner lining of the uterus thickens in response to the secretion of progesterone, eventually gaining the capacity to support an embryo should fertilisation occur. If the egg cell is not fertilised, estrogen and progesterone levels drop, triggering menstruation.

Hormonal changes at the time of menstruation can cause women painful physical problems. For example, the production of *prostoglandins* during menstruation causes uterine contractions. Many of these go unnoticed, but when they are strong and unrelieved, they can be particularly uncomfortable. Fortunately, such pain can be relieved through the use of prostaglandin-inhibiting drugs such as *Ibuprofen*. Much more controversial is the claim that the menstrual cycle can cause psychological problems such as irritability and poor judgement.

The term *pre-menstrual syndrome* (PMS) has been used to describe the behavioural and emotional effects associated with menstruation, although its status has been challenged by some writers. As Karen Paige (1973) has observed:

> 'Women, the old argument goes, are eternally subject to the whims and wherefores of their biological clocks. Their raging hormonal cycles make them emotionally unstable and intellectually unreliable. If women have second-class status, we are told, it is because they cannot control the implacable demands of that bouncing estrogen'.

The menstrual cycle is an example of a bodily rhythm called an *infradian rhythm*. In Chapter 9, we will discuss the evidence concerning pre-menstrual syndrome in more detail.

In some people, the sex hormones are out of balance and this leads to changes in behaviour and physical appearance. Oversecretion of estrogen in males and androgens in females causes the development of secondary sex characteristics of the opposite sex. Females, for example, may grow facial hair, develop a deeper voice and experience shrinkage of the breasts. Males may develop higher pitched voices, begin to grow breasts, and lose facial hair.

In a condition called *Adrenogenital Syndrome* (AGS), the adrenal glands produce a hormone that begins to masculinise the foetus irrespective of its genetically determined sex. Thus, both AGS boys and girls become more masculinised. At birth, the internal reproductive organs of a girl may be female, but their outward appearance is that of a male. Even when surgery is performed and they are raised as females, AGS girls appear to retain some masculine characteristics (if we assume that large amounts of outdoor play, which is enjoyed by AGS girls, is an indicator of 'masculinity'). The evidence (e.g. Money & Erhardt, 1972) also suggests that AGS girls prefer to play with boys, describe themselves as 'tomboys', and are less interested in playing with 'typical' girls' toys such as dolls and more interested in playing with 'typical' boys' toys such as trucks and guns. AGS boys seem to be involved in much rougher outdoor activities than their non-AGS counterparts.

THE HEART

Traditionally, we think of the heart as being a finely tuned and essential pump. However, Cantin & Genest (1986) have argued that it may also be a major endocrine gland. They discovered that the heart secretes a powerful peptide hormone called *atrial natriuretic factor* (ANF). According to Cantin and Genest, this hormone plays an important role in the regulation of blood pressure and blood volume, and in the excretion of water, sodium and potassium. The effects exerted are wide and involve the blood vessels themselves, the kidneys, the adrenal glands, and a large number of regulatory glands in the brain. If Cantin and Genest are right in their views about the heart, there is clearly much we have still to learn about the endocrine system.

Conclusions

In this chapter we have examined the ways in which the peripheral nervous system operates and the ways in which it interacts with the endocrine system. We should note that our look at the hormones secreted by the endocrine system has been selective rather than exhaustive. However, we will encounter more hormones throughout this book. One of these, *melatonin*, is secreted by a tiny structure called the *pineal gland*, a small gland deep within the body. As we will see in Chapter 9, this hormone has been found to play an important role in the regulation of certain biological rhythms.

SUMMARY

- The peripheral nervous system (PNS) consists of the nerves connecting the CNS with the sense organs, muscles, and glands. It sends information to the CNS from the outside world (via the sense organs) and transmits information from the CNS to the muscles.

- Humans have 31 pairs of **spinal nerves**, which are attached to the spinal cord and serve the whole body below the neck. The 12 pairs of **cranial nerves** are directly attached to the brain and serve sensory receptors and muscles in the neck and head.

- The PNS is divided into the **somatic nervous system** (SNS), or skeletal NS, and the **autonomic nervous system** (ANS).

- The SNS connects the CNS to sensory receptors and the skeletal muscles, which allows us to move voluntarily. Sensory and motor neurons are combined in the same nerves for most of their length, allowing the brain to act on sensory information.

- Damage to sensory and motor neurons can cause permanent loss of sensation and paralysis respectively.

- The nerves of the ANS connect the CNS to the **viscera**, glands, and 'smooth' muscled organs; their main function is to regulate internal bodily processes but it is the CNS that ultimately controls things.

- Many of our bodily processes are controlled by the ANS without the need for conscious effort (in an **autonomous** way). The two structurally different branches are the **sympathetic**, which forms a long vertical chain on each side of the spinal cord, and **parasympathetic**, whose nerve fibres originate at either end of the spinal cord and are more widely distributed

- The **sympathetic branch** inhibits salivation, digestion and bladder contraction, accelerates breathing, increases heart rate and blood pressure, stimulates the secretion of adrenaline and noradrenaline, releases sugar from the liver into the blood, and increases blood flow to the muscles used in physical activity. These changes tend to occur together.

- Most of these changes are designed to mobilise the body for an emergency (Cannon's **fight-or-flight response**).

- The **parasympathetic branch**, which acts less as a unit than the sympathetic branch, helps the body to conserve or restore energy, rather than expend it; it is said to be **antagonistic**, although there are exceptions to this general rule. The parasympathetic branch also controls the elimination of waste products and tissue repair.

- Since most internal organs are connected to both branches, the ANS plays a major role in **homeostasis**.

- There is some evidence that the ANS is not completely 'automatic', such as the operant conditioning of rats to alter their heart rates, and yogis surviving under conditions that would normally kill. **Biofeedback** represents a major application of these findings, although there are doubts as to how it produces its effects.

- The ANS exerts its effects by direct neural stimulation of body organs and by stimulating the **endocrine glands** to secrete **hormones**. These glands are ductless and hormones are secreted directly into the bloodstream.

- **Hormones** are powerful chemical messengers that affect physical state and behaviour. They have much in common with **neurotransmitters**, and **norepinephrine** can be classified as both neurotransmitter and hormone. But hormones take much longer to have their effect than neurotransmitters.

- Hormones help to maintain the body's steady states through **negative feedback loops**, whereby the gland is instructed to stop secreting when the required amount of hormone has been released.

- The endocrine system is essentially regulated by the **hypothalamus**, which exerts its influence through control of the **pituitary gland**. The pituitary gland is connected to the hypothalamus via the **infundibulum/pituitary stalk**, and consists of the **anterior** and **posterior** parts.

- The **anterior pituitary** is controlled by **releasing hormomes/factors** from the hypothalamus. It produces several hormones, including **somatotrophin/growth hormone**, **prolactin/lactogenic hormone** and **adrenocorticotrophic hormone** (ACTH). It also releases a hormone which causes the **gonads** to produce still others, which in turn affect the hypothalamus; this demonstrates the interaction between the endocrine and nervous systems.

- The **posterior pituitary** secretes **oxytocin**, which is involved in the production of breast milk via a **neuroendocrine reflex**. Antidiuretic hor-

- mone (ADH) is made in the hypothalamus but stored in the posterior pituitary; it plays a crucial role in drinking and thirst.
- The **adrenal glands** consist of an outer **cortex** and an inner **medulla**. The **cortex** is regulated by ACTH (itself released in response to **corticotrophin-releasing hormone**, produced by the hypothalamus); it secretes **corticosteroids**, which increase resistance to stress, and promote muscle development.
- The adrenal **medulla** is stimulated by the ANS to produce **epinephrine** and **norepinephrine**. Epinephrine is made exclusively by the adrenal glands and activates the sympathetic branch of the ANS; norepinephrine stimulates the anterior pituitary to release more ACTH, thus prolonging the stress response.
- The **thyroid gland** produces **thyroxin** (resulting from the anterior pituitary's production of **thyrotrophic hormone**), which plays a vital role in the body's **metabolism**; overproduction results in **hyperthyroidism**, underproduction in **hypothyroidism** (which, if untreated in infants, can lead to **cretinism**).
- The **parathyroid glands,** four small organs embedded in the thyroid gland, secrete **parathormone**; this controls calcium and phosphate levels in the blood and tissue fluid, affecting the excitability of the NS.
- The **pancreas** plays a major role in controlling blood-sugar and urine-sugar levels by secreting **insulin** and **glucagon.** Oversecretion of insulin results in **hypoglycaemia** (too little blood-sugar), which is often confused with anxiety.

Hyperglycaemia involves too much blood sugar and is associated with **diabetes mellitus**, which can be treated by insulin injections.

- The **gonads** (**ovaries** and **testes**) are stimulated by the **luteinizing hormone**, and the **follicle-stimulating hormone** causes egg cells to ripen; both hormones are produced by the anterior pituitary.
- All three main types of sex hormone are produced in both males and females, but in different amounts; they control both **primary** and **secondary sex characteristics.** The most potent of the male hormones (**androgens**) is **testosterone**; the female hormones are **estrogen** and **progesterone**, both of which regulate the menstrual cycle (an example of an **infradian rhythm**).
- Other hormones produced during menstruation, such as **prostoglandins**, can cause physical problems. The term **pre-menstrual syndrome** (PMS) refers to the behavioural and emotional effects of menstruation. The syndrome is, however, the subject of much controversy.
- In **adrenogenital syndrome** (AGS), the adrenal glands have produced a hormone that masculinises the foetus, so that a genetic female may have the external appearance of a male. AGS girls tend to think and behave in more 'masculine' ways, even when raised as females.
- The **heart** may be a major endocrine gland; it secretes **atrial natriuretic factor** (ANF), a hormone which regulates blood pressure and volume and the excretion of water, sodium and potassium.
- The **pineal gland** secretes **melatonin**, a hormone which regulates certain biological rhythms.

PART 2
Cortical functions

4

SOME METHODS AND TECHNIQUES USED TO INVESTIGATE CORTICAL FUNCTIONS

Introduction and overview

In Chapter 2, we examined the human brain in some detail, describing the relationship between brain structures and behaviour. Although we are still some way from completely understanding the mechanisms of the brain, our knowledge about it grows on an almost daily basis. But how do we know what we know? Our aim in this chapter is to look at some of the methods and techniques that have advanced our understanding.

There are a number of ways in which the various methods could be sub-divided. We will discuss them under three separate headings. First, we will look at methods involving 'accidental interventions' such as injury to and disease of the brain, and will use the term *clinical and anatomical methods* to describe these. Then we will look at methods involving 'deliberate intervention', such as stimulating the brain either electrically or chemically or causing deliberate injury to it. We will term these *invasive methods*. Finally, we will look at methods which involve recording the brain's activity. Since these do not involve making deliberate interventions to it, we will discuss these methods and techniques under the heading of *non-invasive methods*.

Clinical and anatomical methods

Perhaps the most obvious way of studying the brain is to look at the behavioural consequences that occur as a result of *accidental* damage to it. The Greek physician Galen, for example, used this method two centuries after the birth of Christ when he noted that damage to the right side of the head affected movement on the left side of the body. It is only in the last two centuries, however, that the results of damage to specific brain sites have been systematically recorded. This approach to studying the brain assumes that if damage to a particular part of the brain causes a particular change in a behaviour, then it is reasonable to conclude that the damaged part ordinarily plays a role in that behaviour.

In the late nineteenth century, the French physician Paul Broca and the German neurologist Carl Wernicke used this method to study patients who had suffered a stroke. A stroke, or *cerebrovascular accident*, occurs when a blood vessel in the brain is damaged or blocked. This causes brain tissue to be deprived of the oxygen and nutrients carried by the blood, and the tissue dies. Broca's patients had difficulty in producing speech but no difficulty in understanding it. Wernicke's patients, by contrast, were capable of producing speech (although it was often unintelligible), but could not understand it. Post-mortems revealed that Broca's patients had suffered damage in one specific part of the brain whilst Wernicke's had suffered damage in a different part. We will look further at the role played by these parts of the brain in Chapter 6.

Clinical and anatomical studies essentially make a comparison between what people could do before the brain was damaged with what they can do afterwards. Unfortunately, with many cases of accidental damage we don't always have precise enough records of people's behaviour before the damage was sustained. As a result, this approach to studying the brain is useful for very obvious behavioural changes (such as the inability to produce language), but is less helpful where more subtle effects are involved (as might be the case with changes in personality, for example).

We should also note that with this approach it is sometimes difficult to determine the precise location and amount of damage that has been caused by a particular injury. More practically, researchers must wait for the 'right kind' of injury to occur so that the role of a particular part of the brain can be investigated. An alternative method of studying the brain involves deliberately interfering with it in some way. These 'invasive methods' are discussed below.

Invasive methods

ABLATION AND LESION PRODUCTION

Essentially, *ablation* involves surgically removing or destroying brain tissue and observing the behavioural consequences. The technique was pioneered by Pierre Flourens in the 1820s, who showed that removal of thin slices of tissue from the cerebellum of rabbits, birds and dogs resulted in the animals displaying a lack of muscular co-ordination and a poor sense of balance, but no other obvious behavioural difficulties. On the basis of this finding, Flourens concluded that the brain part he had removed must play a vital role in muscular co-ordination and balance and as we saw in Chapter 2, Flouren's conclusion was essentially correct.

Surgical removal can be achieved in several ways, including cutting the tissue with a knife, burning it out with electrodes, and sucking it away through a hollow tube attached to a vacuum pump. Although ablation studies are still conducted on non-human animals, they are limited in what they can tell us about the human brain. Another problem is the issue of *control* versus *involvement* in behaviour. Behaviour changes may occur as a result of part of the brain being removed, but we cannot be completely certain that the removed part controlled the behaviour or was merely involved in it. Since many parts of the brain might work together to produce a particular behaviour, we cannot be really sure what it means when behaviour changes as a result of a part being removed.

Lesion production involves deliberately injuring part of the brain and then observing the consequences of the injury or *lesion* on behaviour. Whilst an animal is under anaesthetic, a hole is drilled in its skull and an electrode inserted into a particular brain site. Then, an electrical impulse of a voltage larger than those occurring naturally in the brain is delivered to the site. The voltage 'burns out' a small area surrounding the electrode. Because the sites involved are usually located deep within the brain, researchers use a *stereotaxic apparatus* (as shown in Figure 4.1 opposite) to enable them to precisely locate the area which is to be lesioned.

Once the animal has recovered from the procedure, its behaviour is observed in order to see whether the lesion has produced immediate, delayed, or no apparent changes in behaviour, and whether any changes are permanent or disappear with time, re-training or therapy. Lesion studies have produced some important findings. As we will see in Chapter 14, research into the physiological basis of hunger, for example, has shown that lesions in part of the hypothalamus cause extreme overeating in rats with the result that the animals become grossly overweight. A lesion in a different area, however, produces the opposite effect and, at least initially, the rats refuse to eat any sort of food.

Whilst lesion production is not used on humans *purely* for research purposes, lesions have been produced for therapeutic purposes. One example of this is the so-called *split-brain* operation in which certain nerve fibres are severed in order to try and reduce the severity of epileptic seizures. In addition to providing some benefit for those who undergo the operation, a number of interesting psychological consequences occur. We will discuss these in Chapter 7.

Lesion production studies tell us something about how different parts of the brain are normally connected. As was the case with ablation studies, however, we must be extremely cautious in interpreting the data from them. Again, since the participants in research studies are

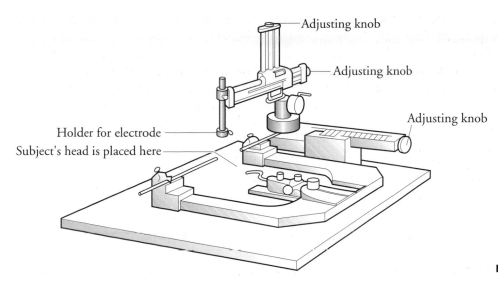

Adjusting knob

Adjusting knob

Holder for electrode

Subject's head is placed here

Figure 4.1   A stereotaxic apparatus

always non-humans the findings obtained may not generalise to human beings. Additionally, whilst a lesion is produced in a specific area, the possibility that behaviour changes occur as a result of other damage caused by the procedure cannot be ruled out. The problem of 'control versus involvement' in the production of behaviour changes is also a concern with lesion studies.

ELECTRICAL STIMULATION OF THE BRAIN

This method, which is abbreviated to ESB, involves inserting one or more electrodes into the brain of a living animal and applying an electric current which is weak enough not to cause any damage. Careful adjustment of the current produces a 'false' nerve impulse and the brain is 'fooled' into thinking that it has received a real impulse from one of its sensory receptors (see Figure 4.2 below).

ESB has produced some dramatic findings. In what can only be described as a very brave experiment, Jose Delgado walked into a bullring equipped with a bull fighter's cape and a radio transmitter. In his book *Physical Control of the Mind* (1969), Delgado revealed that he had implanted a radio-controlled electrode into the limbic system (see Chapter 2) of a 'brave bull', that is, a variety of bull bred to respond with a raging charge in response to the sight of a human being. When the bull charged, Delgado pressed a button on his transmitter which sent an impulse to the electrode in the bull's brain. Fortunately for Delgado, the bull stopped its charge. We will discuss the implications of Delgado's findings in Chapter 16 when we look at the role of the brain in the experience of emotion.

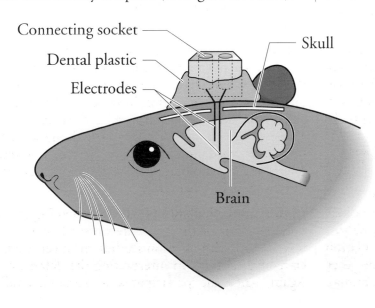

Connecting socket

Dental plastic

Electrodes

Skull

Brain

Figure 4.2   Electrical stimulation of the brain

In a series of experiments conducted in the 1950s, James Olds and Peter Milner found that electrical stimulation of the *hypothalamus* (see Chapter 2) caused a rat to increase the frequency of whatever behaviour it happened to be engaged in. In another experiment, Olds & Milner (1954) connected the implanted electrode to a control mechanism that the rat could operate. Stimulation of one part of the hypothalamus appeared to be extremely pleasurable for the rat, since it would forego food, water and sex to carry on stimulating its brain at a rate of 100 times a minute and over 1,900 times an hour. As well as discovering an apparent 'pleasure centre' in the brain, Olds and Milner also discovered that placing the electrode in a different location led to an animal that had operated the control mechanism once never operating it again, suggesting the existence of a 'pain centre' in the brain (see Chapters 16 and 17).

The studies described above illustrate the sorts of things that researchers have found as a result of stimulating structures located deep within the brain. However, in some studies the surface of the brain (which is called the *cerebral cortex* and is described in detail in the following chapter) has also been electrically stimulated. The impetus for this research came from the discovery in 1870 that applying a weak electric current to the surface of the brain produced movements of the body. The discovery was made by Gustav Fritsch and Eduard Hitzig, two German physicians, who were treating a soldier injured in the Franco-Prussian war. Using this method, Fritsch and Hitzig attempted to draw a 'map' of the brain functions relating specific areas of the cortex to particular muscle activity.

The classic research in this area was conducted by Wilder Penfield, a Canadian neurosurgeon, in the 1940s and 1950s. Penfield routinely performed surgery on epileptics, and in order to minimise the disruption of normal functions as a result of the surgery, Penfield would stimulate the cortex and observe what happened. Because there are no pain receptors in the brain, the person awaiting surgery could be kept conscious whilst the stimulation was given, and was able to report on the experiences produced by the stimulation. Figure 4.3 below shows a photograph taken during surgery conducted by Penfield. The numbers refer to the parts of the cortex he stimulated.

ESB has provided us with a great deal of information about the brain's workings, and has also been used to treat a variety of conditions. For example, claims have been made that ESB can be effective in the treatment of certain psychological disorders. Perhaps its most useful application has been in the reduction of pain. Restak (1975), for example, has shown that ESB can be used to 'block' pain messages in the spine before they reach the brain and that this is effective in relieving the severe pain experienced by people with illnesses such as cancer.

Clearly, ESB is a useful way of 'mapping' the connections between various areas or structures of the brain since, if the stimulation of one area produces increased activity at another, it is reasonable to assume that the two are connected. Equally, it is reasonable to suggest that if the stimulation of a specific brain site produces a

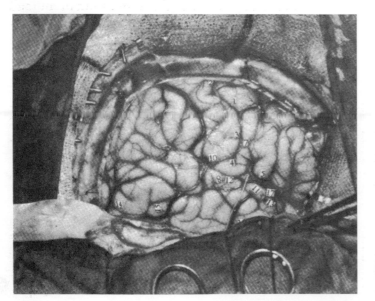

Figure 4.3   Photograph taken during surgery carried out by Wilder Penfield. The numbers refer to the parts of the cortex stimulated

behaviour, that site must be at least involved in the behaviour. However, we must be careful about drawing too many conclusions from research findings.

Valenstein (1977) offers three cautions. First, no single area of the brain is likely to be the sole source of any given behaviour or emotion. Second, ESB-provoked behaviour does not perfectly mimic natural behaviour. Rather, it produces compulsive and stereotypical behaviour. For example, an animal whose eating behaviour is initiated by ESB might only eat one type of food. Third, the effects of ESB may depend on many other factors. Research has shown that people exhibit very different behavioural responses to identical stimulation administered at different times. As Valenstein has observed:

'The impression that brain stimulation in humans can repeatedly evoke the same emotional state, the same memory, or the same behaviour is simply a myth. The brain is not organised into neat compartments that correspond to the labels we assign to behaviour'.

MICRO-ELECTRODE RECORDING

Instead of stimulating the brain, some researchers insert tiny electrodes, called *micro-electrodes*, to record the activity of a single neuron in the brain of a living animal. Micro-electrodes are about one ten-thousandth of a millimetre in diameter and enable the 'sound' of the neuron that has been accessed to be recorded without the 'noise' emanating from neighbouring neurons.

Using a stereotaxic apparatus (see pages 34–35), the electrode is inserted into the brain. It is then attached to an electrical connector cemented to the brain. Finally, the scalp is sewn together. The electrical connector is attached to a wire leading to apparatus that records the electrical activity of the cell as various tasks are performed. Micro-electrodes are so sophisticated that they can detect an electrical charge of one-millionth of a volt.

Recordings of the activity of single neurons have produced a number of interesting findings, particularly into the workings of the visual system. In Chapter 8 we will look at the research conducted by Hubel and Weisel into the workings of the visual system. As we will see, these researchers have been able to build up a detailed picture of some of the ways in which the monkey's brain sorts out visual information. However, since the brain has billions of neurons each of which connects with many others, building up a picture of how the brain works using this method is very slow indeed.

Moreover, since micro-electrodes can destroy brain tissue, their use has been confined to non-human animals making the generalisation of research findings difficult.

CHEMICAL STIMULATION OF THE BRAIN

This technique, used with non-human animals involves introducing a chemical into the brain in order to determine its behavioural and physiological effects. Typically, a thin tube (or micro-pipette) is inserted into the brain with the open end touching the area being studied. A smaller tube is filled with a few crystals of a chemical substance and inserted into the implanted tube. The chemical is then released at the site being stimulated.

Chemical stimulation has been used to trace anatomic pathways in the brain using radioactive 2-deoxyglucose, a form of sugar. Following the injection, the animal is made to perform a certain task. Those brain cells involved in the task use more sugar and so radioactivity builds up in them. After the task has been completed, the animal is 'sacrificed'. The brain is then frozen and thin slices of it are pressed against photographic film (which is sensitive to radioactivity). This indicates which brain cells were particularly active during the performance of the task.

The chemical used depends, of course, on the nature of the study. Perhaps the most commonly used chemicals are those believed to affect synaptic transmission. These produce effects that last longer than those induced by electrical stimulation and allow researchers to make their observations over longer periods of time. However, the data from such studies are often difficult to interpret, with different animals responding differently to the same chemical. Since non-human animals respond differently to one another, we should be cautious in generalising the results to humans.

As well as the practical problems involved in the various methods described above there are, of course, serious ethical issues. Both practical and ethical issues have led researchers to look for alternative ways of studying the brain which do not involve 'direct intervention'. These 'non-invasive' methods are considered below.

Non-invasive methods

RECORDING THE ELECTRICAL ACTIVITY OF THE BRAIN

In Chapter 1 we saw that nerve cells in the brain communicate with one another by releasing neurotransmitters. In 1875, Richard Caton, an English physician, discovered that these chemical changes also produce electrical discharges that can be recorded. Half a century later, a German neurologist, Hans Berger, devised a technique which allowed the electrical activity to be continuously recorded.

Working on the assumption that the part of the brain which is electrically active during some behaviour presumably plays a part in that behaviour, Berger attached two flat silver plates (which acted as electrodes) to the scalp of his son Klaus. The electrodes were attached to a galvanometer, an instrument for measuring small electric currents. After much effort, Berger was successful in recording regular electrical activity from the electrodes, and suggested that the electrical activity was affected by *conscious experience.*

Berger's work was largely ignored until 1934 when Adrian and Matthews confirmed his findings using a newly invented device called an *electroencephalogram* (or *EEG*). Literally, electroencephalography, or the use of the EEG, means 'electrical-in-the-head-writing'. An EEG machine measures the changes in the electrical activity of different parts of the brain. As we will see shortly, there are characteristic patterns of electrical activity which are common to everyone at a particular age or stage of development. However, we should also note that everyone's brain activity is as unique and distinctive as their fingerprints.

With the help of special jelly, small disc-like electrodes are attached to the scalp. Via wires, these electrodes pass electrical information to an amplifier which is capable of detecting impulses of less than $\frac{1}{10000}$th of a volt and then magnifying them by a factor of one million. The amplifier passes its information to pens which trace the impulses on paper that revolves on a drum. The outcome is a permanent record of the oscillating waves produced by the electrical activity. Box 4.1 below describes the ways in which 'brain waves' are measured and the main types of wave that have been identified.

Box 4.1 The measurement of 'brain waves'

EEG activity can be described in two main ways. *Frequency* refers to the number of complete oscillations of a wave that occur in one second. This is measured in cycles per second or Hertz (Hz). The more oscillations that occur in one second, the higher the frequency. *Amplitude* describes half the height from the peak to the trough of a single oscillation. Whilst amplitude is important as a measure of electrical activity, frequency is much more commonly used to describe the brain's electrical activity. The four main types of brain wave are:

- DELTA (1–3 Hz) – mainly found in infants, adults in 'deep' sleep, or adults with brain tumours
- THETA (4–7 Hz) commonly seen in children aged between two and five. In adults, the activity has been observed in a personality disorder called anti-social personality
- ALPHA (8–13 Hz) – this wave can be found in adults who are awake, relaxed, and whose eyes are closed
- BETA (13 Hz and over) – this pattern of activity is found in adults who are awake, alert, whose eyes are open, and who may be concentrating on a task.

The EEG allows researchers to examine the activity of the brain in response to specific experiences as they occur, and it has been found that whilst we are awake our brain's electrical activity changes in response to sights, sounds and other sensory information. As well as being used for research purposes, the EEG is extensively used in clinical diagnosis to detect abnormal brain activity, since research has shown that the EEG patterns from tumours and damaged brain tissue, for example, are very distinctive. Indeed, the EEG has proved invaluable in the diagnosis of *epilepsy*, a condition characterised by abnormal bursts of electrical activity (which may be 20 times that of normal) occurring in rapidly firing individual nerve cells.

In addition to recording the electrical activity in the brain, some researchers also attach electrodes to the skin beneath the chin and near the outer corners of the eyes. The activity recorded from the chin muscles is called an *electromyogram* (EMG) and provides information about muscle tension or relaxation. The activity recorded from near the outer corner of the eyes is called an *electrooculogram* (EOG) and shows the electrical activity that occurs when the eyes move. Any machine that measures more variables than the electrical activity of the brain is called a *polygraph.*

As well as being extensively used for diagnostic purposes, the EEG is also the indispensable tool of researchers who are interested in understanding the nature and functions of *sleep* and *dreaming*. In Chapters 9, 10 and 11 we will discuss research findings related to sleep and dreaming and will make considerable reference to EEG, EMG and EOG measures. As we will see, the activity of our muscles, eyes, and brain is not constant over the course of a night's sleep.

From Chapter 1 we know that the brain contains over 10 billion neurons. Recordings from the scalp therefore reflect the *gross* and simultaneous electrical activity of millions of neurons. For some psychologists, the EEG is analogous to standing outside Wembley Stadium on the day of the Cup Final and hearing a great roar go up from the crowd. A goal could have been scored, but by which side? It could be a penalty, but who to? It might even be the crowd's response to a streaker running across the pitch! In other words, the EEG tells us that *something* is happening but does not enable us to say exactly what.

Recently, however, researchers have found a way of at least partially overcoming this problem. This involves repeatedly presenting a stimulus and having a computer filter out (or 'clean up') the activity unrelated to the stimulus. This technique is known as *computerised electroencephalography*. The filtering out of the extraneous activity leaves what is called an *evoked potential* which can be extremely useful in identifying patterns of activity associated with particular behaviours.

In one study, Donchin (1975) recorded the EEG activity of participants who were exposed to various familiar or predictable stimuli occasionally interspersed with unfamiliar or unpredictable stimuli. Donchin found that the perception of an unexpected event was consistently associated with the production of an evoked potential called P300. Donchin's research suggests that evoked potentials can be helpful to our understanding of the relationship between brain activity and mental processes.

More recently still, researchers have taken advantage of the fact that the brain's electrical activity creates magnetic fields that can be detected outside the skull. *Magnetoencephalograms* (or MEGs) attempt to detect these very weak magnetic fields (which are of the order of one billionth of the earth's magnetic field) that are caused by the passage of electricity. The electrical signals emanating from the brain are distorted when they pass through the skull, making it difficult to identify their point of origin. Magnetic fields are unaffected by bone, and the MEG measures both the strength of the magnetic field and its source. The biggest weakness of MEG is that the magnetic fields are easily disrupted, and this makes measurement extremely difficult. Despite this limitation, MEG has been used successfully to detect disorders such as epilepsy, multiple sclerosis and Alzheimer's disease.

A technique called *EEG imaging* is also proving to be useful in the study of the brain. According to Fischman (1985), this technique allows researchers to measure the functioning of the brain 'on a millisecond by millisecond basis'. The activity recorded by 32 electrodes placed on the scalp is fed to a computer which translates the information into coloured moving images on a television monitor. The technique was originally developed for research into convulsive seizures, but it has also been used to predict learning disabilities in children and for mapping the brain activity of people suffering from psychological disorders (Morris, 1988).

SCANNING AND IMAGING DEVICES

As Carlson (1988) has noted, psychologists know the location of lesions in the brains of laboratory animals because they put them there. Prior to the 1970s, the location of lesions in the human brain could only be identified when the individual died and if the family gave their permission for an autopsy. Since the 1970s, however, a new approach to studying the brain has allowed researchers to identify the location of lesions in *living* individuals, as well as providing other information about the workings of the brain.

For many years, neurologists took X-rays of the head to study brain damage, usually using dyes injected into the circulatory system to make the blood vessels in the brain more visible. However, the flat picture produced by a standard X-ray was not always informative. In the early 1970s *Computerised Axial Tomography* (CAT) was introduced and made the use of X-rays much more informative.

In CAT, the brain is examined by taking a large number of X-ray photographs of it. As shown in Figure 4.4 overleaf, a person's head is placed in a large doughnut-shaped apparatus which has an X-ray source located on one side and an X-ray detector on the other. As the doughnut-shaped apparatus is rotated through many different orientations (or axes), the amount by which the X-rays penetrate the brain is recorded by the detector. This information is fed to a computer which creates detailed images – the CAT scan – which are

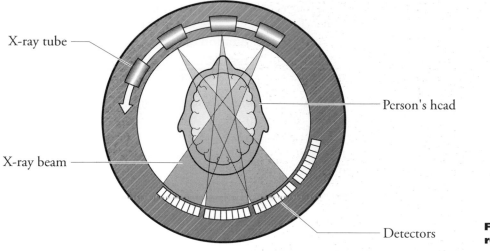

X-ray tube

X-ray beam

Person's head

Detectors

Figure 4.4   Diagrammatic representation of CAT

displayed as a three-dimensional representation of the brain's structures.

CAT is helpful to surgeons because amongst other things it aids decision-making about the procedures that will be followed in an operation on the brain. For psychologists, CAT can help to determine whether a particular behavioural problem has an identifiable physical basis.

A more sophisticated approach than CAT is *Magnetic Resonance Imaging* (MRI). Like CAT, MRI provides a three-dimensional image of brain structures. Although MRI uses similar equipment to CAT, a strong magnetic field rather than X-rays is used to form images of the living brain. The person undergoing MRI is placed in a doughnut-shaped tunnel that generates a powerful magnetic field. Then, harmless radio waves are introduced which excite hydrogen atoms in the brain. This excitation causes changes in the magnetic field which are recorded by a computer and then transformed to an image on a television monitor.

MRI is also used to identify structural disorders and to study the normal brain. One of its advantages over CAT is its sensitivity and the clarity of the images produced. MRI can, for example, identify the smallest tumour with pinpoint accuracy, and locate the slightest reduction in blood flow in an artery or vein. Unfortunately, both CAT and MRI can only provide us with a still image of a cross-section of the brain. Whilst this provides useful information about the brain's structure, it tells us very little about its function.

Positron Emission Tomography (PET) is a method which allows researchers to examine the relationship between activity in the brain and mental processes. PET works by measuring the level of metabolic activity occurring within the brain. A person undergoing PET is first injected with a small amount of harmless radioactive material 'bonded' to a substance, such as glucose, that is metabolised in the body. Since the brain's primary form of energy is glucose, the areas which are most active absorb more of it.

The glucose is broken down by the brain but the radioactive material is not. As it decays, the radioactive material emits positively charged particles called *positrons*. These are detected by sensors arranged about the head. This information is then fed to a computer which produces coloured images of the level of activity occurring throughout the brain, different colours indicating different levels of activity. Figure 4.5 opposite shows a PET machine designed specifically to investigate the human brain. Like CAT and MRI, PET is of great help in diagnosing abnormalities. For example, it is used to locate tumours and growths to give surgeons vital information about the likelihood of essential brain structures being damaged by surgery.

As we noted, PET takes advantage of the fact that at any given time some areas of the brain will be more active than others. PET's biggest advantage over CAT and MRI is that it can be used to provide us with images of what is going on in the brain *during* various behaviours. For example, when a person shuffles a pack of cards there is increased activity in the part of the brain concerned with the regulation of skilled performance. When a person looks at a picture, the area of

Figure 4.5   A typical PET device designed specifically for the study of the human brain. From Gregory (1987)

the brain concerned with the processing of visual information becomes active.

We can also use PET to identify those areas of the brain that are active when we are *thinking*. In one study, Restak (1984) showed that when a person is asked to move the right hand, the front part of the brain and the part that produces movement become active. However, when the person is instructed to 'think about moving the hand' the part of the brain that produces movement is not active but the front part is. In another study, Martin & Brust (1985) asked people to listen to, and attempt to remember, a Sherlock Holmes story. As well as producing activity in the part of the brain responsible for processing auditory information, activity was also observed in the *hippocampus* which, as we saw in Chapter 2, plays an important role in *memory*.

PET has also been shown to be useful in revealing possible differences between the brains of people with and without psychological disorders. For example, it has been shown that the pattern of neural activity in the schizophrenic brain is different to that in the non-schizophrenic brain, suggesting that this particular psychological disorder may have a physical cause.

PET has also been used to explore differences between the sexes. In a study conducted by Robin Gur and his colleagues (1995) at the University of Pennsylvania, PET showed that men have a more active metabolism than women in the primitive brain centres that control sex and violence (see also Chapter 16). Although the results obtained by Gur are reliable, the researchers only studied the brain at rest. However, the potential applications of PET suggest that it will be a useful way of investigating the brain for many years to come.

New imaging and scanning devices are presently being developed and tested. These include the *Superconducting Quantum Imaging Device* (SQUID) and *Single Positron Emission Tomography* (SPET). Like PET, SPET and SQUID are able to map the different brain areas that are either functioning or not functioning during the performance of a task. Although the machines are very expensive (costing around £350,000), their advantage is that they can focus on very small areas of the brain, areas which occupy less than a fiftieth of a cubic inch in volume.

SPET measures the blood that flows into different areas of the brain. When mental activity takes place a great deal of blood is needed. In areas where there is little activity, less blood is required. To use SPET, a person is first injected with a small amount of radioactive iodine which makes the blood vessels, including those in the brain, mildly radioactive. The person is then placed so that the head lies in a ring of detectors, each of which turns the radiation emitted by the iodine into a pulse of light which itself is transformed into a minute electronic signal. By carefully analysing the signals, a computer builds up cross-sections of the brain at various depths depending on the part of the brain researchers are interested in.

SPET has already produced some spectacular results. For example, prolonged and heavy use of alcohol causes a condition known as *Korsakoff's psychosis,* a severe impairment in memory. Using SPET, researchers have been able to show that there is a significant loss of functioning in the front part of the brain. SPET is also proving to be useful in detecting the areas of the brain that are affected in Alzheimer's disease. As George

Fink, director of the brain metabolism unit at the Royal Edinburgh Hospital has observed:

'Really we are just beginning to learn all the different things we can do with these machines. The potential is enormous'.

Conclusions

In this chapter we have discussed the ways in which the brain can be investigated. Although the methods and techniques we have looked at can all tell us something about the way in which the nervous system functions, each has weaknesses which limit the power of the conclusions we can draw from research findings.

SUMMARY

- Three major kinds of methods used to investigate the brain are **clinical and anatomical methods** ('accidental interventions'), **invasive methods** ('deliberate interventions'), and **non-invasive methods** (recording the brain's activity).
- Looking at the behavioural consequences of **accidental** brain damage has a very long history. An assumption made is that, if damage to a specific brain site causes a particular behavioural change, then the damaged part normally plays a role in that behaviour.
- Broca and Wernicke used this method to study patients who had suffered a **cerebrovascular accident** or stroke. Broca's patients had difficulty in **producing** speech and had suffered damage to a different part of the brain from Wernicke's patients, whose main difficulty was in **understanding** speech.
- With many cases of accidental damage, not enough is known about what the patient could do before the damage, especially when the effects are quite subtle. The precise location and amount of damage may be difficult to determine, and researchers cannot choose which brain areas will be affected.
- **Ablation**, which was pioneered by Flourens, involves surgically removing/destroying brain tissue (by cutting with a knife, burning with electrodes, or sucking out through a tube) and observing the behavioural consequences.
- Ablation using non-human animals can tell us little about the human brain. Such studies also face

the problem of **control** versus **involvement**; many parts of the brain might work together to produce a particular behaviour, so we cannot be sure what it means when behaviour changes as a result of one part being removed. These problems also apply to lesion production studies.
- In **lesion production**, an **injury** to the brain is deliberately created by inserting an electrode, using a **stereotaxic apparatus**, which allows precise location of the electrode inside the brain. Changes in behaviour are then observed. Destruction of different sites in the rat's hypothalamus have differential effects on eating behaviour.
- In humans, **split-brain** operations have been used in the treatment of severe epilepsy; they also have interesting consequences for psychology.
- **Electrical stimulation of the brain** (ESB) involves inserting electrodes into the brain of a living animal and passing a non-damaging electric current. Olds and Milner found that stimulating part of the rat's hypothalamus caused an increase in the frequency of whatever it was doing. When the rat could control stimulation of its 'pleasure centre', it would forego food, water, and sex; a different location seemed to act as a 'pain centre'.
- Fritsch and Hitzig pioneered electrical stimulation of the **cerebral cortex**, but the classic research was carried out by Penfield in the course of surgery on epileptics. His conscious patients reported what they experienced as different parts of the cortex were stimulated. ESB has been used

- in the control of severe pain, as experienced by cancer patients.
- ESB is a useful way of mapping the connections between various brain structures. However, no single area is likely to be solely responsible for any given behaviour/emotion. ESB-produced behaviour is often more stereotyped than natural behaviour, and stimulation of the same area can produce different effects at different times.
- The activity of **single** neurons is recorded by using **micro-electrodes,** which are inserted using a stereotaxic apparatus and cemented in place. This has increased our understanding of the visual system in monkeys, but the vast number of connections between neurons makes this a painstaking process.
- **Chemical stimulation of the brain** involves the insertion of a micro-pipette with a smaller tube inside containing a chemical substance, often one which is thought to affect synaptic transmission. The resulting effects last longer than those produced by electrical stimulation, but different non-human animals respond differently to the same chemical, making interpretation difficult.
- All methods involving direct intervention raise serious **ethical** problems, as well as facing practical problems.
- **Recording the electrical activity of the brain** is a non-invasive alternative to direct intervention, pioneered by Berger, who placed silver electrodes, attached to a galvanometer, on his son's scalp. Later, the **electroencephalogram** (EEG) was used; this amplifies the brain's electrical activity which is recorded in the form of oscillating waves on a revolving drum.
- Brain waves can be defined in terms of **frequency** (measured in cycles per second or Hertz/Hz) and **amplitude**, with the former much more commonly used. The four main types are **delta, theta, alpha,** and **beta** waves.
- The EEG records the brain's electrical activity in response to different sensory information, and is widely used in clinical diagnosis of abnormalities, such as tumours, brain damage, and epilepsy.
- The **electromyogram** (EMG) records electrical activity in the chin muscles, and the **electrooculogram** (EOG) records electrical activity from eye movements. These, together with the EEG, are essential tools used in the study of **sleep** and **dreaming**.
- The EEG measures the simultaneous activity of millions of neurons and so provides only very generalised information; **computerised electroencephalography** provides much more specific information, in the form of **evoked potentials**, which can help understand the relationship between brain activity and mental processes.
- **Magnetoencephalograms** (MEGs) try to detect the very weak magnetic fields created by the brain's electrical activity and detectable outside the skull. Despite difficulties, MEG has been used to detect disorders, including multiple sclerosis and Alzheimer's disease.
- **EEG imaging** translates information from 32 electrodes on the scalp into coloured moving images on a TV monitor. It has been used to predict learning disabilities and to chart the brain activity involved in psychological disorders.
- **Computerized Axial Tomography** (CAT) allows researchers to identify the location of lesions in living human brains. Several X-ray photographs are taken in rotation, which are fed to a computer which creates detailed three-dimensional images of the brain's structures.
- **Magnetic Resonance Imaging** (MRI) is more sophisticated than CAT. It produces much clearer, more precise, three-dimensional images based on a strong magnetic field, rather than X-rays. Both MRI and CAT are limited to still images of the brain's structure.
- **Positon Emission Tomography** (PET) measures the level of metabolic activity in the brain following the injection of a radioactive material, which, as it decays, emits **positrons**. A computer produces coloured images of the level of activity throughout the brain, different colours indicating different levels of activity **during the performance of a task**, either physical or mental.
- **PET** has been used to study brain differences between people with and without schizophrenia, as well as sex differences.
- **Superconducting Quantum Imaging Device** (SQUID) and **Single Positron Emission Tomography** (SPET) are among new imaging and scanning devices that are being developed; they are able to focus on tiny areas of the brain. SPET has located the areas involved in Korsakoff's psychosis and Alzheimer's disease.

THE CEREBRAL CORTEX

Introduction and overview

At the end of Chapter 2, we noted that the cerebral cortex is most developed in human beings and is without doubt what separates us from other animals. As well as being the last part of the brain to stop growing and differentiating, it undergoes greater structural change and transformation after birth than any other part of the brain. As we will see, research indicates that certain areas of the cortex are specialised for particular mental processes and behaviours and this offers support for what is known as the *theory of localisation*.

We will begin this chapter by outlining the theory of localisation. After this, we will look at specific processes and behaviours which have relatively precise and circumscribed cortical locations. The cortex can be conveniently divided up into *primary areas* and *association areas*. Following a consideration of the primary *motor* area and the various primary *sensory* areas, we will look at the motor and sensory *association* areas which are intimately associated with the primary areas. We will conclude our discussion of the cortex by examining other areas of it which do not seem to be involved in either motor or sensory functions, but which appear to play a role in the higher cognitive processes such as learning, thinking, and memory. The role of the cortex in *language* will be considered in Chapter 6.

The theory of localisation

According to the theory of localisation, different areas of the brain and cortex are specialised for different psychological functions. This idea is not new and can be traced back to the work of an Austrian physician, Franz Joseph Gall (1758–1828). When he was a young boy, Gall noticed that some of his friends who seemed to have particularly good memories also had large protruding eyes. His explanation for this was that the front of their brains (which he believed to be the location of memories) was so well developed that it had pushed out the eyes. As he wrote in 1812, 'I was forced to the idea that the eyes so formed are the mark of an excellent memory'. On the basis of this and other observations, Gall developed the discipline of *phrenology*.

Phrenologists saw the brain as being composed of a number of separate organs, each of which was responsible for a different psychological trait. The unusual growth of any of these organs would create a bump on the skull, and a person's character could therefore be determined by the pattern of bumps on the skull. For example, a bump on the back of the head indicated that a person was 'cautious' whilst a bump on the side of the head indicated a 'secretive' individual. A bump just above the ears meant, as far as phrenologists were concerned, that a person was 'destructive' and, potentially, a 'criminal'.

Although fashionable in the early nineteenth century, the discipline of phrenology fell into disrepute on the quite reasonable grounds that it was wrong. However, as some psychologists have noted, it was 'just right enough' to continue further interest in the idea that psychological functions are localised in certain parts of the brain. The findings that have been obtained are described in detail below.

THE PRIMARY MOTOR AREA

As we saw in the previous chapter, electrical stimulation of the brain has been used extensively as a way of attempting to understand its function. One finding we briefly described in Chapter 4 was that some areas of the cortex seem to be specialised in governing motor activity, that is, our actual movement.

In his studies carried out in the 1940s and 1950s, Wilder Penfield showed that stimulation of part of the cortex at the back of the frontal lobe and just in front of the central fissure in one cerebral hemisphere caused his patients to twitch specific muscles in the opposite side of the body. In a dramatic illustration of this, Delgado (1969) stimulated a particular part of the primary motor area in the left hemisphere of one of his patients. This caused the patient to form a clenched fist with his right hand. When asked to try and keep his fingers still during the next stimulation of his cortex, the patient could not achieve this and commented, 'I guess, Doctor, that your electricity is stronger than my will'.

You may recall that control of one side of the body by the opposite hemisphere is called a *contralateral connection* (and is contrasted with an *ipsilateral connection* in which information from one half of the body is received, processed, and acted upon by the same side of the body). You may also remember that the crossing over of the nerve fibres connecting each hemisphere to the opposite side of the body takes place in the *medulla oblongata* (see page 17). This phenomenon is known as *corticospinal decussation*.

Penfield discovered that when he stimulated the *top* of the primary motor area (or *motor strip*), a twitching in the *lower* part of the body (such as the leg) occurred. However, stimulation of the *bottom* part of the motor strip produced movement in the *upper* part of the body (such as the tongue). On the basis of these findings, Penfield concluded that the body is represented in an approximately upside down fashion in the primary motor area. Of equal interest was his finding that those areas of the body which require precise control, such as the fingers and the mouth, have more cortical area devoted to them than those requiring less precise control.

It is important to note that the primary motor area itself is not responsible for the 'command' to move the 600 muscles in the body that are involved in voluntary movement. These commands are initiated in other parts of the cortex. However, once a command has been given, nerve cells in the primary motor area are activated, and send their information to the muscles that perform movements. What Penfield's research identified, then, was exactly where the response messages from the brain start their return trip to the muscles and glands of the body. Damage to the primary motor area does not produce complete paralysis. However, it often results in a loss of control over 'fine' movements (especially of the fingers).

THE PRIMARY SENSORY AREAS

In the same way that some parts of the cortex are specialised for motor functions, others govern sensory functions and receive their information in a precise, orderly way from the thalamus (see page 19).

The primary somatosensory area

As we have just seen, the primary motor area *transmits* information out to the body. Certain types of incoming information are *received* by the part of the cortex called the *primary somatosensory area*. This is found in the parietal lobe, just across the central fissure, and is a thin 'strip' along which information from the skin senses (such as touch, temperature, pressure, and so on) is represented. It also receives information concerning *taste*.

Micro-electrode stimulation of the primary somatosensory area might produce the sensation that the arm, for example, is being touched or pinched or that the leg 'feels hot'. Careful investigation has revealed that, like the primary motor area, the body is represented in an approximately upside-down fashion and that those parts of the body which are more sensitive (such as the face and genitals) have more cortex devoted to them. Relatively insensitive parts of the body, such as the trunk, have considerably less area devoted to them.

We should also note that there is a clear relationship between the *importance* of a body part and the amount of cortex devoted to it. In animals that use their forepaws to explore the environment (such as the racoon), there is a large amount of forepaw cortical representation. In rats, the amount of primary somatosensory area devoted to the whiskers is very large. If a human, say, is unfortunate enough to lose a finger, the somatosensory part responsible for receiving input from that finger becomes available to receive input from other fingers. As a result, the other fingers become *more sensitive* (Fox, 1984). Similarly, Robertson (1995) reports that in Braille readers the cortical area devoted to the tip of the right forefinger is considerably enlarged as compared with the left and is larger than that in non-Braille readers.

As was the case with the primary motor area, the primary somatosensory area in the left hemisphere registers information about the right side of the body, that is, the connections are *contralateral*. If the primary somatosensory area is damaged, deficits or disturbances in the sense of touch result. The extent of these deficits or disturbances depends on the amount of damage. With very mild damage, a person might not be able to make fine distinctions between the temperature of objects but could tell the difference between 'hot' and 'cold'. With more severe damage, a person might not be able to distinguish between different temperatures at all.

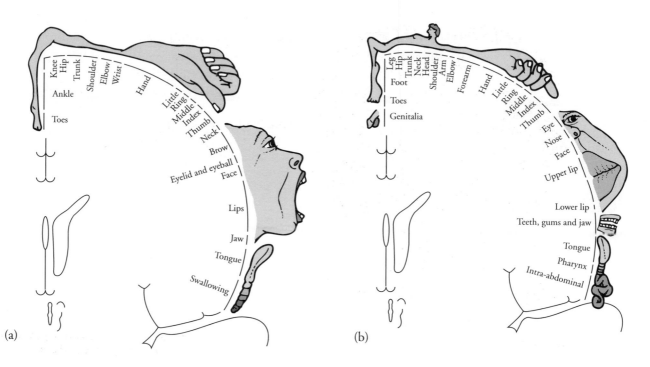

Figure 5.1 (a) and (b)   A cross-section through the cortex. Part (a) shows the primary motor area and the parts of the body it is concerned with. Part (b) shows the primary somatosensory area and the parts of the body it is concerned with

Figure 5.1(a) above shows a cross-section through the cerebral cortex just anterior to (or forward of) the central fissure. This part of the cortex is the primary motor area. Figure 5.1(b) shows a cross-section through the cortex just posterior to (or behind) the central fissure. This part is the primary somatosensory area.

The primary auditory area

The primary auditory area of the cortex lies in the temporal lobe of each hemisphere, along the lateral fissure. When auditory information is detected by the ear it is transmitted via the thalamus to the primary auditory area and causes neurons in that area to be activated. Penfield discovered that stimulation of neurons in this area caused his patients to report hearing sounds such as 'the ringing of a door bell' or 'the engine of a car'. The neurons in the primary auditory area are highly specialised. Micro-electrode recording studies have shown that some neurons respond only to low-pitched sounds whereas others respond only to high-pitched sounds.

Most of the auditory information from one ear travels to the primary auditory area in the hemisphere on the opposite side. However, some information is processed on the same side. In hearing, then, there are both contralateral and ipsilateral connections. Slight damage to the primary auditory area produces 'partial hearing loss'. The more extensive the damage, the greater is the loss. Figure 5.2 opposite illustrates the major pathways of the auditory nerve fibres.

The primary visual area

One of Penfield's first findings was that parts of the cortex are specialised to receive visual sensory information. For example, when a stimulating electrode was applied to the occipital lobe his patients reported 'seeing' different kinds of visual displays. Penfield (1947) reported the descriptions given by his patients as follows:

'Flickering lights, dancing lights, colours, bright lights, star wheels, blue-, green-, and red-coloured discs, fawn and blue lights, radiating grey spots becoming pink and blue, a long white mark, and so on'.

Although Penfield's patients never reported a complete picture of the visual displays they experienced, his findings were sufficient to convince him that the primary visual area of the brain is located in the occipital lobe. When the visual area is damaged, blindness (or a 'hole') occurs in part of the visual field. The rest of the visual sense is, however, intact. Indeed, by moving the eyes,

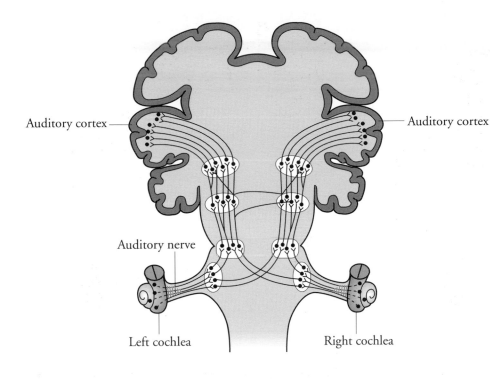

Auditory cortex

Auditory cortex

Auditory nerve

Left cochlea

Right cochlea

Figure 5.2   The major pathways of the auditory nerve fibres

those aspects of the visual world which cannot be seen can be brought into view, although the person will still be blind in some part of the visual field.

In Chapter 8, we will take a detailed look at the structures and processes involved in visual perception. However, it is worth briefly describing the way in which visual information reaches the primary visual area of the cortex. When light strikes the *retina* of the eyes, it is converted into electrical information which then passes along the *optic nerve* of each eye. At a point called the *optic chiasma*, the nerve fibres from each eye meet and divide up in a special way.

For each of our eyes, the fibres from the half of each retina closest to the nose cross over and continue their journey in the hemisphere on the opposite side. The fibres from each half of the retina closest to the temples do not cross over and continue their journey in the hemisphere on the same side. Now, our visual world can be divided into a *left visual field* and a *right visual field*. As Figure 5.3 overleaf illustrates, information from the left visual field is processed by the right cerebral hemisphere whereas information from the right visual field is processed by the left cerebral hemisphere.

As you can see, this occurs because of the crossing over of the fibres at the optic chiasma. This arrangement means that each hemisphere receives information from

each eye. Although it might be simpler if each eye transmitted information to the hemisphere on the same side, damage to one eye would mean that a hemisphere would no longer receive any visual information. By having the more complex arrangement we have described, damage to one eye does *not* result in a hemisphere 'missing out' on visual information. As we mentioned in Chapter 2, visual sensory information travels to the thalami, and is sent on from there to the primary visual area via the lateral geniculate nucleus (see Chapter 8).

ASSOCIATION AREAS IN THE CORTEX

The primary motor and sensory areas account for a relatively small proportion of the surface area of the cortex. The primary motor area sends information to adjacent areas of the cortex called the *motor association areas*. Each of the primary sensory areas sends information to adjacent *sensory association areas*.

Motor association areas

These are involved in the planning and execution of movements, the information about which movements are to be executed being sent to the primary motor area. The motor association areas receive their information from several areas and integrate this information into plans and actions. One region of the cortex is

47

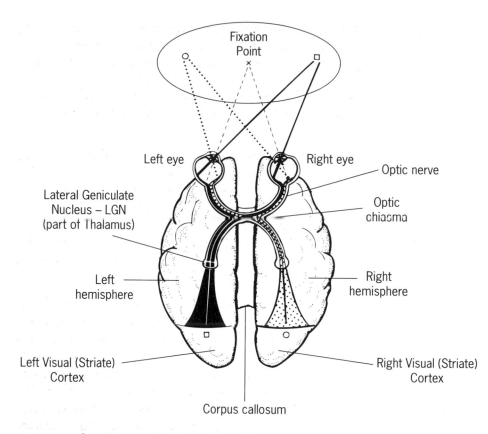

Fixation
Point

Left eye   Right eye   Optic nerve

Lateral Geniculate
Nucleus – LGN
(part of Thalamus)

Optic
chiasma

Left
hemisphere

Right
hemisphere

Left Visual (Striate)
Cortex

Right Visual (Striate)
Cortex

Corpus callosum

**Figure 5.3   The major pathways of
the visual nerve fibres**

necessary for the production of spoken language, and
we will describe it in detail in the following chapter.

Damage to the left parietal lobe results in a person
being unable to make his or her hand go where it
should. One illustration of this is in attempts by people
with left parietal lobe damage to draw. In Figure 5.4
we can see the attempts of a person with left parietal
lobe damage to draw a bicycle. Although the propor-
tions of the elements that make up the bike are quite
good, the drawing looks clumsy and might have been
done by a child. Quite possibly, then, the motor association area's ability to integrate information into plans

and actions is disrupted when the left parietal lobe is
damaged.

According to Carlson (1988), the motor association
areas in the left parietal lobe play an important role in
our ability to keep track of the location of the moving
parts of the body. This view is strengthened by the
finding that people with left parietal lobe damage often
have difficulty with tasks which require them to point
to a part of the body. They may, for example, point to
the shoulder when asked to point to the elbow. Quite
possibly, damage to the left parietal lobe results in
'faulty data' being sent to the primary motor area, and
this leads to poor execution of movement.

Sensory association areas

Each of the primary sensory areas we described above
sends information to adjacent sensory association areas.
As we saw earlier on, the primary somatosensory area
mediates our awareness of what is happening in the
body and on its surface. Severe damage to the
somatosensory association areas produces a disorder
called *sensory neglect*. In this, the affected person loses
all awareness of the opposite side of the body. For
example, Halligan (1995) reports that a person having
a shave will shave only one side of the face. Food will
be eaten on only one side of the plate, and drawings of

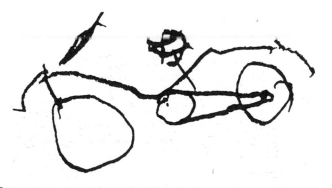

**Figure 5.4   Drawing of a bicycle by a person with
damage to the left parietal lobe**

Figure 5.5   Drawing of a parrot by a person with left-side neglect

objects show inadequate representations of one half of the thing being drawn, as illustrated in Figure 5.5.

Associations in the parietal lobe appear to play a role in the *integration* of complex sensory functions. This can be shown in a simple task called *cross-modal matching*. If an object is placed in your hand but kept out of sight you would, when you were *shown* an array of objects in which it was included, be able to pick it out. This is because ordinarily we are able to integrate visual and tactile information. People with damage in the association areas of the parietal lobe, however, find this task extremely difficult.

The *auditory association area* is located towards the back of the occipital lobes on the side of the temporal lobes. If the auditory association area in the left hemisphere is damaged, severe disturbances of language occur. For example, the ability to comprehend speech is lost, presumably because the neurons that play a role in decoding speech sounds have been destroyed. Additionally, the ability to read is lost and whilst the person may still be capable of producing language, its quality is very poor indeed and just a meaningless jumble of words.

Damage to the right hemisphere, by contrast, does not

affect the production or reception of speech to any great degree. It does, however, affect the ability to perceive the *location* of sounds and the ability to recognise non-speech sounds such as rhythms and tones. As we noted earlier, we will return to the issue of the brain structures involved in language in the following chapter.

In contrast to the effects produced by damage to the primary visual area, the *visual association area* (which includes parts of the temporal and parietal lobes in addition to the occipital lobes) does not produce blindness. However, whilst the primary sensory function of vision is not impaired, the ability to *recognise* objects by sight is impaired. This condition is called *visual agnosia* ('agnosia' means 'failure to know').

In one famous case, the neurologist Oliver Sacks described a person who could not even recognise his own wife. At the end of one testing session, the person started to look for his hat. He reached over to his wife and began to lift her head, seemingly believing it to be his hat. Evidently, the man had mistaken his wife's head for his own hat (Sacks, 1985). It would seem, then, that damage to some parts of the visual association area produces deficits in the visual recognition of familiar objects.

Damage to the occipital lobes results in the inability to recognise the elements of a visual scene such as curves and angles whilst damage to the right parietal lobe results in great difficulty integrating the parts of an object into a consistent whole. In contrast to the drawing of the bicycle produced by a person with left parietal lobe damage (see Figure 5.4), a person with a damaged right parietal lobe produces a drawing which is smoothly executed and well-detailed, but does not have all of the parts placed appropriately. This is illustrated in Figure 5.6.

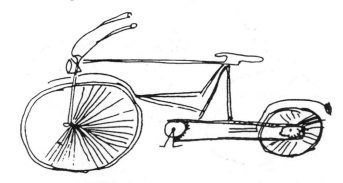

Figure 5.6   Drawing of a bicycle by a person with right parietal lobe damage

From what we have said, it is clear that sensory association areas are located near to their primary sensory area counterparts and receive information only about one sense modality. However, there are other sensory association areas which receive information from more than one sense modality. These perform higher-order analyses of sensory information and represent abstract information in ways that are independent of individual sense modalities.

When we think about the word 'dog', for example, we can picture a visual image of a particular dog, the sound of its bark, and (perhaps) the pain we felt when it bit us. We can also think about the visual representation of the word 'd-o-g' and the sound of the word 'dog'. Our thoughts can be stimulated when we actually see a dog, hear the word being said, or read a book in which the word is printed. The centres of higher-order analysis include areas on the borders between the temporal, parietal and occipital lobes.

ASSOCIATION AREAS NOT INVOLVED IN MOTOR OR SENSORY FUNCTIONS

Even given what we have described, there are still large areas of the cortex that do not seem to be involved in either motor or sensory aspects of behaviour. Although our knowledge is still limited, we do know that these other parts of the cortex are involved in the more complex psychological functions of learning, thinking, memory, and so on. Indeed, the term 'association areas' was originally used to describe these areas because it was strongly believed that they were used in higher cognitive processes such as forming associations between things. We shall now briefly review some of the knowledge that has been gained about these areas.

The frontal lobe is larger in humans than in any other species. For that reason it was once thought to be 'the seat of intelligence'. However, a number of studies have revealed that frontal lobe damage does not cause significant impairments in intellectual functioning. Rather, it seems to affect the ability to set goals, plan actions, and make decisions. Put another way, frontal lobe damage affects our *intentions*.

Research also indicates that damage to the frontal lobes results in the inability to change a behaviour in response to a change in a situation. In one study, for example, Cotman & McGaugh (1980) described a person who worked in a carpenter's shop. Although this person could sand a piece of wood, he did not know to stop when the sanding was complete. As a result, he sanded completely through the wood and continued sanding the work bench below. In another study, Luria (1980) reported the case of a man who kept trying to light a match that was already lit. The term *perseveration* has been used to describe these behaviours.

Card-sorting tasks also illustrate perseveration. In these, a person is given a series of cards each of which has one or more patterns on it (such as squares, triangles, and so on) in one of several colours. People with frontal lobe damage have few difficulties in sorting the cards according to colour, but when asked to sort them according to shape, they have great difficulty and continue sorting according to colour. Studies of the effects of frontal lobe damage in non-humans have shown the inability to remember the solution to a simple problem for more than a few seconds (Rosenkilde & Divac, 1976). Similarly, humans have been shown to have difficulties in remembering the solutions to problems, especially those which require switching back and forth from one solution to another (Passingham, 1985).

Frontal lobe damage is also associated with changes in personality. For example, a person may show a lack of restraint, and a general lack of 'social graces'. Personality can also be affected in other ways. For example, frontal lobe damage may cause a person to react with indifference to emotionally-provoking events. Being informed of the death of a close relative may, for example, produce no over-emotional reaction from a person with frontal lobe damage even though he or she understands what has happened.

Other consequences of frontal lobe damage include a lack of insight and an uncritical acceptance of the failure to solve a task. Excessive damage produces *behavioural inertia* in which a person lacks spontaneity, remains motionless and stares vacantly into space. At a conference of neurologists held in 1935, Jacobsen and Fulton reported that removal of a monkey's frontal lobes produced a reduction in the amount of frustration that was shown when the monkey failed to perform a task correctly. Egas Moniz, a Portuguese neuropsychiatrist, wondered if the removal of the frontal lobes would produce similar effects in humans.

Surgically damaging the frontal lobes became a 'popular' way of treating psychological disorders in the 1930s and 1940s. A large number of operations were carried out, especially by the Americans Freeman and Watts.

Freeman in particular saw the *frontal lobotomy* as *the* way of treating psychological disorders. Indeed, he developed one procedure which he suggested could result in a lobotomy 'being done in a couple of minutes'. He further suggested that 'an enterprising neurologist (could) lobotomise ten to fifteen patients in a morning'. Although surgically damaging the frontal lobes for therapeutic purposes does still take place, the ethical issues that surround *psychosurgery* have resulted in it becoming very much a therapeutic approach of absolutely the last resort.

One final consequence of frontal lobe damage worthy of mention is the production of reflexive behaviour which is normally seen only in babies, such as sucking an object placed near the mouth. Quite possibly, one role of the frontal lobes is to suppress such activities (which are presumably the result of activity in the more 'primitive' parts of the brain) when they are no longer needed.

The association areas in the temporal lobes play an important role in memory. Stimulation of these areas results in a person recalling a 'dream-like' reliving of a past event. For example, when Penfield stimulated a particular area of a young woman's temporal lobe she said, 'I think I heard a mother calling her little boy somewhere. It seemed to be something that happened years ago . . . in the neighbourhood where I live'. When the same part was stimulated moments later, the woman said, 'Yes. I hear the same familiar sounds. It seems to be a woman calling; the same lady'. When Penfield moved the electrode slightly and stimulated the woman's cortex she said, 'I hear voices. It is late at night, around the carnival somewhere – some sort of travelling circus. I just saw lots of big wagons that they use to haul animals in'.

Association areas in the temporal lobe also play a role in both social behaviour and certain emotional responses (Carlson, 1987). In certain types of damage to the temporal lobe, a person becomes a compulsive talker who harangues anyone who is (or potentially could be) listening, even if listeners have not the slightest interest in what is being said. As Carlson has observed, this finding suggests that the association areas of the temporal lobe (especially, it seems, of the right hemisphere) play a role in evaluating the appropriateness of thoughts and speech. If the temporal lobes are damaged, the inability to carry out such evaluations is impaired.

Holism as an alternative to localisation

The findings we have discussed relating to cortical areas lend strong support to the theory of localisation we outlined at the beginning of this chapter. However, localisation has not been universally accepted. According to supporters of *holistic theory*, psychological functions are controlled by neurons throughout the brain rather than being concentrated in specific locations. In the 1920s, Karl Lashley studied the effects of destroying various parts of rats' brains on their ability to remember the way through a complex maze. Although the rats displayed some difficulties as a result of the damage, Lashley discovered that destruction of one particular area did not lead to a greater difficulty than destruction of any other area.

In follow-up experiments, Lashley varied the *amount* of cortex he destroyed in rats who had learned their way through the maze. He found that the greater the amount of cortex that was destroyed, the greater were the effects, and he called this the *law of mass action*. However, he also found that even rats with considerable damage could still find their way through the maze. In 1950, Lashley gave up his search for the part of the brain where memories were stored and remarked that, on the basis of his studies, the only conclusion 25 years of research led him to was that 'learning just is not possible!'

From what we have seen in this chapter, it seems undeniable that at least *some* mental processes and behaviours are localised in certain parts of the brain. However, this does not necessarily mean that we can reject holism as an alternative to localisation. We shall return to this issue in the following chapter.

Conclusions

Quite clearly, the cerebral cortex plays a vital role in our behaviours and mental processes. As well as dealing with motor and sensory aspects of behaviour, the cortex is also responsible for our higher cognitive processes. When the cortex is damaged, various effects are produced depending on the part of the cortex affected. With the introduction of the non-invasive methods of studying the brain we described in Chapter 4, we can confidently expect our knowledge of the cortex and its functions to increase dramatically in the next few years.

In the remainder of this part of the book, we will look in more detail at some of the processes that occur in the cerebral cortex.

SUMMARY

- The cerebral cortex is the last part of the brain to stop growing and differentiating; it also undergoes the greatest structural change after birth.
- According to the **theory of localisation**, different areas of the cortex are specialised for different psychological functions. This idea can be traced to Gall, who developed **phrenology**, according to which bumps on the skull were caused by enlargement of different organs, each of which determined a particular psychological trait.
- Penfield and Delgado showed that stimulation of the **primary motor area** (or **motor strip**) in one cerebral hemisphere caused muscle twitches in the opposite side of the body. This **contralateral control** (as opposed to **ipsilateral connection**) is sited in the medulla oblongata through **corticospinal decussation**.
- Stimulating the **top** or **bottom** of the primary motor area causes twitching in the **lower** or **upper** part of the body respectively. Penfield concluded from this that the primary motor area represents the body in an upside-down fashion.
- Those areas of the body which require precise control have more cortical area devoted to them. Although damage to the primary motor area does not produce complete paralysis, it often results in loss of control over fine movements, especially of the fingers.
- The **primary somatosensory area** receives incoming sensory information, via the thalamus, regarding the skin senses and taste. The body is represented in an upside-down fashion, with more sensitive and **important** body parts having more cortex devoted to them, such as rats' whiskers and the tip of the right forefinger in Braille readers.
- The primary somatosensory area also operates according to **contralateral control.** The extent of deficits in the sense of touch, such as discriminating temperature, will depend on the amount of damage to the area.

- The **primary auditory area** receives auditory information from the ear via the thalamus. Stimulation of the area, which contains highly specialised neurons, produces experience of quite specific sounds. Both contralateral **and** ipsilateral connections are involved.
- Stimulation of the **primary visual area** produces different kinds of visual displays. Damage to the visual area produces a 'hole' in part of the visual field, but moving the eyes can bring the 'missing' aspects of the visual world into view.
- Light striking the **retina** is converted into electrical information which passes along the **optic nerve** of each eye. At the **optic chiasma**, the fibres from the half of each retina closest to the nose cross over to the opposite hemisphere, while those closest to the temples stay on the same side.
- Information from the **left (right) visual field** is processed by the **right (left) cerebral hemisphere**; this means that each hemisphere receives information from each eye, so that damage to one eye does **not** result in a hemisphere receiving no visual information.
- Each of the primary sensory areas sends information to adjacent **sensory association areas**. **Motor association areas** are involved in the planning/execution of movements, receiving their information from several areas, integrating it, then instructing the primary motor area to execute particular movements.
- The integration of information into plans and actions is disrupted as a result of damage to the left parietal lobe, which also seems to be involved in the ability to keep track of the location of the moving parts of the body.
- Severe damage to the **somatosensory association areas** produces **somatosensory neglect**, in which the person loses awareness of the opposite side of the body. Damage in the association areas of the parietal lobe prevents **cross-modal matching**.

- Damage to the **auditory association area** in the left hemisphere results in severe language disturbances, such as the inability to comprehend speech, to read, and to produce meaningful speech. Damage to the right hemisphere affects the ability to perceive the **location** of sounds and to recognise non-speech sounds.
- Damage to the **visual association area** does not produce blindness, but does cause **visual agnosia.** Damage to the occipital lobes produces inability to recognise the elements of a visual scene, while damage to the right parietal lobe results in difficulty in integrating the parts of an object into a consistent whole.
- Some association areas receive information from more than one sense modality; they perform higher-order analyses of sensory information and represent information in abstract ways.
- There are large areas of the cortex that are not obviously involved in either motor or sensory aspects of behaviour, but are involved in more complex psychological functions, such as learning, thinking, and memory.
- The frontal lobe seems to be involved in setting goals, planning actions, and making decisions (i.e. our **intentions**); frontal lobe damage results in inability to change behaviour in response to situational change, as in **perseveration**.
- Frontal lobe damage is also associated with changes in personality, a lack of insight, uncritical acceptance of failure to solve a problem, the production of reflexive behaviour, and, in extreme cases, **behavioural inertia**.
- **Frontal lobotomy** involves surgically damaging the frontal lobes in the treatment of psychological disorders. The ethical issues surrounding the use of **psychosurgery** make it a 'last resort' treatment.
- **Temporal lobe** association areas play an important role in memory, social behaviour, and certain emotional responses. Damage impairs the ability to evaluate the appropriateness of thoughts and speech.
- In contrast with the theory of **localisation**, **holistic theory** maintains that psychological functions are controlled by neurons **throughout** the brain. Lashley's **law of mass action** stresses the **amount** of cortex destroyed, rather than the particular area involved.

LANGUAGE AND THE BRAIN

Introduction and overview

In the previous chapter we described the role that certain areas of the cortex play in our mental processes and behaviour. The cortical areas we described in Chapter 5 are found in *both* cerebral hemispheres. However, research indicates that for the overwhelming majority of people some functions and processes are associated with *one or other* of the cerebral hemispheres rather than both. One of these processes is the production and comprehension of language. In this chapter we will extend our consideration of the cortex by looking at the areas of it that are associated with language and some of the disorders that arise when these areas are damaged.

Cortical areas, language, and language disorders

As we noted in the previous chapter, Gall's theory of phrenology fell into disrepute because it was wrong. However, Gall did make some suggestions which most psychologists would consider to be more or less correct. One of these concerned speech. Gall argued that the frontal lobes of the brain were specialised for speech. An admirer who was particularly impressed with the theory of phrenology offered the (ridiculously large at the time) sum of 500 French francs to anyone who could find a person with frontal lobe damage who did *not* have a speech disorder.

The offer of the money led a young French physician called Paul Broca (see Chapter 4) to begin examining patients who had difficulty in producing speech. His first case, 'Tan', was so named because this was the only word he could say. 'Tan' was originally admitted to the hospital in which Broca worked because he had a serious leg infection, but it was his difficulty in producing speech that most interested Broca.

Shortly after his admission, 'Tan' died as a result of his infection and Broca conducted a post-mortem on him. The post-mortem indicated that 'Tan' had suffered strokes which caused multiple *lesions* in a small area of

the cerebral cortex in the frontal lobe of the left hemisphere. In the next three years, Broca reported a number of other cases, all with the same problem as 'Tan' and all with lesions in a specific part of the left frontal lobe.

At around the same time that Broca was reporting his findings, a German surgeon, Carl Wernicke (see Chapter 4), described patients who had difficulty in understanding language but no difficulty in producing it, even though what was produced was more often than not meaningless. Wernicke identified a region in the temporal lobe as being responsible for the deficit and the parts of the cortex identified by him and Broca are now known as *Wernicke's area* and *Broca's area* respectively. These areas are shown in Figure 6.1 below.

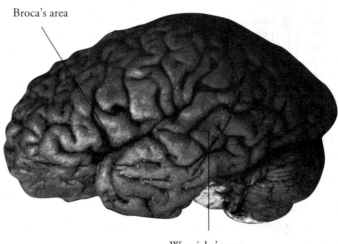

Broca's area

Wernicke's area

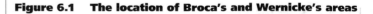

Figure 6.1   The location of Broca's and Wernicke's areas

Disorders of language arising from brain damage are called *aphasias*. However, there are some psychologists (such as Milner, 1971) who argue that the term should only be used to describe a complete loss of language, *dysphasia* being a more accurate term to describe a partial loss of language (the word aphasia comes from the Greek word 'aphitos' which means 'speechless'). A variety of aphasias, resulting from one or more lesions to the brain, have been identified and there have been several attempts to classify them.

Some classifications are based on the presumed location of the lesion(s), whilst others are based on the general sensory and/or motor functions which are impaired. A third, the *Boston Classification* (Kertesz, 1979) is based on the particular linguistic skill the affected individual has lost. Box 6.1 (adapted from Beaumont, 1988) summarises the five types of aphasia recognised by the Boston Classification.

Box 6.1   The five types of aphasia recognised by the Boston Classification

	Type of aphasia				
	Broca's	Wernicke's	Conduction	Anomic	Transcortical (MTA)
Is the person fluent?	No	Yes	Reasonably	Yes	No
Is speech and writing normal?	No	No	Yes	Yes	No
Can the person repeat back words?	Limited ability	Limited ability	No	Yes	Yes
Can the person name things?	Limited ability	Limited ability	Limited ability	No	No
Can the person comprehend speech?	Yes	No	Yes	Yes	No

In some cases, where there is a gross disturbance of language abilities, people do not fit neatly into the Boston Classification. Such individuals are termed *global aphasics*. In other cases, however, it is possible to use the Boston Classification to identify a person as having one of five types of aphasia, which we briefly describe below.

BROCA'S APHASIA

A person with damage to Broca's area experiences *Broca's aphasia*, which is sometimes termed *ataxic*, *expressive*, *non-fluent* or *motor aphasia*. Usually, a Broca's aphasic is able to comprehend spoken or written language either normally or nearly normally. However, the person has great difficulty in producing speech (as Broca observed over one hundred years ago). Typically, speech production is slow, laboured, non-fluent, and difficult for the listener to understand.

For example, Geschwind (1979) reported the case of a Broca's aphasic who was asked about his dental appointment. He replied, 'Yes ... Monday ... Dad and Dick ... Wednesday nine o'clock ... ten o'clock ... doctors ... teeth'. As this example shows, Broca's aphasics find it difficult to produce 'function words', that is, words with grammatical meaning such as 'a', 'the' and 'about'. Their language consists almost entirely of what are called 'content words', that is, words which convey meaning such as nouns, verbs, adjectives and adverbs. As a result, Broca's aphasia has a *telegraphic* quality to it.

In milder cases, the person might be aware that speech is not correct, and may become irritated by being unable to produce the intended words. Another characteristic of Broca's aphasia is the production of *phonemic paraphrasias*. In these, certain words are mispronounced. For example, instead of saying 'lipstick' the person might say 'likstip'. In some cases, Broca's aphasia is accompanied by difficulty in writing, which is termed *agraphia*. Broca's area stores the 'motor plans' for the formulation of words. Normally, these plans are passed to the primary motor area which initiates the processes that will convert them to spoken language. When Broca's area is damaged, 'faulty data' are sent to the primary motor area and this results in the characteristic deficits in speech production we described above.

WERNICKE'S APHASIA

Damage to Wernicke's area produces *Wernicke's aphasia*, which is also known as *receptive*, *sensory*, or *fluent aphasia*. Its major characteristic is a difficulty in understanding spoken and written language. Luria (1973), for example, described a patient who was puzzled by the question 'Is an elephant bigger than a fly?' He told Luria that he 'just didn't understand the words smaller or bigger' and that he 'somehow thinks the expression "a fly is smaller than an elephant" means that they're talking about a very small elephant and a big fly'.

In a much more serious case, Kertesz (1979) reported the response given by a person who was asked, 'What kind of work did you do before you came into the hospital?' The patient replied:

'Never, now mista oyge I wanna tell you this happened when he rent. His – his kell come down here and is – he got ren something. It happened. In these ropiers were with him for hi – is friend – like was. And it just happened so I don't know, he did not bring around anything. And he did not pay for it. And he roden all o these arranjen from the pedis on from his pescid. In these floors now and so. He hadn't had em round here.'

Similarly, Rochford (1974) reports the case of a person who was asked why he had been admitted to hospital. The patient replied:

'Boy I'm sweating, I'm awful nervous, you know, once in a while I get caught up, I can't mention the tarripoi, a month ago, quite a little I've done a lot well. I'm pose a lot, while, on the other hand, you know what I mean.'

As we can see from these examples, Wernicke's aphasics have difficulty in understanding language and the language they produce is, at least in some cases, virtually unintelligible and lacking coherence. Thus, when asked to describe a picture of two boys stealing biscuits behind a woman's back, a patient of Geschwind's replied, 'Mother is away here working her work to get better, but when she's looking the two boys looking in the other part. She's working another time' (Geschwind, 1979).

The noted neurologist John Hughlings Jackson described the verbal outpourings of Wernicke's aphasics as 'a peculiar and outwardly meaningless language form'. Sigmund Freud described such utterances as 'an impoverishment of words with an abundance of speech impulse'. It has been suggested that Freud saw such verbal behaviour as an indication of a serious mental disorder. However, and as Williams (1981) has noted:

'The aphasic patient nearly always tries hard to communicate, whereas in (the seriously psychologically disturbed individual) communication seems to be irrelevant'.

One characteristic of Wernicke's aphasia which is evident in some of the examples given above is the production of *jargon*, that is, nonsense words or *neologisms*. For example, when Rochford (1974) asked a Wernicke's aphasic to name a picture of an anchor, the patient called it a 'martha argeneth'. Similarly, in a study reported by Kertesz (1979) a patient asked to name a toothbrush and a pen responded with 'stoktery' and 'minkt'.

We should note that merely because a Wernicke's aphasic does not give the correct answer to a question, it does not necessarily mean that the question has not been understood. Wernicke's aphasia is also charac-

terised by what are termed *semantic paraphrasias*, in which the word that is produced does not have the intended meaning although it may be related to the intended word. For example, instead of producing the word 'table', the word 'chair' may be produced. In order to assess comprehension, non-verbal responses must be elicited. One test asks the patient to point to various objects on a table in front of him or her. If the patient is asked to 'point to the one you unlock a door with' and responds by pointing to an object which is not a key, the request has not been understood.

Wernicke's aphasics, then, are capable of using some language including function words, complex verb tenses, and subordinate clauses. However, there are few content words and the words that are produced often do not make sense. Since people with damage to Wernicke's area have difficulty in understanding language (and may themselves be unaware that they have a speech deficit), it is possible that they are unable to monitor their own language and this accounts for its incoherence.

It seems reasonable to suggest that Wernicke's area stores memories of the sequences of sounds contained in words. This allows us to recognise individual words when we hear them and produce words ourselves. If Wernicke's area is damaged, sounds cannot be recognised as speech and thus the individual cannot comprehend what has been said.

ANOMIC APHASIA

In terms of producing and understanding language, *anomic* (or *amnesic* or *nominal*) *aphasics* have few problems. However, in this type of aphasia the person is unable to find correct nouns and name objects. The anomic aphasic will, for example, hesitate whilst nouns are being sought and will sometimes produce an inaccurate noun. Alternatively, things may be expressed in a clumsy way as the person tries to get around the difficulty.

Most of us experience this to a degree. For example, ex-president of the United States George Bush's use of phrases such as 'the vision *thing*' and the 'law enforcement *thing*' caused much mirth amongst the American electorate. In severe cases of anomic aphasia, however, the person has difficulty in naming common objects such as a pen or a pair of scissors. In some cases, the anomic aphasic will *circumlocute* or speak in a roundabout way. A shoe, for instance, might be described as 'something to put one's foot in'.

Interestingly, Penfield & Roberts (1959) encountered an anomic aphasic who could not name a comb, but could describe it as 'something I comb my hair with'. Thus, the word could be used as a verb but not as a noun. According to Beaumont (1988), this suggests that:

> 'there is obviously a part of the language system which, given a particular meaning, retrieves the appropriate word from some store and it is this which is disordered in anomic aphasia'.

Anomic aphasia seems to be the result of damage to a part of the cortex called the *angular gyrus*, which is located in the posterior part of the parietal lobe, and it is this which plays the role described by Beaumont. The location of the angular gyrus in relation to Broca's and Wernicke's areas is shown in Figure 6.2.

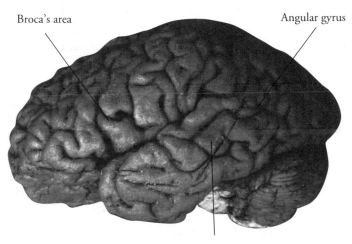

Broca's area

Angular gyrus

Wernicke's area

Figure 6.2   The location of the angular gyrus in relation to Broca's and Wernicke's areas

CONDUCTION APHASIA

The typical symptom of *conduction* (or *central*) *aphasia* is difficulty in repeating a sentence that has just been heard. Although the conduction aphasic can understand and produce speech relatively well, and give an account of a presented sentence in his or her own words, *exact* reproduction is not possible. For example, an American conduction aphasic tested in the 1960s was simply asked to repeat the word 'president'. The aphasic replied, 'I know who that is – Kennedy' (Geshwind, 1972). Another patient, asked to repeat the sentence, 'The auto's leaking gas tank soiled the roadway', responded with, 'The car tank's leaked and made a mess on the street'. It has been suggested that this

type of aphasia occurs as a result of lesions interrupting the nerve fibres (the *arcuate fasciculus* or 'arch-shaped bundle') which connects Broca's area with Wernicke's area. The arcuate fasciculus, then, is yet another structure that can be implicated in language.

TRANSCORTICAL APHASIA

The final type of aphasia identified in the Boston Classification is called *transcortical aphasia*. People with this type of aphasia have few comprehension skills (*transcortical sensory aphasia* or *TSA*), cannot produce normal speech (*transcortical motor aphasia* or *TMA*) or, more usually, both (*mixed transcortical aphasia* or *MTA*). They are, however, able to repeat back what somebody has said to them. Although TSA is similar to Wernicke's aphasia and TMA to Broca's aphasia, the essential difference is that the damage has occurred beyond Wernicke's and Broca's areas.

As well as the aphasias recognised by the Boston Classification, a number of other language disorders have been identified. Space does not allow us to consider all of these, but one very rare form is worthy of consideration. In *isolation aphasia*, the brain's speech mechanisms receive auditory input and can control the muscles used for speech. However, they receive no information from the other senses or from the neural circuits containing memories about past experiences and the meaning of words. In one investigation, Geschwind, Quadfasel & Segarra (1968) studied a patient who had suffered severe brain damage after inhaling carbon monoxide from a faulty water heater. Although there was no damage to the primary auditory cortex, Broca's and Wernicke's areas, and the connections between them, large parts of the visual association cortex were damaged and the woman's speech mechanisms were isolated from other parts of the brain.

The woman remained in hospital for nine years until she died. In that time she made few voluntary movements except with her eyes, which were able to follow moving objects. The woman never said anything meaningful on her own, did not follow verbal commands or otherwise give signs of understanding them. By all available criteria 'she was not conscious of anything that was going on' (Carlson, 1988). However, if somebody recited the first line of a poem such as 'Roses are red, violets are blue', she would respond with 'Sugar is sweet and so are you'.

In addition to being able to finish poems, she could

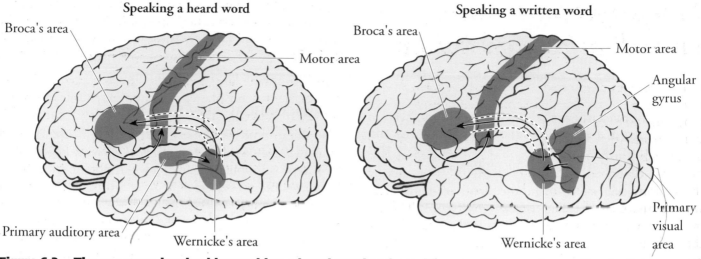

Figure 6.3   The processes involved in speaking a heard word and speaking a written word according to the Wernicke–Geschwind theory of language

also repeat words that were spoken to her. This was not done parrot-fashion since, if someone made a grammatical error while saying something to her, she would repeat what had been said *without* the grammatical error. Because she gave no signs of understanding anything she heard or said, her case suggests that:

'consciousness is not simply an activity of the brain's speech mechanisms; it is an activity prompted by information received from other parts of the brain concerning memories or events presently occurring in the environment' (Carlson, 1988).

The relationship between cortical areas and language

Over one hundred years ago, Carl Wernicke formulated a model of how the brain produces language. More recently, Wernicke's original model was refined by the late Norman Geschwind. According to the *Wernicke-Geschwind theory of language*, when we are asked to repeat a word we have just heard, the word is passed (via the thalamus and the auditory area of the cortex) to Wernicke's area. Activity in Wernicke's area allows us to recognise the words and understand their meaning. The formulation of the word we are to repeat is then passed to Broca's area, where memories of the sequence of movements necessary to produce the word are stored. Broca's area then passes this information to the motor

area of the cortex which programmes the various muscles in the face, tongue, and larynx to reproduce the word. This theory explains why damage to Wernicke's area leaves speech intact but disrupts the understanding of language and the formation of meaningful sentences. It also explains why damage to Broca's area affects the production of language.

When we are asked to repeat a word we have read, a slightly different process occurs. First, the words are registered in the visual area of the cortex. Then, they are sent to the angular gyrus. As we noted earlier on, this part of the cortex transforms the visual appearance of a word into a code which is recognised and understood in Wernicke's area. Once Wernicke's area has received the code and understood the meaning of the word, the formulation is then sent to Broca's area and the sequence of events we described previously occurs. These processes are shown in Figure 6.3.

As Damasio & Damasio (1993) have observed, the last two decades have seen significant progress being made in understanding the brain structures responsible for language. In particular, research using PET (see Chapter 4) has proved to be especially revealing. Studies conducted by Marcus Raichle and his colleagues have shown that when people are asked to say a particular word, a particular part of the cortex becomes highly active. This part is Broca's area. However, when asked to generate a verb that would be appropriate for a particular noun (such as 'cook' for 'oven') other areas of the cortex become active as well.

Language: localisation, lateralisation and holism

In the previous chapter we introduced the term *localisation* to describe the fact that some specific functions and processes have relatively precise and circumscribed locations. From what we have said in this chapter, we can consider language to be a localised function along with those we described in Chapter 5. At the beginning of this chapter we noted that the cortical areas associated with language are, for the vast majority of people, found in one or other cerebral hemispheres rather than both of them. This phenomenon is called *lateralisation*. Thus, as well as being localised, language is also lateralised.

In most of us, language is lateralised in the left hemisphere. However, there are some exceptions to this general rule as Satz's (1979) review of research conducted between 1935 and 1975 discovered. All but around 5% of us are right-handed, and in around 95% of right-handers language is localised in the left hemisphere. In the remaining 5% of right-handers, language is localised in the *right* hemisphere. In left-handers, Satz found that the situation is more complex. In about 75% of left-handers, language is localised in the left hemisphere. Although none of the studies reviewed by Satz indicated that left-handers had language localised in the right hemisphere, the remaining 25% showed *bilateral representation*, that is, the language structures were more or less equally represented in *both* hemispheres.

To add to this already complex picture, more recent research (Kimura, 1993) has reported that some left-handers show a localisation of language which is exactly the opposite of that observed in the vast majority of right-handers. In other words, some left-handers do have language localised in the right hemisphere. We should also note that there seems to be a difference between the sexes with respect to the way in which the brain is organised for speech production!

Kimura (1993) has shown that speech is more bilaterally organised in women and that women are less likely to incur aphasia than men. However, Kimura does not believe that it is the bilateral representation which explains this effect. Her research shows that women are more likely to suffer aphasia when the front part of the brain is damaged whilst in men damage to the back part of the brain is more likely to produce aphasia. Since restricted damage within a hemisphere more fre-quently affects the back part of the brain in both men and women, speech functions would be less likely to be disrupted in the latter because the cortical area is less often affected.

Explaining why language sometimes appears in the left and/or right hemispheres is not an easy task. However, research suggests that the brain has remarkable *plasticity*. When an area is damaged, other areas seem to be able to reorganise themselves and take over the damaged part's functions, and this appears to be particularly true of language. Lashley called this phenomenon the *law of equipotentiality* and Luria argued that the process occurred through *functional reorganisation* whereby surviving brain circuits reorganise themselves to achieve the same behavioural goal in a different way (Robertson, 1995). This would explain why some victims of a minor stroke recover at least some of the abilities that were seemingly lost as a result of the stroke.

It would appear that the brain is particularly flexible during childhood. In one study, a five-year-old boy had his entire left cerebral hemisphere removed in order to treat his severe epilepsy. Even without one hemisphere, the boy completed college and went on to become a company executive (Smith & Sugar, 1975). Presumably, the language functions in his left hemisphere were taken over by the right hemisphere.

As you will have probably guessed, *holistic theories* (which we outlined in the previous chapter as an alternative to the theory of localisation) are capable of explaining the brain's plasticity. Perhaps, then, both localisation and holism are true to some extent. We must wait and see what research into language reveals in the future.

Conclusions

Our ability to produce and comprehend language is one of many remarkable human abilities. In this chapter, we have identified a number of cortical structures that play a role in language production and comprehension and we have described the behavioural consequences of damage to these structures. We also suggested that the cortical areas involved in language are usually found only in the left cerebral hemisphere, although there are some people for whom the opposite is the case and some for whom the areas are present in both hemispheres!

SUMMARY

- Unlike the association areas which are found in both hemispheres, for the great majority of people, certain functions are linked to **one or other** hemisphere, one of these being language.
- Gall claimed that the frontal lobes were specialised for speech. Broca, based on post-mortems, concluded that lesions in a small area of the cortex in the frontal lobe of the left hemisphere (**Broca's area**) were responsible for deficits in speech **production.**
- Wernicke identified damage to a region in the temporal lobe (**Wernicke's area**) as responsible for a deficit in **understanding** language.
- Disorders of language arising from brain damage are called **aphasias** (although some prefer the term **dysphasia**). Classifications of aphasias are based either on the presumed location of the lesion(s), the general sensory and/or motor impairments, or the particular linguistic skill that is lost (the **Boston Classification**).
- **Broca's** (**ataxic, expressive, non-fluent,** or **motor**) **aphasia** involves great difficulty in **producing** speech, which is very difficult for listeners to understand. Speech is **telegraphic**, consisting almost entirely of **content** words, and may also involve **phonemic paraphrasias** and **agraphia**. 'Faulty data' are sent to the primary motor area which initiates the processes that will convert the 'motor plans' for formulating words into speech.
- **Wernicke's** (**receptive, sensory,** or **fluent**) **aphasia** involves difficulty in **understanding** spoken and written language. But Wernicke's aphasics also produce speech that may be almost incomprehensible and incoherent (**jargon/neologisms**, and **semantic paraphrasias**).
- Wernicke's aphasics are capable of using some quite complex language, but there are few content words; they seem unable to monitor their own speech, which may account for its incoherence. They have apparently lost the ability to recognise speech sounds.
- **Anomic** (**amnesic** or **nominal**) **aphasia** involves the inability to retrieve the appropriate word from some store and, hence, failure to find correct nouns and name common objects; the person **circumlocutes**. The part of the cortex which is damaged is the **angular gyrus**.
- **Conduction** (or **central**) **aphasia** involves difficulty in repeating a sentence that has just been heard **exactly**. The sentence can, however, be repeated, if put into the person's own words. The damaged area might be the **arcuate fasciculus**, which connects Broca's and Wernicke's areas.
- People with **transcortical aphasia** have few comprehension skills (**transcortical sensory aphasia** – similar to Wernicke's aphasia), cannot produce normal speech (**transcortical motor aphasia** – similar to Broca's aphasia) or, more usually, both.
- In **isolation aphasia,** although the brain's speech mechanisms receive auditory input and can control the muscles used for speech, they receive no information from the other senses or from neural circuits containing memories of past experiences and word meaning. This has important implications for the nature of **consciousness**.
- According to the **Wernicke-Geschwind theory of language**, when we are asked to repeat a word we have just **heard**, it is passed to Wernicke's area, which allows us to understand its meaning. Formulation of the word is then passed to Broca's area, which passes on information regarding the movements needed to produce the word to the motor cortex, which then programmes the muscles in the face, tongue, and larynx to reproduce the word.
- Repeating a word we have **read** involves the word being registered in the visual cortex, from which it is sent to the angular gyrus. This sends a code to Wernicke's area, which then sends formulation of the word's meaning to Broca's area; the sequence of events is then the same as for repeating spoken words.
- Language is a **localised** function (there are specialised language areas in the cortex) as well as a **lateralised** function (Broca's area etc. are only found in one or other hemisphere).
- For most people, who are right-handed, language is lateralised in the **left** hemisphere. But about 25% of left-handers show **bilateral representation**, and some have language localised in the **right** hemisphere. There is also a sex difference regarding how the brain is organised for speech production.
- The brain's **plasticity** is particularly marked in the case of language; Lashley called this the **law of equipotentiality**, which occurs through **functional reorganisation**. This flexibility is at its height during childhood, and even removal of the entire left hemisphere does not prevent normal language development; this is consistent with **holistic theories** of brain function.

ASYMMETRIES IN THE CEREBRAL HEMISPHERES AND THE 'SPLIT-BRAIN'

Introduction and overview

In the previous chapter, we noted that for most people language is *lateralised*, that is, the cortical areas associated with it are found in one or other of the cerebral hemispheres rather than both. The question of whether the two cerebral hemispheres play the same or different roles in other aspects of our mental processes and behaviour is one that has attracted much research interest and, although the two hemispheres look to be mirror images of one another, it has been argued that they are *functionally different*.

Our main aim in this chapter is to examine what research has told us about the specific abilities of the left and right cerebral hemispheres. However, we will also look at the intriguing question of whether the two cerebral hemispheres represent two kinds of 'mind'.

Cerebral asymmetries and the 'split-brain'

Gustav Fechner, one of the founding fathers of experimental psychology, knew that the brain was *bilaterally symmetrical*, that is, that it consists of two cerebral hemispheres which are apparently mirror images of each other. In 1860, Fechner asked what would happen if the brain of a living person could be split in half. His own answer was that each half of the brain would have a different conscious experience, that is, he believed that two 'minds' existed inside the one brain.

In Fechner's day, the experiment that would answer his question was thought to be impossible to conduct. In the 1960s, however, it became possible to look at the effects of dividing the brain in two as a by-product of surgery performed in order to control epileptic seizures. Up until the 1960s, attempts to control epilepsy involved removing what were presumed to be the disordered parts of the brain. However, this approach was limited in its success and researchers sought other methods for treating the disorder.

In the early 1960s, two American neurosurgeons, Philip Vogel and Joseph Bogen (see, for example, Bogen, 1969), suggested that epileptic seizures were caused by an amplification of brain activity that 'bounced' back and forth between the two hemispheres. As a therapy of last resort, when all else had failed, they suggested severing the $\frac{1}{2}$ inch wide and $3\frac{1}{2}$ inches long corpus callosum, an operation called a *commissurotomy*. Their rationale was that severing the 250 million or so axons of the corpus callosum would prevent the reverberation of the brain activity, and cause it to be confined to one cerebral hemisphere. Since the operation involved splitting the two hemispheres apart from one another, people who underwent it became known as *split-brain patients*.

Research carried out on cats and monkeys by Robert Sperry, Reginald Myers and Michael Gazzaniga had revealed that commissurotomy did not seem to cause any apparent ill-effects. When the same operation was carried out on epileptic patients, the results also suggested that there were no ill-effects apart from, as one patient joked, producing a 'splitting headache'! (Gazzaniga, 1967). As Sperry (1964) remarked:

> 'In casual conversation over a cup of coffee and a cigarette, one would hardly suspect that there was anything unusual about (the patient).'

From a therapeutic perspective, the operation was a great success in that the severity of the epileptic seizures was dramatically reduced, if not eliminated. From a psychological perspective, the operation also provided the opportunity to investigate whether or not the two cerebral hemispheres were specialised for particular functions, as well as allowing the question posed by Fechner to be addressed. As we shall see, the results of many investigations also laid to rest the view of some eminent researchers, such as Karl Lashley, that the corpus callosum served no function other than 'to keep the hemispheres from sagging'.

In their research with cats, Sperry and his colleagues also severed part of the nerve fibres connecting the eyes and the brain (see page 46). This operation meant that the cat's left and right eyes sent information exclusively to the left and right hemispheres respectively. In one experiment, they placed an eye patch over a cat's left eye and then taught it to perform a particular task. When the task had been learned, the eye patch was switched over to the other eye and the cat was tested on the task it had just learned. It behaved as though it had *never* learned the task at all.

On the basis of this finding, the researchers concluded that one half of the brain did not (literally) know what the other half was doing, and that ordinarily the corpus callosum functions as a means by which information can be transmitted back and forth so that each hemisphere is aware of the sensations and perceptions of the other. Gazzaniga and his colleagues wondered if the corpus callosum performed the same function in humans. Of course, it would be unethical to sever some of the optic nerve fibres in humans if it could not be justified on therapeutic grounds (and even then, some would still consider it to be unethical).

Under normal circumstances, we constantly move our eyes and hence both cerebral hemispheres receive information about the visual world whether we have experienced a commissurotomy or not. In 1967, however, Gazzaniga devised a way of sending visual information to one cerebral hemisphere at a time. Before we look at the methodology used, we need to remind ourselves of two findings we described earlier in Chapter 5.

The first concerns the connections between the brain and the body. As we saw, each cerebral hemisphere is primarily connected to the opposite side of the body. Thus, an object placed in the left hand is sensed by neurons in the right cerebral hemisphere. The second finding concerns the transmission of information from the eyes to the primary visual areas of the cortex.

In Chapter 5 we noted that the nerve fibres from the half of each retina closest to the temples sends information to the hemisphere on the same side. However, the nerve fibres from each half of the retina closest to the nose sends information to the opposite hemisphere. We also noted that it is possible to divide up the visual world into a left visual field and a right visual field. As Figure 5.3 illustrates (see page 48), each hemisphere only receives information about the visual field on the opposite side. Thus, visual sensations in the left visual

field are processed only by the right hemisphere, whereas the left hemisphere processes information only from the right visual field.

Normally, each hemisphere more or less immediately shares its information with the other. In 'split-brain' patients, however, the severing of the corpus callosum means that information cannot be conveyed from one hemisphere to another. As we noted, we are constantly moving our eyes and this allows both hemispheres to receive visual information whether the corpus callosum has been severed or not. Sperry's method of delivering information only to one cerebral hemisphere involved presenting a stimulus to just one visual field at a speed that was too quick for eye movements to allow it to enter both visual fields and hence be perceived by both hemispheres. Sperry discovered that presenting a visual stimulus for about one tenth of a second allowed it to be perceived by one of the hemispheres, but was too fast for eye movements to allow it to be perceived by both hemispheres.

In the basic procedure, a patient is seated in front of a projector screen with the hands free to handle objects that are behind the screen, but which are obscured from sight by it. The patient is asked to gaze at a spot (or 'fixation point') in the centre of the screen. Visual stimuli are then 'back-projected' to the left of the fixation point (the left visual field) or to the right of it (the right visual field) for one tenth of a second or less. As we noted, this speed allows the word to be perceived, but is too quick for any eye movements to allow the stimulus to enter both visual fields.

When a picture of an object is shown to the right visual field and the patient is asked to verbally report what was shown, the task is done with ease. However, when a picture of an object is shown to the left visual field, the task cannot be done and the patient typically reports that 'there is nothing there'. Such a finding appears bizarre, but can be easily explained by applying what we know about the organisation of the visual system and what we learned in the previous chapter about the location of the structures responsible for the production and comprehension of language.

All of the split-brain patients studied by Gazzaniga and his colleagues had their language functions located in the left hemisphere (to which right visual field information goes). Thus, when an object is shown in the right visual field, the left hemisphere responds verbally and correctly. However, since the right hemisphere does

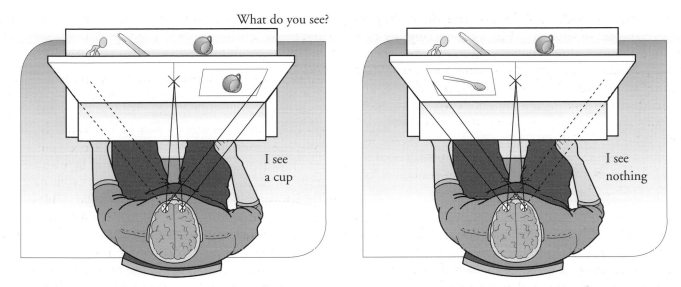

Figure 7.1   Responses given by a split-brain patient when material is presented to the right and left visual fields

not contain the language centres it cannot respond verbally. Thus, when an object is shown in the left visual field, the verbal response to the question 'What did you see?' comes from the left hemisphere. Since nothing was presented in the right visual field, the left hemisphere truthfully responds by saying that it saw nothing! This is shown in Figure 7.1 above.

The apparent difference in the ability to produce spoken language between the two hemispheres led some researchers to use the terms *major* or *dominant* and *minor* or *subordinate* to describe the left and right hemispheres respectively, as though the right hemisphere was some sort of 'second-class citizen' (Nebes, 1974). However, subsequent studies revealed that whilst the right hemisphere might not be able to respond verbally, it is far from being linguistically incompetent.

For example, in another study a picture of an object was shown in the left visual field and hence was perceived by the right hemisphere. When the patient was asked what had been seen, the response 'nothing' was given, a response which emanated from the left hemisphere which had indeed seen nothing in the right visual field. However, when the patient was asked to use the left hand (which was placed beneath the screen so that it could not be seen) to select the object from a variety of objects, the object was correctly selected. The left hand, of course, is controlled by the right hemisphere. Since the left hand was able to select the object, the right hemisphere must have at least some understanding of language. This is shown in Figure 7.2 overleaf.

In a variation of the study we have just described, a picture of a cigarette was presented to the right hemisphere. The patient was then asked to use the left hand (which was again placed beneath the screen so that it could not be seen) to pick out an object which was *most closely related* to the picture that had been presented. Of all the objects that could have been selected, an ashtray was the one that was consistently selected by the patients. However, when asked to verbally identify the picture that had been shown or the object that the left hand had selected, the patient was unsuccessful, the right hemisphere being unable to verbalise a response and the left being in complete ignorance of the picture that had been presented.

As well as showing that the right hemisphere does have some verbal abilities even if these cannot be articulated, the findings of this study also suggest that the left hemisphere seemingly had no idea of, or access to, the perceptions and memories of the right hemisphere. This was shown in other studies using the *divided field technique*. In this, one word or picture is presented to the left visual field (right hemisphere) and a different word or picture is simultaneously presented to the right visual field (left hemisphere).

In one study using this technique, the word 'case' was presented to the right visual field and the word 'key' was presented simultaneously to the left visual field. When asked to report what had been seen, the patient replied 'case'. However, when asked to use the left hand to write the word that had been presented, the patient wrote 'key'. When asked what particular kind

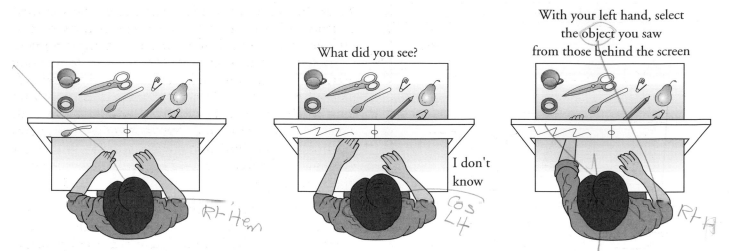

Figure 7.2   Responses given by the left and right hemispheres to material presented in the left visual field

of 'case' he was thinking of, the patient's left hemisphere would respond with 'in case of fire' or 'the case of the missing corpse' and so on. Any reference to 'key case' was purely fortuitous.

Yet another study required the patient to find the objects that corresponded to the words shown to the left and right visual fields using the left and right hands (both of which were behind the projector screen and could not be seen). When the right-hemisphere-controlled left hand came across the object that had been shown to the left hemisphere it ignored it completely, as did the left-hemisphere-controlled right hand when it came across the object that the left hand was looking for!

In 1983, Michael Gazzaniga suggested that on the basis of 20 years of empirical research, 'the cognitive skills of a normal disconnected right hemisphere without language are vastly inferior to the cognitive skills of a chimpanzee'. However, the results of many other studies have shown that whilst the right hemisphere might not be able to report verbally on its experiences, it has linguistic and cognitive capabilities which far exceed Gazzaniga's claims. As Levy (1983) has remarked, this is hardly surprising. As she notes, it seems unlikely that the 'eons of human evolution' would have left 'half the brain witless'.

Eran Zaidel has been one of those critical of Gazzaniga's claims. Zaidel (1983) developed a technique of presenting stimuli to the left or right visual field using a special contact lens that moves with the eye. This allows a stimulus to be presented for a much longer period than is the case using the original method of studying split-brain patients. In one study, Zaidel gave vocabulary questions that required the right hemisphere to choose a picture that corresponded to a particular word.

Although the right hemisphere did not perform as well as the left hemisphere, its performance was roughly equivalent to that of a ten-year-old child. This, and other findings, led Zaidel to conclude that 'the precise limits of right hemisphere language capacity are not yet known' and that 'there is increasing evidence for right hemisphere involvement in normal language'. Indeed, the right hemisphere has been shown to be better than the left at understanding familiar idioms and metaphors such as 'turning over a new leaf'. The right hemisphere may, therefore, play an important (if underrated) role in language.

Other research has shown that the right hemisphere is superior to the left at copying drawings. Figure 7.3 opposite shows its superior talents. Although the left hand was not as dextrous as the right hand (which was the preferred hand in the patients that were studied) it was better able to reproduce the spatial arrangement of the example it had been shown. The more coordinated right hand seemed to be incapable of duplicating three-dimensional forms.

The right hemisphere has also been shown to be superior at recognising faces. Using the divided field

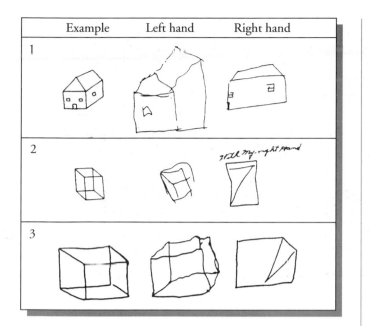

Figure 7.3   The abilities of the right and left hemispheres to reproduce a visual stimulus using the left and right hands respectively

technique, pictures of different faces were presented to the left and right visual fields. When asked to select which face had been presented from an array of several other faces, the picture shown to the right hemisphere was consistently chosen by patients whereas the one shown to the left hemisphere was consistently ignored. A slightly different approach to studying face recognition was taken by Levy,

Trevarthen & Sperry (1972). These researchers showed patients *chimerics,* that is, composite pictures of two different faces, one half of the face being projected to each of the hemispheres. When asked to verbally describe the picture that had been seen, the left hemisphere dominated. When asked to select a picture that had been seen, the right hemisphere dominated. This indicates that the left hemisphere processes information in linguistic terms whereas the right responds to the face as a total picture. This is shown in Figure 7.4 below.

This has led some researchers to use the terms *analyser* and *synthesiser* to describe the left and right hemispheres respectively. It would seem that the left hemisphere is particularly skilled at handling discrete information that can be stated verbally (or, research indicates, in the form of mathematical propositions). A face, for example, is analysed in terms of its components ('deep-set eyes', 'blonde hair' and so on). The right hemisphere is superior when information cannot be adequately described in words or symbols. In the case of a face, for example, the right hemisphere synthesises all the information and recognises it as a whole. The perceptual superiority of the right hemisphere was also demonstrated in a study conducted by Sperry (1974). When the right hemisphere is instructed to arrange some blocks to match a picture, the left hand is highly competent. When the left hemisphere performs the same task using the right hand, its performance is

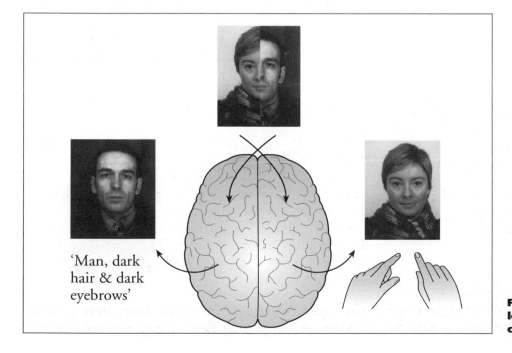

'Man, dark hair & dark eyebrows'

Figure 7.4   Responses given by the left and right hemispheres to a chimeric

so bad that, via the left hand, the right hemisphere 'interrupts' and takes over!

It is also worth noting that outside the laboratory the left and right hemispheres occasionally do battle. The left hand of a female patient might pick out a particular dress to wear, only for the right hand to push the dress away and select another. This finding alone supports the view that the left and right hemispheres may be simultaneously conscious in different ways, and partly answers the question asked by Fechner over one hundred years ago that we noted at the beginning of this chapter. We shall return to Fechner's question at the end of this chapter.

We should also note that the evidence suggests that split-brain patients can sometimes perform *better* than people who have not had a commissurotomy. In one experiment, Ellenberg & Sperry (1980) sent one simple decision task to the right hemisphere and simultaneously sent another to the left hemisphere. The results showed that split-brain patients were much better able to perform both tasks than were people with an intact corpus callosum. It would seem that under normal circumstances the two hemispheres work together at solving tasks whereas in split-brain patients they are able to work independently.

As interesting as the data from split-brain studies are, some researchers have suggested that we should treat such data with caution, on the grounds that those who have been studied might not be representative of people in general. We mentioned earlier that split-brain patients have all had a history of epileptic seizures, and it could be that the observed differences between the hemispheres occur as a result of changes in brain organisation brought about by the epilepsy. If we are to talk about 'cerebral asymmetries' and 'hemispheric specialisation', we need to show that the same phenomena occur in people who have not had a history of epilepsy and/or undergone a commissurotomy. We shall review the findings about people with an intact corpus callosum now.

Cerebral asymmetries and the intact brain

There are several ways in which asymmetries in the intact brain can be studied. One of these is called the

Wada test (after its originator, Julian Wada). This involves injecting sodium amytal (a barbiturate – see Chapter 13) into the left or right carotid artery. Because the carotid artery sends blood primarily to the cerebral hemisphere on the same side, it is possible to temporarily anaesthetise a hemisphere and observe what happens. Just before the injection, the person receiving it is instructed to put his or her arms in the air and begin counting backwards from one hundred. One of the arms will suddenly fall limp depending on which carotid artery was injected. For example, if the left carotid artery was injected the right arm falls limp (see page 45). If the person is able to continue counting backwards, then we know that the language functions must be in the non-injected hemisphere since the injected hemisphere has been temporarily anaesthetised.

The Wada test is only used prior to surgery on the brain in order to assess whether language functions might be affected. Other ways of assessing asymmetries include the use of EEG, measurements of blood flow and glucose consumption (see Chapter 4), and the study of people who have suffered strokes. It is also possible to use variations of the techniques originally employed to study 'split-brain' patients.

In one of these, different stimuli are simultaneously presented to the left and right visual fields. In some cases, the stimulus to the right visual field will be reported by the person, whereas in others the stimulus presented to the left visual field will be reported. Reporting of the right visual field stimulus implies that the left hemisphere is better at processing the type of information presented. If the left visual field stimulus is reported this implies that the right hemisphere is better.

This finding is *not* inconsistent with the claim that the right hemisphere cannot verbalise its responses. In the normal brain, the two hemispheres communicate with one another. Information about the stimulus presented to the right hemisphere must cross into the left hemisphere in order to be verbalised. The fact that the stimulus presented to the right hemisphere is verbally reported first, even though the information has had to travel a greater distance than information presented to the left hemisphere, must mean that the processing has been more efficient.

In the same way, auditory information can be simultaneously presented to the left and right ears. The results of studies using *dichotic listening tasks* indicate that there is a definite 'right ear advantage' for words, which indicates a left hemisphere superiority for processing verbal material. However, non-verbal auditory material (such as music) tends to produce a left ear advantage indicating a right hemisphere superiority in processing this sort of information.

On the basis of many studies using people with intact brains, Ornstein (1986) had concluded that the left hemisphere seems to be specialised for analytic and logical thinking, especially in verbal and mathematical functions. It also processes information sequentially (that is, one item at a time) and its mode of operation is linear. By contrast, the right hemisphere seems to be specialised for synthetic thinking in which it is necessary to bring different things together in order to form a whole. This appears to be particularly true for spatial tasks, artistic activities, body image and face recognition. The right hemisphere also processes information more diffusely, that is, it processes several items at once, and its mode of operation is more holistic than linear.

The conclusions drawn by Ornstein, coupled with the results of many studies we have not described, seem to suggest that our cerebral hemispheres perform somewhat different functions. This has led to the notion of people being 'logically left-brained' or 'intuitively right-brained' depending on the ways in which they behave. Indeed, (best-selling) books have been published which claim to show us how to 'unlock the door to the neglected right side of the brain'.

Although the differences between the hemispheres seems to be well-established, psychologists generally believe the claims made in popular books to be both exaggerated and grossly oversimplified. Whilst the terms 'verbal' and 'non-verbal' hemispheres are reasonable first approximations, the data are actually much more complicated. Under normal circumstances, the two hemispheres work together and communicate by means of the corpus callosum and their functions overlap to at least some degree. Moreover, some of the tasks which are ordinarily dealt with by one hemisphere can be performed by the other. As Sperry (1982) has observed, 'the left-right dichotomy is an idea with which it is very easy to run wild'.

An answer to Fechner's question?

The results from the many studies on split-brain patients seem to agree with the answer Fechner gave to the question he posed over one hundred years ago. What we see when the brain is bisected is, according to Sperry, essentially a divided organism with two mental units each possessing its own private sensations, perceptions, thoughts, feelings and memories. The mental units arc, Sperry argues, each competing for control over the organism.

Ornstein (1986) has asked whether a commissurotomy produces a 'splitting' (or 'doubling') of mind or whether the operation helps to manifest a duality that is actually present all the time. As we have seen, Sperry and at least some of his colleagues, clearly believe the former. Others, however, take the latter view. For example, Pucetti (1977) has argued that split-brain patients are not special in having two minds because even when the hemispheres are connected, we *are* two minds. Normally, Pucetti argues, we appear to be unified and synchronised beings because the separate existence of the two selves is undetectable. All the commissurotomy does is to make apparent the duality that is there all the time. According to this *double brain theory*, the mind, 'self', or personality can be essentially 'reduced' to a hemisphere of the brain.

Other researchers (such as Parfit, 1987) accept the idea that the split-brain patient has two streams of consciousness, but do not believe that we should regard them as constituting two persons because in a sense, Parfit argues, there is *none*. Parfit distinguishes the *ego theory* (a theory of what people are) from the *bundle theory* (which explains the unity of consciousness by claiming that ordinary people are, at any time, aware of having several different experiences). At any time, split-brain patients do not have one state of awareness of several different experiences. Rather, they have two such states (and *not* two separately existing egos). As Parfit has observed, split-brain patients have great theoretical importance because they 'challenge some of our deepest assumptions about ourselves'.

Conclusions

In this chapter, we have looked at the claim that the two cerebral hemispheres are functionally different. Research with split-brain patients suggests that the left and right hemispheres do play different roles in our mental processes and behaviour. However, split-brain patients are not representative of the population in general. Yet, when we look at hemisphere asymmetries in the 'normal' brain a similar picture emerges, although we should note that some researchers have cautioned against making too much about the left–right hemisphere differences. We also looked at the question of whether dividing the brain results in a doubling of consciousness. There are a number of viewpoints on this, and it seems that further research will be needed in order to support or reject them.

SUMMARY

- Fechner understood that the brain is **bilaterally symmetrical**, i.e. the two hemispheres are mirror images of each other; he also believed that each hemiphere 'contained' a separate mind.

- Vogel and Bogen believed that epileptic seizures were caused by an amplification of brain activity travelling back and forth between the two hemispheres; as a last resort, the corpus callosum should be cut (**commissurotomy**), thereby confining the brain activity to one hemisphere. Such patients became known as **split-brain patients**.

- There were apparently no ill-effects of such surgery, and it reduced, if not eliminated, the seizures. It also allowed psychologists to investigate some crucial questions about the brain and the mind.

- Based on experiments with cats, in which part of the optic nerve was cut, Sperry concluded that usually the corpus callosum transmits information between hemispheres, so that each knows what the other is sensing and perceiving.

- Each hemisphere, in fact, only receives information about the visual field on the **opposite** side, but normally, we constantly move our eyes, such that both hemispheres receive information about the whole visual world. In split-brain patients, information can no longer be conveyed between hemispheres, so that if only one hemisphere receives visual input, the other will know nothing about it.

- In his studies of split-brain patients, Sperry presented stimuli to just one visual field so quickly that eye movements did not allow both hemispheres to perceive them. While gazing at the fixation point, stimuli are back-projected onto a screen that obscures from sight the patient's hands which are free to handle objects behind the screen.

- When a picture of an object is shown to the **right** visual field, the patient can easily report verbally what was shown, but if presented to the **left** visual field, this cannot be done. Since the visual information from the left field goes to the **right** hemisphere, and since langauge functions are located in the **left** hemisphere, the right hemisphere cannot answer.

- The left hemispere is said to be **major/dominant**, and the right **minor/subordinate**, but split-brain patients are able to select the appropriate object with their left hand, showing that the right hemisphere must have at least some understanding of language, even if this cannot be articulated.

- Using a special contact lens that allows the stimulus to be presented for much longer than Sperry's method, Zaidel found that the right hemisphere performed as well as a 10-year-old child on a task in which a picture had to be matched to a particular word (although not as well as the left hemisphere).

- There is increasing evidence for right hemispere involvement in normal language, and it may be superior to the left at understanding idioms and metaphors.

- The right hemisphere is superior at copying drawings and recognising faces, as shown by the **divided field technique** and **chimerics**. While the left hemisphere processes pictures of faces linguistically, the right hemisphere responds to the face as a total picture.

- The left and right hemispheres have been described as **analyser** and **synthesiser** respectively. The left is particularly skilled at handling discrete information that can be stated verbally (such as analysing facial features), while the right is superior when information cannot be described in words or symbols, as in synthesising different information into a whole (as in recognising the whole face).

- If two simple decision tasks are sent simultaneously to the two hemispheres, split-brain patients perform **better** than people with an intact corpus callosum; in the former, the two hemispheres are able to work independently.

- Generalising the results of split-brain studies is complicated by the fact that such patients have a long history of epilepsy. Asymmetries in the intact brain have been studied by use of the **Wada test**, which involves injecting sodium amytal in order to temporarily anaesthetise one hemisphere. But it is only used prior to brain surgery to assess whether language functions might be affected.

- Other methods include use of EEG, measurements of blood flow and glucose consumption, and the study of stroke victims. Also, variations of the procedure used in split-brain studies have been employed. **Dichotic listening tasks** show that there is a definite right ear advantage for words, indicating a left hemisphere superiority for processing verbal material, but right hemisphere advantage for processing non-verbal auditory material, such as music.

- Ornstein concludes that the left hemisphere seems to be specialised for **analytical** and logical thinking; it processes information **sequentially** and in a **linear** fashion. The right hemisphere is specialised for **synthetic** thinking; it processes information more **diffusely** and in a **holistic** way. People may differ in terms of being 'logically left-brained' or 'intuitively right-brained'. But normally, the two hemispheres work together and their abilities tend to overlap.

- Sperry sees the bisected brain as two mental units (a doubling or splitting of mind) competing for control of the organism. Pucetti believes that we **are** two minds even when our hemispheres are connected: the commissurotomy simply makes obvious the duality that is there all the time (**double brain theory**).

- According to the **bundle theory**, we are normally aware of having several different experiences, which accounts for the unity of consciousness. Split-brain patients have **two** states of awareness of several different experiences, as opposed to being two distinct egos (**ego theory** claims that we **are**, normally, an ego).

THE NEUROPHYSIOLOGICAL BASIS OF VISUAL PERCEPTION

Introduction and overview

Vision is a dominant sense in humans, and much of what we do depends on the possession of an adequately functioning visual system. The importance of the visual system is reflected by the fact that a greater proportion of the brain is devoted to vision than any other sense. Indeed, such is the importance of vision to us that if we wear lenses that distort a square object into a rectangle, we perceive it as a rectangle even though we can feel it is square with our hands, a phenomenon known as *visual capture*.

We will begin this chapter by looking briefly at light, the 'messenger' that tells us about the colour, size, shape, location and texture of objects and surfaces. Then we will discuss the structure of the eye, the organ responsible for vision. However, our main aim in this chapter is to examine the way in which light information is transformed by the brain. We will conclude our consideration of visual perception by examining the perception of colour and the theories that have been proposed to explain it and the phenomenon of colour constancy.

Light

Light consists of particles of energy called *photons*. Because these particles have both electrical and magnetic properties, light is an example of *electromagnetic radiation*. Photons travel in waves that move forward and oscillate up and down. There are two important *characteristics* of light. The number of photons in a pulsating stream determines the *intensity* of a light wave. The distance between successive peaks of a light wave determines its *wavelength*. Wavelength is measured in *nanometres* (nm). One nanometre is one thousand millionth of a metre.

Light has three *properties* that are important to psychologists. These are *brightness*, *hue*, and *saturation*. The intensity of a light wave determines our experience of brightness. The more photons that a light source emits, the brighter it appears. Hue is the colour we perceive something to be and is in part determined by wavelength. Visible light is a very narrow section of the electromagnetic spectrum that includes radio waves, radar, microwaves and x-rays. Light visible to humans has a wavelength ranging from about 380 nm to 760 nm. Longer wavelengths look red to us, whereas shorter wavelengths are perceived as violet. In between these extremes, the other colours of the rainbow can be found. For example, 600 nm appears yellow-orange. The electromagnetic spectrum is illustrated in Figure 8.1 opposite.

Some colours we perceive, however, are not in the spectrum of light. Included here would be colours like brown and white. Colour, then, cannot be just a matter of wavelength. As we will see later on in this chapter, colours such as brown are produced by a complex process in which various wavelengths are mixed by the visual system. White light is, in fact, radiation that includes all wavelengths within the visible range. Saturation, the third property of light, determines how colourful light appears. White is a completely colourless state, and the more white that is present in a colour the less saturated it is. For example, when we mix mint and vanilla chocolate, the green colour gradually diminishes to a very light green shade. Saturation, then, is the proportion of coloured (or *chromatic*) light to non-coloured (or *achromatic*) light.

Amongst his many other important discoveries, Sir Isaac Newton demonstrated that white light is a mixture of wavelengths corresponding to all colours in the visible spectrum. Newton showed that when light is passed through a prism, the longer wavelengths are refracted least by the prism whilst the shorter wavelengths experience most refraction. By casting the light emerging from a prism on to a screen, Newton revealed the full spectrum of colours. We shall discuss Newton's contributions further when we look at colour vision.

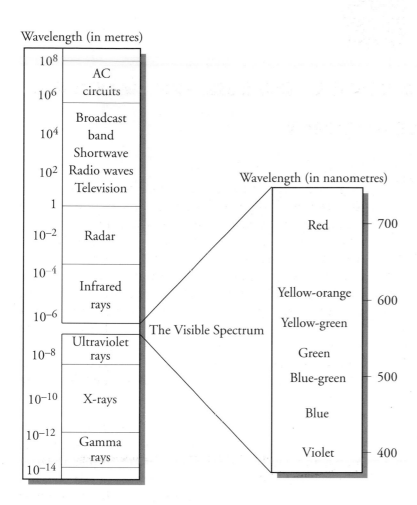

Wavelength (in metres)

Wavelength (in nanometres)

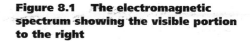

Wavelength (in nanometres)

Figure 8.1   The electromagnetic spectrum showing the visible portion to the right

The eye

The sense organ of vision is the eye. A cross-section of the human eye is shown in Figure 8.2 below.

According to Ornstein (1986), the eye 'is the most important avenue of personal consciousness'. It has been estimated that about 90% of the information we receive about the external world reaches us through the eye. We will now trace the path followed by light as it passes through the eye.

The eyeball is enclosed by a tough outer coat called the *sclera*. Although the sclera is mainly opaque, at the front of the eye it is not, and bulges out to form a

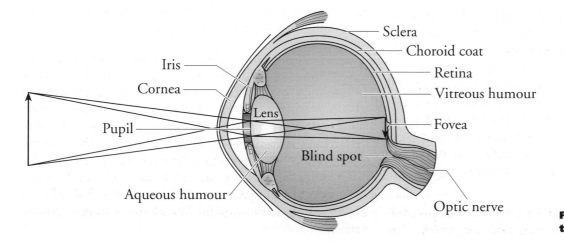

Figure 8.2   Cross-section of the human eye

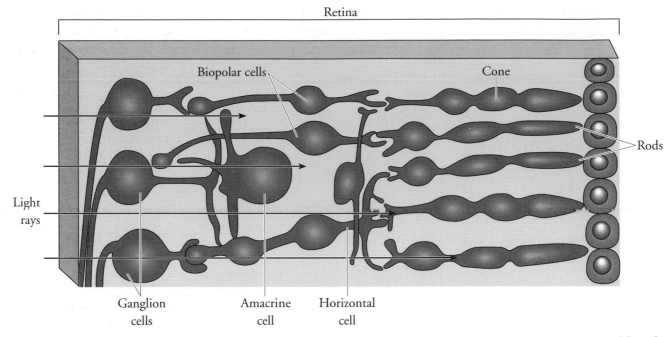

Figure 8.3   The layers of cells in the retina. Note how light must travel through several layers before reaching the photoreceptors

transparent membrane called the *cornea*. It is through the cornea that light enters the eye. Via the cornea, light waves pass through a clear, watery fluid called *aqueous humour*, and are refracted to bring them into sharper focus. The amount of light entering the eye is controlled by the *iris*. This contracts or expands to vary the size of the aperture (the black opening in the eye called the *pupil*) through which light waves pass. The amount of pigmentation of the eye gives our eyes their characteristic colour. Heavy pigmentation produces brown eyes, whereas little or no pigmentation results in blue eyes. Pupil size adjusts automatically to the amount of light and is under the control of the *autonomic nervous system* (see Chapter 3). In low lighting the pupil dilates to allow more light to enter. In bright light, it contracts to limit the amount that enters.

After passing through the pupil, light strikes the *lens* of the eye. This is a crystalline structure which serves to further focus light waves. The lens is held in place by *ciliary muscles* that control its shape. Looking into the distance causes the lens to be made thinner. Looking at objects close to us causes the lens to be made thicker. This process, which is called *accommodation*, brings the image of objects into focus. Abnormalities in eye shape often make it impossible for the lens to accommodate correctly. This results in *short-sightedness* (in which a person can see distinctly for only a short distance) or

long-sightedness (in which distant objects can be seen clearly but near objects cannot).

After being refracted by the lens, light waves pass through a jelly-like substance called *vitreous humour* before striking the *retina*, a delicate membrane which lines the back of the eye. The main parts of the retina are *cones*, *rods*, *bipolar cells*, and *ganglion cells*, all of which are neurons. Rods and cones form one layer of the retina and are *photosensitive cells* (or *photoreceptors*) whose job it is to convert light energy into electrical nerve impulses. Bipolar and ganglion cells form the other two layers of the retina. The bipolar cells are connected to the ganglion cells and to rods and cones. The axons of the ganglion cells form the beginning of the *optic nerve*, the pathway by which information is sent to the brain.

We might expect the photoreceptors to be at the *front* of the retina where they would be in the best position to intercept light waves. However, and as Figure 8.3 above illustrates, they are at the *back*. This means that light waves must pass through the other two layers and the blood vessels that serve them. One reason for this arrangement is that the work done by the photoreceptors requires amounts of energy that cannot be supplied by the fluid of the eye. Thus, the photoreceptors are next to the *choroid coat* of the retina, which is rich in blood vessels. The oxygen and other nutrients carried by the blood provide the photoreceptors with the necessary energy.

In each retina we have about 120 million rods and 7 million cones. Rods help us to see *achromatic colour*, that is, black, white and intermediate grey, and are specialised for vision in dim light (so-called *scotopic vision*). Rods are sensitive only to the intensity of light and therefore contribute to our perception of brightness but not colour. The photosensitive chemical contained in rods, *rhodopsin*, changes its structure in response to low levels of illumination. Different cones respond to different wavelengths and this helps us see *chromatic colour*, that is, red, green, blue, and so on. This provides us with *photopic vision*. The cones are specialised for bright light vision and contain a chemical called *iodopsin*.

Rods and cones are distributed differently in the retina. Cones are much more numerous towards its centre. The *fovea*, a pit-like depression is part of a cone-rich area called the *macula lutea* in which around 50,000 cones can be found. This dense packing helps to explain the *acuity* (or sharpness) of vision. The more densely packed the receptors are, the finer are the details of a pattern of light intensity which can be transformed into electrical energy. The falcon, for example, has cones which are three times more densely packed than in humans. This gives the falcon its acute vision.

Rods are distributed fairly evenly around the periphery of the retina and none are found in the fovea. When we want to focus on an object in bright light, our most sharply defined image will be obtained by looking directly at the object so that light is projected on to the cone-rich fovea. In dark light, however, the sharpest image of an object will be obtained if we look slightly to one side of it in order to stimulate the rods in the retina's periphery.

When a photon strikes a receptor, a *photochemical reaction* occurs. This reaction *transduces* light energy into neural signals. These signals are passed to the bipolar cells which in turn pass them to the ganglion cells. Ganglion cells travel across the inner surface of the retina and converge to form the optic nerve which carries signals to the brain. The *optic disc* is the part of the retina where the optic nerve leaves the eye. There are no visual receptors at this point and the optic disc is thus the eye's *blind spot*. Normally, we do not notice

the blind spot, one reason being that our eyes are constantly moving which allows us to receive the image that would fall on the blind spot in another part of the retina.

There are many more rods and cones than there are bipolar cells, and there are more bipolar cells than there are ganglion cells. What this means is that many rods (and cones) send their information to the same bipolar cell, and ganglion cells receive their information from many bipolar cells. Two other kinds of neuron in the retina, *horizontal cells* and *amacrine cells*, transmit information across the retina and allow interactions between adjacent rods, cones, bipolar cells and ganglion cells.

The number of photoreceptors sending information to the same bipolar cell varies. Around the retina's periphery, several hundred rods may send their information to one bipolar cell. At the fovea, however, individual bipolar and ganglion cells may serve only one cone. This one-to-one relationship accounts for the better acuity of cone vision as compared with rod vision. However, because many rods send information to one bipolar cell, the cell is more likely to 'fire' and hence rods are better at detecting faint light.

In the 1960s, David Hubel and Torsten Weisel (e.g. 1965) identified the type of visual stimulus to which individual retinal cells were most sensitive. The researchers inserted micro-electrodes (see Chapter 4) into the optic nerve of an anaesthetised cat. What they found was that some cells responded maximally when a spot of light fell on one particular, and usually circular, part of the retina. If the spot was moved to the surrounding part of the retina, the ganglion cells gradually stopped responding. Hubel and Weisel called the sensitive areas the cell's *receptive field*, and concluded that a ganglion cell is connected to all or most of the rods and cones within a receptive field.

At least three types of ganglion cell have been shown to exist, each of which has a different kind of receptive field. One type has an *on-centre* and an *off-surround*. This cell is more active when light falls in the centre of the receptive field and less sensitive when it falls on the edge. A second type has an *off-centre* and *on-surround*. A third type has a larger receptive field and seems to respond to movements, especially sudden ones. This is called a *transient cell*. As Beaumont (1988) has observed, the combined activity of on- and off-centre cells provides a clear definition of contours where there is a sudden change in brightness. Such contours are essential in defining the shape of objects to be perceived.

From the eye to the brain

As we saw in Chapters 2 and 5, visual sensory information travels to the *thalamus* and from there to the *primary visual area* of the cortex. The fibres of the optic nerve terminate at synapses with cells of a part of the thalamus called the *lateral geniculate nucleus* (or *LGN* – see Chapter 2). The LGN in each of the two thalami combines the information from both eyes before sending it to the cortex along the *geniculostriate path*. This pathway and the visual area must be intact for the conscious experience of vision. However, in the phenomenon of *blindsight*, the visual area may be extensively damaged but a person can identify objects without being consciously aware of them. Weiskrantz (1986), for example, has reported a case in which a person was able to detect whether a visual stimulus had been presented even though he was subjectively blind! This suggests the existence of another pathway which carries enough information to guide some actions in an unconscious way.

Hubel and Wiesel found that cells in the LGN had circular receptor fields just like ganglion cells. However, when they investigated cells in the cortex, a slightly different picture emerged. Using micro-electrodes to record the activity of single cells in the primary visual area of monkeys and cats, Hubel and Wiesel suggested the existence of three types of cortical cell that play a role in decoding light information.

The first of these, the *simple cell*, responds only to particular features of a stimulus in a particular orientation and in a particular location in the visual field. For example, a straight line which was vertical and in a specific location in the visual field might cause a particular neuron to 'fire'. However, if the straight line was in the same part of visual field but was horizontal, the neuron would not respond.

The *complex cell*, as its name suggests, is more sophisticated in terms of the stimuli to which it responds. It responds to a particular feature of a stimulus in a particular orientation *no matter where* it appears in the visual field. A complex cell, then, might respond to a vertical line wherever it was in the visual field. However, if the line's features or orientation changed, the cell would stop responding. Presumably, complex cells receive inputs from many simple cells which show the same feature and orientation features, and this accounts for their ability to respond to stimuli no matter where they appear in the visual field.

The *hypercomplex cell* is held to be even more sophisticated in that it responds to corners, angles, or bars of a particular length moving in a certain direction. Such cells presumably receive inputs from large numbers of complex cells. Although the existence of hypercomplex cells has been questioned (Bruce & Green, 1990), Hubel and Wiesel's research showed that the visual area of the cortex is not a homogeneous mass of tissues with randomly scattered cells. Rather, it shows precise and regular arrangement of different cells which Hubel and Wiesel termed the visual area's *functional architecture.*

In later research, Hubel & Wiesel (1977) showed that it was possible to identify six main layers of the visual area of the cortex that could be seen beneath the microscope. Hubel and Weisel have argued that the visual area is divided into roughly 1 mm square blocks of tissue that extend from the surface of the cortex down to the white matter below, and they use the term *hypercolumns* to label these. Within the hypercolumns, cells have different receptive fields. Although there is a good deal of overlap of these receptive fields, all fall within some single retinal area (or what Hubel and Wiesel term an *aggregate field*).

There are two further patterns of organisation which are worthy of mention. First, cells fall into two groups according to which eye is most effective in eliciting a response. Although cells in some layers have *binocular fields*, which means that they respond to their optimal stimulus whichever eye it is presented to, they always respond more strongly to the stimulus on one eye or the other (a phenomena termed *ocular dominance*). Cells sharing the same ocular dominance are grouped together into bands running across the visual area.

The second pattern of organisation is that cells are arranged in columns about 0.5 mm across according to their 'orientation preference'. If an electrode penetrates the cortex at right angles to the surface, then all the cells it encounters will have the same orientation preference regardless of whether they are simple or complex. As well as the primary visual area, there are other visual association areas in the occipital, temporal and parietal lobes (see Chapter 5). Maunsell & Newsome (1987) have suggested the existence of at least 19 visual

Figure 8.4   A black and white version of 'Enigma'. There appears to be a rotating movement in the solid rings of the picture

areas, each of which sends output to several others, and most (if not all) of which are matched by reciprocal connections running in the opposite direction. According to one estimate (van Essen, 1985), there are as many as ninety-two pathways linking the visual areas!

It has been suggested that each area has its own specified function. Obviously, we cannot describe anywhere near all of the research in this area, so we will confine ourselves to one illustrative example of the progress being made. Psychologists have long suspected that *visual illusions* are caused by the breakdown of the rules used by the brain to process signals from the eye. One illusion, 'Enigma', is a painting in blue, black and white by the artist Isia Leviant. When this illusion is looked at, there seems to be a rotating movement within the solid rings of the picture. A black and white reproduction of the illusion is shown in Figure 8.4.

Semir Zeki and his colleagues were particularly inter-

ested in an area of the cortex at the back of the head called V5, an area known to be involved in the analysis of moving visual stimuli. Using PET (see Chapter 4), Zeki and his colleagues showed that the black and white version of the illusion as presented in Figure 8.4 stimulated V5 and surrounding areas. It seems that, for some reason, the static picture causes activity in V5 and this accounts for the sensation of the circular movement even though there is no objective motion. The interested reader is directed to Zeki (1993) for a more detailed consideration of recent findings in this area of research.

Colour vision

Earlier on, we mentioned one contribution to our knowledge of light made by Sir Isaac Newton. In further experiments, Newton investigated the effects of mixing various components of the spectrum. The

surface for about 30 seconds and then look at a sheet of white paper, the sheet will appear green. Thus, the persistent sensation of a colour results in the perception of the complimentary colour when the first is removed. Hering's theory explains this by proposing that staring at red (say) forces the red-green receptors into 'red phase'. After a while, the red component tires. When our gaze is directed to a neutral surface, the light it reflects stimulates the red and green components equally, but only the green components are 'fresh' enough to fire.

Psychologists believe that both of the theories we have discussed are correct to a degree, and that colour vision may actually be a product of the mechanisms proposed by each of them. *Microspectrophotometry* research supports the Young-Helmholtz theory by showing that some cones are sensitive to the blue, green and yellow-green parts of the spectrum. Studies of bipolar, ganglion, and some cells in the LGN, however, suggest that the messages from the cones are relayed to parts of the brain in opponent-process fashion (DeValois & Jacobs, 1984).

For example, some neurons that transmit information to the brain are excited by red light but inhibited by green light whilst others work in the opposite way. A red-sensitive neuron excited by red light for half a minute might switch briefly to 'inhibitory mode' when the light is removed. This would result in us perceiving green as an after-image even if no light was present (Haber & Hershenson, 1980). Opponent-process theory does not seem to operate at level of the cones, but rather it operates along the neural path from the cones to the visual area.

It seems possible, then, that colour vision may be the result of a trichromatic system working at the level of the photoreceptors and an opponent-process mechanism working at later stages. It may even be that the trichromatic system itself interacts in an opponent-process way. Norman, et al. (1984), for example, have shown that in the turtle at least, red and green cones are *directly* connected to one another.

Colour constancy

The colours we perceive are not *solely* determined by the wavelength of light reflected from an object. Amongst several other factors that affect perception are our *familiarity* with and *knowledge* of an object's colour. This is part of the psychological phenomenon called *colour constancy*. As McCann (1987) has observed, 'Our visual system is built to tell us about the permanent colours of objects as opposed to the spectral composition of light falling on a local area of the retina'.

A powerful demonstration of colour constancy was provided by Edwin Land (1977), inventor of the Polaroid camera. Land used a large complex display (called a *colour Mondrian*) consisting of a patchwork of randomly arranged and differently coloured matt papers. The display was illuminated by mixed light from projectors with red, green and blue filters. An independent brightness control was also available for each of the projectors.

Observers then selected one of the colours and Land measured the amounts of red, green and blue light coming from it. A second colour was then selected and the same measurements taken. The illumination was then changed so that the amount of red, green and blue light coming from the second colour was the *same* as that from the first colour. When all three projectors were turned on, observers were asked to report what colour they saw. All observers reported seeing the second colour, even though the physical properties of the light coming from it were the same as the first colour!

If perceived colour was determined solely by the spectral composition of the reflected light, the second colour would have been seen as the first. However, it was not and the observers displayed colour constancy. In order to explain this, Land proposed what he called the *retinex theory of colour constancy* ('retinex' is a combination of 'retina' and 'cortex'). According to this, there are three separate visual systems or retinexes, one responsive primarily to long-wavelength light, one to medium-wavelength light, and one to short-wavelength light. Each of these produces a separate lightness image and a comparison of these images is carried out.

The comparison determines the colour which is perceived. The three lightnesses provide the coordinates of a three-dimensional space and, whereas a colour space based on the *absolute* absorptions in the three classes of receptor will predict only whether two stimuli will *match*, a space based on the three lightnesses will predict how colours actually *look*. This is because between them they give the reflectance of the object in different parts of the spectrum (that is, they give a measure of their *relative absorptions*). Land's theory implies that the formation of lightnesses could occur in the retina or cortex and that the retina-cortical structure acts as a whole.

Interestingly, recent research by Zeki (1993) has shown that an area of the cortex called the *fusiform gyrus* (or V4 area) shows increased cerebral blood flow when people are shown 'colour Mondrians' suggesting the existence of a colour centre in the cortex. Of equal interest is the finding that the response from V4 is more pronounced in the left than the right hemisphere. The fact that the response in V4 is not accompanied by increased activity in the temporal lobes (which play an important role in memory – see Chapter 5) suggests that responses to colour do not necessarily trigger previous memories or experiences.

Conclusions

In this chapter we have examined the nature of light and the structure of the eye, the sense organ of vision. We have seen that light information is transduced into electrical energy in the retina of the eye and is then passed on to the brain where it is decoded. Neurons specialised for various functions play an important role in this decoding process, and recent research has begun to identify areas of the cerebral cortex which are specialised for particular aspects of visual perception. We have also discussed colour vision and colour constancy, and presented theories which attempt to explain them.

SUMMARY

- The importance of the visual system is reflected in the fact that a greater proportion of the brain is devoted to vision than to any other sense; its importance is also illustrated by **visual capture**.
- Light consists of **photons** and is a form of **electromagnetic radiation**. Two important characteristics of light are **intensity** and **wavelength**, which is measured in **nanometres** (nm).
- The intensity of a light wave determines its **brightness**. **Hue** is the colour of an object and is partly determined by wavelength. Visible light is a very narrow section of the electromagnetic spectrum, within the range 380–760 nm. Some colours, such as brown and white, are not in the light spectrum, so there is more to colour than wavelength. **Saturation** is the proportion of **chromatic** to **achromatic** light. Newton showed that white light is a mixture of wavelengths of all colours in the visible spectrum.
- About 90% of information about the external world reaches us through the eye; light enters the eye through the **cornea**; the **iris** (which gives our eyes their characteristic colour) contracts or expands to vary the size of the **pupil**; pupil size adjusts automatically to the amount of light and is controlled by the **autonomic nervous system**.
- Light then travels through the **aqueous humour**, which brings it into sharper focus before striking the **lens**, which further focuses the light waves. **Accommodation** is controlled by the **ciliary muscles**; defective accommodation results in either **short-** or **long-sightedness**.
- Light passes through the **vitreous humour** onto the **retina** at the back of the eye; it consists of **cones, rods, bipolar cells**, and **ganglion cells**. Rods and cones are **photosensitive cells/photoreceptors**, converting light energy into electrical nerve impulses. Being situated at the back of the retina, the rods and cones are provided with necessary energy from the blood vessels of the **choroid coat**.
- Bipolar cells are connected to the ganglion cells and to rods and cones. The axons of the ganglion cells form the beginning of the **optic nerve**.
- Each retina contains about 120 million rods, which help us to see **achromatic colour** and are specialised for **scotopic vision**, and 7 million cones, which help us to see **chromatic colour** and are specialised for **photopic vision**. The rods contain **rhodopsin**, which changes its structure in reponse to low levels of illumination, while the cones contain **iodopsin**, which is sensitive to bright light.
- Cones are concentrated in the **macula lutea**,

towards the centre of the retina, particularly in the **fovea**; this helps to explain visual **acuity**. There are no rods in the fovea; instead they are evenly distributed around the outside of the retina.

- When a photon strikes a receptor, a **photochemical reaction** occurs which **transduces** light energy into neural signals; these are passed to the bipolar cells which in turn pass them to the ganglion cells. The **optic disc** has no visual receptors and so is the eye's **blind spot**.

- **Horizontal** and **amacrine cells** transmit information across the retina, allowing interactions between adjacent rods, cones, bipolar and ganglion cells.

- In the periphery of the retina, many hundreds of rods send their information to the same bipolar cell, which makes rods more likely to detect faint light, but at the fovea, individual bipolar and ganglion cells serve a single cone, which accounts for the greater acuity of cone vision.

- Hubel and Wiesel inserted micro-electrodes into the optic nerve of an anaesthetised cat. Some cells were most likely to respond to a spot of light falling on the cell's **receptive field**; a ganglion cell is connected to all/most of the rods and cones within a receptive field.

- One type of ganglion cell has an **on-centre/off-surround** receptive field; another type has an **off-centre/on-surround** receptive field; these are essential for defining object contour. **Transient cells** have a larger receptive field and are most responsive to sudden movements.

- The fibres of the optic nerve terminate at synapses with cells in the **lateral geniculate nucleus** (LGN); combined information from both eyes is sent to the **primary visual area** via the **geniculostriate path**. This pathway must be intact for conscious visual experience, but **blindsight** suggests the existence of another pathway which allows 'unconscious' vision.

- The primary visual area of monkeys and cats contains three kinds of cell that decode light information in different ways. **Simple cells** respond only to particular orientations of a stimulus in a particular location in the visual field. **Complex cells**, which receive input from many simple cells, respond to a particular orientation **wherever** it appears, while **hypercomplex cells** respond to corners, angles, or bars of a particular length moving in a certain direction.

- The visual area of the cortex is arranged in a precise and regular manner (**functional architecture**). It comprises six main layers, divided into **hypercolumns**, within which cells have different receptive fields, all falling within an **aggregate field**. The primary visual area is also organised in terms of **binocular fields** and **ocular dominance**, as well as orientation preference.

- There are additional visual association areas in the occipital, temporal, and parietal lobes; according to one estimate, there are 19 visual areas, and according to another, there are 92 pathways linking them.

- As well as discovering that white light is a mixture of all the colours of the spectrum, Newton found that mixing just two colours produced white, although this only occurred when the colours were at opposite ends of the diameter of his **colour circle**; these are called **complementary colours**.

- Perceived hue is determined by the wavelength of light that is **reflected** (as opposed to the wavelengths that are **absorbed/subtracted**). When different colour paints are mixed, the perceived colour is based on **subtractive colour mixing** (i.e. what the surface/object reflects); when different wavelenghts of light simultaneously stimulate the eye, **additive colour mixing** takes place (i.e. what the visual system does).

- Humans with normal vision can distinguish up to 150 colours, formed from 4 basic hues and 2 hueless colours. While wavelengths can be varied **continuously**, changes in colour are **discontinuous**.

- According to the **Young-Helmholtz trichromatic theory of colour vision**, there are three types of receptor (cones), corresponding to red, blue, and green hues; the perception of colour is determined by the ratio of these receptors that are activated. Each type of cone contains a slightly different **photopigment**.

- The Young-Helmholtz theory can explain the effects of mixing colours of different wavelengths, but **colour blindness** and **negative after-images** are better explained by the **opponent process theory**.

- According to Hering, the three types of receptor are responsive to **pairs** of colours: red-green, yellow-blue (responsible for colour vision), and black-white (responsible for brightness and saturation perception). When one member of a pair is excited, the other is inhibited (i.e. they are **opposed**).

- The most common type of **colour-blindness** is red-green; yellow-blue is much rarer but does occur; people with either type are **dichromatic**, while those who are totally colour-blind are **monochromatic**. Normal vision is **trichromatic**.

- Staring at a particular coloured surface will produce an **after-image** of the opposite (complementary) colour; according to Hering's theory, this is caused by the firing of the first component, followed by firing of the second component.
- Both theories are probably valid, working in a complementary way at different levels or stages. **Microspectrophotometry** research shows that different cones are sensitive to different wavelengths, while there is evidence that messages from the cones are relayed along the neural path to the visual area of the brain in opponent-process fashion.
- Perceived colour is only partly determined by the wavelength of reflected light from an object; our **familiarity/knowledge** of the object's colour are also involved, part of **colour constancy.** This was demonstrated by Land's **colour Mondrian**. According to his **retinex theory of colour constancy**, three separate visual systems, responsive to long, medium, and short wavelengths respectively, produce separate lightness images which are then compared. It is the comparison that determines the perceived colour.
- The **fusiform gyrus** is activated when people are shown colour Mondrians; this is more pronounced in the left hemisphere. The absence of increased activity in the temporal lobe suggests that responses to colour do not necessarily trigger memories of an object's colour.

PART 3
Awareness

BODILY RHYTHMS

Introduction and overview

As Marks & Folkhard (1985) have noted, 'rhythmicity is a ubiquitous characteristic of living cells. In the human it is evident within the single cell, in individual behaviour, and at the population level'. We can define a bodily rhythm as *a cyclical variation over some period of time in physiological or psychological processes*. A number of these rhythms have been identified. Our aim in this chapter is to look at five types of bodily rhythm which have been the subject of research interest.

Circadian rhythms

Circadian rhythms, that is, consistent cyclical variations over a period of about 24 hours (the word circadian comes from the Latin 'circa' meaning 'about' and 'diem' meaning 'a day') are a feature of human and non-human physiology and behaviour. As Aschoff & Wever (1981) have noted, 'there is hardly a tissue or function that has not been shown to have some 24-hour variation'. Such functions include heart rate, metabolic rate, breathing rate, and body temperature, all of which reach maximum values in the late afternoon and early evening and minimum values in the early hours of the morning. It might seem fairly obvious that such a rhythm would occur since we are active during the day and inactive at night. However, many studies have demonstrated that the rhythms persist if we suddenly reverse our activity patterns by, for example, sleeping during the day and being active at night.

The concentration of the body's hormones also varies over the course of the day. However, the time at which a hormone is concentrated varies from one hormone to another. In women, *prolactin* (which stimulates the production of milk) peaks in the middle of the night. This helps to explain why it is more likely for a woman to go into labour during the night rather than the day. We can also explain why certain medications are more effective at certain times of the day. Anticoagulant medication, for example, has been shown to be more effective at night when the blood is a little thinner in density (and note that there is a tendency for heart attacks to occur in the morning when the blood is more prone to clotting).

Ordinarily, we are surrounded by *external cues* as to the time of day. These are known as *Zeitgebers* (which comes from the German, meaning 'time-giver'). But what would happen if all cues to time were eliminated? Would we continue to show a 24-hour cyclical variation in our physiology and behaviour? In 1972, Michel Siffre, a French geologist, spent seven months underground in a cave where no natural sounds or light could reach him. Although he had adequate food, drink, exercise equipment, and so on, and whilst he was in contact with the outside world via a permanently staffed telephone, he had no means of knowing what time it was.

In these conditions, Siffre's physiology and behaviour remained cyclical but his day was 25 rather than 24 hours long. Thus, once every 12 days Siffre ate breakfast when the world immediately above him was tucking into an evening meal! So where is the *internal clock* that must exist? How does it operate, and how is it reset each day to the cycle of the 24-hour world in which we live?

It has long been believed that the body's *master clock* lies in two tiny structures called the *suprachiasmatic nuclei* (SN) located in the hypothalamus (see Chapter 2). The SN receives information directly from the retina of the eye and it is this information about light and dark which synchronises our biological rhythms with the 24-hour cycle of the outside world. If the SN is damaged or the connection between the SN and retina is severed, circadian rhythms disappear completely, and eating, drinking, and other rhythmic behaviours become completely random over the course of the day.

Recent evidence has suggested that the cycle length of rhythms is dependent on genetic factors. In one study, hamsters were given brain transplants of the SN from a mutant strain whose biological rhythms had a shorter cycle than those of the recipient hamsters. The recipients adopted the same activity cycles as the mutant strain. Other studies with non-humans have shown that there are limits beyond which the length of 'day' cannot be environmentally manipulated.

We can, however, adjust our bodily rhythms if necessary. If we were to reverse our pattern of sleep and waking, as happens with shift-work or travelling from (say) England to Australia, we would find that our circadian rhythms eventually became synchronised to the new set of external cues. Unfortunately, some people take much longer than others to adapt to a change in their activity patterns (and in the case of travelling from one time zone to another we use the term *'jet lag'* to describe this). Indeed, it seems that some people never achieve a complete reversal. It is also the case that not all of our physiological functions reverse at the same time. For example, whilst body temperature usually reverses within a week for most people, the rhythm of *adrenocortical hormone* (see Chapter 3) production takes much longer.

The finding that animals transplanted with the SN of others adopt the same activity patterns as their donors, coupled with the fact that the circadian rhythm cannot be experimentally manipulated beyond certain limits, strongly suggests that bodily rhythms are primarily an internal (or *endogenous*) property that do not depend on external (or *exogenous*) cues.

One of the most interesting circadian rhythms is the sleep-waking cycle. Although Meddis and his colleagues (1973) have found that some people have as little as 45 minutes of sleep each night, the average person has around seven to eight hours per 24-hour day. People in all cultures sleep, and even those which take a midday 'siesta' have an extended period of five to eight hours sleep each day.

We also know that the need for sleep does not seem to be *determined* by the cycle of light and darkness. For example, Luce & Segal (1966) found that people who live near the Arctic circle, where the sun does not set during the summer months, sleep about seven hours during each 24-hour period. *External* cues, then, would not seem to be of primary importance as far as sleep and waking are concerned. This has led researchers to try and discover the *internal* events associated with sleep and waking. We will not examine the findings in this chapter. We will, however, devote some of the following chapter to an examination of the physiology of sleep.

Infradian rhythms

Infradian rhythms are those which last for *longer* than one day. Infradian rhythms have been known about for centuries. A seventeenth-century doctor, Sanctorius, for example, used a fine scale to weigh healthy young men over long periods of time. Sanctorius discovered a monthly weight change of 1–2 pounds. The infradian rhythm that has attracted most research interest is menstruation. Menstruation is an example of an endocrine cycle and there are several such cycles that are experienced by everybody. However, none are as well marked as menstruation and other cycles have therefore been much more difficult to study.

Every 28 days or so, female bodies undergo a sequence of changes with two possible outcomes: conception or menstruation. Over the course of a lifetime, menstruation will occur approximately 400 times. Conventionally, we portray menstruation as the *beginning* of a cycle. In fact, the menstrual period is the end of a four-week cycle of activity during which the womb has prepared for the job of housing and nourishing a fertilised egg (see Chapter 3, page 29).

The onset of the 28-day cycle is often irregular at first, but becomes well established in most girls in a matter of months. Some evidence suggests that the cycle can change to fit in with events in the environment. For example, women who spend a lot of time together often find that their menstrual periods become synchronised (Sabbagh & Barnard, 1984). Why this happens is not known, but one hypothesis attributes it to the unconscious detection of some chemical scent secreted by women at certain times during the menstrual cycle.

As we mentioned in Chapter 3, the term *pre-menstrual syndrome* (PMS) has been used to describe a variety of effects that occur at several phases of the menstrual cycle. Typically, the effects occur around four to five days before the onset of menstruation, and it has been estimated that around 60% of all women experience some sorts of effects around this time. These include mild irritation, depression, headaches, and a decline in alertness or visual acuity. One commonly reported experience is a day or so of great energy followed by lethargy that disappears with the onset of menstrual bleeding. Other effects include insomnia, vertigo, and even nymphomania (Luce, 1971). PMS has also been associated with a change in appetite. Some women develop a craving for certain types of food whereas others lose their appetite completely.

The most pervasive social impact of PMS are the psychological and behavioural changes which occur. In an early study, Dalton (1964) reported that a large proportion of crimes were clustered in the pre-menstrual interval along with suicides, accidents, a decline in the quality of schoolwork, and intelligence test scores. However, more recent research (e.g. Keye, 1983) has suggested that whilst a small percentage of women experience effects that are strong enough to interfere with their normal functioning, they are not, contrary to the claim made by Dalton, more likely to commit crimes nor are they more likely to end up on psychiatric wards.

Thirty or more years ago, PMS was commonly attributed to a denial of femininity or a resistance to sexual roles. However, research by Oscar Janiger showed that the effects of PMS occurred in all cultures, suggesting quite clearly that it is a physiological cycle rather than a pattern of behaviour imposed by culture. Support for this view comes from Janiger's further discovery that effects similar to those experienced by women can be found in primates.

We know that it is the pituitary gland which governs the phases of the menstrual cycle by influencing changes in the endometrium (the walls of the uterus) and the preparation of the ovum. A study conducted in Helsinki by Timonen and his associates (1964) showed that during the lighter months of the year conceptions increased whilst in the darker months of the year they decreased, suggesting that light levels might have some influence (either directly or indirectly) on the pituitary gland which then influenced the menstrual cycle.

In a study reported by Reinberg (1967), a young woman spent three months in a cave relying on only the dim light of a miner's lamp. The woman's day lengthened to 24.6 hours and her menstrual cycle shortened to 25.7 days. Even though she was in the mine for only three months, it was a year before her menstrual cycle returned to its normal frequency. Reinberg speculated that it was the level of light in the cave which had influenced the menstrual cycle. Consistent with this was his finding that among 600 girls from northern Germany, *menarche* (the onset of menstruation which occurs at puberty) was much more likely to occur in winter. Interestingly, menarche is reached earlier by blind girls than sighted girls. We will attempt to explain these findings later on in this chapter.

Ultradian rhythms

A third type of bodily rhythm is called an ultradian rhythm. Ultradian rhythms are *shorter* than a day in length. They have been demonstrated in many physiological and behavioural processes including oral activity (such as smoking cigarettes), renal excretion and heart rate. The most well-researched ultradian rhythms are those that occur during *sleep*. To the layperson, sleep is a single state which typically occupies around eight hours of every day (and, as we saw above, the sleep-waking cycle is an example of a circadian rhythm). However, within a single night's sleep, a number of shorter rhythms occur. The rhythms and cycles that occur during sleep have, like the sleep-waking cycle itself, been the subject of extensive research. We will now look at the findings that have been obtained.

Before the invention of the EEG (see Chapter 4), sleep was an impossible phenomenon to study scientifically because there was no way of accessing what was going on inside the sleeper's head. In 1937, however, Loomis, Harvey & Hobart used the EEG to record the electrical activity in the brain of a sleeping person. The researchers discovered that the brain was not electrically inactive during sleep, and that certain types of electrical activity seemed to be related to changes in the type of sleep a person was having. It seemed that the waves tended to get 'bigger' as sleep got 'deeper'.

In 1952, 8-year-old Armond Aserinsky's father Eugene connected him to an EEG machine in order to see if repairs carried out on it had been successful. Electrodes were also placed near Armond's eyes in order to try and record the rolling eye movements that were believed to occur during sleep. After a while, the EOG started to trace wildly oscillating waves. Aserinsky senior thought that the machine was still broken, but after several minutes had elapsed the EOG fell silent. Periodically through the night, however, the wildly oscillating waves returned. When Armond was woken by his father during one such period, Armond reported that he had been dreaming.

Aserinsky senior eventually realised that the EOG was indicating fast, jerky eye movements beneath Armond's closed eyelids, and he further observed that whilst the EOG was active, Armond's EEG indicated that his brain was highly active as well, even though Armond was sound asleep. In a series of experiments, Aserinsky & Kleitman (1953) reported that the same phenomenon occurred when EOG and EEG measurements in adults were recorded. They used the term rapid eye movement sleep (or *REM* sleep) to describe the period of intense EOG activity.

In later experiments, Dement & Kleitman (1957) showed that when people were woken up during REM sleep and asked if they were *dreaming*, they much more often than not replied that they were. When they were woken at other times during the night, in non-rapid eye movement sleep (or *NREM* sleep), they occasionally reported dream-like experiences, but their descriptions usually lacked the vivid visual images and fantastic themes that were described during REM sleep awakenings.

The EEG allows sleep researchers to measure the electrical activity occurring in the brain over the course of a night's sleep. In 1968, Rechtschaffen and Kales devised a set of criteria that could be used to describe changes in the brain's electrical activity. These criteria allowed NREM sleep to be divided into four stages, each of which is characterised by distinct patterns of electrical activity. Note that most of the research in this area is carried out in *sleep laboratories*. Although researchers try to make the setting as much like 'home' as they can, it is clearly a different environment for all of us. We typically take around two nights to get adjusted to the new surroundings and for this reason reliable measures of our sleep patterns can only really be obtained from the third night onwards.

When we are awake and alert, the EEG shows the low amplitude and high frequency *beta waves* (see Chapter 4, page 38 for a description of beta waves and the waves that follow). Once we are in bed and relaxed, beta waves are replaced by *alpha waves* of higher amplitude but slower frequency. Gradually, we begin to fall asleep. Our breathing and heart rate slow down, body temperature drops, and our muscles relax. The onset of sleep is marked by the appearance of irregular and slower *theta waves*, and we have now entered *Stage 1* of sleep.

The transition from relaxation to Stage 1 is sometimes accompanied by a *hypnagogic state* during which we experience dream-like and hallucinatory images that resemble vivid photographs. Such images have been linked to creativity. We may also experience the sensation of falling, and our bodies might suddenly jerk. Although the EMG indicates that the muscles are still active, the EOG indicates slow, gentle, rolling eye movements. Because Stage 1 sleep is the lightest stage of sleep, we are easily awakened from it. If this occurs, we might feel that we have not been sleeping at all.

After about a minute, the EEG shows another change which marks the onset of *Stage 2* sleep. Although the waves are of medium amplitude with a frequency of around 4–7 cycles per second (cps), Stage 2 sleep is characterised by brief bursts of activity with a frequency of 12–14 cps. These are called *sleep spindles* and why they appear is not precisely understood.

Another characteristic of Stage 2 sleep is the presence of *K-complexes*. These are the brain's response to external stimuli such as a sound in the room in which we are sleeping or internal stimuli such as a muscle tightening in the leg. Whilst it is possible to be woken fairly easily from Stage 2 sleep, the EOG registers minimal eye movements and the EOG shows little activity in the muscles. Figure 9.1 overleaf shows the response of a person in Stage 2 sleep to the presentation of several names, one of which is his wife's.

After around 20 minutes in Stage 2, electrical activity in the brain increases in amplitude and becomes even

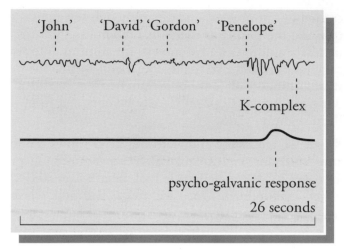

'John'   'David' 'Gordon'   'Penelope'

K-complex

psycho-galvanic response

26 seconds

Figure 9.1   EEG response of a person is Stage 2 sleep to the presentation of several names, one of which is his wife's

slower, dropping to around 1–3 cps. When these slow *delta waves* account for 20–50% of the EEG, we have entered *Stage 3* sleep. After a brief period of time, delta waves will account for more than 50% of the EEG and will slow to around $\frac{1}{2}$–2 cps which marks the onset of *Stage 4* sleep. In both Stages 3 and 4 of sleep we are extremely unresponsive to the environment and it is very difficult for us to be woken up. The EOG shows virtually no eye movements and our muscles are completely relaxed. Noises and lights do not disturb us as they would have done in the earlier stages of sleep.

In Stage 4, our heart rate, blood pressure and body temperature are at their lowest. We have descended what researchers term the *sleep staircase* and have moved from a very light to a very deep sleep. Our first episode of Stage 4 sleep lasts for around 40 minutes. At the end of this time we begin to 'climb' the sleep staircase passing briefly through Stage 3, before entering Stage 2 in which we spend around ten minutes.

Instead of re-entering Stage 1, however, something very different registers on the EEG machine and we start showing the irregular eye movements and brain activity first observed by Aserinsky. We are now experiencing our first episode of REM sleep. Research has shown that REM sleep occurs in all mammals except the dolphin and spiny anteater, but does not occur in fish, reptiles and amphibians, and occurs only briefly in a few birds of prey. It therefore seems likely that REM sleep is related to the development of brain structures found in mammals.

Interestingly, the EMG in REM sleep indicates that the muscles of the body are in a state of *virtual paralysis,*

which occurs as a result of inhibitory processes (the occasional twitches of our hands and feet are presumably a result of the inhibitory processes weakening briefly). We will discuss the probable function of this paralysis in Chapter 11. Although our muscles may be paralysed, our heart rate and blood pressure begin to fluctuate rapidly, and our respiration alters between shallow breaths and sudden gasps. Males may experience an erection and females corresponding changes in their sexual organs. The EMG, EEG and EOG recordings for each of the stages we have described is shown in Figure 9.2 opposite.

The fact that the eyes and brain of a person in REM are very *active* whilst the muscles are virtually *paralysed* and the observation that a person in REM is *very difficult to wake up* has led to REM also being termed *paradoxical sleep*. Our first period of REM sleep lasts for about 10 minutes. The end of it marks the completion of our first sleep *cycle.*

When REM sleep ends, we enter Stage 2 sleep again and spend around 25 minutes in that stage. After passing briefly through Stage 3, we enter Stage 4 and will spend about 30 minutes in a very deep sleep. After ascending the sleep staircase once more, another episode of REM sleep occurs which also lasts for around 10 minutes. We have now completed our second sleep cycle.

The entry into Stage 2 sleep marks the beginning of the third cycle. However, instead of descending the sleep staircase (after about an hour in Stage 2) we enter REM and might spend as long as 40 minutes in that stage. Again, the end of REM marks the end of another cycle. Unlike the first two cycles, then, the third cycle does not involve any Stage 3 or 4 sleep. This is also true of the fourth cycle. The cycle begins with around 70 minutes of Stage 2 sleep which is immediately followed by a fourth episode of REM which might last as long as an hour. By the end of the fourth cycle we will have been asleep for around seven hours. Our fifth cycle will probably end with us waking up and for that reason it is known as the *emergent cycle* of sleep. We may awake directly from REM or from Stage 2 and might experience *hypnopompic images*, that is, vivid visual images that occur as we are waking up (cf. the hypnagogic images mentioned earlier). As was true in the third and fourth cycles, the emergent cycle does not consist of any Stage 3 or 4 sleep.

Typically, then, we will have five or so cycles of sleep,

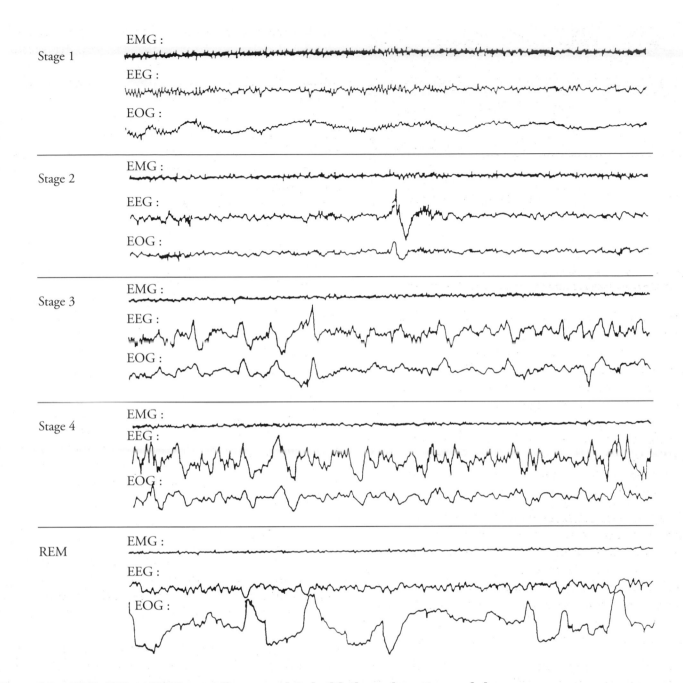

Figure 9.2   EMG, EEG and EOG recordings associated with the various stages of sleep

each of which lasts, on average, for around 90 minutes. The exact pattern of sleep varies from person to person and what we have described above is very much an 'average' since the time between REM and NREM varies both between and within people. So, as well as people differing in terms of their sleep cycles, the pattern can vary within the same person from night to night. What does seem to be true for everyone, though, is that Stages 3 and 4 of sleep occur only in the first two cycles of sleep and that whilst REM occurs in every cycle, episodes increase in length over the course of the night. Figure 9.3 overleaf illustrates the sleep cycles of a person who went to bed at 11.10 p.m. and awoke at 6.30 a.m.

Our pattern of sleeping also changes as we get older. Newborn infants sleep for around 16 hours a day and spend approximately half this time in REM. At one year of age infants sleep for around 12 hours a day and REM occupies about one-third of this time. In adult-

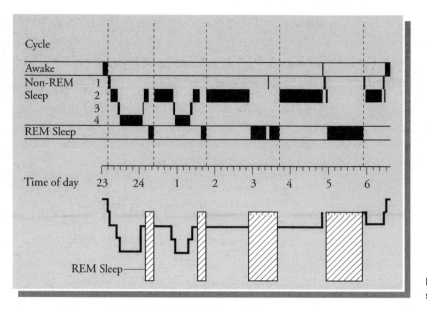

Figure 9.3   A characteristic profile of a night's sleep. From Borbely (1986)

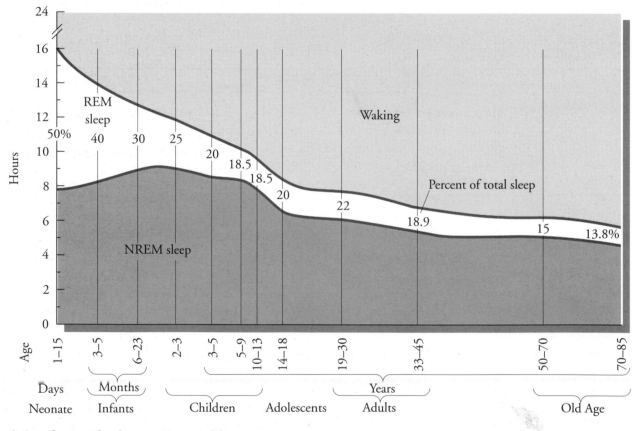

Figure 9.4   Changes in sleep patterns with age

hood, we spend only around a quarter of an eight-hour period of sleep in REM and in very old age the amount of REM time decreases even further. Stage 4 sleep also changes as we get older. At age 60, Stage 4 sleep has all but disappeared. As a result, we tend to be more easily awakened when we are older even though we may have been very sound sleepers when younger. Figure 9.4 above shows the major changes in sleep patterns with age.

Diurnal rhythms

Diurnal rhythms, that is, rhythms which occur during the *waking day*, have been the subject of research interest since the nineteenth century. The main question that has been addressed is whether the time of day at which a particular cognitive task is carried out makes a difference to how well that task is carried out. Because of its potential practical applications, psychologists have paid particular attention to the ways in which performance of complex 'real-world' tasks varies over the waking day.

Some evidence suggests that our immediate memory for realistic events is better in the morning than the afternoon. In a study conducted by Barry Gunter and his associates, participants were tested for their immediate recall of television news information. The results showed a decline across the three times of the day that were tested (09.00, 13.00 and 17.00). However, other research has failed to demonstrate any 'time-of-day' effects. Adam (1983), for example, found that the information remembered from lectures did not differ over the day. It did not seem to matter whether a lecture was attended first thing in the morning or last thing in the afternoon, there was no difference in how much was remembered (or not remembered). Whilst the time of day did not affect how much was remembered, Adam did find that it influenced students' ability to extract the main *theme* from a lecture. Students were considerably better at this in the afternoon than in the morning.

Using their 'Morningness-Eveningness' questionnaire, Horne & Osterberg (1976) have argued that there are two *diurnal types*. Extreme 'morning types' are characteristically tired in the evening, go to bed early, and wake in the morning feeling alert. By contrast, extreme 'evening types' perform best in the evening, go to bed late, and feel tired in the morning. Marks & Folkhard (1985) have proposed that these differences may be due to a *phase advance* in the circadian system. It seems that morning types 'peak' two or more hours earlier than evening types on a number of variables including, for example, body temperature.

It has also been suggested that introversion and extroversion are associated with diurnal differences. Such differences might be attributable to differences in sleeping and waking behaviour. Whilst the time at which we go to bed is influenced by our internal clock, it can also be influenced by psychosocial factors. Differences between introverts and extroverts in terms of how long they sleep for and how regular their sleep is could, therefore, be explained in terms of psychosocial influences (such as going to a lot of parties) and this might account for the differences between them with respect to their diurnal rhythms.

Researchers believe that the differences in performance that have been found on a number of cognitive tasks performed during the waking day cannot be *solely* explained in terms of a circadian variation in how aroused we are. Rather, such differences appear to be the result of a combination of many different rhythms which reflect the various cognitive functions contributing to observed performance. Exactly how the different components of the human information processing system change over the course of the day has, however, yet to be determined.

Circannual rhythms

The word circannual describes rhythms that have a period of about a year. Research has shown that when members of some species are kept under constant conditions the yearly cycle repeats itself like a circadian rhythm (Manning, 1975). Gwinner (1971), for example, has found that when the willow warbler is kept under a constant day consisting of 12 hours of light followed by 12 hours of darkness, it will go through its usual cycle of moulting and migratory restlessness.

The most extensively investigated case of a circannual rhythm in mammals is that of the gold-mantled ground squirrel of the Rocky Mountains. The rhythm was first noted by Pengelley & Fisher (1957) while they were studying the hibernation of squirrels. In August, a squirrel was placed in a small, windowless room which was illuminated for a period of 12 hours and then darkened for the same length of time. The temperature of the room was kept constant at 0 °C (32 °F).

Initially, the squirrel remained active. It ate and drank normally and its temperature remained constant at 37 °C (98.6 °F). In October, the squirrel ceased its activities and hibernated, its body temperature dropping to 1 °C (33.8 °F). In April, the squirrel became active again and its body temperature rose to 37 °C. Finally, in September, it resumed hibernation. The alternating period of activity and hibernation typically lasts for about 300 days, and is clearly a circannual rhythm. What seems to be the key to this rhythm is temperature rather than light. This makes sense given that the squirrel, which spends a great deal of time in its burrow, is probably not much affected by changes in the length of the day.

Other circannual rhythms include the establishment of territories, the formation of colonies and pair bonding. A review of other processes which exhibit circannual rhythms, such as suicide and mortality rates, can be found in Aschoff & Wever (1981). Another rhythm which could be considered circannual is *Seasonal Affective Disorder* (or *SAD*). There is a growing body of evidence to suggest that some disorders of mood are under *seasonal* control. Boyce & Parker (1988) have described two types of SAD, both of which have *depression* as the primary psychological effect. People experiencing *winter SAD* also show a craving for carbohydrates, gain weight, and oversleep. Those who experience *summer SAD* show a loss of appetite (with a consequent reduction in weight) and insomnia, as well as severe depression.

The 'culprit' might be a hormone (see Chapter 3) called *melatonin* which is released by the *pineal gland*. Research indicates that this hormone affects mood and subjective energy levels and that its production is controlled by the presence or absence of direct light stimulation to the eyes. When it is dark, melatonin is produced, but when it is light, its production is suppressed. It has been proposed that in winter SAD the production of melatonin occurs earlier and ends later than is normally the case. Quite possibly, the excessive production of melatonin could be responsible for winter SAD.

One way of treating winter SAD, then, might be to move to a location where the day is much longer since this would suppress melatonin production. The idea that people suffering from depression should move from their habitat during winter is not new. Esquirol (1845), for example, once advised a sufferer of depression to 'be in Italy before the close of October, from where you must not return until the month of May'. Unfortunately, not everybody can afford to follow Esquirol's advice! However, a new form of therapy has been shown to be successful in the treatment of winter SAD. In *phototherapy*, sufferers of winter SAD are seated in front of extremely bright lights (the equivalent to the illumination of 2,500 candles on a surface one metre away being the most effective – Wehr & Rosenthal, 1989). Presumably, the suppression of melatonin production by the artificial lights is responsible for the therapy's success.

The role played by melatonin may also explain some of the findings we described earlier when we looked at infradian and circannual rhythms. Recall that Reinberg (1967) hypothesised that it was the level of light that influenced the menstrual cycle of the young woman who spent three months in a cave, and that evidence exists to suggest that menarche is much more likely to occur in winter and occurs earlier in blind than sighted girls. It seems reasonable to suggest that the pineal gland is somehow affected by the secretion of melatonin and that this affects both the menstrual cycle and, given the finding concerning increased conceptions during the lighter months of the year, the reproductive system in general.

Conclusions

In this chapter we have looked at a variety of bodily rhythms. We have identified several physiological and psychological effects associated with these, and some of the ways in which disruption of these rhythms can affect behaviour.

SUMMARY

- **Circadian rhythms** can be seen in both human and non-human physiology and behaviour. Heart rate, metabolic rate, breathing rate, and body temperature all reach a peak in the late afternoon/early evening and reach their lowest values in the early morning. These rhythms persist even if activity patterns are reversed.

- Hormone concentrations also vary over a 24-hour period, but these vary between hormones. **Prolactin** peaks in the middle of the night, and anti-coagulant drugs are more effective at night when the blood is thinner.

- Even if all **Zeitgebers/external cues** about time were removed, we would continue to show a circadian rhythm, as demonstrated by Siffre's experience underground. However, our **internal/master clock** appears to run for **25** hours (rather than 24).

- The internal/master clock is located in the **suprachiasmatic nuclei** (SN) in the hypothalamus. The SN receives information directly from the retina which synchronises our biological rhythms with the outside world's 24-hour cycle. Damage to the SN or to the connection with the retina results in elimination of all circadian rhythms.

- Studies of hamsters suggest that the cycle length of rhythms depends on genetic factors; other animal experiments show that the length of 'day' cannot be manipulated beyond certain limits.

- Bodily rhythms can be adjusted, as in shift-work or crossing time zones, eventually becoming synchronised to the new set of external cues; people differ in their ability to adjust, as in **jet-lag**. Also, particular physiological functions, such as body temperature, reverse much more quickly than others, such as the rhythm of **adrenocortical hormone**.

- Bodily rhythms are primarily **endogenous**/internal, not dependent on **exogenous**/external cues. The sleep-waking cycle is largely independent of culture and the cycle of light and darkness, but determined by **internal** events.

- **Infradian rhythms** last **longer** than 24 hours. Menstruation is a well-marked endocrine cycle and is the most carefully researched infradian rhythm. It in fact marks the **end** of a four-week cycle of activity, although the cycle can change to fit in with certain environmental events.

- **Pre-menstrual syndrome** (PMS) refers to a large variety of bodily and psychological symptoms, some or all of which are experienced by about 60% of women 4–5 days before the onset of menstruation. The early claims that PMS predisposes women to criminal behaviour or psychiatric disorders are not supported by more recent evidence. PMS appears to be a universal physiological cycle, independent of culture, and also found in primates.

- The phases of the menstrual cycle are controlled by the pituitary gland, which might itself be influenced by (seasonal) light levels. One study found that **menarche** was much more likely to occur in winter; it is also reached earlier by blind than sighted girls.

- **Ultradian rhythms** are **shorter** than 24 hours. The most well-researched ultradian rhythms are those that occur during a night's **sleep**, which consists of a number of shorter rhythms. The EEG made the scientific study of sleep possible, showing that the brain is electrically active during sleep and that certain types of electrical activity are related to different kinds of sleep.

- Aserinsky and Kleitman reported that fast, jerky eye movements under the closed lids (**rapid eye movement**/REM sleep, based on the EOG) are associated with an active EEG pattern. Dement and Kleitman found that people woken from REM sleep usually reported **dreaming**, and in a much more vivid way than in **non-rapid eye movement**/NREM sleep.

- NREM sleep consists of four stages, each characterised by a distinct pattern of electrical activity. When we are awake and alert, the EEG shows **beta waves**, which are replaced by **alpha waves** when we are in bed and relaxed. As we begin to fall asleep, we may enter a **hypnagogic state**, then **theta waves** mark the onset of **Stage 1 sleep**, the lightest stage, from which the sleeper can easily be woken.

- **Stage 2 sleep** is characterised by **sleep spindles** and **K-complexes**. There are minimal eye movements and little muscle activity (based on the EMG); this is also a light stage of sleep lasting about 20 minutes.

- When slow **delta waves** account for 20–50% of the EEG, **Stage 3 sleep** has begun; when delta waves account for over 50% of the EEG, **Stage 4 sleep** has begun. It is very difficult to wake someone from Stage 3 or 4; there are almost no eye movements and the muscles are completely relaxed. The sleeper has now descended the **sleep staircase**.

- After about 40 minutes in Stage 4, we climb the staircase again, passing briefly through Stage 3, then Stage 2 (for about 10 minutes). But instead of entering Stage 1, we enter our first episode of REM sleep (which seems to be related to the development of brain structures found only in mammals).

- The EMG in REM sleep shows that the muscles are **virtually paralysed**, (although there is considerable physiological activity taking place); this, combined with a very **active** brain and eye movements, has led REM sleep to be called **paradoxical sleep**. The end of the first period of REM sleep brings to an end the first sleep **cycle**.

- Another descent of the sleep staircase then takes place, followed by another ascent and a second stage of REM sleep. With entry into Stage 2 (where we spend about an hour), the third cycle has begun; but instead of descending again, we re-enter REM sleep which lasts up to 40 minutes.

- The fourth cycle involves about 70 minutes in Stage 2, followed by a fourth episode of REM, which may last as long as an hour. The fifth cycle is the **emergent cycle** and may involve **hypnopompic images**.

- A typical night's sleep comprises five or so cycles, each lasting about 90 minutes. Although there are important individual differences, Stages 3 and 4 only occur in the first two cycles, and the length of REM episodes, which occur in every cycle, increases as the night progresses.

- There are important developmental changes in sleep patterns. Newborns spend about half of their 16 hours of sleep per day in REM, while in adulthood we spend only about a quarter of our eight hours' sleep in REM. REM time shrinks as we get older, and Stage 4 sleep virtually disappears.

- **Diurnal rhythms** occur during the **waking day** and have been studied in relation to the efficiency of particular cognitive tasks in relation to time of day; for example, immediate memory for realistic events (such as TV news) may be better in the morning. But any such differences are likely to be the result of a combination of many different rhythms, not just the circadian.

- People may differ as to when they function most efficiently (**diurnal types**), and such differences may be due to a **phase advance** in the circadian system. Differences between introverts and extroverts in terms of the length and regularity of their sleeping could be due to psychosocial influences.

- **Circannual rhythms** last about one year, as illustrated by the alternating periods of activity and hibernation of the Rocky Mountain gold-mantled ground squirrel; this rhythm lasts about 300 days and is influenced largely by temperature. Other examples are territory and colony formation and pair-bonding.

- **Seasonal Affective Disorder/SAD** could be considered a circannual rhythm; **winter SAD** and **summer SAD** both involve **depression** as the main psychological effect. The cause may be **melatonin**, released by the **pineal gland** in response to direct light stimulation of the eyes; since melatonin is produced when it is dark, winter SAD may be caused by excessive melatonin production. **Phototherapy** is designed to suppress its production through the use of artificial light.

THE FUNCTIONS OF SLEEP

Introduction and overview

As we saw in the previous chapter, all of us experience the altered state of consciousness we call sleep at least once a day. Spending approximately seven to eight hours in this altered state of consciousness means that around one third of our lifetime is spent fast asleep! Given this, it seems reasonable to suggest that sleep must be important in some ways.

Our aim in this chapter is to look at the various theories that have been offered to explain the functions of sleep. If sleep does serve useful functions then we ought to be able to identify these by *depriving* people of sleep. In the first part of this chapter, we will look at the effects of total sleep deprivation and theories which have been proposed to explain the functions of sleep in general. In the second part, we will look at the effects of depriving people of the most interesting stage of sleep, REM sleep, and at theories that have been offered to explain the function of this stage of sleep. The final part of this chapter looks briefly at what is known about the physiological processes that occur during sleep.

Studies of total sleep deprivation

Most of us have experienced going without sleep for longer than normal, and most of us would agree that sleep is probably necessary for our well-being. But what are the functions that sleep serves? One way to try and answer this question is to deprive a person of sleep and observe the consequences of that deprivation. As Borbely (1986) has noted, it has long been known that depriving people of sleep can have detrimental effects. Indeed, sleep deprivation has served dubious military purposes over the ages. The ancient Romans, for example, used *tormentum vigilae* (or the *waking torture*) to extract information from captured enemies, whilst in the 1950s the Koreans are known to have used sleep deprivation as a way of 'brainwashing' captured American airforce pilots.

Our susceptibility to the need for sleep also appears in legends around the world. In order to be granted immortality, Gilgamesh, a character in Mesopotamian legends, was required to go without sleep for six nights. He didn't manage it and his wish for immortality was denied. In certain cultures the urge to overcome sleep is seen as a desirable though difficult goal. In one Australian culture, for example, young men are not permitted to sleep for three consecutive nights as part of their initiation rites.

The first attempt to investigate sleep deprivation experimentally was conducted by Patrick and Gilbert as long ago as 1898. They deprived three 'healthy young men' of sleep for 90 hours. The men reported a gradually increased desire to sleep, and from the second night onwards two of them experienced illusions and other perceptual disorders. When they were allowed to sleep normally, all three slept for longer than they usually did and the psychological disturbances they reported disappeared.

In 1959 Peter Tripp, a New York disc-jockey, staged a charity 'wakeathon' in which he did not sleep for eight days. Towards the end of his wakeathon Tripp began to show some disturbing symptoms, such as hallucinations and profound delusions. The delusions were so intense that it was impossible to give him any psychological tests in order to assess aspects of his psychological functioning. In 1965 Randy Gardner, a 17-year-old student stayed awake for 264 hours and 12 minutes, his aim being to get himself into the *Guinness Book of Records*. For the last 90 hours of his successful world record attempt he was studied by William Dement and his colleagues. Although Gardner had difficulty in performing some tasks, his lack of sleep did not produce anything like the disturbances experienced by Peter Tripp.

After his record attempt, Gardner spent 14 hours and 40 minutes asleep. When he awoke he appeared to have recovered completely from his efforts. On subsequent nights, Gardner returned to his usual pattern of sleeping for eight hours per day and did not seem to suffer any permanent physiological or psychological effects from his long period without sleep. The feat of going without sleep for over 200 hours has subsequently been achieved by a number of people, none of whom appear to have experienced any long-term detrimental effects. This finding has led one leading sleep researcher (Webb, 1975) to conclude that the major consequence of going without sleep is to make us want to go to sleep!

As interesting as the cases of Tripp, Gardner, and others are, they do not tell us much about the effects of *total sleep deprivation* because they did not take place under carefully controlled conditions. However, a large number of carefully controlled studies have been conducted and the effects of sleep deprivation over time have been summarised by Hüber-Weidman (1976). The effects are described in Box 10.1.

Box 10.1 The effects of sleep deprivation over time (after Hüber-Weidman, 1976)

Night 1: Most people are capable of going without sleep for a night. The experience may be uncomfortable, but it is tolerable.

Night 2: The urge to sleep becomes much greater. The period between 3–5 a.m., when body temperature is at its lowest in most of us, is crucial. It is during this period that we are most likely to fall asleep.

Night 3: Tasks requiring sustained attention and complex forms of information processing are seriously impaired. This is particularly true if the task is repetitious and boring. If the task is interesting, or we are encouraged to try and do well by the experimenter, performance is less impaired. Again, the early hours of the morning are most crucial.

Night 4: From this night onwards periods of *micro-sleep* are often observed. We stop what we are doing and stare into space for anywhere up to three seconds. The end of micro-sleep is accompanied by a return to full awareness. We may be confused, irritable, and misperceive things. We may also experience the *hat phenomenon*. In this we feel a tightening around the head as though we were wearing a hat that was too small.

Night 5: In addition to the effects described above, we may experience delusions. However, our intellectual and problem-solving abilities seem to be largely unimpaired.

Night 6: We begin to experience symptoms of depersonalisation and lose a clear sense of our identity. It becomes difficult to relate to the normal world. The term *sleep deprivation psychosis* has been used to describe this phenomenon.

We should note that the effects described above are psychological rather than physiological. There is little evidence to suggest that our bodies suffer any measurable physical harm as a result of being deprived of sleep. Reflexes are unimpaired and functions such as heart rate, respiration, blood pressure and body temperature show little change from normal. Hand tremors, droopy eyelids, problems in focusing the eyes, and heightened sensitivity to pain seem to be the major bodily consequences of sleep deprivation.

We should also note that the effects of sleep deprivation do not accumulate over time. If we normally sleep for eight hours a day and are deprived of sleep for three days, we will not sleep for 24 hours afterwards. Thus, we do not need to make up for *all* the sleep that has been missed, though we do make up for some.

The experience of Peter Tripp, described in the text, seems to be unusual. As we have seen, some temporary psychological disturbances do occur when we are deprived of sleep but there is little evidence to support the view that sleep deprivation has any significant long-term consequences on normal psychological functioning. Tripp's experiences are, therefore, unlikely to be *solely* attributable to a lack of sleep. It is more likely that *stress*, which sleep deprivation can also cause, produces abnormal behaviour in susceptible individuals.

On the basis of what has been presented in Box 10.1, it might be tempting to conclude that sleep has little value and that a lack of it has few harmful effects. However, studies conducted by Allan Rechtschaffen and his colleagues (1983) suggest that such a conclusion is not justified. Rechtschaffen's research team deprived rats of sleep by means of an ingenious device. The rat was placed on a disc protruding from a small bucket of water and an EEG monitored its brain activity. Every time the rat showed a brain wave pattern indicative of sleep, the disc began to rotate. This forced the rat to walk if it wanted to avoid falling in the water. The experimental apparatus is illustrated in Figure 10.1 opposite.

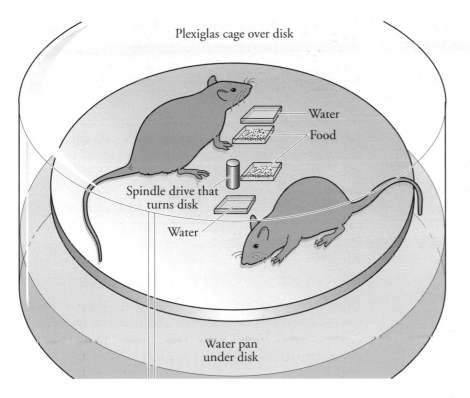

Plexiglas cage over disk

Water

Food

Spindle drive that turns disk

Water

Water pan under disk

Figure 10.1 Apparatus used in the experiment conducted by Rechtschaffen, et al.

The rat was not alone on the disc. Another rat, also connected to an EEG, was present. However, whenever this rat showed brain wave activity indicative of sleep the disc did *not* rotate. Thus, one rat was allowed to sleep normally whereas the other was not. After 33 days, all of the sleep-deprived rats had died, whereas the rats allowed to sleep normally did not appear to have suffered at all. The cause of death could not be precisely determined by the researchers, but on the basis of their observations of the progressive physical deterioration of the rats, they speculated that their ability to regulate their own heat was fatally impaired.

Unfortunately, the results of a sleep deprivation study on rats tells us little about the effects of sleep deprivation on humans, and there would clearly be ethical implications of subjecting humans to anywhere near the length of time the rats were deprived of sleep. However, Lugaressi, et al. (1986) have reported the case of a man who abruptly began to lose sleep at the age of 52. The man became increasingly exhausted and eventually developed a lung infection from which he died. A post-mortem examination revealed that neurons in two areas of the brain linked to sleep and hormonal circadian rhythms were almost completely destroyed.

Irrespective of the effects of sleep deprivation, it is true to say that unless we are constantly encouraged to remain awake, we fall asleep and we do so in virtually any position in any place. People do not like to be kept awake and there does seem to be a need to sleep even though sleeplessness itself does not, at least as far as we know from experimental studies, appear to be particularly harmful. Again, as Webb (1975) has suggested, perhaps people sleep in order to avoid feeling sleepy. However, such a conclusion isn't particularly helpful and psychologists have tried to understand exactly what functions sleep might serve. Two broad theories of sleep function have been advanced. We consider these below.

Evolutionary theories of sleep function

Meddis (1975) has pointed to evidence indicating that different species characteristically sleep for different periods of time and that the amount of time spent asleep is related to an animal's need and method of obtaining food and its exposure to predators. Animals that cannot find a safe place to sleep, have high metabolic rates that require a lot of food gathering, or are at risk from predators, sleep very little. As Woody Allen observed in his film *Love and Death*, 'the lion and the lamb shall lie down together, but the lamb will not be very sleepy'.

The short-tailed shrew, for example, has a safe burrow, but sleeps very little since its high metabolic rate means that it must eat around the clock or die. Animals that are preyed upon, such as cattle, sheep and deer, sleep only about two hours a day, and even then take only 'brief naps'. By contrast, predator species or those species that have safe sleeping places or can satisfy their needs for food and water fairly quickly, sleep for much longer periods. Like the short-tailed shrew, the ground squirrel has a safe burrow but, being a larger animal, it has a lower metabolic rate and does not need to eat so often. It sleeps for 14 hours a day. The gorilla, which does not need to sleep in a burrow to protect itself, also sleeps for 14 hours a day.

In a variation of this theory, Webb (1982) has suggested that sleep enables us to conserve energy when there is no need to expend it or when expending energy would probably do more harm than good. According to Webb, sleep is an instinctual behavioural response which does not satisfy a physiological need in the way that food does, for example. Rather, natural selection would favour an organism that kept itself out of danger when danger was most likely to occur. Sleep can therefore be seen as a response which is useful for the survival of a species.

Since we do not (tend to) walk or roam about whilst we are asleep and (usually) sleep at night, sleep can be seen as an adaptive instinctual behaviour that keeps us quiet and out of harm's way. This has been termed the *hibernation theory of sleep function*. In our evolutionary past, the enforced inactivity of sleeping allowed us to survive for a least two reasons. First, sleeping at night would reduce the risk of predation or accidents. Second, since the likelihood of finding food at night would be much reduced, more energy would have been spent hunting than would have been gained by the results of hunting.

However, even though we may be quiet and out of harm's way whilst asleep, we are *potentially* vulnerable. As Blakemore (1988) has observed:

> 'Our planet is a dangerous place; there is ruthless competition for limited resources and only the fittest survive. And yet all the most advanced animals, normally alert, shrewd, watchful, drop their defences to sleep. Even human beings, the most spectacularly successful species, spend one third of their lives more or less paralysed and senseless.'

More succinctly, Evans (1984) has remarked that 'the behaviour patterns involved in sleep are glaringly, almost insanely, at odds with common sense'.

There is a problem with evolutionary theories of sleep function concerning the predator-prey relationship. Some evolutionary theorists argue that the evidence indicates that preyed upon species sleep for short periods of time because of the constant threat of predation. Others argue that preyed upon species sleep for longer periods of time in order to keep out of the way of predators. The sleep pattern of any species can be explained in one of these two ways by evolutionary theories which suggests that, as far as the functions of sleep are concerned, evolutionary theory is *non-falsifiable*: whatever sleep pattern a species has can be explained in 'evolutionary' terms.

Even though evolutionary theories of sleep function can be criticised, most psychologists find it difficult to believe that sleep does not have an important function. An alternative approach to evolutionary theory is presented below.

Restoration theories of sleep function

Safety and energy conservation might, as evolutionary theories suggest, be two of the functions served by sleep. However, whilst the neural mechanisms for sleep might have evolved to satisfy such needs, they may well have taken on additional functions. Most of us spend around 16 hours a day using up energy. According to Ian Oswald (1966), the purpose of sleep is to restore our depleted reserves of energy, eliminate waste products from the muscles, repair cells, and recover physical abilities that have been lost during the day.

At first sight, this theory seems to make sense. The length of time we remain awake is related to how sleepy we feel, and at the end of a busy day all of us are 'ready for bed'. Research findings support this. In one study, Shapiro and his colleagues (1981) found that people who had competed in an 'ultra-marathon', a running race of 57 miles, slept an hour and a half longer than they normally did for two nights following the race. The researchers also found that stage 4 sleep occupied a much greater proportion of total sleep time (about 45%) than normal (about 25%), whilst the proportion of time spent in REM sleep decreased.

Exactly what restorative processes occur during sleep is not precisely known. Some studies have shown that a lack of exercise does *not* substantially reduce sleep, which it might be expected to do if sleep served an exclusively restorative function. In a study conducted by Ryback & Lewis (1971), for example, healthy individuals spent six weeks resting in bed with no changes observed in their sleep patterns. Some researchers (e.g. Adam & Oswald, 1977, 1983) have suggested that certain kinds of tissue restoration, such as cell repair, occurs during sleep. Others (e.g. Webb & Campbell, 1983) believe that neurotransmitter levels are restored during sleep.

We do know, however, that the pituitary gland (see Chapter 3) releases a hormone during stage 4 sleep which is important for tissue growth, protein and RNA synthesis, and the formation of red blood cells. This suggests that stage 4 sleep may play a role in the growth process. Certainly, as we saw in the previous chapter, our total time spent in stage 4 sleep decreases with increasing age, and this might be related to our relative lack of need for growth hormone. It has also been found that disruption of stage 4 sleep in healthy people produces symptoms similar to those experienced by fibrositis sufferers who are known to experience a chronic lack of stage 4 sleep (Empson, 1989). Since fibrositis is a disorder which causes acute inflammation of the back muscles and their sheaths, which is experienced as pain and stiffness, it is tempting to accept the suggestion that sleep serves a restorative function.

A slightly different approach to restoration theory suggests that sleep may serve a psychological as well as (or instead of) a physiological restorative function. For example, Kales and his colleagues (1974) have shown that insomniacs suffer from far more psychological problems than healthy people, whilst Hartmann (1973) has reported that we generally need to sleep more during periods of stress, such as occurs when we change a job or move house. A detailed study conducted by Berry & Webb (1983) found a strong correlation between self-reported levels of anxiety and 'sleep efficiency' and also discovered that the better the sleep attained by the participants in their study, the more positive were their moods on the following day.

Although the evidence presented above is not conclusive, it seems possible that one function of sleep is to help us recover from the psychological as well as the physiological exertions of our waking hours.

Studies of REM sleep deprivation

In the previous chapter we saw that REM sleep has been of particular interest to researchers, largely because of its paradoxical nature. Some researchers have suggested that REM sleep might serve particular functions and a great deal of research has been conducted towards this end. As was the case with sleep in general, the easiest way to address the role of REM sleep has been to deprive people of it and observe the consequences of this deprivation.

In an early experiment, Dement (1960) had volunteers spend several nights at his sleep laboratory. The volunteers were allowed to sleep normally except that whenever they entered REM sleep they were woken up. A control group of volunteers was woken up the same number of times over the course of the investigation but only during NREM sleep. The results showed several differences between the two groups. Compared with the control group the REM-deprived group became increasingly irritable, aggressive, and unable to concentrate on performing various tasks. As the experiment progressed, the REM-deprived group started to show what might be described as *REM starvation*. Thus, after several nights they attempted to go into REM sleep as soon as they went to sleep, and it became increasingly difficult to wake them when they did manage to enter REM.

On the first night, Dement had to wake the REM-deprived sleepers an average of 12 times each, but by the seventh night they had to be woken an average of 26 times, suggesting that over the course of the experiment the need for REM sleep was steadily increasing. A similar effect was reported by Borbely (1986). In his study, an REM sleep-deprived individual made 31 attempts to enter REM on the first night, 51 attempts on the second, and over 60 on the third!

When people are allowed to sleep without interruption after an REM sleep deprivation study most, but not all, show a REM *rebound effect*, that is, a much longer period of time is spent in REM sleep than is usually the case. This finding suggests that we try to make up for 'lost' REM sleep time, although we must be careful not to draw firm conclusions from this since, as we have said, the rebound effect is *not* observed in all people. In general, the evidence suggests that we seem to be able to adjust to REM sleep deprivation in much the same way as we can adjust to not eating for several days if necessary (Webb, 1975). REM sleep seems to be necessary, though depriving people of it does not appear to be psychologically harmful.

There are several other findings concerning the effects of REM sleep deprivation that should be mentioned. In non-humans, the evidence suggests that learning occurs more slowly and forgetting more quickly following REM sleep deprivation. In humans, learning does not seem to be affected by the ability to integrate newly acquired information with existing memories and information does seem to be impaired.

Some researchers have looked at the effects of REM sleep deprivation on the reduction of anxiety. In one study Greenberg, et al. (1972) had participants watch a film of a circumcision rite performed without anaesthetic. On first viewing the film elicits a high level of anxiety which gradually subsides on repeated viewing. However, Greenberg and his colleagues found that people deprived of REM sleep did *not* show a reduction in their anxiety when they viewed the film on subsequent occasions. This finding suggests that REM sleep may act, at least in part, to reduce the anxiety of events that have occurred during the waking day.

Certain drugs, such as *alcohol* (see Chapter 13), suppress REM sleep without affecting NREM sleep. When heavy alcohol users abstain, the REM rebound effect occurs. For many heavy users the effect is very disturbing and the sharp increase in dreaming which occurs as a result of a change in REM sleep time leads them to resume their drinking behaviour. In cases of severe alcohol abuse, it has been suggested that a kind of REM rebound effect occurs during the waking hours. The rebound effect manifests itself as the disturbing hallucinations experienced during alcohol withdrawal (Greenberg & Pearlman, 1967).

As we noted earlier, in general the evidence suggests that there are few harmful effects as a result of REM sleep deprivation. Indeed, according to William Dement (1974), research 'has failed to prove substantial ill-effects result from even prolonged selective REM deprivation'. Whilst this may be true, the occurrence of the REM rebound effect and the fact that REM-deprived sleepers try to enter REM more and more over the course of time suggests that REM sleep has some functions. We will explore the possible functions of REM sleep next.

Restoration theories of REM sleep function

Ian Oswald (1966) has suggested that REM sleep is related to brain 'restoration' and growth. Studies have shown a greater rate of *protein synthesis* during REM sleep than is the case in NREM sleep. Rossi (1973) has suggested that protein synthesis 'serves as an organic basis for new developments in the personality'. However, whether REM sleep *causes* increased protein synthesis or whether increased protein synthesis is the *result* of the increased activity of nerve cells that occurs during REM sleep is less clear.

REM sleep does, however, differ over the lifespan and, as we noted in the previous chapter, accounts for around 50% of the total sleep time (TST) of a newborn baby as compared with only 20% of the TST of an adult (see Chapter 9, page 88). Indeed, in almost every mammalian species, adults not only sleep less than infants but spend less time in REM sleep as they get older. Quite possibly, then, REM sleep promotes the protein synthesis necessary for cell manufacture and growth, which is essential to the maturation of the developing nervous system. The decline that is observed in adulthood may reflect a decrease in the rate of development of the brain's information processing capabilities.

As was mentioned earlier, deprivation of REM sleep has the effect, in non-human species at least, of impairing learning. Some research (e.g. Bloch, 1976) has shown that REM sleep increases when animals are given training on a new task and that the increase in REM sleep is greatest during the steepest part of the learning curve. Perhaps, then, the protein synthesis that occurs during REM sleep is a contributory factor in the formation of long-term memories. In humans, the consequence of a massive 'insult' to the brain by, for example, a drug overdose, results in an increase in the amount of time spent in REM sleep, as though some attempt was being made to repair the damage done.

Even those who support the restoration theory of REM sleep function accept that REM sleep involves the use of a substantial amount of energy such as the increased blood flow to the brain which we know occurs during REM sleep. Such activity would actually *prevent* high levels of protein synthesis. Researchers are still trying to reconcile these contradictory observations.

Memory consolidation theory of REM sleep function

According to some researchers, REM sleep stimulates neural tissue and consolidates information in memory. In a study conducted by Empson & Clarke (1970), participants heard unusual phrases before bedtime and were given a memory test about them the next morning. The results showed that those who were deprived of REM sleep remembered less than those who were woken the same number of times during the night but from stages of sleep other than REM. This finding has been replicated on a number of occasions using a variety of material (e.g. Tilley & Empson, 1978), although we should note that there is no evidence to suggest that *hypnopaedia* – learning whilst we are asleep – takes place (Rubin, 1968).

As we noted in the previous chapter, REM sleep occurs in all mammals except the spiny anteater and dolphin, but not in animals such as fish whose behaviour is less influenced by learning. We also noted that the proportion of time we spend in REM sleep declines with increasing age when, possibly, the need to consolidate memories is of less importance. The evidence concerning memory consolidation during REM sleep is mounting, and it may well be that memory consolidation is an important function of REM sleep.

The sentinel theory of REM sleep function

Observing that EEG patterns in REM sleep resemble the patterns of activity observed during waking, and that short periods of wakefulness sometimes occur as the *end* of REM sleep, sleep researcher Fred Snyder has suggested that it serves the function of allowing animals to check their surroundings periodically for signs of danger. Snyder thus sees the end of REM acting as a *sentinel* (or look-out) to ensure that we are free from danger. Whilst this is an interesting suggestion, its main weakness lies in the fact that it sees only the end of REM sleep as serving any function. The time we spend in REM sleep presumably, as far as Snyder is concerned, serves no function at all. It is unlikely that many sleep researchers would agree with this view.

The oculomotor system maintenance theory

Some researchers who might agree with Snyder are those who subscribe to the oculomotor system maintenance theory of REM sleep function. According to this theory the function of REM sleep is to keep the eye muscles toned up. About once every 90 minutes during sleep the eye muscles are given some exercise to keep them in trim! Although this theory may be tongue-in-cheek, it highlights one important point about theories of sleep function, namely that they are difficult to test and therefore falsify: as we saw earlier on, evolutionary theories of sleep seem to be capable of accommodating all of the findings concerning sleep patterns. It is difficult to see how Snyder's theory and the oculomotor system maintenance theory could be tested.

The physiology of sleep

In the previous chapter (see page 83) we suggested that external cues are not of primary importance as far as the sleep-waking cycle is concerned. However, external cues do play a role. When night falls, the eyes inform the *Suprachiasmatic Nuclei* (*SN*) and, via a neural pathway travelling through the hypothalamus, the *pineal gland*. As we noted in the previous chapter, the pineal gland secretes the hormone melatonin. Melatonin influences neurons that produce the neurotransmitter serotonin which is concentrated in a brain structure called the *raphe nuclei*. Serotonin is then released and acts on the *reticular activating system* (or *RAS* – see Chapter 2).

It has long been known that the RAS is involved in consciousness. Moruzzi & Magoun (1949), for example, showed that stimulation of the RAS caused a slumbering cat to awaken whereas destruction of the RAS caused a permanent coma. In 1967, Jouvet showed that destruction of the raphe nuclei produces sleeplessness and, on the basis of the finding that serotonin is concentrated in this brain structure, he concluded that serotonin must play a role in the induction of sleep. Since serotonin is a *monoamine* neurotransmitter,

Jouvet advanced what he called the *monoamine hypothesis of sleep*.

Jouvet discovered that *paracholorophenylalanine* (or *PCPA*), a substance which inhibits serotonin synthesis, prevents sleep. However, if its effects are reversed (by means of *5-hydroxytryptophan*) then sleep is reinstated. Such a finding suggests that whilst serotonin may not play *the* role in the induction of sleep, it certainly plays *a* role. Other experiments conducted by Jouvet showed that destruction of the *locus coeruleus* (a small patch of dark cells located in the pons – see Chapter 2) caused REM sleep to disappear completely suggesting that the pons plays a role in the regulation of REM sleep. Moreover, if neurons in a different part of the pons were destroyed, REM remained but muscle tension (which, as we saw in the previous chapter, is ordinarily absent during REM sleep) was *maintained*. This resulted in a cat moving around during REM sleep, even though it was completely unconscious.

For reasons that are not well understood, the inhibitory processes that normally operate during REM sleep do not operate in some people (and this is termed *REM Behaviour Disorder*). According to Chase & Morales (1990) such people 'may thrash violently about, leap out of bed, and may even attack their partners'. As we mentioned in the previous chapter, dreaming is correlated with REM sleep and, presumably, being paralysed during REM sleep serves the useful biological function of preventing us from acting out our dreams. Quite possibly, the cat we described above was acting out a dream! 'Sleepwalking', then, cannot occur during REM sleep because the body's musculature is in a state of virtual paralysis. The stage in which it does occur is identified in Chapter 12.

The locus coeruleus produces the neurotransmitters *noradrenalin* and *acetylcholine*. Jouvet proposed that these were responsible for the onset of REM sleep and the associated loss of muscle tone. The fact that *carba-chol*, a chemical which imitates the action of acetylcholine but has a more *prolonged* action, results in much longer periods of REM sleep, supports this view. Moreover, *scopolamine*, a substance which *inhibits* the action of acetylcholine, leads to a dramatic *delay* in the onset of REM sleep.

Jouvet (1983) believes that the cycles of sleep we described in the previous chapter occur as a result of the relationship between the raphe nuclei and locus coeruleus. The raphe nuclei is believed to initiate sleep (by acting on the RAS). Thereafter, interactions between the raphe nuclei and the locus coeruleus generate the NREM-REM sleep cycle. When one mechanism overcomes the other, wakefulness occurs.

The picture is, perhaps, slightly more complicated than we have painted it. For example, it has been shown that stimulation of the *thalamus* (see Chapter 2) can induce sleep, and stimulation of other areas can prevent waking. Nonetheless, the view that sleep is a passive process can certainly be dismissed. Both sleeping and waking must be the result of complex interactions between a variety of brain structures.

Conclusions

In this chapter we have looked at a variety of theories that seek to explain the functions of sleep in general and REM sleep in particular, and we have examined some of what is known about the physiology of sleep. At the moment, none of the theories that have been offered is firmly supported by the experimental evidence, and it is not really possible to claim that there is a single adequate theory of the functions of sleep. For some, however, the question of why we sleep has a very simple answer. We sleep because we need to dream. If this is the case, another interesting question arises, concerning the function of dreaming. We turn our attention to this question in the following chapter.

SUMMARY

- One way of trying to understand the functions of sleep is to **deprive** someone of sleep and observe the consequences. Sleep deprivation was used by the Romans to extract information from captured enemies, and the Koreans used it as part of 'brainwashing' captured American pilots.

- The importance of sleep is also reflected in myths and legends.

- The first experimental study of sleep deprivation involved three young men, who, during 90 hours of deprivation, reported an increasing desire to sleep, and sometimes illusions and other perceptual disorders; these disappeared after being allowed to sleep normally.

- Peter Tripp's eight-day **wakeathon** produced hallucinations and intense delusions. Randy Gardner broke the world record by staying awake for over 264 hours; he showed much less disturbance than Tripp and seemed to have recovered completely after sleeping for over 14 hours. Like others who have since gone without sleep for over 200 hours, Gardner suffered no permanent physiological or psychological harm.

- Controlled studies of **total sleep deprivation** suggest a pattern of **psychological** reactions: the urge to sleep becomes much greater on the second night, with 3–5 a.m. being the crucial time. On the third night, attention and complex information processing are seriously impaired, although interesting tasks and encouragement can reduce the deficit.

- From night four onwards, people have **micro-sleeps**, they are increasingly irritable and confused, are likely to misperceive things, and may experience the **hat phenomenon**. Delusions may occur on night five, but intellectual/problem-solving abilities are largely unimpaired. By night six, people suffer **sleep deprivation psychosis**.

- There is little evidence that our bodies suffer any measurable harm from prolonged deprivation, with basic physiological functions showing little change from normal. Also, the effects of deprivation are **not** cumulative, so that we do not need to make up for **all** the sleep that has been missed.

- This evidence should not be seen as implying that sleep has little value. Rechtschaffen's research suggests that long-term sleep deprivation fatally impairs the rat's ability to regulate its own heat. The case of a man who abruptly began to lose sleep at age 52 and subsequently died, having suffered almost total destruction of brain areas linked to circadian rhythms, suggests that sleep might be vital.

- **Theories of sleep** try to account for the undeniable **need** to sleep. According to Meddis, different species typically sleep for different periods of time according to their metabolic rate, method of obtaining food, and exposure to predators. Animals with a high metabolic rate, like the short-tailed shrew, and those that are preyed upon, like cattle, sheep and deer, sleep very little. Those with a lower metabolic rate, like the ground squirrel and gorillas, which have no natural predators, sleep for 14 hours per day.

- According to Webb's **hibernation theory of sleep function**, sleep is an instinctual response that does not satisfy a physiological need in the way that food does, but natural selection would favour an organism that kept itself out of danger: sleep has survival value. In our evolutionary past, the enforced inactivity of sleeping reduced the risk of predation/accidents, and it helped us conserve energy that would have been wasted trying to hunt at night. However, we are still **potentially** vulnerable when asleep.

- Some **evolutionary theorists** believe that preyed upon species sleep for short periods of time because of the threat of predation, while others argue that such species sleep longer in order to keep out of the way of predators. This means that evolutionary theories are **non-falsifiable**.

- According to Oswald, the purpose of sleep is to **restore** depleted energy reserves, eliminate waste products from the muscles, repair cells, and recover lost physical abiities. This is supported by the longer sleeping time, including a greater proportion of Stage 4 sleep, that follows excessive physical exertion.

- Although the precise **restorative** processes that occur during sleep are unknown, and lack of exercise does **not** reduce sleep, the pituitary gland is known to release a hormone during Stage 4 sleep that is important for tissue growth, protein and RNA synthesis, and red blood cell production. The reduced time spent in Stage 4 as we get older may reflect a reduction in the need for growth hormone. Deprivation of Stage 4 produces fibrositis-like symptoms in healthy people, consistent with the view that sleep serves a restorative function.

- Sleep may also serve a **psychological** restorative function. Insomniacs suffer more psychological problems than healthy people, and more sleep is needed during periods of stress and anxiety.
- REM sleep might serve particular functions. When Dement deprived volunteers of REM sleep, they became increasingly irritable, aggressive, and unable to concentrate. They began to show **REM starvation**, trying to enter REM as soon as they fell asleep and becoming more difficult to wake from it. The need for REM increases with continued REM deprivation.
- Most REM sleep-deprived participants show a **rebound effect**, representing an attempt to make up for lost REM sleep time. Although necessary, REM sleep deprivation does not seem to be psychologically harmful; learning is not affected as it is in non-humans, but the ability to integrate newly acquired information seems to be impaired. REM sleep may help to reduce the anxiety of events that have occurred during the day.
- Certain drugs, such as **alcohol**, suppress REM sleep without affecting NREM sleep; heavy drinkers who abstain experience the REM rebound. Extremely heavy drinkers may experience a kind of rebound effect while awake, and during withdrawal it takes the form of hallucinations.
- Oswald proposes that REM sleep is related to brain restoration and growth, as demonstrated by the greater rate of **protein synthesis** during REM compared with NREM sleep. The reduction in REM sleep as humans (and most other mammals) get older suggests that REM sleep promotes maturation of the developing nervous system and increases in the brain's information processing capabilities.
- Research with non-humans shows an increase in REM sleep during learning, especially during the steepest part of the learning curve; this implies that REM may be involved in the formation of long-term memories.
- The increased blood flow to the brain during REM sleep would actually **prevent** protein synthesis; this is a problem for restoration theories of REM function.
- REM sleep may stimulate neural tissue and consolidate information in memory, although there is no evidence for **hypnopaedia**. The role of REM sleep in memory consolidation is supported by the decreasing amount of REM with increasing age.
- According to Snyder, REM sleep allows animals to check their surroundings periodically for signs of danger, i.e. it acts as a **sentinel.** But this cannot account for the time we spend **in** REM, only its end.
- According to the **oculomotor system maintenance theory**, the function of REM sleep is to keep the eye muscles toned up. But both this and Snyder's theory are very difficult to test.
- When it gets dark, the eyes inform the **suprachaismatic nucleus/SN,** and, in turn, the **pineal gland**, which secretes melatonin; this influences production of serotonin concentrated in the **raphe nuclei**, which then acts on the **reticular activating system/RAS**.
- The RAS is involved in consciousness. Stimulating the RAS of a sleeping cat wakes it up, while destroying it causes permanent coma. Destruction of the raphe nuclei causes sleeplessness, which led Jouvet to infer that serotonin (a **monoamine**) must play a role in sleep induction (**monoamine hypothesis of sleep**).
- **Paracholorophenylalanine/PCPA** prevents serotonin synthesis and, hence, sleep, but its effects can be reversed (using **5-Hydroxytryptophan**). Destruction of the **locus coeruleus** (in the pons) causes disappearance of REM sleep, suggesting that the pons is involved in REM regulation, including muscle tension.
- Some people fail to show the normal inhibitory processes in REM sleep (**REM behaviour disorder**); the paralysis that usually occurs serves to prevent us from acting out our dreams.
- **Noradrenalin** and **acetylcholine**, produced by the locus coeruleus, are involved in the onset of REM sleep and the associated loss of muscle tone. This view is supported by the REM-prolonging effects of **carbachol** and the REM-delaying effects of **scopolamine**.
- Jouvet believes that the raphe nuclei initiates sleep, after which interactions with the locus coeruleus generate the NREM-REM sleep cycle. The **thalamus** is also involved in what is a complex interaction between a variety of brain structures.

THE FUNCTIONS OF DREAMING

Introduction and overview

Dreams have long held a fascination for both the layperson and the professional psychologist. Some cultures, for example, believe dreams to be the experiences of a world that is not available to us during our waking hours. Others see dreams as messages from the gods. Attempts to discover the meaning of dreams can be found in Babylonian records dating back 5,000 years before the birth of Christ. The Bible, the Talmud, Homer's *Illiad* and *Odyssey* all give accounts of the meaning of dreams. In the Bible, for example, dreams provided revelations. It was during a dream that Joseph learned there was to be a famine in Egypt. Our main aim in this chapter is to look at the various theories that have been proposed to explain the functions that dreaming might serve. We will begin, however, by looking at some of the basic research findings that have been obtained in this area of research.

Dreams: some basic research findings

The pioneering research of Dement, Aserinsky, and Kleitman which was described in Chapter 9 discovered much about the phenomenon of dreaming. Instead of relying on the sometimes hazy recall of a dreamer waking at the end of an eight-hour period of sleep, the method of waking someone during an episode of REM sleep enabled a vivid account of a dream to be obtained. Space does not permit us to describe in detail anywhere near all of the findings that have accumulated concerning dreaming. In Box 11.1 we summarise a selection of some of the findings.

Box 11.1   Dreams: what do we know about the vivid images that occur in the absence of external stimulation?

The realism of dreams: Some dreams can be so realistic and well organised that we feel they must be 'real'. On the other hand, some dreams can be disorganised and unformed. Dreams can occur in black and white and full colour. Some dreams may be very powerful in their emotional effects, but the majority are quite ordinary in content.

Dreams and all of us: Everyone dreams, even though some people claim not to. Not only do EEG records indicate that claimed 'non-dreamers' show the ordinary pattern of four or five episodes of REM sleep per night, but the people themselves report dreaming when awoken during REM sleep. It is more likely that some of us are better at *remembering* dreams than others. We do quickly forget our dreams, but those we remember are the ones that occur closest to waking up. Dreams about recent events occur closest to the waking period. Dreams involving childhood or past events tend to occur earlier in the night.

Dreams and the stages of sleep: Recall from Chapter 9 the discovery that REM sleep is correlated with dreaming. When woken from REM sleep, people report dreaming about 80% of the time. However, some dreaming does occur in NREM stages of sleep. REM and NREM dreams differ in terms of both 'quality' and 'content'. REM dreams are clearly and highly detailed and consist of vivid images. They are often reported as fantastic adventures with a clear plot. NREM dreams consist of fleeting images, are not well detailed, and have vaguer plots. Typically, they are unemotional and involve commonplace things. The nature of the REMs we show during a dream are *sometimes* correlated with the content of a dream, but there is no one-to-one correspondence between dream content and eye movements.

Dreams and pre-sleep events: The content of a dream can be modified by pre-sleep events. Hauri (1970) reported that people who had engaged in strenuous physical exercise before going to sleep tended to have dreams involving little physical activity. In another study, Bokert (1970) found that people deprived of water tended to dream of drinking. Both studies suggest that what we dream compliments and compensates for our waking experiences, although such effects seem to be temporary. People who have been paralysed for a long period of time report less physical activity in their dreams than those who have only recently been paralysed.

Dreams, the sexes, and sex: Men and women seem to differ in terms of their dreams. Cohen (1973), amongst others, has reported that female dreams tend to be about indoor settings whilst males tend to dream about outdoor settings. Male dreams tend to be much more aggressive than females dreams. Contrary to popular belief, only a small proportion of dreams are sexual in content. A study conducted by Hall & Van de Castle (1966) indicated that around 1 in 10 dreams among young men and 1 in 30 among young women had clear sexual overtones.

The duration of dreams: Most dreams last as long as the events would in real life. Although time seems to expand and contract during a dream so that the content ranges from days to weeks, dreams tend to take place in 'real time'. Thus, 15 minutes of events occupies 15 minutes of dreaming time. Perhaps when we dream, something plays the role of a 'film director'. We have all seen films where the cut from one scene to another is accompanied by a phrase like 'New York, ten days later'. Perhaps the 'film director' in our dreams seemingly expands time in a dream in this way.

External events and dreams: Our brains are relatively insensitive to outside sensory input. However, certain sorts of external stimuli can either wake us up or be incorporated into a dream. In one study, Dement & Wolpert (1958) lightly sprayed cold water onto dreamers' faces. Compared with sleepers who were not sprayed, they were more likely to dream about water, incorporating waterfalls, leaky roofs and, occasionally, being sprayed with water into their dream! Significant external stimuli, such as our names, are much more likely to bring about awakening than non-significant external stimuli such as the sound of a lorry in the street below.

Lucid dreaming: Some people, termed *lucid dreamers*, report having dreams in which they knew they were dreaming and felt as if they were conscious during the dream. Lucid dreamers can test their state of consciousness by attempting to perform an impossible act such as floating in the air. If the act can be performed, a lucid dream is occurring. Some lucid dreamers can control the course of events in a dream, and skilled lucid dreamers can signal the onset of a lucid dream by moving their eyes in a way pre-arranged with the sleep researcher.

Dreaming and sleepwalking: Contrary to popular belief, sleepwalking does not occur during REM sleep. It can't since, as we saw in Chapter 10, the musculature is in a state of virtual paralysis during REM sleep. As we noted, the paralysis presumably prevents us from *acting out* a dream. We also saw in Chapter 10 that when the part of the brain responsible for the inhibition of movement is damaged, a cat, for example, will move around during REM sleep. Perhaps, then, animals dream too! Sleepwalking occurs during the deeper stages of sleep when the musculature is not paralysed.

Dreams and the blind: People who have been blind from birth have auditory dreams which are just as vivid and complex as the visual dreams of people with sight.

As Box 11.1 illustrates, we know a great deal about the process of dreaming, but what possible functions might dreaming serve? Some researchers believe that dreaming does not have a purpose. Nathaniel Kleitman, for example, has suggested that 'the low-grade cerebral activity that is dreaming may serve no significant function whatsoever'. Other researchers believe that dreams have important psychological functions. We will review the theories that have been offered for dream function below.

Sigmund Freud's theory of dream function

The first person to seriously consider the psychology of dreaming was Sigmund Freud, whose book *The Interpretation of Dreams* was published in 1900. Freud argued that a dream was a sort of 'psychic safety valve' that allowed a person to harmlessly discharge otherwise unacceptable and unconscious wishes and urges.

During the waking hours such wishes and impulses are excluded from consciousness because of their unacceptable nature. During sleep, such impulses are allowed to be expressed through the medium of dreams. As we noted above, Freud saw dreams as relieving psychic tensions created during the day and gratifying our unconscious desires. He also saw dreams as 'protecting sleep', by providing imagery that would keep disturbing and repressed thoughts out of consciousness.

Freud argued that our unconscious desires are not gratified directly in a dream. What he called the *manifest content* of a dream (that is, the dream as reported by the dreamer) is a censored and symbolic version of its deeper *latent content* (that is, its actual meaning). According to Freud, the meaning of a dream had to be 'disguised' because it consisted of drives and wishes that would be threatening to us if they were expressed directly. Freud believed that the process of 'censorship' and 'symbolic transformation' accounted for the sometimes bizarre and highly illogical nature of dreams.

For Freud, dreams provided the most valuable insight into the motives that directed a person's behaviour, and he described a dream as 'the royal road to the unconscious'. The task of a dream analyst was to decode the manifest content of a dream into its latent content. Analysts term the objects that occur in a dream and which camouflage its meaning, *symbols*. A gun, for example, might actually be a disguised representation of the penis. A person who dreamt of being *robbed* at gunpoint might be unconsciously expressing a wish to be sexually dominated. A person who dreamt of *robbing* someone at gunpoint might be unconsciously expressing a wish to be sexually dominant. Some examples of sexual dream symbols in Freudian dream interpretation are shown in Table 11.1.

Freud believed that no matter how absurd a dream appeared to be to the dreamer, it always possessed meaning and logic. However, he did accept that there was a danger in translating the symbols and warned that dreams had to be analysed in the context of a person's waking life as well as his/her associations with the dream's content: a broken candlestick may well represent a theme of impotence, but as Freud himself (a lover of cigars) famously remarked, 'sometimes a cigar is only a cigar'.

| Table 11.1 Sexual symbols in Freudian dream interpretation |

Symbols for the male genital organs

aeroplanes	fish	neckties	tools	weapons
bullets	hands	poles	trains	
feet	hoses	snakes	trees	
fire	knives	sticks	umbrellas	

Symbols for the female genital organs

bottles	caves	doors	ovens	ships
boxes	chests	hats	pockets	tunnels
cases	closets	jars	pots	

Symbols for sexual intercourse

climbing a ladder	entering a room
climbing a staircase	flying in an aeroplane
crossing a bridge	riding a horse
driving a car	riding a roller coaster
riding an elevator	walking into a tunnel or down a hall

Symbols for the breasts

apples	peaches

Quite possibly dreams do have some meaning and might reveal important conflicts and issues in a person's life. However, Freud's view that conflicts and issues are always disguised has been criticised. For Fisher & Greenberg (1977), a person who is concerned with impotence is just as likely to dream about impotence as s/he is about broken candles. As they note, 'there is no *rationale* for approaching a dream as if it were a container for a secret wish buried under layers of concealment'.

We should also note that Freud's claim that part of the function of dreaming is to 'protect sleep' has also been challenged. As Foulkes (1971) and Cohen (1973) have observed, the evidence suggests that disturbing events during the day tend to be followed by related disturbing dreams rather than 'protective imagery'. Calvin Hall (1966), amongst others, has noted that the content of most dreams is consistent with a person's waking behaviour. Thus, there is little evidence to support the view that the primary function of dreaming is to act as a release for the expression of unacceptable impulses.

The major problem for Freud's theory of dream function

is that the *interpretation* of a dream is not something that can be *objectively* achieved even if the interpreter is a trained psychoanalyst. Collee (1993) has this to say:

'Metaphor is a notoriously ambiguous form of communication. You can suggest to me the meaning of having luminous feet, but the image will almost always mean something entirely different to you from what it means to me. So dreams end up in much the same category as tarot cards or tea leaves: just a system of images which the dream expert can manipulate to tell you exactly what they think you need to hear'.

Another theory of dreams developed by Freud derives from practices in ancient Greece. At the Temple of Aesculapius, the physician Epidaurus administered drugs to people who, having slept and dreamt, then told Epidaurus about their dreams. On the basis of the descriptions provided, Epidaurus was able to tell them the nature of their illness. Like the ancient Greeks, Freud believed that dreams were the body's way of telling us about physical illness.

A 'problem-solving' theory of dreaming

According to Rosalind Cartwright and her colleagues (e.g. Webb & Cartwright, 1978) dreams are a way of dealing with problems relating to work, sex, health, relationships, and so on that occur during our waking hours. Cartwright argues that whatever is symbolised in a dream *is* the dream's true meaning and, unlike Freud, she sees no reason to distinguish between the manifest and latent content of a dream. Like Freud, however, Cartwright's theory makes much use of the role of metaphor in dreaming.

A person dreaming of, say, being buried beneath an avalanche whilst carrying several books might, Cartwright would argue, be worried about being 'snowed under' with work. Dreaming of a colleague trying to stab you in the neck might simply reflect that the colleague was a 'pain in the neck'. Cartwright has claimed support for her theory from a number of studies. In one (Cartwright, 1978), people were presented with common problems which needed solving. Those who were allowed to sleep uninterrupted generated far more realistic solutions than those who were deprived of REM sleep.

Additionally, several studies (e.g. Hartmann, 1973) have shown that people experiencing interpersonal or occupational problems enter REM sleep earlier and spend longer in it than people without such problems. For Cartwright, then, dreams are a way of identifying and dealing with many of life's problems. As she has noted, people going through crises need the support of friends and family, a little bit of luck, and 'a good dream system'.

'Reprogramming' theories of dreaming

According to Evans (1984), the brain needs to periodically shut itself off from sensory input in order that it can process and assimilate new information and update information that has already been stored. The shutting off is REM sleep during which the brain 'mentally reprograms' its memory systems. The dreams we experience are the brain's attempts at interpreting and updating.

Support for this theory of dreaming has been claimed from a number of studies which have shown that REM sleep increases following activities requiring intense or unusual mental activity, such as performing complex and frustrating tasks. In a study conducted by Herman & Roffwarg (1983), participants spent their waking day wearing distorting lenses that made the visual world appear upside down. After this experience, which demands considerable mental effort to adjust to, the participants spent longer than usual in REM sleep. Evans' theory would explain this in terms of the brain needing to spend a longer period of time 'off-line', processing and assimilating the experience. The finding that older people spend shorter periods of time dreaming is also consistent with Evans' theory: presumably, the older we get, the less need there is to reprogram our memory systems.

An alternative 'reprogramming' theory has been offered by Foulkes (1985). Like some other sleep researchers, Foulkes argues that dreams occur as a result of spontaneous activity in the nervous system. Foulkes argues that such activity can be related to our cognitive processes. The activation that occurs in the brain may well be spontaneous and random, but our cognitive systems are definitely *not* random. According to Foulkes, these systems, which we use in interpreting new experiences, themselves try to interpret the brain activity that occurs during REM sleep. Because of the structure imposed on the activation by our cognitive systems, dreams consist of events that generally occur in a way that makes at least some sense.

For Foulkes, dreams have at least four functions. First, most dreams usually refer to and reflect the memories and knowledge of the dreamer. One function of dreaming might therefore be to relate *newly* acquired knowledge to one's own self-consciousness. Second, a dream might help to integrate and combine specific knowledge and experiences acquired through the various senses with more general knowledge that has been acquired in the past. Third, we know that dreams often contain events that could or might have happened to us, but did not. By dreaming about something that has not yet occurred, but which might, a dream may serve the function of programming us to be prepared for dealing with new, unexpected events. Finally, since dreams are shaped by basic cognitive systems, Foulkes believes they may reveal important information about the nature of our cognitive processes.

A third 'reprogramming' theory, which is a variation of the second possible function of dreams suggested by Foulkes, has been proposed by Koukkou & Lehman (1980). The argue that during a dream we combine ideas and strategies of thinking which originated in childhood with recently acquired relevant information. For them, a dream is a restructuring and reinterpretation of the data already stored in memory. Like some other theorists, Koukkou and Lehman clearly see dreams as being *meaningful* rather than *meaningless* phenomena.

Some sleep researchers have challenged the view that dreams represent meaningful psychological activity and argue instead that they reflect biological activity. We will consider these theories next.

Hobson and McCarley's 'activation synthesis' theory of dreams

One of the best known biopsychological theories of dream function is that originated by J. Allan Hobson and Robert McCarley (1977) which they termed the 'activation synthesis' theory. Research conducted by Hobson (1989) showed that in cats certain cells deep within the brain fire in a seemingly random manner during REM sleep. The firing of these nerve cells *activates* adjacent nerve cells which are involved in the control of eye movements, gaze, balance, posture and activities such as running and walking.

As we saw in the previous chapter, most of these body movements are inhibited during REM sleep. However, the signals are still sent to the parts of the cerebral cortex which are responsible for visual information processing and voluntary actions when we are awake. Thus, although the body is not moving, the brain is receiving signals which suggest that it is. In an attempt to make sense of this contradiction, the brain, drawing on memory and other stored information, attempts to *synthesise* and make sense out of the random bursts of neural activity. The result of the brain's effort is the dream we experience.

The process of synthesis results in the brain imposing some order on the chaotic events caused by the firing of nerve cells, but it cannot do this in a particularly sophisticated way. This would explain why dreams often comprise of shifting and fragmentary images. As Hobson & McCarley (1977) have noted, the dream itself is the brain's effort 'to make the best out of a bad job'. For Hobson and McCarley, then, dream content is the by-product of the random stimulation of nerve cells rather than the unconscious wishes suggested by Freud. Whereas Freud saw dreams as 'the royal road to the unconscious', Hobson and McCarley see them as inherently random and meaningless.

Hobson (1988) has also offered an explanation as to why the brain is periodically activated during the sleep cycle. He argues that *giant cells*, which are found in the reticular activating system of the pons are responsible for the onset of REM sleep, and that these nerve cells are sensitive to the neurotransmitter *acetylcholine* (see Chapter 1). When acetylcholine is available, the giant cells fire in an unrestrained way, but when there is no more of the neurotransmitter available the cells stop.

Hobson uses the analogy of a machine gun which can fire bullets very quickly when the cartridge is full, but can do nothing once the cartridge has emptied. The end of REM sleep occurs, to use Hobson's phrase, because there is no more 'synaptic ammunition'. When synaptic ammunition, in the form of acetylcholine, becomes available again the giant cells start firing and another period of REM sleep begins.

Hobson and McCarley's theory has attracted considerable support because of its apparent explanatory power. For example, our strong tendency to dream about events that have occurred during the day presumably occurs because the most current neural activity of the cortex is that which represents the concerns or events of the day. Dreams about falling are, presumably, the brain attempting to interpret activity in the nerve cells involved in balance, whilst dreams about floating might be the brain's attempt to interpret the firing of neurons in the inner ear.

The activation synthesis theory is also capable of explaining why we do not experience smells and tastes during a dream. This is because the neurons responsible are not stimulated during REM sleep. Our inability to remember our dreams occurs because the neurons in the cortex that control the storage of new memories are turned 'off'. Finally, as we saw in Chapter 10, the evidence concerning the role of acetylcholine in REM sleep is also consistent with Hobson and McCarley's theory.

Yet whilst Hobson believes that the activation synthesis theory has 'opened the door to the molecular biology of sleep' (and as Bianchi, 1992, has suggested, closed it on the Freudian approach to dreaming), it has not escaped criticism. According to Foulkes (1985), whose own theory we described earlier, the content of dreams is influenced by our waking experiences and therefore dreams cannot be as random and psychologically meaningless as Hobson and McCarley suggest.

In response to this, Hobson (1988) has accepted that 'the brain is so inexorably bent upon the quest for meaning that it attributes and even creates meaning when there is little or none in the data it is asked to process'. However, although dreams might contain 'unique stylistic psychological features and concerns' which provide us with insights into our 'life strategies' and, perhaps, ways of coping, the activation synthesis theory most definitely sees dreams as the result of brain stem activities rather than unconscious wishes.

Crick and Mitchison's 'reverse learning' theory of dreams

According to Francis Crick and Graeme Mitchison (1983), the function of dreaming is to enable the brain to erase information it doesn't need by weakening undesirable synaptic connections and erasing what they call 'inappropriate modes of brain activity' which have been produced either by the physical growth of brain cells or by experience. During REM sleep, random firing of nerve cells in the brain is held to set off undesirable connections, such as hallucinations and fantasies, that have overloaded the cortex. By 'flushing out' the excessive accumulation of what they call 'parasitic information', more space is made available in memory for useful information. 'We dream in order to forget', they write, and they call this process *reverse learning* or *unlearning*.

Crick and Mitchison argue that their theory is supported by the finding that all mammals except the spiny anteater and dolphin have REM sleep (when dreaming is most likely to occur). Both of these mammals have an abnormally large cortex for their size, and Crick and Mitchison argue that this is because they do not dream. With no way of disposing of the useless information they have accumulated, the spiny anteater and dolphin need an especially large cortex to accommodate all the useless information they have accumulated.

For Crick and Mitchison, then, dreams serve a biologically useful process in that they keep the nervous system functioning effectively. However, the content of a dream is an accidental result that does not lend itself to meaningful interpretation. Indeed, remembering dreams is *bad* for us in that we simply store again the very information we were trying to dispose of!

One problem for theories which see dreams as meaningless events is that history is littered with stories of discoveries or creations that come to people during a dream. The chemist August Kekulé once dreamed of six snakes chasing each other in such a way that the snake in front was biting the snake behind it. From this, he deduced the structure of the benzene ring. Robert Louis Stevenson is said to have dreamed the plot of *Dr Jekyll and Mr Hyde*. His wife told him he was talking in his sleep. Angrily, he replied 'What did you wake me for? I was dreaming a fine wee bogy tale'.

A problem that *all* theories of dreaming have difficulty in accounting for is the observation that something very much like REM sleep occurs in the developing foetus. What unconscious wishes could a developing foetus have? What 'parasitic information' can the foetus be dispensing with? According to Michel Jouvet, the only possible explanation is that REM sleep serves to program processes in the brain necessary for the development and maintenance of genetically determined functions, such as instincts. As Borbely (1986) notes, this theory suggests that REM sleep generates a sensory activity pattern in the brain – the dream – that is independent of the external world. Jouvet sees the activity of nerve cells that occurs in REM sleep as representing a code which is capable of activating information stored in the genes. This inborn instinctive behaviour is 'practised' during REM sleep. When we are born it is combined with acquired or learned information.

Conclusions

In this chapter, we have reviewed a large number of theories which seek to explain the function of dreaming. These theories see dreams as either being meaningful or meaningless. Because of the difficulty in testing the theories that have been offered, we are not in a position to disqualify or, indeed, accept any of them. A final answer to the question we posed at the beginning of the chapter is not, at present, available. As Collee (1993) has observed:

'There is a danger in thinking about the body in teleologial terms – imagining that everything has a function, whereas we know that a lot of what happens is accidental. Yawning is one example of such accidents of nature, seeming to be just the useless by-product of various important respiratory reflexes. Dreams might have no function at all or they might have a heap of different functions all jumbled together so that one obscures the other. They might just be the films your brain plays to entertain itself while it is sleeping.'

SUMMARY

- Both the layperson and the professional psychologist have been fascinated by dreams for a very long time. Some of the world's greatest religious books and works of literature give accounts of the meaning of dreams.
- Scientific studies of sleep made possible the vivid recall of dreams by waking the dreamer from REM sleep. Some dreams are very realistic, others are disorganised. They can occur in black and white and full colour. Everyone dreams, as indicated by EEG records, including those who believe that they do not, but some are better at **remembering** their dreams.
- People woken from REM sleep report dreaming about 80% of the time. Although dreaming also occurs in NREM stages, there are important differences of quality and content between REM and NREM dreams. REMs are only sometimes correlated with dream content.
- There is some evidence that what we dream complements and compensates for our waking experiences, although such effects tend to be temporary. There are sex differences in the content and themes of dreams, but for both sexes, only a small proportion are about sex.
- Most dreams last as long as the events would in real life, although the experience of time in dreams is often very different; perhaps some kind of 'film director' controls this aspect of dreams. Certain external stimuli can either wake us up or be incorporated into the dream, such as the sound of our names.
- **Lucid dreamers** claim that they know that they are dreaming, sometimes controlling the course of events in a dream. **Sleepwalking** occurs during the deeper stages of (NREM) sleep when the musculature is not paralysed (as in REM sleep). People blind from birth have auditory dreams which are as vivid as the visual dreams of sighted people.
- While Kleitman believes that dreaming serves no significant purpose, other researchers argue that it is psychologically very important. **Freud** saw dreams as a psychic safety valve, allowing the harmless discharge of otherwise unacceptable,

unconscious wishes and urges. In this way, dreams protect sleep.

- Freud distinguished between the **manifest** and **latent content** of dreams, the former being a disguised, symbolic version of the latter which is what the dream actually means; the manifest content is often bizarre and illogical because of the censorship and symbolic transformation involved.

- Freud described dreams as the 'royal road to the unconscious'. The **symbols** in the manifest content must be decoded/interpreted to reveal the unconscious, latent content; this must be done in the context of the dreamer's waking life, as well as his/her associations to the manifest content.

- Not everyone agrees with Freud that conflicts and important issues are always disguised, or that part of the function of dreaming is to protect sleep; disturbing daytime experiences are often repeated in dreams. Also, interpreting a dream cannot be achieved **objectively**, even by a trained psychoanalyst.

- According to Cartwright, dreams are a way of **solving problems** in our lives. She rejects Freud's distinction between latent and manifest content, but like Freud, she stresses the role of **metaphor** in dreaming. Support for her theory comes from studies which show that people experiencing interpersonal/occupational problems enter REM sleep earlier and spend longer in it than those without such problems.

- Evans' **reprogramming theory** maintains that the brain needs to periodically shut itself off from sensory input in order to process and assimilate new information and update already-stored information. This happens during REM sleep, and dreams are the brain's attempts at interpreting the updating. This is supported by studies which find that REM increases following activities requiring intense/unusual mental activity, such as wearing distorting lenses.

- Foulkes' reprogramming theory states that our cognitive systems, which are used in interpreting new experiences, try to interpret the often spontaneous and random brain activity that occurs during REM sleep. Dreams usually make some sense because of the structure that our cognitive systems impose on the otherwise meaningless brain activity.

- According to Foulkes, dreams (a) usually refer to/reflect the dreamer's memories/knowledge; (b) might help to integrate specific knowledge/experiences to more general knowledge we already possess; (c) can help prepare us for new, unexpected events; (d) may reveal important information about our cognitive processes.

- Koukkou and Lehman argue that dreams involve the restructuring/reinterpretation of the data already stored in memory from childhood in the light of recently acquired experiences.

- In contrast with all the above-mentioned theories, which see dreams as **meaningful**, Hobson and McCarley's **activation synthesis theory** argues that dreams reflect biological activity and are, essentially, meaningless.

- In cats, certain neurons deep within the brain fire randomly during REM sleep, which **activates** adjacent neurons which control eye movements, balance, running and walking etc. Although these body movements are mostly inhibited during REM, the signals are still sent to the relevant parts of the cortex. The brain attempts to **synthesise**/make sense of this random activity, resulting in what we call a dream, which is often fragmented and meaningless.

- **Giant cells** in the RAS of the pons are responsible for the onset of REM sleep and are sensitive to **acetylcholine**; when this is available, the giant cells fire freely, but they stop (and, hence, so too does REM sleep) when there is no more available. This accounts for the periodic activation of the brain during sleep.

- The activation synthesis theory can account for common dreams of falling and floating, as well as the tendency to dream about that day's events; it can also explain why we don't experience smells and tastes in dreams. Yet, if dream content is influenced by our waking experiences, dreams cannot be as random/meaningless as all that.

- According to Crick and Mitchison's **reverse learning/unlearning theory**, dreams enable the brain to erase information that is no longer needed by weakening certain synaptic connections. REM sleep involves the random firing of neurons which produce hallucinations and fantasies that have overloaded the cortex; flushing out 'parasitic information' provides more space for useful information.

- According to Crick and Mitchison, the abnormally large cortex of the spiny anteater and dolphin are needed to accommodate all the useless information which they are unable to flush out, since they do not have REM sleep.

- Historical accounts of discoveries and creations coming to people in dreams suggest that dreams **are** meaningful. The REM-like sleep that occurs in the foetus poses problems for **all** theories of dreaming. According to Jouvet, the neural activity involved in REM sleep represents a form of practice of instinctive behaviour which, after birth, is combined with experience.

HYPNOSIS AND HYPNOTIC PHENOMENA

Introduction and overview

Like dreaming, hypnosis has long held a fascination for both laypeople and professional psychologists. Our aim in this chapter is to review what is known about hypnosis and hypnotic phenomena. We will begin by briefly looking at the history of hypnosis and, after describing the induction of a hypnotic state, we will consider some of its major characteristics. We will then look at two very different theories of hypnosis before concluding this chapter with an examination of some of the potential practical applications of hypnosis and the issue of hypnosis and behaviour control.

A brief history of hypnosis

Although the Cult of Aesculapius (400 B.C.) provides us with the first known reference, serious scientific interest in what we now call hypnosis can be traced back to 1784, when King Louis XVI of France established a committee to investigate the work of an Austrian physician working in Paris called Franz Anton Mesmer. Like some present-day physicists, Mesmer believed that the universe was connected by a mysterious form of 'magnetism'. He also believed that human beings could be drawn to one another by a process called *animal magnetism*.

According to Mesmer, illnesses were caused by imbalances in the body's own magnetic fields. Since he considered himself to possess a very large amount of 'magnetic fluid', Mesmer reasoned that by rechannelling his own magnetism people who were ill would be cured, because their 'magnetic fluxes' would be restored. *Mesmerism*, the treatment devised by Mesmer, was unusual. In a darkened room, patients, who held on to iron bars, were seated around wooden barrels filled with water, ground glass, and iron filings. With soft music playing in the background Mesmer, dressed in a lilac taffeta robe, would walk around the room and occasionally tap the patients with his bar. Often, they would suffer convulsions and enter a trance-like state. When this occurred, Mesmer's assistants removed them

to a mattress-lined room so that they would not harm themselves during the convulsion.

Using Mesmerism, Mesmer was able to cure some minor ailments. However, Louis XVI's committee did not believe that 'animal magnetism' was responsible. In their view, cures probably occurred through 'aroused imagination' or what would nowadays be called the *placebo effect*. Although the committee's conclusions led to a decline of interest in Mesmer, 'Mesmerism' and 'animal magnetism' physicians remained interested in the possibility that similar techniques had a use, especially in order to reduce pain during surgery.

In 1842, Crawford Long, an American surgeon, operated on an etherised patient, the first instance of anaesthesia being used in medicine. In the same year, W.S. Ward, a British physician, reported that he had amputated a man's leg without causing any discomfort and without anything other than 'hypnosis' (a word coined by another British physician, James Braid, and taken from the Greek *hypnos* meaning 'to put to sleep'). Between 1845 and 1851, James Eskdale performed many operations in India using hypnosis as his only anaesthetic. The technique's success was indicated by the fact that Eskdale's patients appeared to show no sign of suffering during their operations, and showed no apparent memory for having been in pain during the operation.

Inducing a hypnotic state

There are several ways of inducing a 'hypnotic state', the only requirement of any of these being that a person understands hypnosis will take place. Typically, the individual is asked to stare upwards and focus attention on a 'target' such as a small light or a spot on the wall. As attention is focussed on the target, the hypnotist will make suggestions of relaxation, tiredness, and sleepiness. Contrary to popular belief, hypnotised people are *not* asleep. Although the eyes are closed, EEG recordings do not show the patterns characteristic of the stages of sleep (see Chapter 9) even though rapid eye movements may be seen beneath the closed eyelids.

The hypnotist may also suggest that the arms and legs feel heavy, warm, and relaxed. Pennebaker & Skelton (1981) have shown that the *expectation* of bodily changes can be sufficient to produce these changes. In all probability, the suggestions reduce the activity of the sympathetic branch of the autonomic nervous system (see Chapter 3) and help bring about the relaxed state. If the person's eyes are still open after ten minutes, the hypnotist will suggest that they be closed. After further suggestions of relaxation, hypnotic tests are administered.

Characteristics of the hypnotic state

A number of characteristics are associated with the hypnotic state, some or all of which may be apparent in a hypnotised person. One of these is termed *the suspension of planning* in which volition, the ability to initiate actions, is lost. Thus, hypnotised people sit quietly and show litle or no activity. If, however, an activity is suggested to them, the suggestion is responded to. Another characteristic is a distortion in information processing. Hypnotised people tend to accept inconsistencies or incongruities that would ordinarily be noticed. A narrowing of attention also occurs and results in less awareness of sensory information. For example, a hypnotised person told to listen to, say, only the hypnotist's voice will apparently hear no other voices. This is a particularly interesting characteristic because it has been shown that there is no reduction in sensory sensitivity and information is *still* analysed by the brain.

Figure 12.1 illustrates this.

Hypnotised people will also respond to suggestions that, for example, their arms are becoming lighter and will rise, or that their hands are becoming 'attracted' to one another. As well as initiating movements, suggestion can be used to inhibit it. A person told that the arm is 'rigid' will report being unable to bend it at all or only with extreme difficulty. Feelings and perceptions suggested by the hypnotist are also experienced even if they are not consistent with actual external conditions. For example, a person who is told that the bottle beneath his or her nose contains water, may report smelling nothing even though the bottle contains ammonia in the concentration found in household bleach.

Other perceptual distortions include the uncritical acceptance of hallucinated experiences. For example, hypnotised people may talk to an imaginary person they are told is sitting next to them without checking if this person is real. When something that is not present is reported as being present, the term *positive hallucination* is used. The term *negative hallucination* refers to instances when a person does not respond to something that is present.

Two other characteristics are worthy of mention. In *post-hypnotic amnesia*, the hypnotist may instruct the hypnotised individual to forget all that has occurred during the hypnotic session. On 'awakening', the hypnotised person may have no knowledge of the hypnotic session and may not even be aware that hypnosis has taken place. When hypnotised again, however, recall of the events of the original session usually occurs.

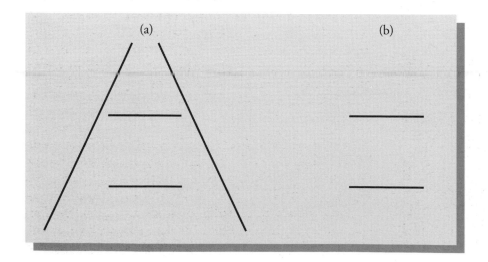

Fig 12.1   In the Ponzo illusion (a), the two parallel horizontal lines are the same length, but the top one looks longer than the bottom one. If, through hypnotic suggestion, the slanted lines are made to 'disappear', participants still report the top line as looking longer. This shows that the visual system continues to process sensory information during hypnosis. If this were not the case, the lines would be perceived as being equal in length, as in (b). The findings were reported by Miller, et al. (1973)

In *post-hypnotic suggestion*, a person is given an instruction during the hypnotic session that, for instance, on hearing the word 'sleep' after the session, he or she will fall into a deep sleep. Responses to post-hypnotic suggestions seem to occur even when the person has been instructed to forget that the suggestions have been made. What is especially interesting is that a person eliciting a post-hypnotic response will, in the absence of any reason for making the response, attempt to justify it. For example, a person instructed to eat a banana whenever the hypnotist says a particular word may justify the behaviour by saying that he or she 'feels hungry'. Not surprisingly, post-hypnotic suggestion has been used with people who wish to stop smoking but have otherwise been unable to do so. Typically, a *hypnotherapist* will make the suggestion that a cigarette will, when lit, taste repulsive.

Individual differences in hypnotic susceptibility

The evidence suggests that not everyone is susceptible to hypnosis. Hilgard (1977) has estimated that 5–10% of people are highly *resistant* and about 15% highly susceptible. The remaining 75–80% fall somewhere between these two extremes. One device for measuring susceptibility is the *Stanford Hypnotic Susceptibility Scale*. Many of the phenomena included in the scale have already been referred to earlier on in this chapter. The items that make up the scale are shown in Box 12.1 below.

Box 12.1   The Stanford Hypnotic Susceptibility Scale

(1) Arm lowering: It is suggested to the participant that an outstetched arm is getting heavier and heavier. The arm should be gradually lowered.

(2) Moving hands apart: The participant sits with arms outstretched in front. The suggestion is made that the hands are repelled from each other as if by magnets. This should lead to them moving part.

(3) Mosquito hallucination: The suggestion is made to the participant that an annoying mosquito is buzzing around. This should lead to the participant trying to 'shoo' it away.

(4) Taste hallucination: The participant should respond to the suggestion that a sweet substance and then a sour one is being tasted.

(5) Arm rigidity: Following the suggestion that an arm held out straight is getting stiffer and stiffer, the participant should be unable to unbend it.

(6) Dream: The participant is told to have a dream about hypnosis while remaining hypnotised. The contents of the dream should be released by the participant.

(7) Age regression: The participant is told to imagine being at different school ages. For each of the ages selected, realistic handwriting specimens should be provided.

(8) Arm immobilisation: Following the suggestion made by the hypnotist, the participant should be unable to lift an arm involuntarily.

(9) Anosmia (loss of smell) to ammonia: Following suggestions made by the hypnotist, the participant should report being unable to smell household ammonia.

(10) Hallucinated voice: The participant should answer questions raised by a hallucinated voice.

(11) Negative visual hallucination: Following suggestions made by the hypnotist, the participant should report the inability to see one of three small coloured boxes.

(12) Post-hypnotic amnesia: The participant should be unable to recall particular information after hypnosis until given a prearranged signal.

After a hypnotic state has been induced, the first of the suggestions is made. If the response is made it is counted as 'present' and the second suggestion is made. The procedure continues until a response is counted as 'absent'. Since the 12 suggestions are ordered in terms of difficulty, a person who does not respond to the first suggestion is unikely to respond to the second, third, and so on.

Some researchers (such as Hilgard, 1979) do not believe that hypnotic susceptibility is related to any particular personality type, but others (such as Kihlstrom, 1985) believe there are several stable personality traits that underlie hypnotic susceptibility. For example, people who score high on *absorption*, defined as the tendency to become deeply absorbed in sensory and imaginative experiences, also score higher on measures of hypnotic susceptibility. *Expectancy* has also been suggested to be an important characteristic. It seems that people are not influenced by hypnotic expectations if they do not expect to be. Those who do usually are, and typically have very positive attitudes towards hypnosis. Finally, people who are *fantasy-prone*, that is, have frequent and vivid fantasies, also tend to be more susceptible to hypnotic suggestion.

These observations do not, of course, indicate that such characteristics *cause* susceptibility to hypnosis. Moreover, at least one of them ('absorption') seems to correlate with hypnotic susceptibility only when people expect to *undergo* hypnosis. In other contexts, the correlation is not obtained (Council, et al. 1986). As a general conclusion, though, a person who becomes deeply absorbed in activities, expects to be influenced by hypnotic suggestions (or 'shows the faith' – Baron, 1989), and has a rich, vivid and active fantasy life, is likely to be much more susceptible to hypnotic suggestions.

The genuineness of hypnosis

According to Orne & Evans (1965), all of the phenomena that can be produced under hypnosis can be produced without hypnosis. Spanos, Gwynn & Stam (1983) have proposed that the essential difference between hypnotised and non-hypnotised people is that the former *believe* their responses are involuntary whereas the latter *know they are pretending*. Although hypnotic phenomena seem to be genuine enough, the genuineness of at least some of them has been questioned.

As we noted earlier, in post-hypnotic amnesia people act as though they cannot remember what happened during a hypnotic episode. Spanos, Jones & Malfara (1982) have explained this in terms of the suggestion *not* to recall information being an 'invitation' to refrain from attending to retrieval cues. However, Coe & Yashinski (1985) have shown that when people are given a 'lie detector' test and led to believe that they will be found out if they do not tell the truth, recall of the hypnotic episode increases dramatically! This, along with other findings, has led to the suggestion that hypnotic phenomena are not real but merely a clever act perpetrated by the hypnotist and the participant, the latter pretending to be 'under the influence'.

A number of attempts have been made to experimentally investigate *trance logic*, that is, the difference in performance between the hypnotised and those who are pretending to be hypnotised. Orne, Sheehan & Evans (1968) used two groups of participants. The first were hypnotised and the second instructed to act as though they were hypnotised. Both groups were told that in the following 48 hours their right hand would touch their foreheads every time they heard the word 'experiment'. Some time later, participants encountered a secretary who said the word 'experiment' three times. On average, participants highly susceptible to hypnosis touched their foreheads an average of 70% of the occasions on which the word was said. For all participants who were hypnotised the figure was 29.5%, whilst for those pretending to be hypnotised it was only 7.7%. More recently, Kinnunen and his colleagues (1995) have used Skin Conductance Reaction (SCR), a crude but effective measure of deception, to investigate hypnosis. The researchers found significantly higher SCRs for 'simulators' as compared with hypnotised individuals.

In another study, Bowers (1976) showed that participants who are told they cannot see a chair *will* bump into it if they are faking hypnosis, but will walk around it (just as a sleepwalker does) if they have been hypnotised. In other studies (e.g. Morgan & Hilgard, 1973) it has been shown that hypnotic susceptibility peaks between 9 and 12 years of age, decreases until the mid-thirties, and then levels off. The finding that hypnotised and non-hypnotised individuals can be shown to differ in terms of their behaviour, and the fact that there is no reason why hypnotic susceptibility should change over time if it is faked, suggests that hypnotic phenomena *may* be real.

A 'state' or 'special processes' theory of hypnosis

According to *state* or *special processes* theorists, hypnosis is a unique and altered state of consciousness. Ernest Hilgard, one of the leading special processes theorists, has advanced what he calls a *neo-dissociation theory of hypnosis*. According to this, hypnosis is the dissociation (or division) of consciousness into separate channels of mental activity. This division allows us to focus our attention on the hypnotist and, simultaneously, enables us to perceive other events peripherally (or 'subconsciously').

Central to Hilgard's theory is the *hidden observer* phenomenon which he first demonstrated in 1973. Hilgard told a male participant that deafness would be induced in him through hypnosis, but that he would be able to hear when a hand was placed on his shoulder. Although the participant was 'hypnotically deaf', he was asked to raise a forefinger if there was some part of him that could still hear. To Hilgard's surprise, and that of a watching audience, a forefinger rose.

In later studies, Hilgard explored the hidden observer phenomenon further using what is called the *Cold Pressor Test* (CPT). In this, one or both forearms is plunged into circulating icy water, and the participant is required to keep the forearm(s) submerged for as long as possible. Initially, the sensation is of coldness. After a few seconds, however, this turns to pain which cannot be tolerated by most people for longer than about 25 seconds. Hilgard found that when participants highly susceptible to hypnosis were told that they would feel no pain, they were able to keep their forearm(s) submerged for an average of around 40 seconds.

However, although the hypnotised participant appeared to be able to withstand the pain for longer than would ordinarily be the case, the hidden observer did not! Thus, when the hidden observer was asked to 'remain out of awareness' and write down ratings of pain on a 10-point scale, the ratings were significantly higher than those reported verbally by the participant. Such a finding is consistent with Hilgard's theory: the part of consciousness accepting and responding to the hypnotist's suggestions becomes dissociated from the pain whilst the hidden observer, which monitors everything that happens, remains aware of it. This could be explained in terms of neural inhibition preventing the transmission of information between the verbal system ('consciousness') and the brain's peripheral and motor systems. Quite possibly, this is the 'dissociation' Hilgard refers to.

Earlier on in this chapter we noted that hypnosis has a long history as an *analgesic* (or 'pain-reliever'). For example, as well as helping children to withstand painful bone marrow transplants for cancer, hypnosis has been used in a variety of surgical procedures including the removal of teeth, tonsils and breast tumours. Indeed, some researchers (such as Gillett & Coe, 1984) have argued that the analgesic effects of hypnosis are more powerful than those of drugs like morphine, and can even act to reduce the emotional upset that accompanies pain as well as the pain itself. Hilgard's findings suggest that hypnosis does *not* eliminate pain, but enables it to be tolerated better because there is no conscious awareness of it. Box 12.2 below describes some other ways in which the analgesic properties of hypnosis have been investigated.

Box 12.2   The analgesic properties of hypnosis

Other ways of explaining the analgesic properties of hypnosis have been advanced. Hypnosis may, for example, relax people. By encouraging them to focus on pleasant images, they might be distracted from thoughts of pain. Relaxation itself might allow the brain to produce *endorphins*, its own natural pain-killers (see Chapter 1). The issue of whether hypnosis really does have analgesic properties has been the subject of much debate. According to Barber (1970), for example, even if people do experience pain when hypnotised, they might not wish to report this for fear of causing offence! Whether people are simply *acting* as though they are anaesthetised was studied by Pattie (1937). He told participants that they would be unable to feel anything with one hand. They were instructed to cross their wrists as illustrated below.

If you try this and ask someone to touch one of your hands very rapidly, you'll find that it is difficult to determine which hand has been touched. Pattie showed that when he touched the fingers on *both* hands and asked participants to count the number of times they had been touched, they included touches made to the 'anaesthetised' hand (which should not have been counted if the hand really was anaesthetised). This finding would seem to suggest a difference between local anaesthesia and hypnotic anaesthesia. In the latter, a person behaves *as though* he or she is anaesthetised.

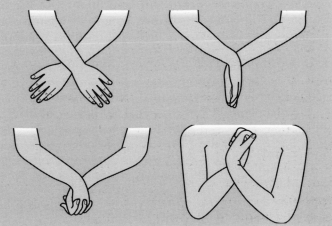

A 'non-state' theory of hypnosis

In contrast to Hilgard's views, some researchers have taken a very different approach to the explanation of hypnotic phenomena. Barber (1979), for example, has argued that if they occur only when a person is hypnotised, it is difficult to see why the brain should have evolved in such a way that people *can* be hypnotised. For Barber, the functional analysis of a behavioural phenomenon usually points to a plausible reason for the occurrence of a behaviour. Thus, as far as Barber and other *non-state* theorists are concerned, hypnosis is *not* an altered state of consciousness.

Barber sees hypnotised people as acting out a *social role* which is defined by their own expectations and the social situation in which they find themselves. The rules of the social situation are governed by the hypnotist's direct instructions or are indirectly implied by his or her words and actions. In Barber's view, hypnosis is not special but people, and their imagination and ability to play roles, are. Non-state theorists argue that hypnosis involves the *suspension of self-control*, a phenomenon which occurs when, say, we allow the actors in a film or the author of a book to lead us through some sort of fantasy. Certainly, the finding that 'suggestible' hypnotic participants have (amongst other things) vivid and absorbing imaginations, lends support to the views of non-state theorists and casts doubt on the claims that hypnosis is an altered state of consciousness.

Barber's theory is supported by the finding that behaviours possible under hypnosis are also possible in non-hypnotic conditions. The 'human plank' trick, for example, in which a hypnotised person remains suspended from chairs placed at the back of the head and ankles, can be accomplished by most people in a normal waking state. Even Martin Orne, a leading researcher in the area, has acknowledged that the behaviour of non-hypnotised people occasionally fooled him:

> 'As a clinician who worked extensively with hypnosis, I never doubted it would be easy for me to recognise those who were, in fact, simulating. It came as a complete surprise to find that (people) were able to deceive me.'

The hidden observer phenomenon has also been challenged by non-state theorists. They argue that it is simply a product of a *script* which is supplied by the hypnotist. Using the CPT, Spanos and his colleagues (1983) instructed hypnotised participants that they would not experience any pain. Some were also given instructions similar to those used by Hilgard to elicit the hidden observer, whilst others were told that the hidden observer was *less* aware of things going on in and around their bodies. The results of the study showed that as compared with participants in whom the hidden observer was not elicited, the hidden observer reported more *or* less pain depending on the instructions that had been given.

Spanos and his colleagues suggest that these findings reflect the playing of *two roles* rather than a division of consciousness. They argue that participants in Hilgard's experiment ignored the pain when instructed it would not be perceived and switched attention to it when the hidden observer was requested. Rather than being a part of consciousness remaining aware of reality, Spanos (1986) argues that the hidden observer is merely following the hypnotist's instructions.

Some practical applications of hypnotic phenomena

Irrespective of the way in which hypnosis can best be explained, a large amount of research has looked at the ways in which the phenomena associated with it can be put to practical use. One application makes use of *hypermnesia*, that is, the apparent ability of a hypnotised person to focus on selected details of an event and reconstruct an entire memory if told to do so. In some police departments, this has been used to prompt the memories of people who have witnessed a crime but cannot recall specific details of the events that occurred. Indeed, in America at least, evidence obtained from hypnotised witnesses has been admitted into court, and some police departments have officers trained in hypnosis.

In the *television technique*, the hypnotised witness is told that he or she will be able to 'zoom in' on details such as a car number plate and 'freeze the frame' to examine the details (Reiser & Nielsen, 1980). Unfortunately, the reports obtained from hypnotised people have not always been helpful. In an American court case (People versus Kempinski, 1980) a hypno-tised witness identified Mr Kempinski as a victim's murderer. However, the defence successfully argued that, given the lighting conditions at the time, it would only have been possible to identify the murderer's face from a maximum of eight yards away. Since the witness was some 90 yards away, the defence challenged the validity of the witness' recall under hypnosis. The challenge was accepted and the evidence dismissed.

Box 12.3 below identifies some of the reasons why evidence gathered under hypnosis should be treated with caution.

Box 12.3   Some cautions against the use of hypnosis in criminal investigations

(Based on findings reported in Laurence & Perry, 1983, Rathus, 1987 and Hassett & White, 1989)

(1) Witnesses may pick up on suggestions communicated by the hypnotist, incorporate these into memory, and recall them as 'factual'. Related to this is the finding that 'leading questions' are even more likely to produce distorted memories under hypnosis.

(2) Although the hypnotically suggestible recall more information than non-hypnotised people, this information is frequently incorrect. Hypnotised witnesses sometimes 'see' things that were not there and fail to report things that were there.

(3) The confidence with which hypnotised people give information is very high (even if it is actually incorrect). This may throw off both the police and a jury.

(4) Hypnosis might not actually affect what people remember, but might make them *less cautious* about what they are willing to guess. If hypnosis does make mental images more vivid, hypnotised people may confuse these images with actual memories.

The conclusion of a panel appointed by the American Medical Association was that whilst hypnosis *sometimes* produces additional details, such information is often unreliable. Rather than accepting recall under hypnosis as evidence itself, the police were recommended to limit its use to the investigative stage of an enquiry where it might produce new clues whose details could be checked by other sources of objective evidence.

Another application of hypnosis has been to *age regression*. People under hypnosis seem to be able to play unusual roles. For example, something requiring increased stamina (such as riding a bicycle) can be done with apparently less fatigue than normal (Banyai & Hilgard, 1976). In age regression, people are asked to play themselves as infants or children. It would seem that some are able to show excellent recall of details such as a long-forgotten toy or speech pattern, and may be able to speak in a language they have not spoken since childhood.

Hypnosis made a significant contribution to the development of *psychoanalytic theory*. Charcot, for example, believed that hysterical disorders (such as apparent blindness in the absence of any damage to the visual system) was caused by some other sort of physical problem even if this was not connected with the visual system. However, his discovery that hysterical symptoms could be simulated under hypnosis led him to conclude that the origins of hysterical disorders were psychological rather than physical.

A little later, Breuer demonstrated that one of his patients could be made to feel better about her problems when she spoke freely of them under hypnosis. Freud believed that hypnosis was a useful way in gaining access to the unconscious and could be used to uncover the causes of psychological disorders. For Freud, psychological problems in adulthood had their origins in early childhood experiences which could not ordinarily be recalled because the memory of them had been *repressed*.

Freud believed that hypnotic states produced *regression*. In this, the conscious control (or 'ego functioning') of behaviour is suspended, and it becomes possible to return to childish modes of behaviour. Although Freud later abandoned hypnosis as a method of gaining access to the unconscious (not least for the reason that he felt it elicited childhood *fantasies* rather than *experiences*) it is still used today to help people discuss memories whose apparent inaccessibility is hindering therapeutic progress. However, the approach has been criticised, and the recent concerns about *False Memory Syndrome* have cast doubt on this particular application of hypnosis.

Hypnosis and behaviour control

According to some researchers, hypnotists are able to induce people to act in ways which grossly violate their moral code, and this is sometimes referred to as the *Hollywood theory of hypnosis* (Hayes, 1994). Such behaviours include harming others or doing damage to themselves. Other researchers, however, believe this to be untrue and also feel that it is impossible for a person to be tricked into behaving in such ways (Barber, 1969).

Reports of 'porno-hypnotist' shows in America, the use of 'striptease' in the stage show of at least one British hypnotist, and reports of indecent assaults on patients by hypnotherapists, have raised serious ethical questions about the extent to which hypnotists can control people's behaviour. Because of this, it is hardly surprising that a Federation of Ethical Stage Hypnotists exists!

It is certainly possible to think of ways in which it might be possible to trick a hypnotised person into behaving in a way which violates ordinary standards of behaviour. For example, a situation could be misperceived by a hypnotised person who is told to shoot a gun at a 'paper target' which is actually another person (Carlson, 1987). What is much more difficult to determine is whether a particular behaviour occurs because the hypnotist has control or because the person actually *wants* to behave in that way.

Consider, for example, a person who is instructed to eat raw onions until told to stop. We might find that these instructions are followed and that the person feels angry and embarrassed by having been 'forced' to behave in such a way. Although it would appear that the hypnotist has been successful in producing a behaviour that would ordinarily not have been performed, we cannot rule out the possibility that the person *wanted* to be 'punished' in this way because of some real or imagined misdeed (Baron, 1989). As with all the other phenomena associated with hypnosis, there is still much for us to discover.

Conclusions

As we have seen, hypnosis has attracted the interest of many psychological researchers, and hypnotic phenomena have been the subject of a large number of experimental investigations. How hypnosis can best be explained is an issue yet to be resolved, although Alden (1995) has suggested that more and more researchers are moving towards accepting hypnosis as a 'non-state paradigm'. Whatever the explanation, hypnotic phenomena have been applied in several areas, although the evidence for their effectiveness of these is far from clear.

SUMMARY

- Serious scientific interest in hypnosis can be traced to 1784, with the establishment of a committee to investigate the work of Mesmer, who believed that human beings could be drawn together by **animal magnetism**.
- Mesmer's treatment for illnesses, supposedly caused by imbalances in the body's own magnetic fields, came to be called **mesmerism**, but the committee concluded that any cure probably occurred through the **placebo effect**. Nonetheless, many doctors began to use hypnosis as a form of anaesthetic during surgery.

- Although there are several ways of inducing a hypnotic state, typically, the individual who is to be hypnotised is asked to focus on a target. This is then followed by suggestions of relaxation, tiredness, and sleepiness. Despite the occurrence of rapid eye movements, the hypnotised person is not asleep.
- One characteristic of the hypnotic state is the **suspension of planning**. Others include the acceptance of inconsistencies that would normally be noticed, a narrowing of attention resulting in less awareness of sensory information, and a respon-

siveness to suggestions to initiate and inhibit movements of the limbs.

- Suggestibility also applies to perceptual distortions, including both positive and negative hallucinations, post-hypnotic amnesia, and post-hypnotic suggestion, which is used by hypnotherapists to help people stop smoking.

- About 15% of people are highly susceptible to hypnosis, 5–10% are highly resistant, and the rest fall somewhere in between. This can be measured by Hilgard's **Stanford Hypnotic Susceptibility Scale**, which is composed of 12 items, including susceptibility to limb movements, hallucinations, post-hypnotic amnesia, and age regression.

- Susceptibility has been shown to be associated with **absorption**, **expectancy**, and being **fantasy-prone**.

- The genuineness of at least some characteristics of hypnosis, such as post-hypnotic amnesia, has been challenged as being nothing more than a clever act. However, experimental studies of **trance logic** show that hypnotised and non-hypnotised individuals do behave differently, with the former displaying similar behaviour to sleepwalkers. This, together with the finding that susceptibility changes with age, points to hypnosis being a real phenomenon.

- According to the **state** or **special processes** theory, hypnosis is a unique and altered state of consciousness. One version of this is Hilgard's **neo-dissociation theory**, according to which hypnosis involves the division of consciousness into separate channels; this allows us to focus our attention on the hypnotist and simultaneously to perceive other events 'subconsciously', as demonstrated by the **hidden observer** phenomenon and the **cold pressor test**.

- Hypnosis has for a long time been used as an analgesic in a range of surgical procedures. One explanation of this pain-relieving property of hypnosis is the neo-dissociation theory; another is that relaxation induces the production of **endorphins,** the brain's natural pain-killers. It is possible that in hypnotic anaesthesia, people merely behave as though they are anaesthetised.

- According to the **non-state** theory, hypnosis is not an altered state of consciousness, but involves people acting out a **social role** defined by their own expectations and the rules of the situation. It also involves the **suspension of self-control**.

- The non-state theory is supported by the finding that suggestible hypnotic participants have vivid imaginations, and the finding that behaviours that are possible under hypnosis are also possible in non-hypnotic conditions; indeed, even experts can be fooled by the behaviour of non-hypnotised people.

- Non-state theorists have explained the hidden observer phenomenon in terms of a **script**, whereby the participant plays two roles determined by the hypnotist's instructions (rather than displaying a division of consciousness).

- Other practical applications of hypnosis include **hypermnesia** and the **television technique**, although these are unreliable, and evidence gathered under hypnosis should be treated with caution. **Age regression** can sometimes produce recall of long-forgotten details from childhood.

- Freud's **psychoanalytic theory** was influenced by Charcot's discovery that hysterical symptoms could be simulated under hypnosis, and by Breuer's account of a patient who came to feel better about her problems when she spoke freely about them under hypnosis.

- Although Freud abandoned hypnosis as a way of unlocking the unconscious, it is still used today to help people remember repressed memories. However, this use of hypnosis has been criticised because of its implication in **False Memory Syndrome**.

- The ethics of using hypnosis to induce behaviour in people in public shows and demonstrations has been called into question. However, it is unclear whether a hypnotist can get someone to act in a particular way if the person does not **wish** to.

SOME DRUGS AND THEIR EFFECTS ON BEHAVIOUR

Introduction and overview

For thousands of years, humans have taken drugs to alter their perceptions of reality and, as Weil & Rosen (1983) have observed, for thousands of years societies have limited this kind of drug use by placing various restrictions on it. Our aim in this chapter is to examine the psychological and physiological effects exerted by some *psychoactive drugs*. The word 'psychoactive' is usually taken to mean any chemical compound which alters perceptions and behaviour by changing conscious awareness. Unfortunately, most drugs fit into this definition of 'psychoactive'. Aspirin, for example, can be considered psychoactive because when it relieves a headache, it changes conscious experience.

For our purposes, we will confine our consideration to those drugs which people use to alter their state of consciousness temporarily for the purpose of *pleasure*. Such drugs might be considered 'recreational', but as Carlson (1988) has noted (and as we will see during the course of this chapter), some of the effects these drugs produce would hardly constitute most people's idea of 'having fun'.

Tolerance, dependence, addiction and withdrawal

Before we look at our chosen psychoactive drugs, it is necessary to familiarise ourselves with four terms that will be used frequently throughout this chapter. All of the drugs we will be discussing alter thoughts, feelings and behaviour by affecting the brain. However, the effects that some of the drugs exert is *lessened* with continued use. Put another way, users need to take increasing amounts of some drugs to achieve the same initial effect. This phenomenon is called *tolerance*.

Tolerance to a drug is sometimes associated with *physiological* (or *physical*) *dependence*. Physiological dependence means that the body cannot do without a drug because it has adjusted to, and becomes dependent on, the presence of that drug. When a person stops taking a drug which produces physiological dependence, a variety of problems occur, such as insomnia, profuse sweating, shaking, and so on. These problems are the symptoms of *withdrawal* (or *abstinence syndrome*). Physical dependence and tolerance together define the medical syndrome called *drug addiction*.

Some drugs are so pleasurable that users feel compelled to continue taking them even though the body is not physically dependent on the drug's presence. This is *psychological dependence*, and being deprived of the drug is anxiety-producing for the user. Since the symptoms of anxiety (e.g. rapid pulse, profuse sweating, and shaking) overlap with the symptoms of withdrawal, people may believe they are physiologically dependent on a drug when in fact they are psychologically dependent.

Types of psychoactive drug

There are four major classes of the psychoactive drugs that are taken for 'recreational' purposes. *Depressants* (or *sedatives*) depress neural activity, slow down bodily functions, induce calmness, and produce sleep. By contrast, *stimulants* temporarily excite neural activity, arouse bodily functions, enhance positive feelings, and heighten alertness. The *opiates* also depress activity in the central nervous system, but in addition have an *analgesic* property, that is, they produce insensitivity to pain without loss of consciousness. *Hallucinogens* produce alterations in perception and evoke sensory images in the absence of any sensory input. As well as looking at the major drugs in each of these four classes, we will also consider the effects of *cannabis*, a drug which defies the system of classification described above.

THE DEPRESSANTS

Depressants are drugs that slow down mental processes and behaviours. The most widely used and abused depressant is *alcohol*, whose psychoactive effects have been known about for over 5,000 years. The effects associated with the consumption of alcohol are shown in Box 13.1 below.

Box 13.1   Alcohol and its effects

How taken: Alcohol is drunk. Over 90% of adults in Britain drink alcohol to some extent.

Psychological effects: There are wide individual differences in the effects of alcohol, which are at least in part dependent on body weight and sex. The effects of alcohol, and other drugs, also depend on *expectations*. For example, those people who believe alcohol has an arousing effect may be more responsive to sexual stimuli even though alcohol *per se* does not increase arousal.

In general, small amounts have a 'stimulating effect' (but note that alcohol is *not* a stimulant – see below). The 'stimulating' effects include a lowering of social inhibitions. This interferes with the ability to foresee negative consequences and results in the inability to recall accepted standards of behaviour. Thus, actions may become more extreme and we become likely to 'speak our mind'. As the ancient Romans said, 'in vino veritas' ('in wine there is truth'). Large amounts have a sedative effect.

Alcohol affects both cognitive and motor functions. For example, its use impairs the ability to process recent experiences into long-term memory. A day after consuming a large amount of alcohol, a person might not remember the events that occurred when alcohol was being taken. Other cognitive impairments include deficits in visual acuity and depth perception, and the subjective experience of time passing more quickly. Even 10 mg of alcohol interferes with the ability to follow a moving target with a pointer. 80 mg slows reaction time by about 10%. Greater amounts result in staggering and a complete loss of motor co-ordination caused by depression of neural activity in the cerebellum – see Chapter 2. Very large amounts can induce a coma and, on occasion, lead to death.

Long-term consequences: Although short-term use may alleviate depressive feelings, long-term use may augment such feelings. Heavy users of alcohol suffer malnutrition because they eat less. Alcohol contains many calories, which suppresses appetite. Since it interferes with the absorption of Vitamin B from the intestines, alcohol causes vitamin deficiency. The prolonged effect of this is brain damage and memory is particularly affected. Other physical consequences include liver damage, heart disease, increased risk of a stroke, and susceptibility to infections due to a suppressed immune system. Women who drink during pregnancy can produce an offspring with *foetal alcohol syndrome*. This is characterised by retarded physical growth, intellectual development, and motor co-ordination. There are also abnormalities in brain metabolic processes and liver functions.

Effects of abstinence: After prolonged and severe intoxication, physiological dependence and withdrawal occur. The symptoms include restlessness, nausea, fever, and the bizarre hallucinations of *delerium tremens*. In some cases, withdrawal produces such a profound shock to the body that death occurs. There is no doubt that tolerance develops, and it is likely that psychological dependence also develops.

Exactly how alcohol exerts its effects is not known. In terms of autonomic nervous system activity, alcohol has a relaxing effect. Its 'stimulating effects' probably occur from a suppression of the brain mechanisms that normally inhibit behaviour. In large amounts, alcohol decreases neural activity, possibly by acting on the cell membrane of neurons (especially those in the reticular activating system – see Chapter 2) and reducing their ability to conduct nerve impulses. Alcohol also seems to increase the sensitivity of post-synaptic receptors for the inhibitory neurotransmitter GABA (see Chapter 1). By increasing the inhibition generated by GABA, alcohol would reduce neural activity in the brain circuits associated with arousal.

The reason why some people abuse alcohol is also not clear. According to the *disease model of alcoholism*, some people have a weakness for the drug that cannot be controlled because of a genetic predisposition. If alcoholism is to be cured, the alcoholic must abstain *completely* (which is the philosophy of the organisation *Alcoholics Anonymous*). The disease model is the one that most members of the public believe to be true. However, an alternative to it sees drinking as a complex category of behaviour that may have different causes and hence different cures. According to the *social model of alcoholism*, one way to treat excessive alcohol consumption is by using *controlled drinking* rather than abstinence. This approach implies that people can be taught to maintain consumption at an acceptable (non-damaging) level. Both of these models have their supporters and opponents, and at the moment the evidence does not favour one model over the other.

Barbiturates are another type of depressant and have similar effects to alcohol. Because they depress neural activity, barbiturates are often prescribed to induce sleep or reduce anxiety. They exert their effects by reducing the release of excitatory neurotransmitters at synapses in several parts of the nervous system. Barbiturates were first used clinically in 1903, having been synthesised in 1862. However, their clinical use is limited since physiological dependence and withdrawal occurs and tolerance develops quickly. Other depressants include the 'minor tranquillisers' (such as *Valium*) and the *aromatic solvents*. 'Minor tranquillisers' have much milder effects than barbiturates and do not induce sleep. Aromatic solvents include some types of glue and paint thinner. Their use in Britain has been associated with a number of deaths and various surveys have estimated that about 6 to 9% of secondary school children (around 500,000) have taken solvents.

THE STIMULANTS

The general effects of stimulants is to stimulate the CNS by increasing the transmission of nerve impulses. The most widely consumed stimulants are *caffeine* and *nicotine*, both of which exert mild effects and both of which are legal. *Amphetamines* and *cocaine* exert considerably stronger effects and are illegal, as are the newer 'designer' stimulants such as *methylenedioxymethamphetamine* (or *MDMA*) which is known as '*ecstasy*'. 'Designer' drugs are synthetic substances produced by altering the chemical structure of an illegal substance without reducing its potency.

The amphetamine group of drugs were first synthesised in the 1920s. Their general effect is to increase energy and enhance self-confidence. As a result, they were used extensively by the military in World War Two to reduce fatigue and give soldiers going into battle more confidence. Another effect of amphetamines is to suppress appetite, and they also found use as 'slimming pills' being marketed under such trade names as Methedrine, Dexedrine and Benzedrine. However,

their effects on consciousness and behaviour led to them being widely abused, with the result that they are now illegal.

Chemically, amphetamines are similar to *epinephrine*, a neurotransmitter that stimulates the sympathetic nervous system (see Chapter 3). This chemical similarity has led to amphetamines being used as a treatment for asthma, since they open respiratory passages and ease breathing. Amphetamines are also used in the treatment of *narcolepsy*, a disorder characterised by brief and unpredictable periods of sleep.

One other use of amphetamines is in the treatment of hyperactivity in children. With hyperactive children amphetamines (and a related stimulant, *methylphenidate* or *Ritalin*) increases self-control and attention span and decreases fidgeting. According to Rapport (1984), such treatment can produce significant academic gains in hyperactive children. Exactly why a stimulant should calm hyperactive children is not entirely clear. According to one hypothesis, hyperactivity is caused by the immaturity of the cerebral cortex. Amphetamines might stimulate the cortex to exert control over primitive structures within the brain (Hinshaw, et al. 1984).

Box 13.2 below describes some of the effects produced by amphetamines.

Box 13.2 Amphetamine and its effects

How taken: Swallowed in pill form, inhaled through the nose in powder form, or injected in liquid form.

Psychological effects: Small amounts cause increased wakefulness, alertness and arousal. Users experience a sense of energy and confidence with the feeling that any problem can be solved and any task accomplished. This effect is, however, illusory, and problem-solving is no easier with the drug than without it. After the drug wears off, users experience a 'crash' (characterised by extreme fatigue and depression). Users counteract this by taking the drug again which can have serious long-term consequences (see below). Large amounts cause restlessness, hallucinations, and *paranoid delusions* (see below).

Long-term consequences: Amphetamine can stimulate aggressive, violent behaviour. This is not due *directly* to the drug itself. Rather, the effect occurs as a result of personality changes that come from excessive use. The paranoid delusions experienced in *amphetamine psychosis* are virtually indistinguishable from those experienced in the psychological disorder known as *paranoid schizophrenia*. Long-term use has also been associated with severe depression, suicidal tendencies, disrupted thinking and, perhaps, brain damage.

Effects of abstinence: Tolerance develops quickly as does psychological dependence. The evidence concerning physiological dependence is mixed. However, according to Blum (1984), the amphetamine 'hangover' (characterised by extreme fatigue, depression, prolonged sleep, irritability, disorientation, and agitated motor activity) is indicative of a withdrawal effect, suggesting that a physiological dependence has developed.

Cocaine, or more properly cocaine hydrochloride, is a powerful CNS stimulant that is extracted from the leaves of the coca shrub which is native to the Andes Mountains in South America. The drug was discovered centuries ago by Peruvian Indians who chewed on the leaves of the plant to increase stamina and relieve fatigue and hunger. Among present-day South Americans, the chewing of the leaf is still practised.

Cocaine became known about in Europe in the middle 1800s, when coca was blended into wine and other drinks. Until 1906, Coca-Cola actually *did* contain cocaine. Today, it is still blended with coca leaves that have had their active ingredient removed! A famous user of cocaine was Sigmund Freud, who used it to fight his own depression and wrote an article entitled *Song of Praise* in which he supported its use as, amongst other things, a cure for alcoholism. Freud eventually became disillusioned with the drug because of its side-effects. One of his friends, however, developed its use as a local anaesthetic: in very high concentrations cocaine blocks the transmission of action potentials in axons (see Chapter 1). Today, this is still the only legitimate use of the drug.

Although cocaine use declined in the early part of this century, it re-emerged as a popular, if expensive, drug in the 1980s. As the manager of a rock group once famously noted, 'Cocaine is God's way of telling you you've got too much money'. Box 13.3 describes the effects associated with the use of cocaine.

Box 13.3   Cocaine and its effects

How taken: Often inhaled through the nose in powder form, injected into the veins in liquid form, or smoked. When smoked the drug reaches the brain in 5–10 seconds, as compared with 30–120 seconds when inhaled and 60–180 seconds when injected (Miller, et al. 1989). Cocaine can also be swallowed, rubbed on the gums, or blown into the throat.

Psychological effects: In general the effects are similar to amphetamine, though of a briefer duration (around 15–30 minutes as compared with several hours). This is because cocaine is metabolised much more quickly than amphetamine. Typically, the user experiences a state of euphoria, deadening of pain, increased self-confidence and energy, and enhanced attention. As with amphetamines, users experience a 'crash' when the drug wears off. Attempts to offset these effects include taking depressants or an opiate.

Long-term consequences: Even in small amounts, the stimulating effects can result in cardiac arrest and death. Repeated inhalation constricts the blood vessels in the nose. The nasal septum may become perforated, necessitating cosmetic surgery. *Cocaine psychosis* (cf. amphetamine psychosis) can also occur with chronic long-term use as can convulsions, respiratory failure, and bleeding into the brain. Bales (1986) has suggested that, at least in rats, cocaine gradually lowers the tolerance for seizures. An interesting effect is *formication*, that is, the sensation that 'insects' (known as 'coke bugs') are crawling beneath the skin. Although this is merely random neural activity, users have been known to try and remove the imaginary insects by cutting deep into themselves with a knife. Cocaine taken in pregnancy has been associated with impaired foetal development.

Effects of abstinence: Whether cocaine produces physiological dependence, tolerance and withdrawal has been the subject of much debate. However, there is no argument that it produces psychological dependence. This probably stems for the user's desire to avoid the severe depression associated with 'crashing'. Note that some researchers see the symptoms associated with 'crashing' as indicative of physiological dependence (Miller, et al. 1989).

Both amphetamine and cocaine stimulate the sympathetic nervous system causing the effects observed with increased autonomic nervous system activity (see Chapter 3). It has been suggested that the increase in brain activation with the drugs is due to heightened activity at synapses that secrete norepinephrine and dopamine. Amphetamine and cocaine facilitate the release of norepinephrine and dopamine but inhibit its re-uptake by the vesicles that released them. This means that there are excesses of these neurotransmitters in the nervous system. This vastly increases the 'firing' of neurons, leading to a persistent state of arousal.

The euphoric effects are probably the result of the drug's effects on dopamine whilst the increased energy is probably caused by norepinephrine. According to Carlson (1987), cocaine activates neural circuits that are normally triggered by reinforcing events such as eating or sexual contact. Cocaine can thus be seen as an artificial producer of some of the effects of these activities. The 'crash' associated with cocaine and amphetamine use is held to be a result of the 'rush', depleting the brain of norepinephrine and dopamine.

Crack is a form of cocaine which first appeared in the 1980s. Crack is made using cocaine hydrochloride, ammonia or baking soda, and water. When the mixture is heated, the baking soda produces a 'cracking' sound. The result is a crystal which has had the hydrochloride base removed (hence the term *free basing* to describe its production). Its effects are more rapid and intense than cocaine. However, the 'crash' is also more intense, and the pleasurable effects wear off more rapidly.

1970 saw the first appearance of MDMA or 'ecstasy'. This chemical relative of amphetamine is popular amongst those who attend 'raves'. Box 13.4 below describes the effects associated with the use of MDMA.

Box 13.4 MDMA (ecstasy) and its effects

How taken: Swallowed in pill or tablet form. Sometimes taken with other mood-altering drugs.

Psychological effects: Small amounts produce a mild, euphoric 'rush', together with feelings of elation. This can last for ten hours. Self-confidence is increased and sexual confidence gained. Large amounts trigger hallucinations. Users report the effects of MDMA to be intermediate between amphetamine and LSD (see Box 13.6). Serotonin and dopamine are the neurotransmitters affected.

Long-term consequences: Ecstasy causes extreme dehydration and hyperthermia which leads to a form of heatstroke. This can produce convulsions, collapse, and death. Blood pressure also rises dangerously. If it becomes too high the taker may suffer a stroke and thereafter permanent brain damage. Over 50 deaths in Britain alone have been attributed to the drug. The high temperature dance environment of Britain's 'rave' scene no doubt increases the hyperthermia. Depression and panic attacks are also associated with long-term use as are kidney and liver failure.

Effects of abstinence: As Parrott & Yeomans (1995) have observed, little research has been carried out into the effects of ecstasy, let alone the effects of abstinence, despite the fact that several million doses of the drug are annually consumed worldwide. According to the Department of Health (1994), tolerance occurs but physiological dependence does not.

THE OPIATES

The psychological effects of the sticky resin produced by the unripe seed pods of the opium poppy have been known about for centuries. Indeed, it was the ancient Sumerians who, 4,000 years before the birth of Christ, gave the poppy its name: it means 'plant of joy'. One constituent of opium is *morphine*. From morphine, two other opiates can be extracted. These are *codeine* and *heroin*.

In general, the opiates depress neural functioning and suppress physical sensations and responses to stimulation. For reasons which will become clear shortly, the opiates are effective in reducing pain (that is, they are *analgesics*). In Europe, morphine was first used as an analgesic during the Franco-Prussian war. However, it quickly became apparent that morphine produced physiological dependence, which became known as 'the soldier's disease'. In 1898, in an attempt to cure this physiological dependence, the Bayer Company of Germany developed heroin (so named because it was the 'hero' that would cure the 'soldier's disease'). Unfortunately, heroin also causes physiological dependence, and has a number of unpleasant side-effects. These are described in Box 13.5 opposite.

Box 13.5 Heroin and its effects

How taken: Can be smoked, inhaled through the nostrils, or intravenously injected.

Psychological effects: Users term the immediate effects the 'rush', which is described as an overwhelming sensation of pleasure similar to sexual orgasm but affecting the whole body. Subjectively, such effects are so pleasurable that they eradicate any thoughts of food or sex. Heroin rapidly decomposes into morphine which produces feelings of euphoria, well-being, relaxation, and drowsiness.

Long-term consequences: Increases in aggressiveness and social isolation have been reported as has a decrease in general physical activity. Although the findings relating to physical damage are mixed, the use of any opiate may damage the body's immune system leading to increased susceptibility to infection. The impurity of heroin sold to users, their lack of an adequate diet, and the risks from contaminated needles also increase the dangers to health. Overdoses are common, but drugs like *naloxone* act as opiate antagonists (see page 12), although their effects are not long-lasting and such drugs cannot control heroin use.

Effects of abstinence: Heroin use produces both physiological and psychological dependence. Tolerance develops very quickly. The symptoms of withdrawal initially involve the experience of flu-like symptoms. These progress to tremors, stomach cramps and chills, which alternate with sweating, rapid pulse, high blood pressure, insomnia and diarrhoea. Often, the skin breaks out into goose bumps resembling a plucked turkey (hence the term 'cold turkey' to describe attempts to abstain). The legs also jerk uncontrollably (hence the term 'kicking the habit'). Such symptoms usually disappear within one week.

As we saw in Chapter 1, the brain produces its own opiates called *opioid peptides* or *endorphins*. When we engage in behaviours important to our survival, endorphins are released into the fluid that bathes the cells of the brain. Endorphin molecules stimulate *opiate receptors* on some of the neurons in the brain. These are similar to those post-synaptic receptors that respond to neurotransmitters. One consequence of this is an intensely pleasurable effect just like that reported by heroin users, which has led some researchers to suggest that endorphins are important in mood regulation. Another consequence is analgesia, the lessening of pain presumably serving to prevent us from running away if we are hurt during fighting or mating (Carlson, 1987).

According to Snyder (1977), the regular taking of opiates overloads the endorphin sites within the brain, with the result that the brain stops its own production of them. When the user abstains, neither the naturally occurring endorphins nor the opiates are available. The internal mechanism for regulating pain is thus severely disrupted, and the person experiences the painful withdrawal symptoms described in Box 13.5.

In order to treat the physiological dependence associated with opiate use, a number of synthetic opiates (or opioids) have been created. These include *methadone*, which acts more slowly than heroin and does not produce the 'rush' associated with heroin use. Whether methadone is a suitable substitute is debatable. While methadone users are less likely to take heroin, they are still taking a drug and are likely to become at least psychologically dependent on it so that the withdrawal symptoms associated with opiate use can be avoided.

THE HALLUCINOGENS

Hallucinogens are the drugs which produce the most profound effects on consciousness. For that reason they are sometimes termed *psychedelics* (which means 'mind expanding' or 'mind manifesting'). The effects include changes in perception, thought processes and emotions. Two of the four most well-researched hallucinogens are naturally derived. *Mescaline* comes from the peyote cactus, whilst *psilocybin* is obtained from the mushroom *psilocybe mexicana* (the so-called 'magic mushroom'). The other two hallucinogens, *lysergic acid diethylamide* (or *LSD*) and *phencyclidine* (or *PCP*) are chemically synthesised. We shall look in detail at these chemically synthesised hallucinogens.

LSD was first synthesised in 1943 by Albert Hoffmann, a Swiss chemist. After accidentally ingesting some of the chemical Hoffmann reported that he 'perceived an uninterrupted stream of fantastic pictures, extraordinary shapes with intense, kaleidoscopic play of colours'. In the 1960s, LSD was used for a variety of purposes including the treatment of emotional and behavioural disturbances, and as a pain reliever for the terminally ill. It was also believed that LSD could serve useful military purposes (see Neill, 1987).

Its popularity as a 'recreational' drug was largely inspired by Timothy Leary, a Harvard University psychologist, who coined the slogan 'turn on, tune in, and drop out', which became the byword of the 1960s hippy movement. Box 13.6 describes the effects associated with the use of LSD.

Box 13.6 LSD and its effects

How taken: LSD is usually impregnated on blotting paper and swallowed. Unlike other drugs, the onset of its effects may be delayed for an hour or more.

Psychological effects: LSD produces heightened and distorted sensory experiences such as sights and sounds being intensified or changing form and colour. Hallucinations may also be tactile. Such effects may be pleasurable or terrifying (a 'bad trip') depending on mood and expectations. The subjective passage of time is distorted and appears to slow dramatically. *Synaesthesia*, the blending of sensory experiences, may also occur. Music, for example, may yield visual sensations. *Depersonalisation* has also been reported and is experienced as a state in which the body is perceived as being separate from the self. Users report being able to see themselves from afar. Impaired judgement also occurs, even though the subjective feeling may be of an 'increased understanding' of the world.

Long-term consequences: Some users experience *flashbacks*, that is, distorted perceptions or hallucinations that occur days or weeks after the drug has been taken. These might be physiological *or* psychological in origin. There is no evidence to suggest that LSD itself can cause death, but there are numerous examples of users being killed as a result of its psychological effects. Reproductive processes also seem to be affected by long-term use, since some women rarely conceive when they are taking the drug. The reason for this is not known.

Effects of abstinence: LSD use does not seem to lead to physiological dependence and withdrawal. However, tolerance can develop rapidly. If taken repeatedly, few effects are produced until its administration is stopped for about a week. Whether LSD produces psychological dependence is hotly debated (McWilliams & Tuttle, 1973).

The chemical structure of some hallucinogens closely resembles the neurotransmitters dopamine and serotonin. According to Jacobs (1987), hallucinogen molecules compete with the normal activity of these neurotransmitters in the brain. It has been suggested that serotonin plays a role in the production of dream-like activity (see Chapter 11). The inhibition of these neurons at any time other than during sleep can explain why we do not dream during the waking hours. However, suppression of serotonin by hallucinogenic drug molecules might cause 'dream mechanisms' to be activated, with the result that the person experiences a 'waking dream' or hallucination (Carlson, 1987).

Siegel (1982) has suggested that all hallucinations, whether caused by drugs, oxygen starvation or sensory deprivation, take the same form. Usually they begin with simple geometric forms (such as a spiral), continue with more meaningful images (such as 'replays' of past emotional experiences) and, at the peak of the hallucination, produce a feeling of separation from the body and dream-like experiences which can appear frighteningly real. The fact that all hallucinations seem to take the same form suggests that the same mechanisms may be involved in their production.

Phencyclidine (or PCP or 'angel dust') was first synthesised in the 1950s for use as a surgical anaesthetic. However, its use was discontinued when its psychoactive side-effects became apparent. Usually combined with tobacco and smoked, it can be classified as a hallucinogen because it produces distortions in body image and depersonalisation. In low doses, users report euphoria, heightened awareness, and a sense that all problems have disappeared. In high doses, however, it has stimulant, depressant, and (not surprisingly given its original purpose) analgesic properties. Effects include violence, panic, psychotic behaviour, disrupted motor activity, and chronic depression. These may persist for weeks after a single dose.

Long-term use of PCP is associated with what Smith and his associates (1978) have termed the four 'Cs': *combativeness* (agitated or violent behaviour), *catatonia* (a muscular rigidity of the body), *convulsions* (epileptic-like seizures) and *coma* (a deep, unresponsive sleep). Users also report difficulty in thinking clearly and emotional blandness. Although PCP does not produce physiological dependence, there is evidence to suggest that users may become psychologically dependent (Bolter, et al. 1976).

CANNABIS

Cannabis is one of the most widely used 'recreational' drugs, second only in popularity to alcohol. The *cannabis sativa* plant grows wild in many parts of the world and was cultivated over 5,000 years ago in China. The psychoactive ingredient of the plant is *delta-9-tetrahydrocannabinol* or *THC*. THC is found in the branches and leaves of the male and female plants (*marijuana*), but is highly concentrated in the resin of the female plant. *Hashish* (or 'hash') is derived from the sticky resin and is more potent than marijuana. The effects associated with cannabis are described in Box 13.7 below.

Box 13.7   Cannabis and its effects

How taken: Usually smoked with tobacco in a 'joint'. Those who prefer not to smoke swallow it. When smoked, the drug finds its way to the brain inside seven seconds.

Psychological effects: Small amounts produce a mild, pleasurable 'high', consisting of relaxation, a loss of social inhibition, intoxication, and a humorous mood. Speech becomes slurred and co-ordination is impaired. Other effects include increased heart rate, lack of concentration, and enhanced appetite ('the munchies'). Short-term memory is also affected, and there is an inability to retain information for later use. According to Weil & Zinberg (1969), it is not unusual for a user to begin a sentence and then forget what the sentence was about before it has been completed. As with other drugs, the effects are somewhat dependent on social context and other factors. Thus, some users report negative effects such as fear, anxiety and confusion.

Large amounts result in hallucinogenic reactions such as the perceived slowing of time and amplified sensitivity to colours, sounds, tastes, and smells. However, these subjective reports are not borne out by objective measures. As well as increased awareness of bodily states (such as increased heart rate), sexual sensations are also heightened.

Long-term consequences: THC remains in the body for as long as a month. Cannabis may disrupt the male sex hormones and, in females, influence the menstrual cycle. Its use during pregnancy has been associated with impaired foetal growth, and cannabis is more damaging to the throat and lungs than cigarette smoking. Long-term use may lead to *amotivational syndrome*, that is, a general lack of energy or motivation. However, this may simply reflect the fact that users differ psychologically from non-users.

Effects of abstinence: There is some debate over whether cannabis leads to a physiological dependence. Tolerance is, as we know, a sign of physiological dependence, but with cannabis *reverse tolerance* has been reported. Thus, regular use leads to a lowering of the amount needed to achieve the initial effects. This could be due to a build-up of THC which takes a long time to be metabolised. An alternative explanation is that the user becomes more adept at inhaling the drug and therefore perceives its effects more quickly. Withdrawal effects (restlessness, irritability, and insomnia) have been reported, but these seem to be associated with the continuous use of very large amounts. Psychological dependence almost certainly occurs in at least some people.

Cannabis has been classified as a hallucinogen because, as Box 13.7 indicates, large amounts can produce hallucinations. However, it could also be classified as a depressant because in low doses it has a sedative effect. In very large amounts, however, it acts as a stimulant, hence our decision to classify it separately. Cannabis has been shown to have some *medical* applications. For example, it is sometimes used with glaucoma sufferers because it reduces fluid pressure in the eyes. The fact that cannabis decreases nausea and vomiting has also led to it being administered to patients with cancer who must receive chemotherapy, a treatment that induces nausea and vomiting. A third medical application is with eating disorders. Since cannabis causes an increase in appetite, the drug has been used to promote eating behaviour.

The precise biochemical mechanisms underlying the behavioural effects of THC are not known. It has been suggested that THC influences the action of the neurotransmitters norepinephrine and serotonin. As we saw in Chapter 1, acetylcholine is held to play a role in memory, and the observation that cannabis interferes with the ability to recall previously learned information might be explained in terms of the disruption of normal activity in acetylcholine-utilising neurons in the limbic system.

Conclusions

As we have seen, there are a variety of psychoactive drugs. We have concentrated on some of the drugs taken for 'recreational' purposes. The physiological and psychological effects produced by the drugs are wide-ranging. As well as being taken for the purposes of pleasure, such drugs have other uses as well.

SUMMARY

- **Psychoactive drugs** are chemical compounds which alter perceptions and behaviour by changing conscious awareness. This definition would cover drugs such as aspirin, but the focus here is on those drugs taken for **pleasure**.
- The effects of some drugs on consciousness are **lessened** with repeated use, so that larger amounts are needed to achieve the same initial effect (**tolerance**).
- **Physiological/physical dependence** refers to the body's inability to do without a drug. When someone who is physically dependent stops taking the drug, they experience **withdrawal/abstinence syndrome**.
- Physical dependence combined with tolerance defines **drug addiction**.
- Some drugs are so pleasurable that users feel driven to take them despite not being physically dependent (**psychological dependence**). Being deprived of the drug causes anxiety, whose symptoms overlap with withdrawal.
- The main classes of psychoactive drugs taken for 'recreational' purposes are **depressants/sedatives, stimulants,** the **opiates**, and **hallucinogens**. **Cannabis** does not fit into any of these categories.
- **Depressants** slow down mental processes and behaviours; **alcohol** is the most widely used. Its effects differ according to body weight, sex, and **expectations**. Usually, small amounts have a stimulating effect, including a lowering of social inhibitions. Large amounts have a sedative effect.
- Alcohol affects both cognitive and motor functions, such as reducing the ability to process recent experiences into long-term memory. Large amounts cause loss of motor coordination, and very large amounts can induce coma, and even death.

- Long-term use may increase depressive feelings, cause malnutrition and vitamin deficiency, which can lead to brain damage and damage to other major organs as well suppressing the immune system. Heavy drinking during pregnancy can produce offspring with **foetal alcohol syndrome**. Withdrawal symptoms include **delirium tremens** and can be fatal.
- In terms of ANS activity, alcohol has a relaxing effect. Its stimulating effects probably result from suppression of the brain mechanisms that normally inhibit behaviour. In large amounts, alcohol decreases neural activity, especially in the RAS; it also reduces arousal by increasing the inhibitiory effects of GABA.
- According to the **disease model of alcoholism**, some people have a genetic predisposition for the drug; **complete abstinence** is the only cure (as advocated by **Alcoholics Anonymous**). But the **social model of alcoholism** sees it as much more complex than this; people can be taught to use **controlled drinking**.
- **Barbiturates** are depressants with similar effects to alcohol. They depress neural activity (by reducing release of excitatory neurotransmitters) and so are often prescribed to induce sleep/reduce anxiety. But physiological dependence, withdrawal, and tolerance are all quite common. The **minor tranquillisers** (e.g. **Valium**) and **aromatic solvents** are also depressants.
- **Stimulants** increase the transmission of nerve impulses. **Caffeine** and **nicotine** are the most widely consumed and are legal, while **amphetamines, cocaine**, and **methylenedioxymethamphetamine/MDMA (ecstasy)**, which have much stronger effects than caffeine and nicotine, are illegal.
- **Amphetamines** increase energy and self-confi-

dence, creating the illusion that any task can be achieved; they were given to soldiers before battle in World War Two. They are also appetite suppressants and so are used as slimming pills. They are chemically similar to **epinephrine**, which stimulates the ANS, and are used to treat asthma and **narcolepsy**.

- Amphetamines and the related **methylphenidate (Ritalin)** are used in the treatment of hyperactivity in children, increasing self-control and attention span. They might work by stimulating an immature cortex to exert control over primitive brain structures.

- After the effects of amphetamines wear off, users experience a 'crash', which may encourage further use. Long-term use can produce personality changes which lead to increased aggressive and violent behaviour. **Amphetamine psychosis** involves **paranoid delusions** that are almost identical to those experienced in **paranoid schizophrenia**. Tolerance and psychological dependence develop quickly, and there is also some evidence of physiological dependence.

- **Cocaine (hydrochloride)** is a powerful CNS stimulant which has been used for centuries by Peruvian Indians who chew the leaves of the coca plant. Freud was an early European advocate of cocaine, but he became disillusioned with its side-effects. The drug is legally permitted as a local anaesthetic.

- The psychological effects of cocaine are similar to those of amphetamine, but shorter-lasting. Users also experience a 'crash' which might be counteracted by taking depressants or an opiate. Even small amounts can produce cardiac arrest and death, and long-term consequences include **cocaine psychosis**, **formication**, convulsions, respiratory failure, and bleeding into the brain. Psychological dependence definitely takes place, but more controversial is whether cocaine also produces physiological dependence, tolerance and withdrawal.

- Both amphetamine and cocaine facilitate the release of norepinephrine (associated with increased energy) and dopamine (associated with euphoria) and inhibit its re-uptake, which can account for the persistent state of arousal. Cocaine can be seen as an artificial producer of some of the pleasurable effects of eating and sexual contact.

- **Crack** is made by removing the hydrochloride base from cocaine (**free basing**), producing more rapid and intense effects than cocaine; but the 'crash' is also more intense.

- Small amounts of **ecstasy (MDMA)** produce euphoria, elation and increased self- and sexual confidence; large amounts trigger hallucinations. Long-term consequences include extreme dehydration and hyperthermia, which can result in convulsions and death. Rises in blood pressure can cause strokes and permanent brain damage. Little is known about the effects of abstinence, but tolerance is likely.

- The **opiates** are derived from the **opium** poppy, one constituent of which is **morphine**, from which **codeine** and **heroin** can be extracted. They are **analgesics.**

- **Heroin** produces an overwhelming sensation of bodily pleasure, similar to sexual orgasm, followed by relaxation and drowsiness. Long-term consequences include aggressiveness and social isolation and reduced physical activity. Any opiate can damage the immune system, and health risks are increased by impurity of heroin, lack of adequate diet, and contaminated needles. Heroin produces both physiological and psychological dependence and tolerance develops very quickly. Withdrawal involves several symptoms, including 'cold turkey' and 'kicking the habit'.

- The brain's own opiates (**opioid peptides/endorphins**) stimulate **opiate receptors** on some brain neurons, producing an intensely pleasurable effect and analgesia. Taking opiates regularly may overload the endorphin sites within the brain, so that the brain stops producing its own. When the user abstains, neither the endorphins nor the opiates are available, which accounts for the painful withdrawal symptoms.

- Synthetic opiates/opioids used to treat opiate physiological dependence include **methadone**; although methadone users are less likely to take heroin, they are likely to become at least psychologically dependent on the methadone.

- **Hallucinogens** are sometimes called **psychedelics**, because of their 'mind expanding' effects. **Mescaline** and **psilocybin** ('magic mushroom') are both naturally derived, while **lysergic acid diethylamide/LSD** and **phencyclidine/PCP** are chemically synthesised.

- **LSD** was widely used in the 1960s for treating emotional/behavioural disturbances and as an analgesic for the terminally ill; it also became widely used as a 'recreational' drug as part of the hippy movement. It produces hallucinatory experiences, which may be visual, auditory, or tactile, and which can be pleasurable or terrifying. Time seems to slow dramatically, and **synaesthesia** and **depersonalisation** are sometimes reported.

- Long-term consequences of LSD can include **flashbacks**, which may be physiological or psychological in origin. Death can occur as a result of the psychological effects of the drug. While tolerance develops rapidly, physiological dependence and withdrawal do not occur; the question of psychological dependence is more controversial.
- The chemical structure of some hallucinogens closely resembles dopamine and serotonin; as a result of competition between these neurotransmitters and hallucinogen molecules, dream mechanisms may be activated, producing 'waking dreams'/hallucinations.
- **PCP** was first used as a surgical anaesthetic. It causes distortions in body image and depersonalisation, and, in small doses, euphoria and heightened awareness. High doses have stimulant, depressant, and analgesic properties, and effects include violence, panic, psychotic behaviour, disrupted motor activity, and chronic depression. Long-term use is associated with **combativeness, catatonia, convulsions,** and **coma**, as well as psychological dependence.
- **Cannabis** is second only to alcohol in popularity as a 'recreational' drug. The psychoactive ingredient of the **cannabis sativa** plant is **delta-9-tetrahydrocannabinol/THC**, which is found in the branches and leaves of the male and female plants (**marijuana**). **Hashish** ('hash') is derived from the resin of the female plant and is more potent than marijuana.
- Small amounts of cannabis produce relaxation, loss of social inhibition, intoxication, and a humorous mood. Short-term memory is impaired, concentration is reduced, and appetite is increased. Large amounts produce a slowing down of perceived time, a heightened sensory sensitivity, increased heart rate and sexual sensations.
- **THC** can remain in the body for up to a month and can disrupt hormonal activity in both sexes. Used during pregnancy, cannabis can impair foetal growth, and it is more damaging to the throat and lungs than tobacco. Long-term use may produce **amotivational syndrome**. There is evidence of **reverse tolerance**; this could be due to a build-up of THC in the body, or the user may inhale the drug more efficiently. Psychological dependence occurs in some people, but withdrawal effects only occur after using very large amounts continuously. It may produce its effects by influencing norepinephrine, serotonin and acetylcholine.
- Cannabis can have depressant, stimulant, and hallucinogenic effects, depending on the amount taken. It has several **medical** applications, in the treatment of glaucoma, cancer (chemotherapy) and eating disorders.

PART 4
Motivation, emotion and stress

MOTIVATION AND THE BRAIN

Introduction and overview

The word 'motive' comes from the Latin 'movere' which means 'move'. Psychologists see motives as inner directing forces that arouse an organism and direct its behaviour towards some goal. Most psychologists would accept Geen's (1995) description of motivation as 'the processes involved in the initiation, direction, and energisation of individual behaviour' and most would agree with Miller's (1962) view of the study of motivation as involving 'all those pushes and prods – biological, social, and psychological – that defeat our laziness and move us, either eagerly or reluctantly, to action'. Put differently, the study of motivation is the study of the *why* of behaviour which, in a sense is what psychology is all about! Our aim in this chapter is to look at the role played by the brain in the motivational states of hunger and thirst. We will also look at the impact that external factors can have on these behaviours.

Hunger

If the body is to survive, it must have appropriate amounts of food, water, air, sleep and heat. Our bodies contain complex mechanisms that maintain proper levels of these essentials. In Chapter 2, we labelled the body's tendency to maintain a steady state *homeostasis,* and noted that it refers to the maintenance of a proper balance of physiological variables such as body temperature, fluid conservation, and the amount of nutrients stored in the body. Early researchers likened homeostasis to a *ther-*

mostat: when room temperature rises above the *set-point,* the heating system switches off and stays switched off until the temperature falls to the set-point. This analogy has dominated much biopsychological thinking and underlies at least some of the proposals concerning hunger (and thirst) that have been advanced.

On the assumption that hunger and eating are at least partially, if not wholly, controlled by some internal homeostatic mechanism, what are the means by which the body's need for food is conveyed to the brain and what part of the brain receives these messages and sends signals to the body to initiate eating?

When we are hungry, the walls of the stomach contract producing 'hunger pangs'. When we have eaten, the stomach is full and we 'feel bloated' or *satiated.* One of the earliest theories of eating proposed that it was the *stomach* which, via the *vagus nerve* (the connection between the stomach/gastrointestinal tract and the brain), sent information to the brain informing it when we are hungry and when we are full. In an experiment conducted by Cannon & Washburn (1912), Washburn swallowed a balloon which was inflated by air introduced through an attached tube. Washburn's stomach contractions forced air out of the balloon and activated a recording device. Whenever Washburn felt a pang of hunger he pressed a key which activated a recording device. The results showed that each time Washburn reported a hunger pang, a large stomach contraction occurred, suggesting that hunger was controlled by the stomach. The experimental set-up in Cannon and Washburn's study is shown in Figure 14.1 overleaf.

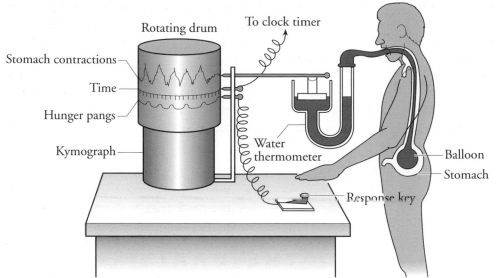

Figure 14.1 The experimental set-up in Cannon and Washburn's (1912) experiment

As appealingly simplistic as this common sense approach to hunger is, the picture is actually much more complicated than Cannon and Washburn's data suggest. For example, people whose stomachs have been surgically removed because of cancer still report feeling hungry, and cutting the connections between the gastrointestinal tract and the brain has little effect on food intake in both human and non-human animals (Pinel, 1993).

Although Cannon exaggerated the importance of stomach contractions in causing hunger, the stomach/gastrointestinal tract does play an influential role. The evidence suggests that even if the *vagus nerve* is cut, signals arising from the gut can be communicated to the brain via the circulatory system. Additionally, the presence of food in the stomach (*stomach loading*) is also important in the regulation of feeding since if the exit from the stomach to the small intestine is blocked, rats will still eat normal-sized meals. It therefore seems that information about the stretching of the stomach wall is passed to the brain (via the vagus nerve) and the brain is able in some way to control food intake.

As well as the stomach, a number of other internal stimuli involved in eating have been identified. Some of these are identified in Box 14.1 below.

Box 14.1 Some internal stimuli involved in eating

The mouth: Clearly, chewing and swallowing must provide some sensations of satiety. If this was not the case we might eat for a long time after we had eaten enough, since it takes the digestive tract time to metabolise food and send signals to the brain about food levels. Janowitz & Grossman (1949), for example, showed that when a tube is implanted into a dog's throat so that food did not reach the stomach, the animals did stop eating (although they resumed eating sooner than normal dogs).

The liver: Russek (1971) has shown that injections of glucose to the liver causes a decrease in eating and that specialised cells in the liver convey information to the brain via a nerve connection.

Hormones: It has been suggested that eating behaviour is influenced by hormones that are released into the bloodstream and circulate to the brain. One hormone, *cholecystokinin* (CCK) is produced by the walls of the intestine. Research conducted by Dockray, Gregory & Hutchinson (1978) has shown that injections of this hormone can cause satiety. CCK may, therefore, be a hormone that informs the brain about food levels in the intestines, although exactly how it does this is not known at present.

It would seem that the depletion of fats, carbohydrates (including glucose), vitamins/mineral salts, and proteins/amino acids may all play some role in initiating action in the stimuli identified in Box 14.1. The effects of changes in *blood-glucose* levels and the amounts of *fat* in the body have received most attention, and several theories have been proposed to explain the way in which such changes relay information about hunger and its converse, *satiety*.

According to *glucostatic theory*, the primary stimulus for hunger is a decrease in the level of blood-glucose *below* a certain *set-point*. Satiety is held to occur when levels rise *above* the set-point. Since glucose is the body's (and especially the brain's) primary fuel, this theory is intuitively appealing. It is also supported by some evidence. Thus, when glucose is injected into the system, eating is usually inhibited. When insulin injections (which lower blood-glucose levels) are given, eating is stimulated.

Glucostatic theory postulates the existence of a *glucostat*, an analogue of the thermostat found in a central heating system. Mayer & Marshall (1956) injected mice with *gold thioglucose* reasoning that the glucose would bind to hypothesised *glucoreceptors* (wherever they happened to be) and, because Gold is a *neurotoxin*, the tissue would be destroyed. When post-mortems were conducted, damage was found in the *ventromedial hypothalamus* (*VMH*). Since the injected mice ate large quantities of food following the injection, and since the injection damaged the VMH, Mayer and Marshall concluded that the VMH must be a *satiety centre* which 'tells' mice to stop feeding (and might possibly serve the same function in humans). We will return to the role of the VMH in eating a little later on in this chapter.

Further support for glucostatic theory came from the finding that a fall in blood-glucose level before a spontaneous meal is not just related to the onset of eating, but actually causes it. For example, Campfield, et al. (1985) found that if very small amounts of glucose were injected into the veins of rats as a decline in their blood-glucose levels occurred, the predicted meal the rat would take was 'postponed' as though the injection had removed the hunger signal.

Mayer saw the *rate* of glucose *utilisation* rather than its *absolute level* as being the most important factor in eating. However, there is little evidence to support this view and at least some to contradict it (Geiselman, 1983). Furthermore, although blood-glucose levels might be important, they cannot be the only signal to stop and start eating. As Carlson (1988) has observed, an animal that eats a meal low in carbohydrates but high in fats or protein still eats a relatively constant amount of calories even though its blood-glucose level is reduced slightly. If eating was exclusively controlled by blood-glucose levels, the animal would overeat and become fat.

A second explanation of the homeostatic mechanism regulating eating concentrates on the role of fats (or lipids) in *adipocytes*. Clumps of adipocytes form the fatty (or *adipose*) tissues of the body, and it has long been known that the level of body fat is normally maintained at a relatively constant level. According to Nisbett's (1972) version of *Lipostatic theory*, everyone has a body-weight set-point around which body weight fluctuates within quite narrow limits. Nisbett argues that this is determined by the level of fats in the adipocytes.

One line of evidence supporting lipostatic theory comes from the observation that short-term dieting programs do *not* produce long-term weight loss. As soon as the dieter stops dieting, the weight that has been lost is regained. Additional evidence comes from studies in which the *lateral hypothalamus* (*LH*) of animals is damaged. When this occurs, the animal stops eating, even when food is freely available, to the point of starvation. This condition is called *aphagia*.

Originally, this finding was assumed to indicate that the LH normally functions to *stimulate* feeding. Keesey & Powley (1975), however, showed that this is not the case. These researchers deprived animals of food so that their body weight was significantly lowered. The LH was then lesioned. Instead of eating less, which should have occurred if the LH does normally stimulate feeding, the rats ate *more*. The most plausible interpretation of this finding is that the LH does not affect feeding directly but does so *indirectly* by altering the body-weight set-point: when an animal's weight is reduced before the lesion is made, its feeding increases after the lesion in order to reach the new and higher set-point. As with the VMH, we will return to the role of the LH a little later on in this chapter.

Glucostatic theory was intended to explain the relatively short-term processes of the initiation and termination of eating, whereas lipostatic theory was a way of explaining long-term feeding habits and body-weight regulation. Both, however, share the belief that predetermined set-points exist. Some researchers do not agree with this and prefer to see body-weight as drifting around a *settling-point*, that is, a level at which the various factors that influence it try to achieve balance or equilibrium. Rather than seeing the processes involved in eating as analagous to a thermostat, Pinel (1993) prefers the analogy of a 'leaky barrel' in which the level of fat in the body is regulated around a natural settling-point just as water is in a leaky barrel.

EXTERNAL STIMULI FOR HUNGER

As if the picture concerning the internal stimuli for eating were not complex enough, it is also clearly the case that eating can be affected by external factors. In Box 14.2, we identify some of the factors that are known to be influential.

Box 14.2   Some external factors that influence eating

Habit: If we miss a meal, our hunger does not continue to grow indefinitely. Rather, it subsides sometime after the meal would normally be taken and then grows just before the scheduled time of the next one. Our hunger, then, increases and decreases according to a schedule of eating that has been **learned**.

Environment: We are much more likely to eat and feel hungry when in the presence of others who are eating. Even when we have just eaten, we may join friends for some company only to find ourselves joining in their meal!

Culture: What is accepted as food is shaped by culture (and, indeed, by habits acquired early in life). Ducks' feet and frogs' legs, for example, are enjoyed by members of some cultures but are rarely eaten in our own culture.

Palatibility: The sight, smell and taste of food can all influence our eating. For example, even when children have just eaten, and do not feel at all hungry, they will still eat M&Ms (Rodin & Slochower, 1976). Pinel (1993) has noted that whilst we have an innate preference for sweet tastes, we can also learn the relationship between taste and the post-ingestinal consequences of eating food. In *taste aversion studies*, for example, findings indicate that animals learn to avoid novel tastes that are followed by illness. By contrast, a sick rat that tastes a novel food and then recovers will display an acquired preference for that flavour, a phenomenon termed the *medicine preference effect*.

As Box 14.2 indicates, eating is far from a straightforward behaviour to explain. The many internal and external factors interact, often in complex ways. For example, however palatable a food is, we find several small but different foods more interesting than one large and specific food. Given access to only one type of food we demonstrate *sensory-specific satiety*, that is, we

become tired of it. Rather than eat four yoghurts of the same flavour, then, we would prefer to eat four different flavoured yoghurts. Sensory-specific satiety encourages the consumption of a varied diet, and we are also capable of learning which diets best meet our biological needs. Mexicans, for example, increased the calcium in their bodies by mixing small amounts of mineral lime to their tortillas.

The fact that we sometimes eat when we are not hungry and some people (such as hunger strikers) do not eat when they are hungry tells us that hunger is neither necessary nor sufficient for eating even though there is usually a close relationship between them. Space does not permit us to explore the relationship between internal and external factors further, but an interesting discussion can be found in Blundell & Hill (1995).

THE HYPOTHALAMUS AND EATING

As long ago as 1902, Alfred Frolich, a Viennese physician, observed that tumours near the hypothalamus caused overeating (or *hyperphagia*) and *obesity*. In the late 1930s, the introduction of stereotaxic apparatus (see Chapter 4) allowed experimenters to assess the effects of experimentally induced damage to particular areas of the hypothalamus on the eating behaviour of non-human animals.

Earlier on, we noted that Mayer & Marshall's (1956) findings suggested that 'glucoreceptors' might be located in the VMH and that the VMH might act as a satiety centre. In fact, the role of the VMH as a satiety centre had been proposed some years previously by Hetherington & Ranson (1942). These researchers showed that a VMH lesioned rat will overeat and become grotesquely fat, doubling or even trebling its normal body weight as shown in Figure 14.2 opposite.

Subsequent research showed that the VMH hyperphagia syndrome has two distinct phases. The *dynamic phase* begins as soon as the animal regains consciousness following surgical damage to the VMH. This phase is characterised by several weeks of grossly excessive overeating and rapid weight gain. As the animal approaches its maximum weight, eating gradually declines to a level just sufficient to maintain a stable level of obesity. The *static phase* is a period of stability in which the animal 'defends' its new body weight. If it is deprived of food until it loses a substantial amount of weight, it will temporarily increase its intake until the lost weight is gained. If, however, the animal is force-

Figure 14.2   A hyperphagic rat

fed, it will temporarily reduce its intake until the excess is lost. Research also revealed that if the VMH is electrically or chemically stimulated (or 'turned on'), a rat will terminate eating until the stimulation is stopped.

We referred to the role of the LH in eating behaviour earlier on when we considered the findings of research conducted by Keesey & Powley (1975). The first researchers to observe the aphagic effects of LH damage were Anand & Brobeck (1951) who found that if the damage was extensive enough rats would actually starve to death. Additionally, it was also discovered that electrically stimulating the LH caused a rat to start eating. These findings led to the conclusion that the LH was the 'start feeding' centre in contrast to the VMH's role as the 'stop eating' centre.

The findings concerning the VMH and the LH led to what is known as the *dual hypothalamic control theory of eating*. According to this, the VMH and LH receive information about nutrient levels in the body and operate together to maintain a relatively constant level of satiety. Thus, the LH 'turns on' hunger and the VMH 'turns' it off. As Green (1994) has noted, it seems likely that the hypothalamus can initiate and terminate eating but that it needs information from peripheral regulatory factors to do this (and glucostatic and lipostatic theories suggest two possible mechanisms). However,

exactly how the VMH and LH interact with respect to eating is still unclear.

Traditionally, biopsychologists have assumed that obesity is a consequence of overeating in VMH lesioned animals. Recently, however, it has been suggested that obesity may be a *cause* of overeating. It is possible that VMH lesions increase *lipogenesis* (the body's tendency to produce fat) and decrease *lipolysis* (the body's tendency to release fats into the bloodstream). Because this would result in calories being converted to fat at a much higher than normal rate, an animal would be forced to keep eating in order to ensure that it had enough calories in its blood for immediate energy needs. One finding which supports this suggestion is that rats with VMH lesions accumulate more fat than controls, even when they eat the same amount of food (Friedman & Stricker, 1976).

The role of the VMH is further complicated by the observation that VMH lesioned rats show an increased 'fussiness' about the *taste* of food. Ordinarily, hungry rats will eat food even if it has an unpleasant taste (as, for example, occurs when bitter-tasting quinine is added to it). Such food will not be eaten by the VMH lesioned rat even if it becomes *underweight* (Teitelbaum, 1955). This suggests that such rats become more sensitive to *external cues* (such as the taste of food) than to *internal cues* (such as blood-sugar level) and therefore the VMH may also play a role in this aspect of eating.

It has also been found that whilst a rat with damage to the VMH does eat more food than normal, it does so only if the food is freely available. If the rat has to work for food by, for example, having to press a lever or lift a heavy lid, it actually eats less than a normal animal. Some obese humans behave in a parallel way and also respond to the availability of food. They are, for example, less willing to find food or prepare it in some way. Although human obesity is almost certain to have physiological correlates, we must remember that eating is influenced by many other factors, and that an account of obesity based only on physiological factors is far too simplistic.

Research findings concerning the LH are also more complex than dual hypothalamic theory proposes. For example, whilst rats with LH lesions initially do not eat, they can be coaxed into eating by first being fed through a tube. After several weeks of this, they begin to eat by themselves provided they are given palatable food (Teitelbaum & Epstein, 1962). These findings challenge the idea that the LH is a discrete 'eating centre' as does the finding that damage to the LH causes changes in behaviour that are not related to eating. The evidence indicates that animals with LH damage fail to groom themselves, have difficulty with balance, and demonstrate *sensory neglect*, that is, they show little interest in almost *any* stimuli. The additional finding that eating can also be elicited by stimulation of other areas of the hypothalamus as well as the amygdala, hippocampus, thalamus and frontal cortex also challenges the simple idea that the LH is a discrete 'hunger centre'.

As we noted earlier on, the evidence suggests that damage to the LH affects weight indirectly by altering the body-weight set-point and it is possible that this is also the case with the VMH. These findings would seem to indicate that the VMH and LH are not *absolutely* essential for regulating hunger and eating. So whilst the immediate effect of VMH and LH lesions might be to destroy the capacity to regulate eating and body weight, this is not necessarily the case over the long term. However, the fact that lesions in these structures appear to affect the set-point does strongly implicate them in long-term weight control.

The belief that the hypothalamus is the neurological key to understanding hunger has, then, not always produced data which can be explained in a simple way. The anatomical complexity of the hypothalamus makes it even more difficult to assess its role. For example, VMH lesions also damage the axons that connect the *paraventricular nucleus* (*PVN*) with certain parts of the brain stem. If CCK (see Box 14.1) is injected into the PVN, food intake is inhibited (Pinel, 1993). Additionally, neurotransmitters (see Chapter 1) in the medial hypothalamus also appear to play an important role in eating behaviour. We tend to eat sweet or starchy carbohydrate-laden foods when we are tense or depressed (Carlson, 1987). Carbohydrates help increase *serotonin* levels, and depression is associated with lower than normal levels of this neurotransmitter. *Noradrenaline*, by contrast, stimulates carbohydrate intake. One potential application of this would be the use of food substitutes that mimic the biochemical effects of carbohydrates to treat stress-related food cravings.

With continued advances in methodology, we are constantly discovering new information about the processes involved in eating and how such processes are regulated in the brain. Current biopsychological thinking sees the hypothalamus as just *one part* of a system in the brain that regulates eating and that other areas (such as the limbic system) also play important roles.

Drinking

As with eating, numerous theories have been proposed to explain the onset and termination of drinking. According to the *dry mouth theory of thirst*, receptors in the mouth and throat play a major role in determining thirst and satiety. However, 'sham drinking' studies, in which liquid swallowed down the throat does not pass into the stomach, indicate that whilst animals drink a normal amount and then stop, they return to drinking quickly afterwards unless water is placed in the stomach. Thus, internal signals rather than the amount that has been swallowed would appear to govern how much is drunk.

THE HYPOTHALAMUS AND DRINKING

One important internal signal in drinking is *cellular dehydration*. It would seem that certain cells in the *lateral preoptic area of the hypothalamus* (*LPH*) are sensitive to cellular dehydration and the activation of these causes us to drink until enough fluid has been consumed to restore the balance. The level of fluid inside the cells is affected by levels of salt in the blood. When these are high, water leaves the cells by *osmosis* (and hence this type of thirst is often referred to as *osmotic thirst*). It is this that causes the cells to become dehydrated.

The *osmoreceptors*, the name given to the cells, seem to shrink themselves when the brain is fluid-depleted and as a result of this two hypothalamic effects are produced. The first is the production of *antidiuretic hormone* (*ADH*) by the pituitary gland (see Chapter 3). This causes the kidneys to reabsorb water which would otherwise be excreted as urine. The second hypothalamic effect is the generation of thirst.

In addition to cellular dehydration, a lowered water level reduces the volume of blood in the body which lowers blood pressure. This *volumetric thirst* is held to stimulate *baroreceptors* which are located in the heart, kidneys, and veins. Volumetric thirst is caused by bleeding, vomiting, diarrhoea, and sweating. The baroreceptors then trigger the secretion of ADH which causes the kidneys to retain water. The kidneys then release the hormone *angiotensin* which circulates to the hypothalamus resulting in the initiation of drinking behaviour.

Whilst we have a reasonable understanding of thirst,

our understanding of what stops us drinking is less clear. The observation that is particularly difficult to explain is that we normally stop drinking well before the new supply of fluid reaches the *extracellular* (that is, blood plasma) or *intracellular* (that is, the fluid portion of the cell cytoplasm) compartments of the body. However, one plausible hypothesis is that cells in the small intestine send a message to the hypothalamus when enough liquid has been consumed (Rolls, Wood & Rolls, 1980).

PRIMARY AND SECONDARY DRINKING

Like hunger, thirst is influenced by external as well as internal factors. *Primary drinking* occurs when there is a physiological need, but we sometimes engage in *secondary drinking*, that is, drinking which is not caused by a physiological need. An example of secondary drinking would be the consumption of many pints of beer during the course of an evening. It is highly likely that secondary drinking occurs as a result of learning and reinforcement. Drinking beer, for example, makes us feel good; drinking tea when offered a cup in the afternoon is a sociable thing to do; we may even drink because we wish to be like someone portrayed in a media 'message'. Moreover, what we drink can be influenced by many external factors. Ice-cold lemonade in February, for example, is as popular a drink as a cup of piping hot cocoa on a sunny August afternoon.

Conclusions

Although the relationship between the body and brain is complex, in the motivated behaviours of eating and drinking it has been at least partially explained by biopsychological research. The important brain structure in eating and drinking would seem to be the hypothalamus which receives information from various parts of the body concerning tissue needs. Yet whilst the hypothalamus is important, we have also seen that external factors play an important role in eating and drinking. Exclusively physiological accounts of these motivated behaviours are, therefore, unlikely to be true.

SUMMARY

- Psychologists see motives as inner directing forces that arouse an organism and direct its behaviour towards some goal. The study of motivation is concerned with the **why** of behaviour.
- For our biological survival, our body needs certain amounts of food, water, air, sleep and heat; **homeostasis** is the process which maintains a proper balance of these physiological variables. The analogy between homeostasis and a **thermostat** has dominated biopsychological theories of hunger and thirst.
- When we feel hungry, the stomach walls contract, producing 'hunger pangs'; when we have eaten, the stomach is full and we feel bloated or **satiated**. An early theory of eating proposed that the **stomach**, via the **vagus nerve**, sends information to the brain as to when we are hungry and full. This seemed to have been supported by Cannon and Washburn's famous experiment, in which Washburn swallowed a balloon used to measure his stomach contractions.

- However, people whose stomachs have been surgically removed still report feeling hungry, and cutting the connections between the gastrointestinal tract and the brain has little effect on food intake in both human and non-human animals. But this does **not** mean that the stomach/gastrointestinal tract does not play an important part; even if the vagus nerve is cut, signals from the gut travel to the brain via the circulatory system, and **stomach loading** also conveys important information about the stretching of the stomach.
- Apart from the stomach, **chewing** and **swallowing** provide sensations of satiety much faster than signals from the digestive tract can reach the brain. The **liver** contains specialised cells which convey information to the brain about satiety, and the walls of the **intestine** produce a hormone called **cholecystokinin/CCK** which is thought to inform the brain about food levels in the intestines.

- The depletion of fats, carbohydrates (including glucose, the body's and especially the brain's primary fuel), vitamins/mineral salts, and proteins/amino acids may all be involved in causing hunger and satiety. Theories of hunger and eating have concentrated on the effects of changes in **blood-glucose** levels and the amount of body **fat.**

- According to **glucostatic theory**, the primary stimulus for hunger is a decrease in blood-glucose **below** a certain **set-point**; satiety occurs when levels rise **above** the set-point. When glucose is injected into the system, eating is usually inhibited; when insulin (which lowers blood-glucose levels) is injected, eating is stimulated.

- The theory proposes a **glucostat**. Mayer and Marshall injected mice with **gold thioglucose**, reasoning that the glucose would bind to hypothetical **glucoreceptors**, and, because gold is a **neurotoxin**, the tissue would be destroyed. Postmortems showed damage in the **ventromedial hypothalamus/VMH**, which, since the mice ate large quantities of food, they inferred must be a **satiety centre**.

- A fall in blood-glucose before a spontaneous meal actually **causes** eating to begin, although there is some debate as to whether it is the **absolute level** that is crucial, rather than the **rate** of glucose **utilisation**. However, if eating was controlled exclusively by blood-glucose levels, an animal that ate a meal low in carbohydrates but high in fats or protein would overeat and become fat; in fact, it still eats a relatively constant amount of calories despite slightly lowered blood-glucose.

- Clumps of **adipocytes** form the body's fatty (**adipose**) tissues; the level of body fat is normally maintained at a relatively constant level. According to **lipostatic theory**, everyone has a body-weight set-point around which body-weight fluctuates within quite narrow limits; this is determined by the fat levels in the adipocytes.

- This is supported by the observation that short-term dieting does not produce long-term weight loss. Damaging an animal's **lateral hypothalamus/LH** causes **aphagia**, even when food is freely available. This does **not** show that the LH usually **stimulates** feeding, because if an animal's body weight is lowered **before** the LH is damaged, it will eat **more**; this implies that the LH affects feeding **indirectly** by altering the body-weight set-point. This is further support for the lipostatic theory.

- Glucostatic theory was intended to explain short-term eating behaviours, while lipostatic theory was intended to explain long-term habits and body-weight regulation. But both believe in predetermined set-points. Others prefer to see body-weight as drifting around a **settling point**, which uses a leaky barrel as an analogy (rather than a thermostat).

- Eating is influenced by several **external** factors, such as **habit**, the social **environment**, **culture**, and the **palatability** of food. Although we have an innate preference for sweet tastes, we can also learn the relationship between taste and the consequences of ingesting certain foods; this is demonstrated in **taste aversion studies** and the **medicine preference effect**.

- There is a complex interaction between internal and external factors. For example, access to only one type of food (however palatible it might be) produces **sensory-specific satiety**, which encourages the consumption of a varied diet. Hunger is neither necessary nor sufficient for eating, although they are usually correlated.

- A VMH lesioned rat will overeat (**hyperphagia**) and become grotesquely fat. This has a **dynamic phase**, in which the animal's maximum weight is attained, and a **static phase**, in which the animal 'defends' its new body weight.

- If damage to the LH is extensive enough, rats will starve to death; electrically stimulating the LH causes rats to start eating. These findings led to the conclusion that the LH is the 'start feeding' centre, while the VMH is the 'stop eating' centre. Together, they operate to maintain a relatively constant level of satiety (**dual hypothalamic control theory of eating**).

- It is possible that VMH lesions increase **lipogenesis** and decrease **lipolysis**; this would result in calories being converted to fat at a much higher than normal rate, causing an animal to keep eating in order to ensure that it had enough calories for immediate energy needs. This suggests that obesity is a **cause**, not a consequence, of overeating.

- VMH lesioned rats, unlike hungry rats with an intact brain, show increased fussiness about the **taste** of food, suggesting that they become more sensitive to **external cues** than to **internal cues**. Also, lesioned rats will only consume more food if they do not have to work for it, and there are some interesting parallels here with obese people.

- Rats with LH lesions can eventually be coaxed into eating, and after several weeks wll eat palatable food by themselves. This challenges the view of the LH as a discrete eating centre, as does the finding that LH damage causes changes in behaviour that are unrelated to eating, including **sensory neglect**. Eating can also be triggered by stimulation of other areas of the hypothalamus, as well as structures in the limbic system.

- VMH lesions also damage the axons that connect the **paraventricular nucleus/PVN** with certain parts of the brain stem. If CCK is injected into the PVN, food intake is inhibited, and the medial hypothalamus also seems to be involved in eating behaviour. The hypothalamus appears to be just **one part** of a larger system.

- According to the **dry-mouth theory of thirst**, receptors in the mouth and throat play a major role in determining thirst and satiety. But **sham drinking** studies suggest that internal signals rather than the amount swallowed determines how much is drunk.

- Cells (**osmoreceptors**) in the **lateral preoptic area of the hypothalamus/LPH** are sensitive to **cellular dehydration**. Fluid levels in the cells are affected by salt levels in the blood; when these are high, water leaves the cells by **osmosis** (**osmotic thirst**), causing cellular dehydration.

- The osmoreceptors shrink when the brain is fluid-depleted. This leads to (a) the production of **antidiuretic hormone/ADH** by the pituitary gland, which causes the kidneys to reabsorb water, and (b) to the generation of thirst.

- A reduced water level reduces the body's blood volume, which lowers blood pressure. This **volumetric thirst** stimulates **baroreceptors** located in the heart, kidneys and veins, in turn triggering the secretion of ADH which causes the kidneys to retain water. The kidneys then release **angiotensin** which reaches the hypothalamus, resulting in drinking.

- Why we stop drinking is much less clear than why we start. We normally stop well before the fluid intake reaches the **extracellular** or **intracellular** body compartments; cells in the small intestine might signal the hypothalamus to stop drinking.

- **Primary drinking** is caused by physiological (internal) need, while **secondary drinking** is caused by non-physiological (external) need, which also determines **what** we drink.

THEORIES OF MOTIVATION

Introduction and overview

One of the major aims of psychological research has been to explain what motivates us to act in certain ways. A number of theories of motivation have been proposed. As we might expect given the findings presented in the previous chapter, some of these adopt a distinctly physiological approach. Others, however, are primarily psychological in their orientation. Our aim in this chapter is to examine these theories and explore the contrast between the various physiological and non-physiological alternatives that have been advanced. We will begin by looking at some types of motive that have been identified and researched.

Types of motive

The range of motivation is very broad. As we will see, some behaviours, such as drinking a glass of water, can be explained in terms of reducing a 'need' (and we will look at the meaning of 'need' shortly). Other behaviours, such as smoking cigarettes when we know this causes disease, must have more complex explanations. To assess the usefulness of theories we need to identify *types* of motive. Three main categories of human behaviour can be identified. These are *biologically-based motives*, *sensation-seeking motives*, and *complex psychosocial motives*.

Biologically-based motives are rooted primarily in body tissue needs (or *drives*) such as those for food, water, air, sleep, temperature regulation, and the avoidance of pain. Although these needs are in-built, their expression is often learned. For example, hunger is caused by food deprivation and we learn to search the environment effectively for food to satisfy this basic need.

Sensation-seeking motives are apparently largely unlearned needs for certain levels of stimulation. These motives, which aim to increase rather than decrease the amount of stimulation, are most evident in the way in which we attempt to create our own sensations when placed in *sensory isolation*. The hallucinations that have been reported in so-called 'sensory deprivation' experiments may be an attempt to compensate for a lack of external stimulation. Box 15.1 identifies some of the sensation-seeking motives that have been the subject of research interest.

> **Box 15.1 Sensation-seeking motives**
>
> These are largely unlearned needs for certain levels of stimulation. These motives depend more on external stimuli than biologically-based motives. Their main function is to deal with (and often change) the environment in general. Examples include:
>
> **Activity**: The need to be active is something that affects all animals. When an animal is deprived of activity it is much more active than normal when subsequently released. Whether activity is a separate motive or a combination of motives, and whether it is unlearned or learned, is unclear. *Sensory deprivation studies*, in which virtually all sensory input is cut off, indicate that sensory deprivation appears to be intolerable for people. As well as hallucinations, people have difficulty in thinking clearly. They also experience boredom, anger and frustration. However, voluntary sensory restriction has also been associated with increased ability to gain control over negative habits such as smoking, but this is much milder than studies in which virtually all stimulation is cut off.
>
> **Curiosity and exploration**: This is a motive activated by the new and unknown, and which appears to be directed to no more a specific goal than 'finding out'. For example, children will play with toys even though there is no extrinsic reward for doing so. The evidence suggests that *unfamiliarity* and *complexity* are sometimes preferred because they are in some way more appealing. The term *novel stimulation* is occasionally used to describe this. Thus, a non-human animal that has just copulated will show an interest in sexual behaviour when presented with a 'novel' sex partner. Non-human animals will learn discrimination problems when the reward is nothing

more than a brief look around the laboratory in which they are housed.

Manipulation: Manipulation is directed towards a specific object that must be touched, handled, or played with before we are satisfied. 'Do Not Touch' signs in museums, for example, are there because curators know that our urge to touch things is irresistible. This motive is limited to primates who have agile fingers and toes and seems to be related to the need to have *tactile experience* and a need to be *soothed*. The 'worry beads' manipulated by Greeks would be an example of the latter.

Play: Many species have this innate motive and many young enjoy *practice play*, that is, behaviour which will later be used for 'serious' purposes. As Bolles (1967) has remarked, such activity might not appear to have any immediate consequences for the fulfillment of biological needs. Much of the behaviour normally associated with play can be thought of in terms of the drives for curiosity, exploration and manipulation.

Contact: This refers to the need to *touch* other people and is broader and more universal than the need for manipulation (see above). It is not limited to touching with the fingers and toes, and can involve the whole body. Unlike manipulation, which is active, contact can be passive.

Control: The need for control is linked to the need to be free from restrictions from others and to declare our own actions and not to be dictated to. When our freedom is threatened, we tend to react by reasserting it, a phenomenon which Brehm (1966) has termed *psychological reactance*. The phenomenon of *learned helplessness* (Seligman, 1975) is important here. Whilst initial negative experiences produce psychological reactance, further negative experiences produce a state in which we perceive ourselves as being unable to do anything else. Rotter (1966) has proposed that all of us have a belief about the things that control events in our everyday lives. His *locus of control* questionnaire attempts to distinguish between *internals*, who see themselves as being responsible for events in their lives and *externals*, who see events in the outside world as being particularly influential.

It is generally believed that the motivation to seek stimulation evolved because of its survival value. Organisms motivated to find out about their environment, and acquire information about it, would be more likely to survive because of an increased awareness of resources and potential dangers. Such behaviour would allow an organism to change its environment in beneficial ways.

Complex psychosocial motives demonstrate little if any relationship to biological needs. They are acquired by learning and are aroused by psychological events rather than body tissue needs. Unlike body needs, which must be satisfied, there is no biological requirement for complex psychosocial motives to be met (although we should note that much of our happiness and misery is associated with them). The attempt to list these motives was begun by Murray (1938) in his book *Explorations in Personality*. Some of the 21 that Murray identified have been more intensely researched than others. The most important of these are briefly described in Box 15.2 below.

Box 15.2   Complex psychosocial motives ('social motives')

Need for achievement (nAch): This refers to the need to meet or exceed some standard of excellence and was one of the motives identified by Murray (1938). McClelland (1958) has claimed that this need can be measured using the *Thematic Apperception Test* (or TAT) which consists of ambiguous pictures about which a story must be told. The content of the story is then scored for achievement and other important motives which are held to reflect 'hidden forces' that motivate behaviour. Differences between individuals have been correlated with *child rearing practices* such as an emphasis on competition, praise-giving, enouragement to take credit for success, and *modelling*, where parents serve as models to their children by being high in nAch themselves. Sex differences have also been claimed, with *fear of success* reported as being more common in women. The evidence is, however, mixed, and at least some studies have shown that men are just as fearful of success as women.

Need for affiliation (nAff): This refers to the desire to maintain close, friendly relations with others. Research conducted by Schachter (1959) suggests that people high in nAff find it painful to make their own decisions or be by themselves over extended periods of time. One

---

exception to this is anxiety-provoking situations. In these, people high in nAff prefer to be with others provided these others are also experiencing anxiety. According to *social comparison theory* (Festinger, 1954), this is because we prefer to affiliate with people with whom we can compare our feelings and behaviours.

Need for power (nPower): The need for power is a concern with being in charge, having status and prestige, and bending others to our will. This has both positive and negative features. For example, leaders high in nPower can impede group decision-making by failing to allow full discussion and by not encouraging full consideration of others' proposals. It is also linked to child rearing. Children whose parents allow them to be aggressive to siblings, tend in turn to produce children high in nPower. This is possibly because allowing the children to exercise power at an early age encourages them to continue to do so later on.

Need for approval (nApp): This is the desire to gain approval or some kind of sign that others like us and think we are good. The characterstics of people with a high need for approval have been studied using Crowne & Marlowes' (1964) *social desirability scale*. This measures the extent to which people try to gain others' approval by behaving in socially desirable ways. There are wide individual differences with respect to this need, but those who are high in the need for approval are conformist and tend to change their behaviour when they know they are being observed.

Instinct theories of motivation

According to instinct theories of motivation, behaviour can be explained in terms of *innate* or genetically pre-determined dispositions to act in a particular way when confronted with a certain stimulus. Instinct theories were popular at the turn of the century, largely due to Darwin's emphasis on the similarity between humans and other animals. Indeed, William James (1890) argued that humans were *more* influenced by instincts than non-humans, because we are motivated by *psy-*chosocial instincts such as 'jealousy' and 'sympathy', as well as biological instincts. James did not bother with systematic evidence to support his view that these traits were inborn. He compiled his list of instincts from arguments about their evolutionary advantages and observations of his own children's behaviour.

A number of attempts were made to identify the instincts that foster self-survival. McDougall (1908), for example, proposed that there were 12 'basic' instincts including 'hunger' and 'sex'. However, the list of instincts grew steadily larger until there were as many instincts as there were psychologists studying them. In fact, and as Tolman (1923) noted, since around 15,000 instincts were identified, there were probably more! Many of these instincts (such as 'cleanliness' and 'modesty') had little to do with basic survival, and the term instinct gradually lost its meaning and became a way of *labelling* rather than explaining behaviour, a basic flaw in any theory. Moreover, the existence of an instinct was inferred from the behaviour it was trying to explain. The existence of a 'cleanliness' instinct, for example, was inferred from the observation that most people keep themselves clean, and the fact that we keep ourselves clean was taken to indicate that we have a 'cleanliness' instinct. This sort of *circular reasoning* did little to enhance the reputation of instinct theory.

In the 1930s, instinct theory was revised by *ethologists*, that is, students of the behaviour of non-human animals in their natural habitats. Instead of using the term 'instinct', ethologists coined the term *fixed action pattern* to describe an unlearned behaviour that is universal to a particular species and occurs (or is *released*) in the presence of a naturally occurring stimulus (a so-called *sign stimulus*). Tinbergen (1951), for example, demonstrated that the sign stimulus of a red belly elicited the fixed action pattern of aggressiveness in the three-spined stickleback.

Ethologists nowadays believe that whilst instinctive behaviour is innate or pre-programmed, it is subject to modification in the face of environmental requirements. The greylag goose, for example, has an innate tendency to retrieve an egg that has rolled from its nest. However, if the egg has rolled to a dangerous place, this behaviour may change.

Whether instincts really are innate is, however, debatable. At least some of the behaviours that ethologists identify as innate are influenced by experiences occurring *before birth*. For example, Gottleib (1975) has shown that the duckling's ability to discriminate maternal calls is linked to its behaviour within the egg. At some point, the duckling's bill penetrates the interior membrane of the egg and the unhatched bird begins to 'talk to itself'. This self-vocalisation is critical to the duckling's ability at birth to identify the maternal call of its species.

More recently, *sociobiologists* have argued that innate patterns or tendencies play an important role in complex forms of *human* behaviour. Sociobiologists see the primary motivation of all organisms, both non-human and human, as ensuring the future survival of their *genes*. Our behaviour is basically *selfish*, because it is designed to ensure the survival of our genes. Far from caring for others and behaving empathically, altruistic acts are actually examples of 'genetic selfishness' designed to ensure that our genes survive. Although sociobiological theory has been influential, some psychologists regard it as oversimplifying human behaviour. They argue that whilst altruism may have a genetic component, the role of situational and personal variables should not be ignored.

Drive theories of motivation

During the 1920s, the concept of instinct was replaced by the concept of *drive*, a term first used by Woodworth (1918). Woodworth likened human behaviour to the operation of a machine. He saw machines (and hence humans) as being relatively passive and drive was the power that made machines (and humans) 'go'. Two major theories using the concept of drive have been particularly influential. These are *homeostatic drive theory*, which is a physiological theory, and *drive reduction theory* which is primarily a theory of learning.

HOMEOSTATIC DRIVE THEORY

Cannon (1929) viewed homeostasis (see Chapters 2 and 14) as an optimum level of physiological functioning that maintains the organism in a constant internal state. When a state of imbalance occurs, something must happen to correct this. For example, if our body temperature deviates from the normal temperature of 98.4°F, sweating occurs in order to bring the tempera-ture down or shivering occurs in order to raise it.

In the case of a rise in temperature, we do not need to 'do' anything since sweating is completely autonomic and purely physiological. However, in the case of an imbalance which is caused by a *tissue need*, that is a physiological need for food or drink, the hungry or thirsty animal must behave in a way which will procure food or water. It is in these cases that the concept of a homeostatic drive becomes important: a tissue need leads to an internal imbalance which causes a homeostatic drive. The homeostatic drive leads to an appropriate behaviour which results in the balance being restored and the tissue need which produced the drive being reduced.

As Green (1980) has remarked, the internal environment requires a relatively regular supply of raw materials from the external world. Some of these, such as oxygen intake, are involuntary and continuous. Others, such as eating and drinking, are voluntary and discontinuous. Although we talk about a hunger and thirst drive, we do not talk about an oxygen drive. Because of the voluntary nature of eating and drinking, hunger and thirst have been the homeostatic mechanisms most researched by biopsychologists and, as we saw in the previous chapter, they are also the drives that have been most researched in terms of the brain structures that are involved in them.

DRIVE REDUCTION THEORY

If an animal is deprived of food, then it is said to be in a state of *need*, that is, it is experiencing a tissue deficit of some sort. According to drive reduction theory, this need state is held to lead to an *unpleasant* state of bodily arousal which is called a *drive state*. Drive states activate behaviour in an attempt to *reduce* the tension associated with them. Behaviours that are successful in achieving this are strengthened whereas those that are not are weakened. According to drive reduction theory, then, organisms are *pushed* into behaviours that arise in connection with tissue needs. An animal that is thirsty is motivated to reduce the unpleasant drive state by drinking. Once this has been achieved, the behaviour ceases and arousal recedes.

It is important to note that whilst drives and needs are mostly parallel, sometimes they are not. A person who is hungry, for example, might have an overwhelming need for food but may be so weak that the drive to search for nutrition is absent. Originally, drive reduction theory focussed on biological needs or *primary drives* such as hunger and thirst. However, through association we also learn *secondary* or *acquired drives* which help in reducing primary drives. A drive for money is an example of a secondary drive that enables us to buy food and drink. These reduce the primary drives of hunger and thirst respectively and eliminate the tension they produce.

Drive reduction theory is still popular with some researchers, not least because biologically-based motives fit in with it. However, there are at least four reasons for doubting its usefulness as a comprehensive theory of motivation. First, whilst it makes sense to conceive of a hunger and thirst drive because they reduce tension or arousal, we would need to invent a drive for all instances of motivated behaviour which reduced a drive. This is as absurd as it is impossible. For example, Sheffield & Roby (1950) found that rats will eat saccharin for hours even though it has no nutritional value and so cannot reduce the physiological basis for hunger or thirst. To talk of a 'saccharin eating drive' (or, for another behaviour, a 'stamp collecting drive') just does not make sense. So whilst some behaviours clearly are motivated by drives associated with physiological need states, other are not (or at least not obviously so) and these are difficult for drive reduction theorists to explain.

Second, at least some of our behaviour *increases* rather than reduces various drives. Some people, for example, will refuse the offer of a biscuit with a mid-morning cup of coffee, even though they are hungry, in order to increase their enjoyment of a lunch-time meal. Others will make lengthy efforts to prepare a meal instead of a snack, even though the snack would reduce the hunger drive much more quickly.

Third, the theory proposes that when tension is reduced the behaviour that led to the reduction will itself be reduced. This does not always happen. For example, when we are given the opportunity to explore our surroundings we engage in *more* exploration rather than less (see Box 15.1). All of the sensation motives we identified in Box 15.1 would seem to go against drive reduction theory unless we argue for the existence of a 'manipulation drive', 'curiosity drive', and so on, which simply labels rather than explains behaviour (and recall that this was one of the criticisms we made of instinct theories of motivation).

The fourth, and perhaps the most compelling evidence against drive reduction theory comes from research conducted by Olds & Milner (1954) into the effects of electrical self-stimulation of the brain (research we briefly described in Chapter 4). Olds and Milner's research findings are discussed in Box 15.3 below.

> **Box 15.3 Electrical self-stimulation of the brain**
>
> One of the most compelling lines of evidence against the drive reduction theory of motivation are the findings reported by Olds & Milner (1954). They discovered that when an electrode is placed in the hypothalamus and rats are able to cause the electrode to stimulate the brain (by, for example, pressing a lever), they will do so thousands of times an hour. This behaviour *never* satiates and is done in preference to anything else. Thus, although exhausted, rats continued pressing the lever, would cross an electrified grid to gain access to it, and would ignore sexually receptive females.
>
> Olds and Milner's findings were subsequently obtained in a variety of other species including goldfish, dolphins, monkeys and humans. On the basis of their results, Olds and Milner proposed the existence of a *pleasure centre* in the brain. Later research has shown that the main reward site for *electrical self-stimulation of the brain* (*ES-SB*) appears to be the *median forebrain bundle* (*MFB*), a nerve tract which runs from the brain stem up to the forebrain and through the lateral hypothalamus.
>
> In other research, Olds and Milner showed that when the electrodes were placed elsewhere in the brain the opposite effects were obtained. Thus, rats would do everything they could to *avoid* stimulation of the brain, suggesting the existence of a *pain centre*. The research reported by Olds and Milner indicates that reinforcement does *not* consist of drive reduction. Rather, it produces what would be labelled as *drive*, since brain stimulation appears to *increase* drive levels.
>
> Research has also shown that stimulation of parts of the hypothalamus activate neurons which release the neurotransmitter dopamine (see Chapter 1) to a part of the brain called the *nucleus acumbens*. It is highly likely that dopamine and the nucleus acumbens are part of some sort of 'reward pathway' and that ES-SB is a 'short cut' to pleasure which eliminates the need

for drives and reinforcers. However, and as Green (1994) has remarked, although ES-SB has been demonstrated in all species that have been studied:

'It remains rather mysterious . . . (and) acts as a reminder that however much we may uncover about motivated behaviours . . . there are still many aspects of motivation, even in the rat, to be uncovered.'

Optimum level of arousal theory of motivation

On some occasions we are, as drive reduction theory proposes, motivated to reduce the tension we are experiencing. As we have noted, however, there are other occasions on which we behave as though we want to *increase* the amount of tension or excitement we experience and this seems to occur without the need to satisfy any biological need. Driving a Formula-1 car at 180 miles per hour, parachuting from an aeroplane, or climbing Mount Everest 'because it is there' are yet other observations which are difficult for drive reduction theory to explain.

The fact that we sometimes want to decrease and sometimes increase what Routtenberg (1968) terms *arousal* suggests that we have a preference for an *optimum level* of stimulation that is neither too low nor too high. Consistent with drive reduction theory, *optimum level of arousal (OLA) theory* proposes that when our level of arousal is too high we seek to reduce it by decreasing stimulation. Inconsistent with drive reduction theory is OLA theory's proposal that when our arousal level falls below a certain level we are motivated to increase it by increasing stimulation.

Although most of us fall between the extremes, there are wide individual differences in the optimum level of arousal that we seek. People with low levels may prefer to lead sedentary lives whereas those with high levels may prefer to engage in activities we mentioned above, such as driving a Formula-1 car or parachuting from an aeroplane. Zuckerman (1979) has coined the term *sensation-seeker* to describe this sort of person.

The major problem with OLA theory also applied to

drive reduction theory. Because we cannot measure an organism's drive or arousal level, we cannot say what its optimum level of arousal should be. Thus, OLA theorists identify an organism's optimum level by the way it behaves. If it seeks out stimulation it must be functioning below its optimum level, and if it avoids stimulation it must be functioning above it. This is clearly an unsatisfactory and circular way of measuring optimum level of arousal.

Incentive theory of motivation

Each of the theories we have considered so far address the internal or biologically-based state of the organism and propose that some level of tension or arousal motivates (or *pushes*) an organism to perform certain behaviours. A very different idea is that *external stimuli* in the environment motivate (or *pull*) us in certain directions in the absence of any known physiological state.

Such stimuli are called *incentives*, and according to the incentive theory of motivation the expectation of a desirable goal motivates us to perform a behaviour (and note that incentive theory has also been termed *expectancy theory* by some researchers). The expectation of an undesirable goal motivates us not to perform a behaviour. The central question asked by incentive theorists, then, is what induces us to act and what inhibits our actions.

Numerous studies have shown that incentives can act as powerful motivators. As we mentioned earlier (see page 144), rats will work hard for a sip of saccharin even though saccharin has no nutritional value and therefore cannot reduce a tissue need. Rats simply like the taste of saccharin and are therefore motivated to experience it! As we know, people who are no longer hungry and whose tissue needs have been satisfied will sometimes eat chocolate after a meal. In the same way that rats enjoy saccharin, people enjoy chocolate and are motivated to eat it.

Incentive theory has found its most important application in *work motivation*, that is, our tendency to expend effort and energy on the job we do. According to Mitchell & Larson (1987), we will demonstrate a high level of work motivation if (a) we believe that hard work will improve our performance, (b) we believe that good performance will yield various rewards (such as a pay increase), and (c) the rewards we receive are the rewards we value.

Some psychologists, and in particular Rotter (1966), have proposed that both expectancies *and* values affect whether a behaviour is performed or not. For example, whether you ask someone out for the evening is determined to some degree by your past experiences. If you have been unsuccessful in the past, your expectancies are low and you would be less likely to try again. However, if you assign great value to the goal of taking someone out for the evening, your expectancies of failure might be overcome.

It is useful to consider the relationship between *intrinsic* and *extrinsic reward* at this point. The former refers to the pleasure and satisfaction that a task brings. It seems that, for whatever reason, some tasks themselves are rewarding to us. The latter refers to the rewards that are given beyond the intrinsic pleasures of the task itself. The relationship between intrinsic and extrinsic reward is not straightforward, and it seems that if we are given rewards for behaviours we intrinsically enjoy, our enjoyment of them lessens.

In some cases, then, extrinsic reward can undermine instrinsic motivation. In other cases, extrinsic rewards can be given without reducing instrinsic motivation. For example, a reward given as a recognition of competence can maintain rather than reduce intrinsic motivation. However, it is important to remember that giving rewards for something that is quite happily done for pleasure can 'rob' a person of that pleasure and reduce intrinsic motivation.

Opponent-process theory of motivation

Some of our motives are clearly *acquired* and become powerful and driving forces in our lives. According to Solomon & Corbit (1974), some acquired motives (such as taking drugs) initially bring about a basic pleasure, but each pleasurable experience eventually triggers some kind of 'pain'. In the case of taking drugs, for example, the pain would be the unpleasant symptoms of withdrawl. Equally, other acquired motives, such as parachuting from an aeroplane for the first time, bring about an initial suffering (in the form of terror) but

eventually trigger a pleasurable experience (the elation of having successfully attempted a parachute jump).

We could easily have examined Solomon and Corbit's opponent-process theory of motivation as a theory of emotion since they are, in essence, suggesting that every emotional experience elicits an opposite emotional experience that persists long after the primary emotion has passed and is more intense than it. Solomon and Corbit argue that the opposite emotion remains for a much longer period of time than the primary emotion it developed from, and acts to diminish the primary emotion's intensity. In the case of parachuting from an aeroplane, for example, each successful jump lessens the fear associated with it whilst the elation of the experience remains. Although we could have considered Solomon's theory in Chapter 17, we have chosen to consider it here because it is similar to theories of motivation we have already discussed that talk in terms of the maintenance of 'steady states'.

Opponent-process theory has been particulary useful in explaining *drug addiction*, although Solomon and Corbit see it as being equally useful in explaining acquired motives such as social attachments and love. In the case of drug addiction, opponent-process theory argues that the initial pleasure produced by a drug is followed by a gradual decline and then a minor craving for the drug. When addiction occurs, the drug is not being taken for the purposes of pleasure, but to avoid the pain of withdrawl and it is this that provides the motivational forces for the continued taking of the drug.

For Solomon and Corbit, then, behaviour is influenced by what happens in the long term rather than the short term. Repeated pleasurable (or unpleasurable) experiences eventually lose their pleasantness (or unpleasantness) and shift the driving force from pleasure to pain or pain to pleasure.

Maslow's theory of motivation

According to Abraham Maslow (1954), one of the problems with many theories of motivation is that they are 'defensive' and see human behaviour as occurring in a mechanical fashion and being aimed at nothing more than survival and tension reduction. In Maslow's view, and the view of other *humanistic psychologists,* our behaviour is also motivated by the conscious desire for *personal growth.* Maslow argued that our needs could be organised into a *hierarchy* as is shown in figure 15.1 below.

At the bottom of the hierarchy are basic physiological needs (such as food and drink) which derive from bodily states that *must* be satisfied. Maslow argues that we all start our lives at this lowest level (and he would see this as being the level at which drive reduction theory operates). As we move up the hierarchy, so the needs change from being basic and biological to complex and psychological. The hierarchy culminates in *self-actualisation,* which is our self-initiated striving to become whatever we believe we are capable of being.

Maslow labelled those behaviours which are related to survival or deficiency needs (*deficiency* or *D-motives*) because they satisfy those needs and represent a means to an end. Behaviours relating to self-actualisation were labelled 'growth' or 'being' (*B-motives*). Maslow saw them as being engaged in for their own sake since they are intrinsically satisfying.

Maslow believed that the needs at one level must be 'relatively satisfied' before those at the next level could direct and control our behaviour. Before enjoying reading a book for example, the 'stomach pangs' of hunger we are experiencing should ideally be attended to first. Maslow considered self-actualisation to be reached by very few people because most are stalled along the way by insurmountable social or environmental barriers. However, he also thought that all of us could reach the final level in the hierarchy for brief periods, and termed these *peak experiences.*

Critics of Maslow have argued that towards the highest level of the hierarchy the ordering is wrong. In a sense, this criticism is trivial because it is the idea of a *need* hierarchy that is useful rather than the exact nature and order of it. Also, we used the term 'relatively satisfied' when we described moving from one level to another rather than 'completely satisfied'. Maslow would accept

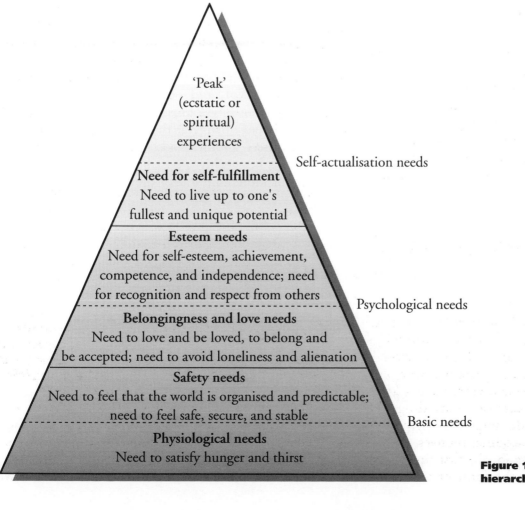

Figure 15.1   One version of Maslow's hierarchy of needs

that basic physiological needs do not need to be completely satisfied for higher needs to be addressed and would, perhaps, use the example of the hungry artist working on a 'masterpiece' in support of this.

Despite its intuitive appeal, Maslow's theory has been criticised on a number of other grounds. For example, some researchers have argued that it is difficult to *operationally define* concepts like self-actualisation, and that without such operational definitions it is not possible to test the theory experimentally. Other researchers have argued that some people don't seem to show any interest in going beyond physiological, safety, and love needs. Thus, it has been proposed that there is too much individual variation for the hierarchy of motivation to apply to everyone.

Maslow's conclusions about 'self-actualisation' have also been criticised. These were based on his observations of people he considered to be 'self-actualised' and included historical figures, famous living individuals, and even some of his friends whom he admired greatly. As Wahba & Bridwell (1976) have observed, such an approach does not exactly follow the traditions of the scientific process.

Freud's theory of motivation

The theories we have so far considered assume that our motives for behaving in particular ways are *conscious*. Freud, however, argued that our behaviour is controlled by *unconscious* (and inaccesible to consciousness) motives. Indeed, we could refer to these as 'instincts'

and Freud's theory could be discussed as an instinct theory of motivation. Originally, Freud saw all of human behaviour as being rooted in *eros*, the drive for 'bodily pleasure'. Later on, he argued behaviour was also directed by *thanatos*, the drive for self-destruction, which he felt was necessary to explain the massive destruction that occurred during World War 1.

Freud's view that behaviour is controlled by unconscious motives has attracted much controversy and stimulated considerable theoretical and research interest. Limitations of space do not allow us to consider Freud's theory in any detail. However, his view that *all*, or indeed any, behaviour is controlled by unconscious motives is difficult to assess because we cannot measure 'unconscious motivation' directly. Thus, whilst such motives might exist, we do not at present have any direct evidence for them and for this reason alone we cannot consider Freud's theory to be a plausible contender to explain human motivation.

Conclusions

In this chapter we have reviewed several theories of motivation, some of which are primarily physiological in their orientation and others of which lay greater emphasis on non-physiological factors. Our consideration would seem to suggest that no one theory offers a uniquely correct solution and that in any given behaviour (such as hunger) it is possible to locate supporting evidence for more than one of the theories we have discussed.

SUMMARY

- Psychologists see motives as inner directing forces that arouse an organism and direct its behaviour towards some goal. The study of motivation is the study of the **why** of behaviour.
- There are several different types of motive, in particular **biologically-based**, **sensation-seeking**, and **complex psychosocial**.
- **Biologically-based motives** are in-built body tissue needs (or 'drives'), such as those for food, water, air, sleep, temperature regulation, and the avoidance of pain.

- **Sensation-seeking motives** are largely unlearned needs for increasing the amount of stimulation and are most evident in situations of sensory isolation or deprivation. They appear in many non-human species, as well as in humans and include **activity**, **curiosity** and **exploration**, **manipulation**, **play**, **contact**, and **control**.
- Threats to our freedom produce **psychological reactance**; repeated negative experiences/loss of control may result in **learned helplessness**.
- **Complex psychosocial motives** are learned

needs, entirely unrelated to bodily needs, that include **need for achievement** (nAch), **need for affiliation** (nAff), **need for power** (nPower) and **need for approval** (nApp).

- Inspired by Darwin's theory, **instinct theories** of motivation explain behaviour in terms of innate, genetically pre-determined dispositions to act. James identified human psychosocial, as well as biological, instincts, and McDougall identified 12 basic instincts, including hunger and sex.

- Attempts to identify instincts stopped being useful when they merely acted as descriptive labels for the behaviour from which they were inferred; instinct theories were circular and explained nothing.

- **Ethologists** used the more precise **fixed action pattern** instead of 'instinct' and recognised the role of environmental stimuli, both before and after birth.

- **Sociobiologists** argue that innate patterns play a crucial role in complex human behaviours; all behaviour, human and non-human, is motivated by the 'selfish gene'.

- 'Instinct' was replaced by **drive**, based on the analogy with machines. Two major drive theories are **homeostatic drive theory** and **drive reduction theory**.

- Some homeostatic needs, such as oxygen intake, are involuntary and continuous, and satisfied automatically. Those which involve **tissue needs**, such as the need for food or drink, are involuntary and discontinuous, and cause a **homeostatic drive,** which leads to appropriate behaviour, such as eating or drinking.

- **Drive reduction theory** maintains that behaviours that are successful in reducing the unpleasant arousal (drive state) associated with a tissue need, will be strengthened. An important distinction is made between **primary** (innate) and **secondary** (acquired) **drives.**

- While some behaviours are motivated by drives associated with tissue needs, others (the majority) are not. Also, some behaviours are aimed at increasing rather than reducing drives, and others do not stop when the drive has apparently been reduced. Drive reduction theory cannot explain such observations.

- According to **optimum level of arousal theory**, we sometimes try to reduce our level of arousal by decreasing stimulation (consistent with drive reduction theory), and sometimes we try to increase it (which contradicts drive reduction theory).

- There are wide individual differences in the optimum level of arousal that people seek.

- According to **incentive theory** (or **expectancy theory**), the expectation of a desirable environmental goal 'pulls' us towards it; the expectation of an undesirable goal, will have the opposite effect. The value we place on the goal is also crucial.

- There is an important distinction between **intrinsic** and **extrinsic rewards**; sometimes, extrinsic rewards can reduce the intrinsic enjoyment of certain behaviours.

- According to **opponent-process theory**, every emotional experience triggers an opposite emotional experience, which persists far longer, is more intense, and which reduces the intensity of the primary emotion. It can help to explain **drug addiction** and other **acquired** motives which develop over a period of time.

- Maslow's **hierarchy of needs**, with **physiological needs** at the bottom, and **self-actualisation** at the top, distinguishes between **deficiency/D-motives** and **being/B-motives**; the former are a means to an end, the latter are intrinsically satisfying.

- Self-actualisation is not achieved by most people, and it is also very difficult to operationalise; the theory as a whole is seen as unscientific.

- Freud believed that behaviour is controlled by **unconscious** motivation, but this is very difficult to measure in a direct way.

EMOTION AND THE BRAIN

Introduction and overview

For over one hundred years, the study of emotion has assumed a prominent position in psychology. Much of the research interest has been concerned with identifying the brain structures that play a role in emotional experience, and our aim in this chapter is to review these research findings. We will begin by looking at data relating to the role played by the hypothalamus and the limbic system. After this, we will look at the reported differences between the cerebral hemispheres with respect to the comprehension and communication of emotion. Finally, we will look at findings related to sex differences, the brain and emotion.

The hypothalamus and emotion

In the early part of this century, research suggested that destroying parts of the cerebral cortex in cats and dogs resulted in a much lowered threshold of emotional excitation. For example, following *decortication* (removal of part or all of the cerebral cortex), a cat would present a typical picture of 'full-blown rage'. It hissed, growled, screamed and spat, arched its back, and displayed elevated heart rate and blood pressure. However, this aggression occurred in response to the slightest provocation and was poorly directed. For example, if the cat had its tail pinched it would hiss, scream, claw, and so on, *but* at the ground in front of it rather than the source of the pinching.

On the basis of this finding, researchers concluded that the cortex normally acts as an *inhibitor* of sub-cortical structures and that it was sub-cortical structures that were responsible for the production of emotional behaviour. The responses elicited by decorticated animals were termed *sham rage* because they seemed to be the integrated expression of rage but without the awareness and peristence characteristic of normal emotion.

Philip Bard (1928) discovered that the rage produced by the removal of the cortex largely disappeared if the *hypothalamus* was also removed. The *involvement* of the hypothalamus in the full expression of emotional behaviour has been shown in many studies of non-human animals. For example, destruction of the *lateral hypothalamus* produces what is termed a *quiet biting attack* (which does not appear to be accompanied by strong emotion and which ends when the prey ceases to move), whereas *affective attack* (the behaviours exhibited by a decorticated cat which were described above) is produced by stimulation in the region of the *ventromedial nucleus* of the hypothalamus. If the *dorsal* part of the hypothalamus is stimulated, an animal exhibits frantic attempts to escape the cage in which it is housed, and displays physiological responses indicative of increased activity in the sympathetic branch of the autonomic nervous system (see Chapter 3). If it is restrained, the animal will frequently attack in an attempt to escape.

As well as cats, such findings have also been obtained in rats, monkeys and several other non-human species. In humans, however, the picture is much less clear. Sem-Jacobsen (1968) found that stimulation of the hypothalamus had little effect on emotional experiences, and studies of people with damage to the hypothalamus caused by disease have also reported little change in subjective emotional reactions. The hypothalamus, then, cannot be *responsible* for the experience of emotion, and it has also been discovered that it is not *uniquely* involved in organising emotional behaviour.

Because large hypothalamic lesions will kill an animal by causing severe disruption to the endocrine system (see Chapter 3), a special piece of apparatus is needed to cut around the hypothalamus to sever all the connections between it and the rest of the brain, whilst leaving it connected to the pituitary gland. The technique devised by Ellison & Flynn (1968) contained two knives that could be rotated around the hypothalamus leaving it as an 'island' in the brain. However, even when the hypothalamus was separated from the rest of the brain, some kinds of aggressive behaviour could still be elicited in cats. These occurred in response to 'natural stimulation' (such as the sight of a mouse) and artificial electrical stimulation of other parts of the brain, although slightly higher levels of electrical current were necessary as compared with those before the isolation.

The limbic system and emotion

In 1937 Heinrich Kluver, a psychologist, and Paul Bucy, a neurosurgeon, reported the results of a number of studies investigating the effects of damage to the *temporal lobes* in monkeys. Essentially, they reported five main consequences which together are known as the *Kluver-Bucy Syndrome*. First, the monkeys ate any sort of food that was presented to them including that which they had rejected prior to the operation, and displayed a tendency to put anything movable into their mouths (a phenomenon known as *hyperorality*). Second, they displayed *visual agnosia* which, as we saw in Chapter 8, is the inability to recognise objects by sight. Third, the monkeys displayed increased, and often inappropriate, sexual activity (or *hypersexuality*). A fourth consequence was that the monkeys became tamer and safer to handle. Finally, they seemed to display a complete lack of fear. For example, they would repeatedly put their fingers into the flame of a burning match.

In later research, Kluver and Bucy investigated the effects of damage to the limbic system which, as we saw in Chapter 2, is a series of structures located between the cerebrum and parts of the hindbrain. Much of the early research into the limbic system was concerned with its role in olfaction (see Chapter 2). However, Kluver and Bucy showed that damage to the limbic system had effects on the emotional behaviour of monkeys. For example, as well as displaying increased sexuality, they also displayed decreased fearfulness and increased aggression towards one another. Researchers thus began to explore the possibility that structures in the limbic system may be responsible for the expression of emotion.

Kluver and Bucy noted that the destruction of one particular part of the limbic system, two small almond-shaped clusters next to the hypothalamus called the *amygdala* (see page 20) changed wild and ferocious monkeys into tame and placid animals. Removing the amygdala from the brain of a monkey dominant in a social group, for example, caused it to lose its place in the dominance hierarchy when it returned to the colony. When the amygdala was lesioned, stimuli that would normally elicit an aggressive response failed to do so. Such effects were not confined to monkeys, and subsequent research showed that lesions to the amygdala in species such as the rat, wolverine, and lynx also resulted in timidity and placidity.

In cats, research has shown that the effects of electrical stimulation of the amygdala depend on the part that is stimulated. In one part, stimulation results in the cat arching its back, hissing, and showing all the signs of preparing to attack. However, stimulation in a part a small distance away results in the cat cowering in terror when caged with a small mouse. Of course, there is always a danger in generalising the results obtained with non-humans to human beings. However, there is some evidence to suggest that the amygdala plays a similar role in humans.

Nearly thirty years ago, Charles Whitman killed his wife and mother before making his way to the campus of the University of Texas. Once there, he killed 15 people he did not know and wounded another 24 before being killed himself by the police. It seems that Whitman was aware of his aggressiveness since, just before he embarked on the killings, he wrote of the agony he was experiencing:

> 'I don't quite understand what compels me to type this letter . . . I am supposed to be an average, reasonable and intelligent young man . . . However, lately I have been a victim of many unusual and irrational thoughts . . . I talked with a doctor once for about two hours and tried to convey to him my fears that I felt overcome (sick) by overwhelming violent impulses. After one session I never saw the doctor again and since then I have been fighting my mental turmoil alone, and seemingly to no avail. After my death I wish that an autopsy would be performed on me to see if there is any visible physical disorder.' (quoted in Johnson, 1972)

After an autopsy had been conducted, a small tumour was discovered in Whitman's brain. Although the wounds caused by the gun fire of the police made it difficult to establish the precise location of the tumour, Sweet, et al. (1969) report that it appeared to be in (or at least close to) the amygdala.

The findings reported by Kluver, Bucy and others concerning the amygdala were instrumental in the development of *psychosurgery*, which we briefly mentioned in Chapter 5. In a case study conducted by Mark & Ervin (1970), a young woman called Julia was admitted to hospital after committing, seemingly without any reason, twelve separate attacks on people. Tests suggested that Julia's amygdala was damaged, and her family agreed to surgeons conducting psychosurgery (in the form of a small lesion in the amygdala) to try and reduce her aggressive behaviour. In follow-up studies of Julia, Mark and his colleagues reported that her aggressive behaviour had been greatly reduced.

As we noted in Chapter 5, the ethics of performing surgery on the amygdala of humans are, of course, highly dubious. The removal of *damaged* areas of the brain which consequently result in aggression being reduced raises little by way of objection. However, in psychosurgery brain tissue is removed without there being any direct evidence to suggest that the tissue was in some way damaged (Carlson, 1987).

Despite the ethical issues involved in psychosurgery, some researchers (such as Culliton, 1976) have argued for its use on the grounds that it can produce beneficial effects (assuming such use is to *improve* rather than *control* a person's condition). Breggin (1973), however, has argued that it is not ethically acceptable to affect behaviour by altering the structure and functioning of the brain. Breggin has predicted that if any country 'ever falls into the hands of totalitarianism, the dictators will be behavioural scientists and the secret police will be armed with lobotomy and psychosurgery.'

Box 16.1 below highlights one of the controversial issues Breggin talks about.

Box 16.1 The surgical treatment of emotional disturbances

'Case 34 was admitted and kept in (hospital) . . . He was a young man of 25 years . . . admitted because he was always violent. He was constantly aggressive and was destructive. He could not be kept in general wards and had to be nursed in an isolated cell. It was difficult to establish any sort of communication with him. *Bilateral stereotaxic amygdalectomy* was performed. Following the operation he was very quiet and could be safely left in the general wards. He started answering questions in slow syllables'. (Balasubramamiam, et al. 1970)

Balasubramaniam, et al's method of assessing the effectiveness of psychosurgery on the hyperactive or violent behaviour of their patients is presented below (after Carlson, 1977):

Grade	Criteria
A	There is no need of any drug. Patient is able to mingle with others.
B	Very much docile and given to occasional outbursts only.
C	Manageable when given drugs although not leading a useful life.
D	Transient improvement.
E	No change.
F	Died.

According to these criteria, 'Case 34' would be graded as an 'A'. Do you think the patient was cured as a result of psychosurgery or does 'manageability' seem to be the criterion of importance? Should there be a category for patients whose condition is made *worse* by psychosurgery?

Another part of the limbic system, the *septum*, has also been implicated in emotional behaviour. Brady and Nauta (1953) found that lesions in the septum resulted in a lowering of a rat's 'rage threshold'. For example, if a person approached the cage in which a septally lesioned rat was housed, it showed signs of extreme emotional arousal such as screaming and jumping wildly. If a person placed a hand into the cage, the rat would launch a vicious attack on it. However, in mice, a septal lesion produces an increase in 'flight' behaviour rather than 'affective rage'. We should also note that in rats, increased emotionality gradually subsides until within a few weeks it is all but absent. In mice, hyperemotionality remains indefinitely (Carlson, 1977).

As well as these differences, it has been shown that most other animals do *not* display emotionality as a result of a septal lesion. Thus, making *general* statements about the role of the septum in emotional behaviour is not possible since the effects of lesions seem to depend on the species studied.

On the basis of the data obtained from animal studies and his own investigations of brain-damaged people,

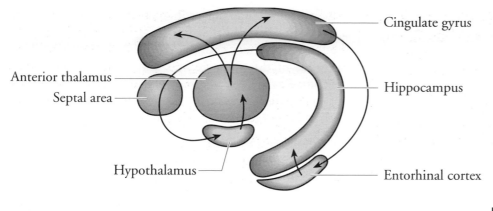

Anterior thalamus

Septal area

Hypothalamus

Cingulate gyrus

Hippocampus

Entorhinal cortex

Figure 16.1   The Papez circuit

Papez (1937) proposed that a complex set of interconnected pathways and centres in the limbic system underlies the experience of emotion. The *Papez circuit* (which is shown in Figure 16.1 above) forms a closed loop running from the *hippocampus* to the *hypothalamus* and from there to the *anterior thalamus*. The circuit continues via the *cingulate gyrus* and the *entorhinal cortex* back to the hippocampus.

Unfortunately, Papez's proposals have not stood the test of careful anatomical study. However, Paul MacLean has modified the circuit and suggested that the amygdala and hippocampus play a central role in the mediation of aggression but the cingulate gyrus does not. Whilst the *Papez-MacLean limbic model* has been influential, researchers have cautioned against the idea that there are specific 'emotion centres' (especially 'aggression centres') in the brain, since the brain is not neatly organised into structures that correspond to our categories of behaviour.

One of those who has claimed evidence for an 'aggression centre' is Delgado (1969), whose research we briefly described in Chapter 4 (see page 35). In a much-publicised demonstration, Delgado showed that stimulating the limbic system of a charging bull resulted in the bull stopping in its tracks. However, researchers such as Valenstein (1973) have challenged Delgado's interpretation of his results. After watching film of Delgado's demonstration, Valenstein noted that the bull always circled to the right when Delgado stimulated its brain. Rather than being pacified as a result of the stimulation, Valenstein argues that the bull was simply 'confused' and 'frustrated' and just gave up!

Recent research has begun to clarify the role that limbic system structures play in emotional behaviour. Much of this research has concentrated on the amygdala, and it has been found that the amygdala has direct connections with *sensory channels*. What function do such connections serve? According to LeDoux (1989), when the amygdala receives sensory information an emotional response can be elicited independently of the cortex. This has been termed a *precognitive emotional response* since it occurs without the cortex having made any appraisal of the appropriateness of a particular emotional response.

Perhaps you have had the experience of someone creeping up on you. On turning round, your initial response is to jump (and perhaps scream), but when the cortex appraises the situation, and recognises the person as someone you know, your initial emotional response disappears (sometimes to be replaced by another response – anger!). LeDoux suggests that we can view the initial emotional response as being mediated by the amygdala which acts as a sort of 'early warning system' and allows us to experience emotion without cognition. The cortex then assesses the situation and determines whether the 'system' is responding appropriately or inappropriately.

Since the development of PET and other non-invasive methods of investigating the brain, it has (as we saw in Chapter 4) been possible to investigate the activity occurring in the brain during the performance of a task. As we noted in Chapter 7, there is some evidence to support the view that the two cerebral hemispheres are not functionally symmetrical but are specialised for the performance of different tasks. In the following section, we will look at the relationship between the cerebral hemispheres and emotion.

The cerebral hemispheres and emotion

In a case study conducted in 1908, a mentally disturbed woman repeatedly tried to choke herself with her left hand. As she did this, her right hand would try to pull the left away from her throat. As well as this self-destructive behaviour, the woman engaged in other forms of destructive behaviour such as ripping her bed pillows and tearing her sheets. However, she only did this with her left hand. After the woman died, a post-mortem was conducted. This revealed that her *corpus callosum* was badly damaged.

As we know from Chapter 7, the corpus callosum connects the two cerebral hemispheres and allows them to exchange information so that each is aware of the activities of the other. When the corpus callosum is surgically divided, the channel of communication is disrupted and the hemispheres are no longer in contact with one another. In a sense, the woman described above was like a split-brain patient, and on the basis of her behaviour, researchers suggested that the two hemispheres might be different in terms of their comprehension and communication of emotion.

Studies of people with brain damage have told us something about the role of the left and right hemispheres in emotion. In Chapter 5 we noted that damage to the motor area of the right hemisphere leads to paralysis of the left side. However, people with right hemisphere damage seem to be completely unmoved by this and continue to make plans as though they could walk normally. This is termed an *indifference reaction*. Damage to the left hemisphere might cause paralysis of the right side. Far from being unmoved by this, people with left hemisphere damage display what is termed a *catastrophic reaction*, that is, an episode of severe anxiety and depression which is probably a result of their awareness of the major damage the brain has suffered.

These findings suggest that the left and right hemispheres differ in terms of the ways in which they react to emotion-provoking stimuli. Because of the way in which the undamaged right hemisphere responds to the consequences of damage to the left hemisphere, it seems reasonable to propose that the right hemisphere is specialised for recognising emotion-provoking stimuli and for organising the appropriate pattern of emotional responses. Equally, because of the indifference

reaction of the left hemisphere to the consequences of damage to the right, it seems reasonable to propose that the left hemisphere cannot recognise the emotional significance of this damage and continues to make plans without taking it into consideration. As we noted, the left hemisphere is *aware* of the damage, but it simply does not seem to be bothered by it.

Studies of people who do not have damaged left or right hemispheres have *generally* confirmed that they do differ in terms of their reactivity to emotion-provoking stimuli. In a study conducted by Ley & Bryden (1979), people were shown drawings of faces displaying different expressions of emotion. The drawings were presented one at a time to either the left or right hemisphere using the modified version of the method employed with split-brain patients which enables information to be presented to one hemisphere only (see page 62). After a drawing had been displayed, it was replaced by another which was shown in the centre of the visual field. This meant that it was perceived by both hemispheres. The task was to decide whether the emotion displayed in the second picture was the same as, or different to, the emotion displayed in the first.

The results showed that when the drawings displayed *clear* emotional states (such as a big smile), fewer recognition errors were made by the right hemisphere. When the drawing displayed no emotion or a 'mild' emotional state, there was no difference in recognition between the hemispheres. These findings would seem to suggest that the right hemisphere has a definite advantage in the recognition of clear or strong facial expressions of emotion. This also appears to be the case when emotions are expressed *paralinguistically*, that is, utterances that convey their meaning in terms of the tone of the voice, emphasis, pausing, and so on (compare the 'Ooh' produced by a soccer crowd when a player makes a valiant effort to score with the 'Ooh' produced when an open goal is missed).

Earlier on we noted that damage to the left hemisphere results in an indifference reaction and, as we have just seen, the right hemisphere seems to be better than the left at recognising facial and paralinguistic expressions of emotion. As Davidson (1992) has observed, to suggest that the left hemisphere is completely non-emotional would, however, be incorrect on the basis of the data reported in some studies.

It would seem that the left hemisphere is more active during the experience of *positive* emotions. For example, research using PET (see Chapter 4) has indicated that when people are given 'good' news, asked to think about 'positive' events, or required to discriminate happy faces from neutral ones the left hemisphere is more active than the right (Tomarken & Davidson, 1994; Gur, et al. 1994). By contrast, the right hemisphere is more active when people are given 'bad' news or asked to think about 'negative' events (and recall from earlier in this chapter that the woman who engaged in destructive behaviour did so only with her right-hemisphere-controlled left hand).

Support for the left/right, positive/negative distinction comes from studies of clinically depressed people in which it has been shown that there is a tendency for the frontal lobes of the right hemisphere to be more active (Miller, 1987). Research has also suggested that different areas of the cortex *within* the right hemisphere play slightly different roles. Ross (1981), for example, describes several examples of people with damage to the frontal lobe of the right hemisphere who had difficulty in *producing* facial gestures and tone of voice to express emotion. However, their ability to *recognise* other people's emotional expression appeared to be unaffected. By contrast, people with damage to the right parietal/temporal lobe seemed to be able to produce emotional expressions but unable to recognise those expressed by other people. Damage to both the right frontal and parietal/temporal lobe resulted in the inability to both produce and recognise emotional expression.

You may have noticed an interesting similarity between the findings reported by Ross and the research we described in Chapter 6 on the localisation and lateralisation of language. Whether there are discrete areas in the right hemisphere for the production and understanding of emotional expression which are analagous to Broca's and Wernicke's areas in the left hemisphere is an interesting possibility, but the findings reported by Ross need to be replicated by other researchers before we can begin to talk about the 'localisation and lateralisation of emotion'.

The apparently differential responses of the right and left hemispheres to positive and negative emotions has also led to much speculation. According to Sackheim (1982), the two hemispheres operate in a *reciprocal* manner with activity in one (caused by either a positive or negative emotion-provoking stimulus) producing reciprocal activity in the other. Such activity might function to ensure that an emotion was not experienced in an inappropriately intense way. Extremely excited reactions might, therefore, be due to the right hemisphere failing to reciprocate the activity in the left hemisphere, whilst extremely sad or angry reactions might result from the left hemisphere failing to reciprocate the activity in the right hemisphere. Such speculations, of course, require considerable investigation to assess their worth.

Sex differences, emotion, and the hemispheres

It has long been known that the average male brain weighs more than the average female brain. Paul Broca (some of whose findings about the brain we discussed in Chapter 6), for example, found an average weight of 1,235 grams for the 292 male brains he measured whereas the 140 female brains he measured had an average weight of 1,144 grams. For Broca:

> 'We might ask if the small size of the female brain depends exclusively on her body. But we must not forget that women are, on the average, a little less intelligent than men, a difference we should not exaggerate but which is nonetheless real'.

At least in part, then, Broca saw the smaller female brain as being due both to a 'physical inferiority' and an 'intellectual inferiority'. Although the evidence indicates that Broca was wrong in claiming that there are sex differences in intelligence, it has been suggested that the sexes do differ in some respects (such as spatial ability and language ability – Kimura, 1993). Recently, physiological differences in the brains of men and women have been linked to differences in emotion.

Robin Gur and his colleagues (1995) used PET (see Chapter 4) to study 51 healthy right-handed volunteers of whom 27 were men and 24 women. All participants were studied in a dimly-lit room and instructed to stay quiet and relaxed without closing their eyes or falling asleep. Brain metabolism between the sexes was identical in all regions except two. In the *temporal-limbic system*, metabolism was higher in men than women, whereas in the *cingulate gyrus* the reverse was true.

It has been hypothesised that the temporal-limbic system is associated with 'action-oriented' emotional responses such as sexual arousal and violence. It has been claimed that the cingulate gyrus plays a role in 'symbolic' modes of expression. Gur and his colleagues have proposed that these findings point to the possibility that men are more biologically inclined to express themselves physically (through, for example, aggressive behaviour) whilst women are biologically disposed to 'talk things through'.

We should, however, recognise that Gur and his colleagues' findings concern the brain *at rest*, and before any firm conclusions can be drawn, it needs to be shown that there are consistent differences between the sexes with respect to activity in the brain during the processing of emotion-provoking stimuli.

Conclusions

In this chapter we have looked at the role played by specific brain structures in the experience of emotion and at the differences between the hemispheres with respect to the communication and comprehension of emotion. We have also looked at the ways in which the brains of males and females might differ in terms of the expression of emotion. Unfortunately, we cannot draw simple conclusions about any of the research we have described. To argue that 'emotional centres' (especially 'aggression centres') exist is an argument that is simply not supported by the evidence.

SUMMARY

- Early research with cats and dogs suggested that destroying parts of their cortex produced a much lower thresold of emotional excitation. For example, **decortication** induced 'full blown rage' in a cat, although it would occur in response to the slightest provocation and was poorly directed (**sham rage**).

- This suggested that the cortex normally **inhibits** sub-cortical structures which are the ones actually responsible for emotional behaviour. Bard found that sham rage largely disappeared if the **hypothalamus** was also removed. Destruction of the **lateral hypothalamus** produces **quiet biting attack**, whereas stimulation near the **ventromedial nucleus** causes **affective attack**. Stimulation of an animal's **dorsal** hypothalamus produces frantic attempts to escape its cage, accompanied by increased sympathetic ANS activity.

- The picture in humans is far less clear than for many non-human species. Neither stimulation of, nor damage to, the hypothalamus has much effect on emotional experience or reaction.

- Even when the hypothalamus is successfully isolated from the rest of the brain (but still connected to the pituitary gland), some kinds of aggressive behaviour can still be elicited in cats, both by natural stimuli and by electrical stimulation of other parts of the brain.

- The **Kluver-Bucy syndrome**, based on studies of monkeys, refers to the effect of damage to the temporal lobes, namely **hyperorality**, **visual agnosia**, **hypersexuality**, a total lack of fear and the monkeys being tamer and safer to handle.

- Kluver and Bucy also investigated the effects of damage to the **limbic system**. As well as increased sexuality, monkeys displayed decreased fear and increased aggression towards one another. Destruction of the **amygdala** changed wild and ferocious monkeys into tame and placid ones, so that a previously dominant group member would lose its place in the hierarchy. Similar results were found using other species.

- Electrical stimulation of a particular part of a cat's amygdala caused it to prepare for attack, while stimulation of a nearby area caused terror when the cat was caged with a small mouse.

- An autopsy on the brain of Charles Whitman revealed a small tumour in or close to the amygdala. Animal experiments such as those of Kluver and Bucy led to the development of **psychosurgery**, which was used to make a lesion in the amygdala of Julia, after which her violent behaviour was greatly reduced.

- There are serious ethical issues involved in psychosurgery, such as manageability and control of the patient versus beneficial effects for the patient.

- Lesions in the **septum** of a rat lower its 'rage threshold', while in mice, it produces an increase in 'flight' behaviour; the effect in rats only lasts a few weeks, while the hyperemotionality in mice remains indefinitely. But most other species do **not** display emotionality as a result of septal lesions.

- Papez proposed that emotional experience is based on the **Papez circuit**, a closed loop in the limbic system, running from the **hippocampus** to the **hypothalamus**, from there to the **anterior thalamus**, on to the **cingulate gyrus** and the **entorhinal cortex** and back to the hippocampus.

- The **Papez-MacLean limbic model** sees the amygdala and hippocampus playing a central role, but not the cingulate gyrus. While this has been influential, researchers argue that the brain does not have specific emotion centres, especially aggression centres. Delgado's claim to have found an aggression centre by stimulating a charging bull's limbic system has been interpreted as the bull being confused and giving up (rather than stopped in its tracks).

- The amygdala has direct connections with **sensory channels**, allowing an emotional response to be elicited independently of the cortex (**precognitive emotional response**); this represents an 'early warning system', followed by the cortex's appraisal of the appropriateness of the response.

- People with damage to the motor area of the cortex of the right hemisphere suffer paralysis of the left side, but they display an **indifference reaction** (with their left). Damage to the left hemisphere produces a **catastrophic reaction** (by the right), reflecting patients' awareness of the major brain damage suffered. This suggests that the right hemisphere is specialised for recognising emotion-provoking stimuli and for organising the appropriate pattern of emotional responses. By contrast, the left hemisphere, while aware of the damage to the right, continues to make plans without allowing for it.

- Studies involving people with intact brains have presented stimuli, such as drawings of faces displaying different emotional expressions, to one hemisphere only. When drawings display **clear** emotional states, the right hemisphere makes fewer recognition errors than the left; this advantage is also demonstrated when emotions are expressed **paralinguistically.**

- However, the left hemisphere is not totally non-emotional. PET scans have shown that the left hemisphere is more active than the right when people experience **positive** emotion; the reverse is true for negative emotion. This is supported by the tendency for the right frontal lobes of clinically depressed people to be more active than the left. Different areas of the right cortex may control different emotional functions, such as **producing** emotional reactions (frontal lobe) and **recognising** them in others (parietal/temporal lobe). The two hemispheres may work in a **reciprocal** way.

- PET scans have revealed that there is a sex difference in brain metabolism in the **temporal-limbic system**, where it is higher in men than women, and the **cingulate gyrus**, where it is higher in women than men. The former is thought to be involved in 'action-oriented' emotional responses, such as sexual arousal and violence, while the latter is involved in 'symbolic' modes of expression, such as 'talking things through'. These findings are, however, only based on the brain **at rest**.

THEORIES OF EMOTION

Introduction and overview

Some theories of emotion try to tell us how emotion-provoking events produce subjective emotional experiences. Others try to explain how emotions develop. Our aim in this chapter is to critically consider some of the theories of *emotional experience* that have been proposed. In everyday language, we use the words 'emotions' and 'feelings' interchangibly. However, psychologists generally agree that 'feelings' are but one element of an emotion, and that it is possible to identify four integral components of human emotions. These are *subjective feelings, cognitive processes, physiological arousal*, and *behavioural reactions*. The way in which these components are related and the relative emphasis given to one or more of them distinguishes the theories we will examine.

We will begin by looking at two theories which emphasise the role of physiological activity in emotion. After this, we will consider two influential approaches which emphasise the role played by non-physiological factors, in the form of cognitive processes, as important determinants in the experience of emotion.

The James-Lange theory of emotion

The relationship between emotional experiences and bodily and/or behavioural changes is surely a straightforward one, isn't it? Suppose, for example, we receive bad news about something. The emotion we experience is sadness, and this causes us to cry. In other words, a *common sense theory of emotion* tells us that a physiological response (crying) occurs because of an emotional experience. However, William James (an eminent American philosopher) and, independently, Carl Lange (a Danish physiologist) offered a theory which runs counter to common sense. According to the *James-Lange theory of emotion*, emotional experience is the *result* of bodily and/or behavioural changes to some

emotion-provoking stimulus rather than the cause. James (1890) put the position quite clearly:

'The bodily changes follow directly the perception of the exciting fact, and . . . our feelings of the same changes as they occur is the emotion. Common sense says that we lose our fortune, are sorry, and weep; we meet a bear, are frightened, and run; we are insulted by a rival, are angry, and strike. The hypothesis to be defended here says that this order of sequence is incorrect, that the one mental state is not immediately induced by the other and that the bodily manifestations must first be interposed between. The more rational statement is that we feel sorry because we cry, angry because we strike, afraid because we tremble, and not that we cry, strike, or tremble because we are sorry, angry or fearful, as the case may be.'

When we experience some stimulus, then, physiological reactions and behaviour responses occur, and it is these that trigger the experience of an emotion. For the James-Lange theory, emotions are a *by-product* (or *cognitive representation*) of automatic physiological and behavioural responses.

James and Lange argued that the brain receives *sensory feedback* from the internal organs *and* parts of the body that respond to emotion-provoking stimuli. The feedback that is received by the brain is recognised and then labelled appropriately. Although this theory runs counter to common sense, you might be able to think of a situation in which you reacted in a fairly automatic way. An example would be slipping down the stairs and grabbing the bannisters. Only when you had stopped yourself slipping would you become aware of feeling frightened, as though the sudden change in your behaviour *caused* the fear (quite apart from *why* you grabbed the bannisters). Figure 17.1 opposite illustrates the James-Lange theory.

Because it was counter-intuitive, the theory received much attention. One critic was Walter Cannon (1927) who identified three major problems with theory. The first of these concerned the pattern of physiological activity fed back to the brain. Cannon argued that each

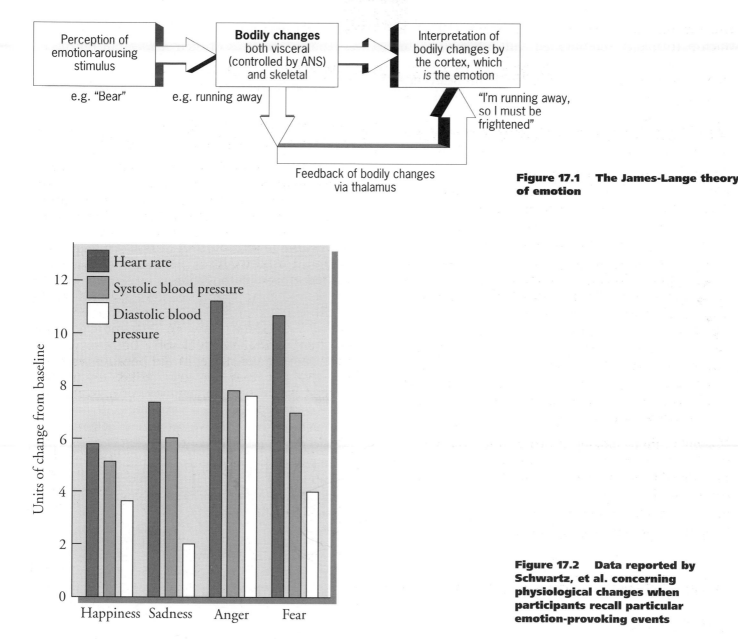

Figure 17.1   The James-Lange theory of emotion

Figure 17.2   Data reported by Schwartz, et al. concerning physiological changes when participants recall particular emotion-provoking events

emotion should have its own distinct pattern of activity otherwise the cortex would not be able to 'determine' which emotion should be experienced. A large number of studies have reported that distinct patterns of physiological activity are associated with different emotional states. However, an equally large number of studies have reported the absence of such differences.

Studies conducted by Ax (1953) and Schwartz, Weinberger & Singer (1981) are amongst those that obtained data supportive of the James-Lange theory. These studies demonstrated that emotions like fear, anger, happiness, and sadness are different in terms of heart rate and body temperature, muscular activity in

the face, blood pressure, and neural activity in the frontal lobes. Figure 17.2 above shows the data reported by Schwartz and his colleagues.

Other researchers (such as Wolf & Wolff, 1947 and Mandler, 1962) have supported Cannon's criticisms by presenting data indicating that different people may show different patterns of physiological activity when experiencing the same emotion, and that the same person may respond in a different way when experiencing the same emotion on several occasions.

Cannon also argued that James and Lange were wrong to maintain that physiological changes themselves produce changes in our emotional states. He based this criticism on a study reported by Maranon (1924), in which participants were injected with *adrenaline*. This causes changes in autonomic nervous system activity (see Chapter 3), such as an increase in heart rate. Following the injection, participants were asked to describe their emotional state. Most reported a physical change with *no* emotional overtones, and those who did report a change in their emotional state described it as an 'as if' change in emotional state rather than an actual change. Such data do not support the James-Lange theory.

Cannon's third criticism was that total separation of the viscera from the central nervous system did *not* result in the absence of emotional experience (the James-Lange theory, of course, would predict that emotional experience would be absent in such conditons). Cannon based this criticism on the finding of his own and others' research indicating that when visceral feedback was abolished in dogs and cats, their emotional experience did not seem to be affected. However, apart from the fact that we do not know about the emotional experiences of non-humans, Cannon seems to have ignored James' views about the body, and in particular the *muscles,* as well as the viscera. Even if visceral feedback was cut off, an animal would still receive feedback from the muscles and this might contribute to some sort of emotional experience.

If feedback from the internal organs through the autonomic nervous system was important, then we would expect that humans with damage to the spinal cord would not be capable of experiencing emotion of the same intensity that they experienced before the damage (if, indeed, they experienced *any* sort of emotion). Hohmann (1966) studied a number of patients with spinal cord injuries. Some of these had damaged relatively low portions of the spinal cord which meant that the feedback from the internal organs still reached the brain through the higher undamaged portions. Others had damaged their spinal cords much further up and received little or no information from the internal organs (see Chapter 1).

Hohmann asked his patients to recall an event that had aroused fear, anger, grief, or sexual excitement before their injury and a comparable event that had occurred after the injury. As measured by self-reports of emotional intensity, the data revealed a diminishing of emotional experience for events occurring after the injury. Also, the higher up the spinal cord the injury

occurred, the less intense were the emotional experiences reported in terms of their *feelings* but not necessarily their *behaviour*. As one patient put it:

'I was at home alone in bed and dropped a cigarette where I couldn't reach it. I finally managed to scrounge around and put it out. I could have burnt up right there, but the funny thing is, I didn't get all shook up about it. I just didn't feel afraid at all, like you would suppose. Now I don't get a feeling of physical animation, it's a sort of cold anger. Sometimes I cry when I see some injustice. I yell and cuss and raise hell, because if you don't do it sometimes I've learned people will take advantage of you, but it doesn't have the heat that it used to. It's a mental kind of anger.'
(reported in Hohmann, 1966)

Hohmann's data seem to cast doubt on Cannon's criticism. However, Hohmann's and other studies finding similar effects (e.g. Jasnos & Hakmiller, 1975) have been criticised on the grounds that they are liable to experimenter and social desirability effects and the possibility that patients might suppress their feelings as a way of coping with their extreme circumstances (Trieschmann, 1980). If we are being generous, we would accept the findings concerning the lack of emotional response in the absence of visceral feedback as being supportive of the James-Lange theory, whilst acknowledging the potential methodological shortcomings in such supportive studies.

Despite the criticisms that have been levelled at it, the James-Lange theory of emotion has stood the test of time remarkably well. In discussing its relevance, James (1890) suggested that it had practical as well as theoretical importance. Since emotions are no more than the perception of physiological and behavioural responses, we could:

'. . . conquer undesirable emotional tendencies . . . by assiduously, and in the first instance cold-bloodedly, going through . . . the *outward movements* of those contrary dispositions which we prefer to cultivate.'

For James, then, by smiling at someone who makes us angry our anger would eventually disappear. It is generally agreed that our emotional states are *reflected* by our facial expressions, but a number of researchers have suggested that the reverse may be true as well. One proponent of this view is Sylvia Tomkins (1962) who argued that specific facial displays are *universally* associated with neural programmes linked to various emotions.

Certainly, some facial expressions of emotion do seem to be recognised by people in all cultures irrespective of their experiences, and studies which induce people to facially express a particular emotion (smiling, for example) are associated with self-reported changes in emotional state and distinct patterns of physiological activity (as we mentioned earlier in the study conducted by Schwartz and his colleagues – see page 159) that are comparable to those that occur during actual emotional experiences.

Facial feedback theory, then, argues that facial expressions can *produce* changes in emotional state as well as mirror them. As James suggested, we do seem to feel happier when we smile, sadder when we frown, and so on. In several studies people have been asked to imagine a pleasurable event such as winning a large sum of money or an unpleasurable event such as being placed in a fear-provoking situation. Then, they were asked to enhance or suppress tension in certain facial muscles. Consistent with facial feedback theory, subjective reports of emotional experience have been shown to change as Figure 17.3 (derived from an experiment conducted by McCanne & Anderson, 1987) illustrates.

Some research suggests that contraction of the facial muscles heightens physiological arousal and it is possible that this leads to us reporting changes in our perceived emotional state. Other researchers have proposed that contraction of the facial muscles affects blood flow to the brain and this influences the release of certain *neurotransmitters* (such as *serotonin* and *norepinephrine* – see Chapter 1) that are strongly believed

to play a role in emotion. However, irrespective of the mechanisms involved, it is not hard to see how facial feedback theory could have applications as a potential treatment for certain emotional disorders.

There is, of course, a danger in exaggerating the claims from any area of research. Critics of facial feedback theory have identified a number of methodological problems with some studies that have been reported (such as the possibility that the participant's expectations and distracting elements in the experimental setting may affect their emotional states) and it has been suggested that while research may show statistically significant effects, these are behaviourally *insignificant*. Nonetheless, the possibility that the British 'stiff upper lip' may influence our emotional experiences cannot be entirely ruled out!

The Cannon-Bard thalamic theory of emotion

As we saw in the previous section, Cannon criticised the proposal that different emotions are associated with different patterns of physiological and bodily activity. He saw all emotions as producing the *same* pattern of responses which correspond to the *fight-or-flight* response (see Chapter 3) and which prepares us to deal with an emergency. According to Cannon and his co-researcher Philip Bard, external stimuli activate the

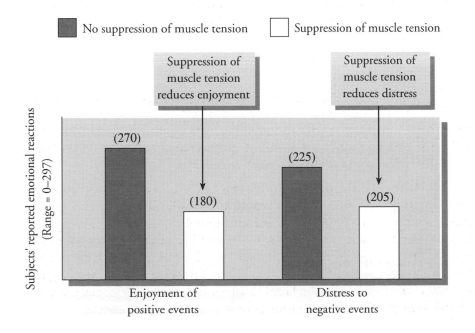

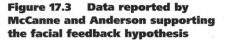
Figure 17.3   Data reported by McCanne and Anderson supporting the facial feedback hypothesis

thalamus which (a) sends sensory information to the cortex for interpretation, and (b) simultaneously sends *activation messages* through the peripheral nervous system to the viscera and skeletal muscles.

The Cannon-Bard theory claims that at the same time as information sent to the cortex produces the sensations of emotion, physiological and behavioural responses are also produced. However, the theory sees these as being *independent* of one another. Thus, the experience of emotion neither causes nor is a result of physiological and behavioural responses. Heightened physiological and behavioural activity occurs in response to the emotion-provoking stimulus rather than the experience of emotion it produces. Figure 17.4 below illustrates the theory proposed by Cannon and Bard.

The claim that physiological and bodily activity is a 'side-effect' of emotion and plays no role in it is, as we saw earlier on, not supported by the evidence. Also, research suggests that Cannon was almost certainly wrong to ascribe a central role to the thalamus. As we saw in Chapter 16, other brain structures, principally the hypothalamus and limbic system appear to be much more directly involved in the experience of emotion. However, despite the limitations of the theory, it does at least point out the important role played by the brain in emotional responses.

Schachter and Singer's theory of emotion

According to Stanley Schachter and Jerome Singer, Cannon was wrong in believing that bodily changes and emotional experiences are independent. Schachter and Singer also saw the James-Lange theory as being mistaken in its claim that changes in physiological activity cause the experience of emotion. According to

Schachter and Singer's theory, emotional experience depends on two factors. The first is physiological arousal in the autonomic nervous system. The second is the *cognitive appraisal* (or interpretation) of the physiological arousal.

Thus, like James and Lange, Schachter and Singer see arousal as preceding the experience of emotion and being necessary for it. However, physiological arousal itself is not sufficient. If an emotion is to be experienced, the arousal must be appraised in an emotional way. In Maranon's study, which we outlined on page 160, the participants had a clear explanation for their physiological arousal, namely the injection that was given to them. For Schachter and Singer, it is hardly surprising that they did not report an emotional experience because their cognitive appraisal of the heightened physiological activity could be explained in a non-emotional way.

Schachter and Singer argued that the degree of arousal determines the intensity of an emotion, provided that arousal is interpreted in an emotional way. The particular interpretation itself determines the emotion that is experienced. Notice how different this is to the James-Lange theory. Whereas the James-Lange theory sees each emotional state as being determined by a *different* pattern of physiological activity, Schachter and Singer's theory assumes that the same physiological changes underlie all emotions and that it is the *meaning* that is attributed to them that generates different emotions. Because Schachter and Singer's theory proposes arousal and cognition as the central elements in the experience of emotion, it is sometimes referred to as the *two-factor theory of emotion*. Figure 17.5 opposite illustrates the Schachter and Singer theory.

The role of the two factors in emotion was tested by Schachter & Singer (1962) in an ingenious experiment. Male college students were informed that they would be participating in an experiment looking at the effects

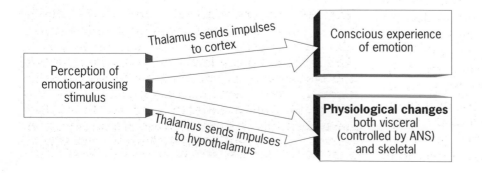

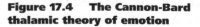

Figure 17.4   The Cannon-Bard thalamic theory of emotion

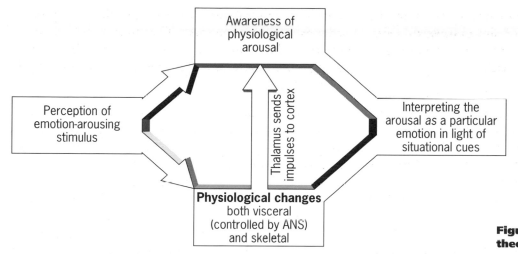

Figure 17.5   The Schachter-Singer theory of emotion

of the vitamin compound 'Suproxin' on vision, and that this would necessitate them receiving a vitamin injection. In fact, the injection they were given was of *epinephrine*, a hormone that causes an increase in heart rate, respiration rate, blood pressure, and produces muscle tremors (see Chapters 1 and 3).

Participants in one condition (termed the *epinephrine-informed condition*) were told of these effects. Participants in a second condition (*epinephrine-misinformed*), however, were given *false* information about epinephrine's effects. These participants were told that the injection would cause 'itching', 'facial numbness' and a 'headache'. In a third condition (*epinephrine-ignorant*), participants were given no information at all about the effects of the injection. Participants in a *control condition* were given an injection of a saline solution (which does not cause changes in physiological activity) and were told nothing about the effects of this injection.

After a participant had received the injection, he was taken to a 'waiting room' before supposedly having his vision tested. Once there, he was introduced to another 'participant' who was actually part of the experimental set-up (and we may use the term 'stooge' to describe him). With some of the participants, the stooge pretended to fill out a questionnaire, a copy of which was also given to the genuine participant to complete. As he completed the questionnaire, the stooge began to act 'angrily' and complain loudly about the personal nature of the questions it contained. After a while, the stooge ripped up the questionnaire and stormed out of the room. With other participants, the stooge pretended to

behave 'euphorically' according to a pre-determined script of behaviours including making paper aeroplanes, throwing crumpled up paper into a basket, and generally 'messing around'. Box 17.1 below outlines the predictions derived from Schachter and Singer's theory as regards the effects of the injection, information, and the stooge's behaviour on the genuine participant.

Box 17.1   Hypothesised effects of the various manipulations in Schachter & Singer's (1962) experiment

Epinephrine-informed condition: These participants have been told of the real effects the 'vitamin' injection will have. Whilst they will show an increase in physiological arousal, they will interpret this arousal in a non-emotional way because the effects they are experiencing are the effects they have been told to expect. Factor 1 (arousal) is present in this condition, but Factor 2 (cognitive appraisal in an emotional way) is not. Therefore, participants in this condition should not experience any change in their emotional state.

Epinephrine-misinformed   condition: These participants have been given *false* information about the effects the 'vitamin' injection will have. An increase in physiological arousal will occur but the participants will not be able to explain it in terms of the effects of the injection, since the effects they are experiencing are not those they have been told to expect. Factor 1 (arousal) is present in this condition as is Factor 2 (cognitive appraisal potentially explaining the arousal in an emotional way). In the absence of a suitable non-emotional explanation for their arousal, participants would be expected to cognitively appraise their environment for a logical explanation and a suitable label for the arousal they are experiencing. In a room with somebody behaving 'angrily' or 'euphorically', the participant might conclude that he too was feeling angry or euphoric. Participants in this condition should experience a change in their emotional state.

Epinephrine-ignorant condition: These participants have been given no information about the effects the 'vitamin' injection will have. Like participants in the epinephrine-misinformed condition, these participants will experience arousal and will have no obvious explanation for it since they have not been told that the injection will produce any change in their physiological activity. Since both Factor 1 (arousal) and Factor 2 (cognitive appraisal potentially explaining the arousal in an emotional way) are present, these participants too should experience a change in their emotional state.

Control condition: Participants in this condition have received a 'vitamin' injection but the substance they have been injected with produces no change in physiological activity (it is merely a saline solution). Therefore Factor 1 (arousal) is not present in this condition. Since arousal is necessary for the experience of emotion, participants should not show any change in their emotional state.

The participant's emotional responses were assessed by observers who watched through a one-way mirror and coded the responses according to a pre-determined schedule which included the extent to which the stooge's behaviours were copied. At the end of the stooge's 'routine', the genuine participant was given a questionnaire to fill in that included questions about his emotional state. The results provided *some* support for Schachter and Singer's theory with participants showing emotional changes which were generally in line with the experimental predictions.

Thus, in the 'epinephrine-misinformed' and 'epinephrine-ignorant' conditions participants appeared to use the stooge's behaviour as a cue for identifying and labelling their own emotional state, at least as regards the measurements taken by the observers. Participants in the 'epinephrine-informed' condition had a ready explanation for their arousal (the effects they were told they would experience) and showed little change in their emotional state. The finding that participants' emotional state seemed to change irrespective of whether they were in the 'angry' or 'euphoric' condition is also important because it supports the view that the same type of physiological arousal can be associated with different emotions (recall the view of James and Lange concerning different patterns of physiological activity being associated with different emotions).

In addition to their own study, Schachter and Singer's theory has been supported by other experiments which have reported data consistent with its predictions. In one of these (Dutton & Aron, 1974), participants were unsuspecting males aged between 18 and 35 who happened to be visiting the Capilano Canyon in British Columbia, Canada. Whilst they were on the extremely unstable suspension bridge 230 feet above the canyon, participants were interviewed by an attractive female who asked them questions as part of a survey she was allegedly conducting on reactions to scenic attractions. In a comparison condition, different participants were interviewed by the same female, but on a solid wooden bridge upstream of the canyon.

One of the things both groups of participants were asked to do was to invent a short story about an ambiguous picture of a woman. This was later scored for the amount of sexual content, which was taken to reflect a participant's sexual attraction towards the interviewer. The results showed that those interviewed on the suspension bridge (the 'high arousal' condition) told stories with significantly more sexual imagery than those interviewed on the solid wooden bridge (the 'low arousal' condition). This study seems to confirm the view that the physiological arousal which accompanies all emotions is similar, and that it is our interpretation of the arousal that is important, even though we may occasionally *misidentify* our emotional state. In this case the participants seemed to mislabel their fear as sexual attraction towards the interviewer.

Findings such as those reported by Dutton and Aron have led to Schachter and Singer's theory being applied as a form of therapy. As Reisenzein (1983) has noted, although Schachter and Singer did not explicitly say so, their theory really identifies *two* cognitive components that must be present for emotion to be experienced.

First, cognitive appraisal must interpret the situation in an emotional way. Second this appraisal must 'connect up' (as Gordon, 1978 terms it) with the arousal and be attributed to the emotional source.

In *misattribution therapy*, people are taught to attribute their arousal to some other source. For example, a therapist dealing with a person who is afraid of spiders might give that person a pill and tell them that the pill causes heightened physiological activity. When the person is in the presence of a spider, the heightened physiological activity that occurs as a result of fear is attributed to the effects of the pill (even though the pill actually produces no effects). By misattributing increased physiological activity to the pill rather than the spider, it would not be labelled as 'fear'. After a programme of exposure to spiders under these conditions, spiders would become much less frightening to the person.

Schachter and Singer's theory has been very influential and has sometimes been described as a 'juke box' theory of emotion in which arousal is the coin we put into the juke box and cognition is the button we press to select an 'emotional tune'. However, although the theory highlights the important role played by cognition in the experience of emotion, we should be cautious about accepting it uncritically.

One important problem concerns the *replication* of the original findings reported by Schachter & Singer (1962). Some studies (e.g. Marshall & Zimbardo, 1979) have failed to report *any* effects of the arousal and cognition manipulations. Others (e.g. Maslach, 1978) have found different effects to those reported by Schachter and Singer. In her experiment, Maslach discovered that participants were less likely to imitate the stooge's behaviour and more likely to apply negative emotional labels to their arousal irrespective of the social situation in which they are placed.

Hilgard, at al. (1979) have documented a number of specific criticisms concerned with Schachter and Singer's original experiment. First, epinephrine does not affect everyone in exactly the same way. Indeed, Schachter and Singer actually eliminated from their analysis the data provided by five participants who later reported they experienced no physiological effects. When the data from these discarded participants are included in the analysis, the difference between conditions disappears! Second, Schachter and Singer omitted to assess the mood of the participants *before* they were given the injection. It is possible that a participant in a good mood to begin with might have responded more positively to the stooge irrespective of any injection. Third, as we know, some people are extremely fearful of injections. Schachter and Singer appear to have assumed that receiving an injection is affectively neutral, an assumption highly unlikely to be true.

We should also note that everyday experience suggests that many of our emotions are triggered spontaneously and do not result from interpreting and labelling unexplained arousal. Some sorts of stimuli might produce the emotion of fear long before we had any opportunity to cognitively assess the reason for our heart beating faster. A more complete theory of emotion, then, needs to take this consideration into account. In the following section, we describe a theory that attempts to do just that.

Lazarus' theory of emotion

Despite the criticisms that have been made of the Schachter and Singer theory, the view that cognitive appraisal is a necessary determinant of emotional experience continues to be influential. Of several cognitively-oriented theories that use cognitive appraisal as a central component, the most well-known is that proposed by Richard Lazarus (1982).

Lazarus argues that some degree of cognitive processing is an essential pre-requisite for the experience of emotion. In his view:

> 'Emotion reflects a constantly changing person–environment relationship. When central life agendas (e.g. biological survival, personal and social values and goals) are engaged, this relationship becomes a source of emotion . . . Cognitive activity is a necessary pre-condition of emotion because to experience an emotion, people must comprehend – whether in the form of a primitive evaluative perception or a highly differentiated symbolic process – that their well-being is implicated in a transaction, for better or worse.'

With some emotions, in some situations, cognitive appraisal occurs in a conscious, rational and deliberate way, and up to a point we are able to exercise conscious control over our emotions. However, the view that cognition has primacy over emotion has been disputed by some researchers. Zajonc (1984), for example, has argued that cognition and emotion (or *affect* as Zajonc prefers to call it) operate as independent systems. He believes that in certain circumstances an emotional response may *precede* the onset of cognition and, in other circumstances, an emotional response may occur in the *absence* of any type of cognitive appraisal. For example, when we meet a person for the first time, we often form a positive or negative impression even though we have processed very little information about that person. In Zajonc's view, we have evolved the capacity to detect affective qualities *without* cognitive mediation (and you may feel that LeDoux's, 1989, research which we described in the previous chapter is relevant here).

Lazarus, however, disagrees and argues that primitive emotional responses such as fear might not involve any conscious processing, but certainly do involve rapid and unconscious appraisal (and as illustrated in the quote above Lazarus uses the term *primitive evaluative perception* to describe this). Zajonc has also been criticised on the grounds that some of the things he identifies as emotional states are not emotional states at all. One of these, 'startle', is essentially a *reflex* response, and Lazarus would not disagree with the view that it occurs in the absence of any cognitive appraisal!

In support of Lazarus, Ekman, et al. (1985) have noted that whilst 'startle' is a response to a sudden loud noise which is produced automatically in *all people*, there is no known stimulus which reliably produces the same emotion in everybody. As Eysenck & Keane (1990) have noted:

'There is no doubt that Lazarus's studies have far more direct relevance to everyday emotional experiences than do those of Zajonc. This provides grounds for assuming (albeit tentatively) that emotional experience is generally preceded by cognitive processes, even if that is not invariably the case.'

Conclusions

In this chapter we have described and evaluated some of the theories that have been offered to explain the experience of emotion. Whilst some theories are almost certainly untrue, others have evidence which generally supports their claims. However, at present we do not seem to have a single comprehensive theory of emotional experience. Nor, perhaps, are we ever likely to have one. The reason for this is that ethical considerations preclude us from inducing strong emotions as part of psychological research. Whilst we can ask participants to make a facial expression corresponding to a particular emotion, we cannot expect them to actually experience such strong emotions. Only those situations which are motivationally relevant for a person can reliably produce strong emotions, and it would be unethical to create these in laboratory settings.

SUMMARY

- Different theories of emotion are distinguished by how they see the relationship between **subjective feelings, cognitive processes, physiological arousal**, and **behavioural reactions**, and the relative emphasis given to one or more of these components.
- A **common sense theory of emotion** claims that a physiological response occurs as a result of an emotional experience. But the **James-Lange theory of emotion** reverses this picture: emotional experience is the **result** of bodily and/or behavioural changes to an emotion-provoking stimulus.
- According to the James-Lange theory, emotions are a **by-product/cognitive representation**

of automatic physiological and behavioural responses. The brain receives **sensory feedback** from the internal organs **and** parts of the body that respond to emotion-provoking stimuli; this feedback is then labelled appropriately.
- Cannon criticised the James-Lange theory on three counts:
   – unless each emotion had its own distinct pattern of physiological activity, the cortex would be unable to identify the emotion. The relevant evidence is mixed: while some studies have shown that different emotions differ in terms of heart rate, body temperature, facial muscular activity, blood pressure, and neural activity in the frontal lobes, others have shown that **different** people

may display **different** patterns of physiological activity when experiencing the **same** emotion, and the **same** person may respond **differently** when experiencing the **same** emotion on **different** occasions

– physiological changes themselves do not produce changes in emotional state. This is supported by Maranon's study in which participants injected with **adrenaline** either reported **no** emotional effects or **as if** emotions

– total separation of the viscera from the central nervous system does **not** result in the absence of emotional experience. This criticism was based largely on studies of dogs and cats, and Cannon overlooked the role of the **muscles** in providing feedback.

- Hohmann's study of patients with spinal cord injuries casts doubt on Cannon's criticism. Based on self-reports of emotional intensity, the study revealed reduced emotional experience for events occurring after the injury, and the higher up the spinal cord the injury occurred, the greater the reduction in **feelings,** though not necessarily in **behaviour**. Hohmann's and other supportive studies have been criticised on methodological grounds.

- An important **practical** implication of the James-Lange theory is that deliberately expressing a particular emotion through our faces will induce self-reported changes in emotional state as well as distinct patterns of physiological activity. There is considerable empirical support for **facial feedback theory.**

- Contraction of the facial muscles might increase physiological arousal, or it might affect blood flow to the brain, which influences the release of **serotonin** and **norepinephrine** (and other **neurotransmitters**). Whatever the specific mechanisms involved, and allowing for methodological criticisms of some of the relevant studies, facial feedback theory could be used as a treatment for certain emotional disorders.

- Cannon believed that all emotions produce the **same** pattern of responses, corresponding to the **fight-or-flight** response. According to the **Cannon-Bard thalamic theory of emotion**, external stimuli activate the **thalamus** which (a) sends sensory information to the cortex for interpretation, and (b) simultaneously sends **activation messages** to the viscera and skeletal muscles. These are **independent** of each other, so that the experience of emotion neither causes **nor** is caused by the physiological/behavioural responses.

- According to Schachter and Singer, Cannon was wrong in claiming that bodily changes and emotional experiences are independent, just as the James-Lange theory was wrong in claiming that physiological changes cause the experience of emotion. According to **Schachter and Singer's theory of emotion, both** physiological arousal in the autonomic nervous system and **cognitive appraisal** (interpretation) of the arousal are necessary for emotional experience.

- Like the James-Lange theory, Schachter and Singer see arousal as preceding emotional experience and being necessary for it; but arousal alone is not sufficient, since emotional experience requires the arousal to be appraised in an emotional way. The same physiological changes underlie **all** emotions; it is the **meaning** that is attributed to them that determines the particular emotion that is experienced.

- Schachter and Singer's theory is sometimes called the **two-factor theory**, and they tested it in the famous **epinephrine experiment**. In three experimental conditions, male college students were given an injection of **epinephrine**: epinephrine-informed/epinephrine-misinformed/epinephrine-ignorant. A **control condition** involved injection of a saline solution. All participants were then exposed to either an **angry** or a **euphoric stooge** and their emotional responses assessed by observers and a self-report questionnaire. The results were mostly in line with the predictions.

- Dutton and Aron's **suspension bridge** experiment supports Schachter and Singer's belief that the physiological arousal which accompanies all emotions is similar, and that it is our interpretation of the arousal that is important, even though we may sometimes **misidentify** our emotional state: Dutton and Aron's male participants seemed to mislabel their fear as sexual attraction.

- In **misattribution therapy**, people are taught to attribute their arousal to a source other than its actual or customary one, as in the arousal associated with a fear of spiders being attributed to a pill with which the therapist pairs the spider.

- A number of attempts to replicate the **epinephrine experiment** have failed. Epinephrine affects different people in different ways. Schachter and Singer failed to assess their participants' mood **before** giving them the injection, and being given an injection is **not** affectively neutral, as they seemed to assume.

- Despite criticisms of Schachter and Singer's theory, many cognitively-oriented theories are based on some form of cognitive appraisal. According to Lazarus, some degree of cognitive processing is an essential prerequisite for emotional experience. Sometimes this occurs in a conscious, rational, and deliberate way.

- Zajonc disputes the view that cognition has primacy over emotion, claiming that cognition and **affect** operate independently, so that sometimes an emotional response **precedes** cognition or may occur in the **absence** of cognitive appraisal. Lazarus claims that emotional responses such as fear may not involve **conscious** appraisal but do involve **primitive evaluative perception**. However, both theorists agree that **reflex** emotional responses, such as startle (which is a universal response), do not involve any cognitive appraisal.

STRESS

Introduction and overview

Sixty years ago, a Canadian researcher, Hans Selye, conducted a series of experiments whose aim was to discover a new sex hormone. In one such experiment, rats were injected with ovary tissue extracts. This caused an enlargement of the adrenal cortex, shrinkage of the thymus gland, and ulcers of the stomach and small intestine. Since no known hormone produced such effects, Selye believed he had discovered a new one. However, when he injected extracts from other tissues or toxic fluids that did not come from tissues, the results were identical.

Instead of abandoning his research, Selye changed his direction. As he noted, 'it suddenly struck me that one could look at (the experiments) from an entirely different angle. (Perhaps) there was such a thing as a non-specific reaction of the body to damage of any kind' (Selye, 1976). Later, Selye showed that when rats were exposed to a variety of adverse conditions such as extreme cold, fatigue, electric shocks, or surgical trauma, the same pattern of physiological responses was observed.

Although Selye's research was undertaken on non-human animals, he pioneered a continuing interest in something we are all familiar with – stress. We have three aims in this chapter. Our first is look at what stress is and at theory and research findings concerning the effects stress has on the body. Following that we will examine the relationship between stress and illness. Our final aim in this chapter is to look at some of the ways in which stress can be reduced and its impact on our health minimised.

What is stress?

Intuitively, we all know what stress is because we have all experienced it at one time or another. However, defining what we mean by 'stress' is no easy task. Physicists see stress as the pressure or force that is exerted on a body. Psychologists take a similar view, but look at stress in terms of the demands it makes on an organism and the efforts the organism makes to adapt, cope, or adjust to those demands. An adequate definition of stress must, therefore, include the interaction between external *stressors* and our physiological and psychological responses to them. An adequate definition must also acknowledge the role played by cognitive factors, since the way in which a potential stressor is *appraised* by people influences the effects it has. Finally, since some stress (or what Selye, 1980, terms *eustress*) is healthy and necessary to keep us alert, an adequate definition must also take into account the fact that stress can be beneficial as well as detrimental.

A definition of stress which meets the requirements outlined above has been offered by Lazarus & Folkman (1984). They define stress as 'a pattern of negative physiological states and psychological responses occurring in situations where people perceive threats to their well-being which they may be unable to meet'. Lazarus and Folkman's definition is generally accepted by those active in the area of research into stress.

THE EFFECTS OF STRESS ON THE BODY

In the introduction to this chapter we noted that the rats studied by Selye appeared to respond in the same way irrespective of the adverse conditions to which they were exposed. On the basis of this, Selye concluded that the body's response to a stressor is *non-specific*. Selye argued that when an organism is confronted with a stressor the body mobilises for action to defend itself against the stressor. If the stressor can be adequately managed, the body returns to its original state. However, if repeated or prolonged exposure to the stressor cannot be managed, the organism suffers tissue damage, increased susceptibility to disease and, in extreme cases, death.

Selye called the non-specific response produced by a stressor the *general adaptation syndrome* or *GAS* and, for reasons which will become clear shortly, it is also known as the *pituitary-adrenal stress syndrome*. The GAS is held to consist of three distinct stages. Because these stages represents an excellent example of the ways in which the *central nervous system, autonomic nervous system*, and *endocrine system* interact, we will consider them in some detail.

The first stage is called the *alarm reaction* and is triggered by the perception of a stressor. It is in this stage that the body is mobilised for action. In the *shock phase* of the alarm reaction the body initially responds with a drop in blood pressure and muscle tension. The shock phase, which lasts only briefly, is replaced by the *counter-shock phase* which is an alerting response to possible threat or physical injury. The bodily reactions in the counter-shock phase are initiated by the *hypothalamus* (see Chapter 2) and regulated by the *sympathetic branch of the autonomic nervous system* and the *endocrine system* (see Chapter 3). Some of the major processes that occur in the alarm reaction are described in Box 18.1 below.

Box 18.1 The major processes occurring in the alarm reaction

The perception of a stressor results in the *hypothalamus*:

(a) releasing *corticotrophic-releasing hormone*. This stimulates the *pituitary gland* to secrete *adrenocorticotrophic hormone* (ACTH). ACTH acts on the *adrenal cortex* of the *adrenal gland,* causing it to enlarge and release *corticosteroids*. These help to fight inflammation and allergic reactions (e.g. difficulty in breathing)

(b) activating the *sympathetic branch of the autonomic nervous system*. This causes the *adrenal medulla* of the *adrenal gland* to enlarge and release *adrenaline* and *noradrenaline* (the 'stress hormones'). This initiates a heightened pattern of physiological activity which includes:

- accelerated heart rate and increased blood pressure in order to send blood to parts of the body that will need it for strenuous activity
- the release of glucose from the liver to provide fuel for quick energy
- accelerated respiration rate to supply more oxygen to the muscles
- a tensing of the muscles in preparation for an adaptive response (such as running away)
- an increase in blood coaguability so that blood will clot more quickly if injury occurs
- perspiration in order to cool the body and allow more energy to be burned
- the curtailing of digestion which makes more blood available to the muscles and brain

- the breaking down of some tissue to provide energy-giving sugars
- the movement of blood from the internal organs to the skeletal musculature.

(Note that the amount of corticosteroids and adrenaline in the body serve as an objective biological measure of stress since they are secreted in response to a stressor. The measurements may be taken from a urine sample.)

The heightened pattern of physiological activity shown in Box 18.1 (which Cannon, 1927, termed the *fight-or-flight response* – see Chapters 3 and 17) cannot be maintained for long. If the stressor is removed, physiological activity returns to its baseline levels (although we should note that the noradrenaline released by the adrenal gland *prolongs* the action of adrenaline, with the result that sympathetic arousal continues for a period even if the stressor is removed). However, if the stressor continues then at some point the *parasympathetic branch of the autonomic nervous system* (*ANS* – see Chapter 3) is activated in an attempt to slow down the internal organs (such as the heart) that have been activated by the sympathetic branch.

Although endocrine and sympathetic activity drop slightly, they are still higher than normal as the body continues to draw on its resources. This is the second stage of the GAS and is called the *resistance stage*. If the stressor can be adequately dealt with or is terminated, the organism is unlikely to suffer any physiological damage. However, the action of corticosteroids aggravates the natural inflammatory reaction and the *immune system's* reaction to infection or physical damage is reduced. Additionally, the repair of cells which have a high turnover is inhibited. So, whilst an organism *appears* to be able to defend itself against the stressor, its body's resources are depleted because they are being used faster than they are being replaced.

If the stressor continues, the adrenal glands enlarge and lose their stores of adrenal hormones. Tissues begin to show signs of wear-and-tear, muscles become fatigued, and the endocrine glands, kidneys and other internal organs are damaged. This is the *exhaustion stage* of the GAS and it is in this stage that what Selye terms *diseases of adaptation* occur. These include ulcers and coronary heart disease (see pages 171–174). The relationship between the three stages of the GAS and an organism's level of resistance to a stressor are shown in Figure 18.1.

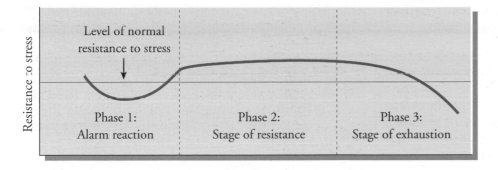

Figure 18.1   The three stages of the general adaptation syndrome

Selye's GAS has been widely acknowledged to offer a useful approach to our understanding of the physiological responses to a stressor. However, it has not escaped criticism. For example, Selye's claim concerning the non-specific responses produced by stressors has been challenged. Taylor (1990), for example, has shown that some stressors produce patterns of physiological activity which are different to those produced by other stressors. It has also been pointed out that Selye's GAS, based as it was on responses to stressors produced in non-human animals, fails to consider the role played by *psychological factors* in the production of the stress response and the fact that stressors may have psychological as well as physiological effects. Box 18.2 below summarises the role of psychological factors and some of the psychological effects that stress exerts.

Box 18.2   Psychological responses to a stressor

Stressors can exert a variety of effects on our *cognitive processes*. Some of these are negative. For example, a person experiencing a stressor might be easily distracted from a task and perform it poorly. However, and as Selye acknowledges, some stress (eustress – see page 169) can be beneficial, at least up to a point.

The *primary appraisal* of a stressor involves deciding whether it has positive, neutral, or negative implications. If it is decided that the stressor has negative implications, it is assessed according to how challenging, threatening, or harmful it is. After this primary appraisal, *secondary appraisal* occurs. This involves considering the extent to which our abilities will allow us to overcome the challenge, threat, or harm that was assessed earlier on. Whether stress is experienced or not depends on these two appraisals.

Stress is also associated with *negative emotional states*. Such states include anger, hostility, embarrassment, depression, helplessness, and anxiety. Of these, anxiety is the most damaging and people who cannot cope effectively with anxiety are more susceptible to a variety of psychological and physical disorders.

Stress affects *behaviour* in a variety of ways. Some behaviours involve an attempt to confront the stressor whilst others involve withdrawing from it (and the terms 'fight' and 'flight' respectively can be used to describe these). Yet other behaviours involve an attempt to adapt to the stressor by, for example, taking avoiding action whenever it occurs. All of these behaviours can be seen as attempts to manage or reduce the effects of stressors, and are discussed further on pages 174–178.

Stress and illness

There is a large body of evidence to suggest that stress plays a *causal* role in certain types of illness. Indeed, according to Frese (1985), stress is involved in around 50–70% of *all* physical illnesses. Research has discovered a link between stress and headaches, asthma, cancer, cardiovascular disorders, hypertension, and the malfunctioning of the immune system. We will now look at some of the findings that have been reported.

STRESS AND THE IMMUNE SYSTEM

The essential function of the immune system is to help us combat disease. When bacteria, viruses, and other hazardous foreign bodies (or *antigens*) are detected, the immune system stimulates white blood cells (or *leucocytes*) to seek out and destroy them. The immune system also produces *antibodies* which bind to antigens and identify them as targets for destruction. In a very clever way, the immune system forms a 'memory' of how to battle the antigens it encounters by maintaining them in the bloodstream.

Another role played by the immune system is in *inflammation*. As a result of injury, blood vessels first contract in order to stem bleeding. Shortly afterwards they dilate, which allows more blood to flow to the damaged area (hence the redness and warmth that characterises inflammation). The increased blood supply carries large numbers of leucocytes to combat any foreign bodies that might use the injured area to gain access to the body. However, if the immune system is suppressed, we are much more vulnerable to the effects of hazardous foreign bodies. If, for some reason, the immune system becomes over-reactive, it turns on itself and attacks healthy body tissues.

The study of the effects that psychological factors (especially stress) exert on the immune system is called *psychoneuroimmunology*. As we saw earlier on, the production of various steroids is increased when the body is exposed to a stressor. Although an intermittent secretion of steroids has negligible effects on the immune system, persistent secretion (as occurs in the GAS) impairs its functioning by interfering with the production of antibodies. This decreases inflammation and suppresses the activity of leucocytes.

Stressful events have been linked to a variety of infectious diseases such as influenza, herpes, and the Epstein-Barr virus which, amongst other things, causes fatigue. Stressful events that appear to compromise the immune system include the death of a spouse, marital discord, and taking examinations. Immunological deficiencies were even shown in American astronauts immediately following the experience of re-entering the earth's atmosphere and splashing down in the ocean (Kimzey, 1975). In non-humans, separation from the mother, electric shocks, and exposure to loud noise have all been shown to cause immunological deficiencies (Esterling & Rabin, 1987).

Given the role of the immune system and the effect that prolonged exposure to stressors has on it, it is hardly surprising that there is a link between stress and illness. Steroid production may not be the only factor involved. Recent research has focussed on the influence that stressors may have on the production of *immunoglobulin A*, one of the body's first defenders against influenza, and *interleukin-b*, a protein which is produced soon after tissue injury and regulates the remodelling of the connective tissue in wounds and the rate of production of collagen, the tough fibrous tissue in scars. In a study reported by Sweeney (1995), two groups of participants agreed to undergo a small skin biopsy on their arms. Compared to a non-stressed control group, it took significantly longer (nine days) for the wound to heal in people experiencing stress as a result of caring for relatives with dementia. This finding suggests that stress impairs the body's ability to heal as well as its response to infectious diseases, and this could have important consequences for people undergoing major surgery.

STRESS AND CANCER

The word 'cancer' refers to over 100 disorders that affect humans, non-humans and even plants. Cancer's essential feature is the rapid development of abnormal cells which deplete the body's nutrients. Although the evidence linking stress and cancer is not conclusive, it is impressive. For example, Visintainer, et al. (1983) have shown that the injection of cancerous cells followed by exposure to an uncontrollable stressor dramatically weakens non-human animals' ability to resist the effects of the cells. Additionally, exposure to a stressor is linked to a higher incidence of malignancy than is observed in non-stressful conditions.

In humans, Jacobs & Charles (1980) have shown that cancer patients have often experienced higher than normal levels of stress prior to the onset of their illness. A significant percentage of children with cancer, for example, had experienced severe changes in their lives, such as the death of a loved one, within one years of the diagnosis. Tache, et al. (1979) have produced evidence suggesting that cancer occurs more frequently among widowed, divorced, or separated adults as compared with those who are married. This might suggest that the stress caused by the absence of a *social support network* (see page 177) plays an important role in the development of cancer.

Unfortunately, one of the principal weaknesses of studies looking at the relationship between stress and cancer is that they tend to be *retrospective*, that is, patients with cancer are asked to discuss events that occurred before they developed the illness. Such discussion may be inaccurate for a number of reasons. Another weakness concerns the cause and effect relationship between stress and cancer. It may be, for example, that stress is the result of cancer developing rather than the cause of it.

In addition to these weaknesses, there is the further problem of identifying the physiological mechanism which links stress and cancer (if, indeed, one exists). According to Levy (1983), the immune system plays a key role. As we have seen, the immune system guards against hazardous foreign bodies and, according to Rogers, et al. (1979), may even produce chemicals specifically designed to defend against cancer cells. Since the relationship between stress and the immune system seems to be well established, it is at least plausible to propose that the immune system may be the mechanism which links stress and cancer.

There is, however, at least one other possibility concerning the stress-cancer relationship. As with certain other illnesses, there appears to be an inherited predisposition towards developing cancer, and it is beyond dispute that certain behaviours (such as smoking cigarettes) heighten the risk for certain types of cancer. Stressful experiences might lead people to engage in behaviours that heighten this risk. Cigarette smokers, for example, might smoke even more in stressful circumstances and increase yet further their risk of developing cancer.

STRESS AND CARDIOVASCULAR DISORDERS

Cardiovascular disorders, such as heart diseases and disorders of the circulatory system, have long been known to be associated with a variety of 'risk factors'. These include diet, heavy drinking, smoking, obesity, and a lack of physical activity. However, since these known risk factors account for only 50% of all diagnosed cases, other factors must be involved and one of these appears to be stress.

In the late 1950s, Meyer Friedman and Ray Rosenman looked at the relationship between diet and cardiovascular disorders. Their findings showed that men were far more susceptible to heart disease than women, even though there seemed to be no significant differences between the sexes as far as diet was concerned. Friedman and Rosenman speculated that the difference might be due to job-related stress since most of the men worked but most of the women did not. When questioned about what they thought had caused their own heart attacks and those of colleagues, respondents seemed to share Meyer and Friedman's speculation.

In a follow-up study, 40 tax accountants had their blood clotting speed and serum cholesterol levels (both of which are used as warning signs in coronary heart disease) monitored over several months. From January to the beginning of April, the levels were within the normal range. However, as the deadline for filing tax returns approached, the levels rose dangerously and then returned to normal once the deadline had passed.

Friedman & Rosenman (1974) then undertook a much larger study lasting for nine years and involving several thousand 39–59-year-old men who were initially physically healthy. On the basis of their responses about eating habits and ways of dealing with stressful conditions, the participants were divided into roughly equal groups which were called 'Type A' and 'Type B'. Type A individuals tended to be ambitious, competitive, easily angered, time-conscious, hard-driving, and demanding of perfection in both themselves and others. Type B individuals tended to be relaxed, easy-going, not driven to achieve perfection, understanding, forgiving, and not easily angered. Subsequent research has identified other ways in which Type A people differ from Type B people, some of which are shown in Box 18.3 below.

Box 18.3   Some of the differences between Type A and Type B behaviour

Compared to Type B individuals, Type A individuals tend to:

- suppress symptoms of tiredness
- show greater expression of aggression and hostility
- eat, walk, and talk rapidly, and become restless when they see others working slowly
- try and dominate group discussions
- be unwilling to surrender control or share power
- be highly self-critical
- seek out negative information about themselves in order to bring about improvements
- constantly strive for achievement
- think negative thoughts about themselves and others.

Friedman and Rosenman found that of the 257 men who died in the nine years after the study began, 70% were members of the Type A group. Other research has generally confirmed the finding that Type A individuals have a greater risk of developing heart disease. The role of the so-called *Type A personality* in 'coronary proneness' has been the subject of much debate. For example, Hicks & Pellegrini (1982) have proposed that

Type A people engage more frequently in behaviours that are known risk factors whilst Krantz & Manuck (1984) have suggested that Type A people are more psychologically reactive to stress and that this contributes to their coronary proneness.

It has also been argued that Type A behaviour is a *response* to, rather than a cause of, physiological reactivity. It seems that even when they are unconscious and undergoing surgery, Type A people show higher blood pressure levels than Type B people experiencing the same surgery. This finding might suggest the existence of a predisposition to respond with heightened physiological activity in the presence of a stressor. If this is the case, then Type A behaviour could be interpreted as a way of *coping* with heightened physiological activity.

Ragland & Brand (1988) have presented findings indicating that there is actually no difference between the incidence of heart attacks and death rates between Type A and Type B men. Indeed, Ragland and Brand argue that their data suggest that Type A men might actually be at a *lower risk* of recurrent heart attacks than Type B men. It has been suggested that the contradictory findings can be reconciled if it is assumed that some Type A characteristics are more influential than others. According to Wright (1988), the most important aspects of Type A behaviour are *hostility* and an *aggressively reactive temperament*. Other researchers (e.g. Carson, 1989) have proposed that *cynicism*, or expecting the worst from other people, is the most important factor.

Clearly, the relationship between stress and cardiovascular disorders is far from straightforward. Stress itself cannot cause cardiovascular disorders, but exactly how it is linked continues to be the subject of research interest. However, it seems likely that activity in the sympathetic branch of the autonomic nervous system is involved.

STRESS AND HYPERTENSION

Consistent with the likely role played by the sympathetic branch of the ANS, it has been suggested that stress is linked to cardiovascular disorders because of the role it evidently plays in hypertension or high blood pressure. An increase in the flow of blood through the veins occurs when activity in the ANS is heightened. This can cause both a hardening and a general deterioration in the tissue of the blood vessels. Although a number of factors contribute to hypertension, the role

of stress has been demonstrated in several studies.

For example, Harburg, et al. (1973) measured the blood pressure of people from 'high' and 'low' stress areas of Detroit in the United States, defining high stress areas as those in which population density, crime rates, poverty and divorce were greatest. The highest blood pressures were found in those who lived in the highest stress areas, although as with much of the research into the relationship between stress and illness, considerable caution needs to be exercised in interpreting health and demographic data.

From our review of the evidence concerning the link between stress and illness, it seems reasonable to conclude that stress almost certainly plays a role in the development of certain types of illness. Given that illnesses are unpleasant, most of us would seek ways of minimising our experience of them. If stress can cause illness, it is important to find ways in which stress can be reduced and its impact on our health minimised. The following section will address this issue.

Reducing stress

One way to reduce stress is to eliminate the factors that give rise to it. However, since there are so many different factors that can cause stress it would be impossible to eliminate all of them completely from our lives! Many ways of managing and reducing stress have been devised. Dixon (1980), for example, has suggested that humour can be beneficial because it stimulates the output of *endorphins* (see Chapter 1). Although the use of humour might seem to be a light-hearted (so to speak) approach to a serious problem, the moderating effects of humour on stress have been demonstrated (e.g. Martin & Lefcourt, 1983). In this section, however, we will briefly examine some approaches to the management and reduction of stress which are more orthodox.

REDUCING PHYSIOLOGICAL RESPONSES TO STRESS

As we have seen, the stress response involves the activation of the sympathetic branch of the ANS, that is, stress increases *arousal*. Several methods for reducing the physiological effects of stress can be identified. One of these involves the use of *psychotherapeutic drugs* which act directly on the ANS. Commonly used are the *benzodiazepine anti-anxiety (or anxiolytic) drugs* (such as *Librium* and *Valium*). However, whilst these and other drugs may reduce the physiological effects of stress, they do lead to a physical dependence in at least some people who take them and may also have unpleasant side-effects. For this reason alone, other methods of reducing physiological responses would seem preferable.

One alternative method is *biofeedback*. The human body is not designed to allow us to be consciously aware of subtle feedback about our internal physiological states that occur when we experience stress. The aim of biofeedback is to provide this information so that we can, at least to a degree, learn how to modify or control our internal physiological states. A biofeedback machine produces precise information (or feedback) about bodily processes such as heart rate and/or blood pressure. This information may be presented in visual or auditory form (or both). For example, a change in heart rate may be indicated by a tone which changes pitch and/or a line on a television monitor that rises or falls when heart rate increases or decreases.

The fact that some people do seem to be able to regulate some internal bodily processes has led to biofeedback being used to reduce many types of disorder associated with stress. These include migraine headaches, tension headaches, and high blood pressure. However, whilst biofeedback might be useful in stress reduction, there are a number of disadvantages associated with it. First, unlike methods we will consider shortly, biofeedback requires physiological measuring devices. Because biofeedback and techniques which do not require specialised equipment are equally effective in stress reduction, biofeedback would seem to be least preferable.

Another disadvantage is that regular practice over a period of months appears to be needed for the development and maintenance of any beneficial effects (although we should note that this is also true of some methods we will consider shortly). Finally, whilst biofeedback may eventually enable a person to learn to recognise the symptoms of, say, high blood pressure without the need for the biofeedback machine, it is not known exactly how biofeedback works. Some sceptics have argued that biofeedback itself exerts no effects and that what is important is a person's commitment to reducing stress and the active involvement of the stress therapist!

Physiological responses to stress may also be reduced through *relaxation*. In a very early study of the physical reactions to stress, Jacobson (1938) observed that people tended to add to the discomfort they were experiencing by tensing their muscles. In order to overcome this, Jacobson devised *progressive relaxation*. In this, the muscles in some area of the body are first tightened and then relaxed. Then, another group of muscles is tightened and relaxed and so on until, progressively, the entire body is relaxed.

Once a person becomes aware of muscle tension and can differentiate between feelings of tension and relaxation, the technique can be used to control stress-induced effects. Progressive relaxation has been shown to lower the arousal associated with the alarm reaction (see page 170) and reduce the number of recurrent heart attacks. As Green (1994) has noted, though, progressive relaxation only has long-term benefits if it is incorporated into a person's lifestyle as a regular procedure.

Another relaxation technique is *meditation*. In this, a person assumes a comfortable position and, with eyes closed, attempts to clear all disturbing thoughts from the mind. A single syllable, or *mantra*, is then silently repeated. Although meditation has attracted controversy, at least some people who use it believe that it helps them to relax. Indeed, Wallace & Fisher (1987) have shown that meditation reduces oxygen consumption and induces electrical activity in the brain indicative of a calm, mental state. Jacob, et al. (1977) have shown that both progressive relaxation and meditation reduce blood pressure more than placebos do, and the fact that both of these techniques do not require specialised equipment gives them, as we noted earlier, an advantage over biofeedback.

In an early study of London bus drivers and conductors, Morris, et al. (1953) showed that the conductors, who moved around the bus collecting fares, were far less likely to suffer from cardiovascular disorders than the drivers, who remained seated in their cabs. Although Morris and his colleagues' study was correlational, subsequent research has confirmed their suggestion that *physical activity and exercise* are beneficial in the reduction of stress.

All forms of physical activity seem to be useful in reducing the incidence of stress-related illnesses. Physiologically, exercise promotes fitness. Although fitness is a complex concept, being fit allows, amongst other things, our bodies to use greater amounts of oxygen during vigorous exercise and pump more blood with each heart beat. As a result, circulation is improved and the heart muscle strengthened. Psychologically, exercise might also be therapeutic, since it has been shown that sustained exercise can reduce depression and boost feelings of self-esteem (Sonstroem, 1984).

REDUCING STRESS BY CHANGING COGNITIONS

Meichenbaum (1985) has devised a three-step procedure, which he calls *stress inoculation*, to control the *catastrophising thoughts* that people often have in potentially stressful situations (an example would be a person about to take a driving test who says, 'I just *know* I'm not going to pass'). The first step (*conceptualisation*) involves a therapist talking with the individual and helping to identify and express feelings and fears. The second step (*skill acquisition and rehearsal*) involves replacing negative self-statements with positive coping statements that are incompatible with them. A person about to take a driving test, for example, might be encouraged to say to his or herself, 'There's no point in imagining the worst. I've prepared as well as anyone, and I'll do the best I can'. The third step (*application and follow-through*) involves the therapist guiding the individual through a series of progressively more threatening situations. The individual rewards him or herself with a 'mental pat on the back' for having produced effective changes in beliefs and thought patterns. Although it may take time to learn to alter negative 'self-talk' successfully, Meichenbaum claims that this method of 'cognitive restructuring' can significantly reduce the amount of stress that, for example, taking tests and examinations can produce.

People seem to differ widely in terms of their ability to resist the effects of a stressor. One characteristic that apparently helps people to resist stress has been termed *hardiness* by Kobasa (1979). According to Kobasa, 'hardy' individuals differ from 'non-hardy' individuals in three main ways:

- they are highly *committed* or more deeply involved in whatever they do and see the activities associated with their endeavours as being meaningful
- they view change as a *challenge* for growth and development rather than a threat or burden
- they see themselves as having a stronger *sense of control* over events in their lives, and feel they can overcome their experiences (to use Rotter's (1966) term, they have a *high internal locus of control*).

By choosing to be in stress-producing situations, interpreting the stress that occurs as making life more interesting, and being in control, the amount of stress experienced can be regulated. Research carried out by Pines (1984) has shown that people high in hardiness tend to be healthier than those low in hardiness, even though the amount of stressful experiences to which they have been exposed does not differ.

On the basis of her own and others' findings, Kobasa has suggested that stress can be reduced if hardiness is increased. One approach to this is to teach people to identify the physical signs of stress, since a stressor can hardly be dealt with if it cannot be identified. Even if we can identify stressors, the way in which we deal with them might not necessarily be beneficial. Another approach is therefore to try and make a more realistic assessment of life's stresses. This involves examining a stressful experience in terms of the ways in which it could have been more and less effectively dealt with.

A third approach identified by Kobasa derives from her view that our perceived abilities to bring about change have important effects on our capacity to withstand stress (a view shared by Bandura, 1984). Kobasa suggests that when the effects of a stressor cannot be avoided, we should take on some other challenge which can be dealt with in order to experience the *positive* aspects of coping with a stressor. What Bandura terms *self-efficacy expectations* regulate problem-solving and allow us to 'bounce back' more readily from failure so that life's stressors are actually experienced as being less stressful.

Another way in which we differ in our ability to resist stress is related to the *coping strategies* we use in trying to manage it. Coping is the cognitive and behavioural efforts to manage specific external and/or internal demands that are appraised as taxing or exceeding our resources. Lazarus & Folkman (1984) have distinguished between *problem-focussed* and *emotion-focussed* coping strategies. In the former, some specific plan for dealing with a stressor is made and implemented and other activities are not engaged in until the stressor has been reduced or terminated. The latter involves implementing strategies that are effective in the short term, but do little to reduce or eliminate a stressor's long-term effects.

Consider, for example, having to revise for an examination as a potential source of stress. A problem-focussed coping strategy would be to organise a revision plan and then adhere to it until the day of the examination. What Moos (1988) terms a *behavioural* emotion-focussed coping strategy might be to go out drinking every night, which would avoid having to confront the stressor. When the results of the examination are published, the stress caused by failure could be reduced by using a *cognitive* emotion-focussed coping strategy such as claiming there was no opportunity to revise. Most of us use a combination of problem- and emotion-focussed strategies, but some people rely almost exclusively on the latter. By teaching them more effective strategies for dealing with stressors, the amount of stress a problem engenders can be significantly reduced.

REDUCING STRESS BY CHANGING BEHAVIOUR

At least some of the stresses we experience in everyday life could be reduced if we simply changed some of our behaviours. *Stress management programmes* have identified a variety of techniques for dealing with the stress that occurs as a result of our behaviour. For example, some people tend to leave things until the last minute and then find themselves under extreme pressure to get a job done. *Time management training* aims to help people pace themselves so as to avoid leaving too much for the last minute.

This approach can also be used to help what has been termed the *superperson syndrome*. Some people take on many tasks and find it difficult to accomplish any one of them. Time management helps us to recognise our limits so that we (a) do not take on more than we can accomplish and (b) delegate at least some of the work to others. Another way in which time management can be used is to help people organise themselves more effectively. This involves training in how to establish goals, avoid wasting time, and become more task-oriented. For those who find it difficult to 'stand up for their rights' and who may be 'boiling inside', *assertiveness training* can be used, the aim being to help people *confront* stress-provoking situations.

A final approach to managing stress by changing behaviour stems from the fact that facing stress alone can be more damaging than facing it with the support of others. The term *social support* refers to the resources provided by others when stress is experienced. Evidence suggests that social supports can be beneficial in the reduction of stress even if the stressful situation remains unchanged. For example, Fleming, et al. (1984) found that residents affected by the nuclear near-accident at Pennsylvania's Three Mile Island reactor plant reported

less stress if they had solid networks of social supports, such as close friends or relatives, with whom they could share their experiences.

The effect of social support has been even more powerfully demonstrated in research reviewed by Berkman (1984). Berkman showed that people with fewer family, friendship, and community ties were significantly more likely to die at a given age than those who had strong ties, irrespective of their physical health. Research conducted by Wolf & Bruhn (1993) has shown that social support can be of considerable help with those people suffering from coronary heart disease. Some of the types of social support that can help to reduce stress are shown in Box 18.4 below.

Box 18.4   Some major types of social support

Showing emotional concern: This involves listening to a person's concerns and expressing feelings of sympathy, care, reassurance, and understanding.

Providing information: This involves giving information that will enhance a person's ability to cope. Some people, for example, turn to religious personnel or psychotherapists for such guidance.

Giving instructional aid: In some cases people may require material support in order to cope with stress. When national disasters occur, government and other aid agencies provide relief support to reduce the stress experienced by the victims. Even those not directly involved in a disaster can be affected by it. Dixon, et al. (1993), for example, showed that cross-channel ferry workers not involved in the *Herald of Free Enterprise* disaster were strongly affected by it.

Providing feedback: This involves an appraisal of how the individual experiencing stress is doing. This kind of support can help people to interpret or 'make sense' of what has happened to them.

Socialising: The provision of social companionship can help even if it is not designed to solve any problems. Such support ranges from simple conversation to accompanying a person on, say, a shopping trip.

Although social support and stress reduction are related, we should again note that the evidence is primarily *correlational*. Social support is a situational variable, but people can *choose* whether or not they seek such support. Those who do might be better at coping anyway. Finally, we should briefly mention those strategies for reducing stress for those who have been identified as 'Type A' (see page 173). Friedman & Ulmer (1984) have advocated approaches based on altering a person's time urgency, hostility, and self-destructive tendencies. According to Friedman and Ulmer, when behaviour patterns can be successfully changed, the likelihood of recurrent heart attacks is significantly reduced.

Conclusions

Stress exerts a variety of physiological and psychological effects. The extensive research into the link between stress and a variety of illnesses suggests almost beyond doubt that a causal link between stress and illness exists. Given the negative effects of stress, we should not be surprised to find that there are a variety of approaches aimed at reducing stress. Such approaches involve reducing physiological responses and changing cognitions and behaviours.

SUMMARY

- In his attempts to find a new sex hormone, Selye discovered that the **same** effects – enlargement of the adrenal cortex, shrinkage of the thymus gland, and ulcers of the stomach and small intestines – were produced by injecting rats with ovary tissue extracts, extracts from other tissues and toxic fluids that did not come from tissues. This led him to the hypothesis that the body reacts in a non-specific way to any kind of damage or adverse conditions, including electric shocks, extreme cold, fatigue and surgical trauma.

- Psychologists see **stress** as an interaction between the demands made on an organism (**stressors**) and the organism's efforts to adapt, cope, or adjust to those demands (physiological and psychological responses). An adequate definition must also acknowledge the role played by cognitive **appraisal** of potential stressors, as well as the positive aspects of stress (**eustress**).

- A widely accepted definition of stress is that of Lazarus and Folkman, according to whom stress is a pattern of negative physiological states and psychological responses, arising in situations where people perceive threats to their well-being beyond their ability to meet them.

- Selye maintained that the body's response to a stressor is **non-specific** and he called it the **general adaptation syndrome (GAS)**, also known as the **pituitary-adrenal stress syndrome**. The GAS involves an interaction between the **central nervous system** (CNS), **autonomic nervous system** (ANS) and **endocrine system** and comprises three distinct stages.

- The **alarm reaction**, in which the body is mobilised for action, is triggered by the percep-

tion of a stressor. In the **shock phase**, there is an initial drop in blood pressure and muscle tension, quickly followed by the **counter-shock phase**, which alerts the body to possible threat or physical injury.

- The counter-shock phase is initiated by the **hypothalamus**, which releases **corticotrophic-releasing hormone** stimulating the **pituitary gland** to secrete **adrenocorticotrophic hormone (ACTH)**; this acts on the **adrenal cortex** which releases **corticosteroids** (which help to fight inflammation and allergic reactions). The **hypothalamus** also activates the **sympathetic branch** of the ANS, causing the **adrenal medulla** to release **adrenaline** and **noradrenaline** (the 'stress hormones').

- Adrenaline and noradrenaline secretion causes a heightened pattern of physiological activity which Cannon called the **fight-or-flight response**. This includes accelerated heart, respiration rate and blood pressure, release of glucose from the liver, tensing of the muscles, increase in blood coaguability, perspiration, inhibition of digestion, breakdown of certain tissues and the re-direction of blood from internal organs to the skeletal muscles.

- The amount of corticosteroids and adrenaline in the body (based on a urine sample) is an objective measure of stress.

- The fight-or-flight response cannot be maintained for long; if the stressor is removed, physiological activity returns to baseline levels (although noradrenaline prolongs the action of adrenaline, so that sympathetic arousal continues beyond the removal of the stressor).

- If the stressor continues, the **parasympathetic branch** of the ANS is activated in an attempt to slow down the internal organs. However, endocrine and sympathetic activity are still higher than normal as the body continues to draw on its resources; this is the **resistance stage** of the GAS.

- Even if the stressor is dealt with or removed, the action of corticosteroids aggravates the natural inflammatory reaction and the **immune system's** reaction to infection/physical damage is reduced. Bodily resources are becoming depleted because they are being used faster than they are being replaced.

- If the stressor continues, the **exhaustion stage** of the GAS occurs: the adrenal glands enlarge and lose their stores of adrenal hormones, tissues begin to show signs of wear-and-tear, muscles become fatigued, and the endocrine glands, kidneys and other internal organs are damaged. **Diseases of adaptation** occur, such as ulcers and and coronary heart disease.

- While widely recognised as being useful, the GAS has been criticised for claiming that all stressors produce the same non-specific responses, as well as for largely ignoring the **psychological** aspects of the stress response (although Selye himself acknowledged the benefit of eustress).

- Stressors can influence **cognitive processes** in various ways, such as distracting us from a task so that we perform it poorly. A stressor receives a **primary appraisal**, which includes an assessment of how challenging/threatening/harmful any negative implications are, followed by a **secondary appraisal**, which involves an assessment of our ability to overcome the challenge. These two appraisals determine whether or not stress is experienced.

- Stress is also associated with **negative emotional states**, the most damaging of which, both physically and psychologically, is anxiety. It also affects **behaviour**, such as trying to confront the stressor or withdrawing from it ('fight' or 'flight' respectively) and other attempts to manage or reduce the stressor's effects.

- There is evidence to suggest that stress plays a **causal** role in much physical illness, including headaches, asthma, cancer, cardiovascular disorders, hypertension and malfunctioning of the immune system.

- When **antigens** are detected, the **immune system** stimulates white blood cells (**leucocytes**) to seek out and destroy them and **antibodies** which bind to antigens, identify them as targets for destruction. If the immune system becomes over-reactive, its normal role in **inflammation** can result in attacks on healthy tissue.

- Persistent secretion of corticosteroids (as in the GAS) impairs the functioning of the immune system by interfering with the production of antibodies, which decreases inflammation and suppresses the activity of leucocytes.

- **Psychoneuroimmunology** studies the effects of stress on the immune system. Stressful events, such as the death of a spouse, marital discord, and taking exams, have been linked to various infectious diseases. In non-humans, separation from the mother, electric shocks and exposure to loud noise all cause immunological deficiences.

- As well as the effects of prolonged production of corticosteroids, stress seems to interfere with the production of **immunoglobulin A**, involved in resisting influenza, and **interleukin-b**, involved in the healing of wounds and scarring.

- There is considerable, although not conclusive, evidence, both human and non-human, linking stress and cancer; in humans, the stressors include extreme life changes, such as the death of a loved one, separation and divorce. However, the studies are mainly **retrospective**. It is unclear whether the cancer is an effect or a cause of stress, and the precise physiological mechanism involved is not known, although it may well be the immune system.

- Stress may only play an indirect role in producing cancer, by, for example, encouraging behaviour, such as smoking, that increases the risk of developing cancer.

- Risk factors, such as diet, heavy drinking, smoking and obesity, only account for about 50% of **cardiovascular disorders**, such as heart disease and circulatory disorders.

- Friedman and Rosenman initially proposed that men's greater susceptibility to heart disease was due to job-related stress. A follow-up study showed that blood-clotting speed and serum cholesterol levels both rose dangerously as stress levels increased. A larger nine-year study led to the classification of participants as **Type A** and **Type B** individuals.

- **Type A** individuals were described as ambitious, competitive, easily angered, time-conscious, hard-driving, and demanding of perfection both in themselves and others. Other differences have subsequently been identified, such as greater expression of aggression and hostility, an unwillingness to surrender control or share power, and the tendency to be very self-critical.

- Friedman and Rosenman found that Type A individuals have a greater risk of developing heart disease and this has been confirmed by others. But the findings have been interpreted in various ways; for example, Type A behaviour is a **response** to/way of coping with, rather than a cause of, a predisposition towards physiological reactivity in the presence of a stressor.
- Findings that Type A individuals are actually **less** prone to heart attacks can be reconciled with the earlier findings by assuming that certain characteristics are more important than others, such as hostility, aggression and cynicism.
- Stress may be linked with cardiovascular disease by its role in producing **hypertension**, which is increased as part of the activation of the sympathetic ANS; increased blood flow through the veins can cause both hardening and a general deterioration of the blood vessels.
- Stress increases physiological **arousal**, so attempts to manage and reduce the effects of stress often aim at reducing arousal, such as **psychotherapeutic drugs** (e.g. the **benzodiazepines/anxyolitics**) which act directly on the ANS. But they can produce physical dependence and unpleasant side-effects.
- **Biofeedback** aims at providing feedback, of which we are not usually aware, about our internal physiological responses to stress, such as heart rate and blood pressure, so that these can be at least partly controlled. It has been used in the treatment of migraine headaches and hypertension.
- Disadvantages of biofeedback include the need for a biofeedback machine and for regular practice over a period of months in order to maintain any beneficial effects. It is not known how biofeedback works; what may be important are the commitment to reducing stress and the active involvement of the therapist.
- **Progressive relaxation** of the muscles in different parts of the body can reduce physiological responses to stress, especially those associated with the alarm reaction; to be beneficial in the long term, as in preventing recurrent heart attacks, it must become a routine feature of a person's lifestyle.
- **Meditation** is another form of relaxation, which can reduce oxygen consumption and induce electrical activity in the brain associated with a calm mental state. Both meditation and progressive relaxation reduce blood pressure more than placebos, and neither needs specialised equipment, unlike biofeedback.
- **Physical activity** and **exercise** can help to reduce stress through promoting fitness, which allows the body to use greater amounts of oxygen during vigorous exercise and pump more blood with each heart beat, improving circulation and strengthening the heart muscle. Exercise can also reduce depression and enhance self-esteem.
- Stress can also be reduced by **changing cognitions** (cognitive restructuring), as in Meichenbaum's **stress inoculation**, designed to control people's **catastrophising thoughts**. It comprises **conceptualisation**, **skill acquisition** and **rehearsal**, and **application** and **follow-through**.
- **Hardiness** helps people to resist the effects of a stressor through being highly **committed**, seeing change as a **challenge** and having a strong **sense of control (high internal locus of control)**.
- Other approaches include trying to make a more realistic assessment of life's stresses, and, when faced with a stressor whose effects cannot be avoided, taking on some other challenge which can be met, so that we experience the positive aspects of coping (**self-efficacy expectations**).
- Lazarus and Folkman's **problem-focussed** coping strategies involve making and implementing a specific plan for dealing with a stressor, while **emotion-focussed** coping strategies are effective in the short term (e.g. denying or avoiding the stressor in some way) but not in the long term.
- **Stress management programmes** help reduce stress by changing people's behaviour, as in **time management training**, which can help people to pace themselves to prevent last-minute panic and to avoid the **superperson syndrome**.
- **Assertiveness training** can help people to **confront** stress-provoking situations, and **social support** can reduce stress by the individual not having to face it alone, even if the stressor itself remains unchanged. However, people who **choose** social support may already be better copers in other ways.
- If the Type A individual's pattern of time urgency, hostility and self-destructive tendencies can be changed, the chances of recurrent heart attacks can be significantly reduced.

REFERENCES

ADAM, K. & OSWALD, I. (1977) Sleep is for tissue restoration. *Journal of the Royal College of Physicians*, 11, 376–388.

ADAM, K. & OSWALD, I. (1983) Protein synthesis, bodily renewal and the sleep-wake cycle. *Clinical Science*, 65, 561–567.

ADAM, M.N. (1983) Time of Day Effects in Memory for Text. D.Phil. thesis, University of Sussex.

ALDEN, P. (1995) Hypnosis – the professional's perspective. *The Psychologist*, 8, 78.

ANAND, B.K. & BROBECK, J.R. (1951) Hypothalamic control of food intake in rats and cats. *Yale Journal of Biological Medicine*, 24, 123–140.

ASCHOFF, J. & WEVER, R. (1981) The circadian system in man. In Aschoff, J. (Ed.) *Handbook of Behavioural Neurology, Volume 4: Biological Rhythms*. New York: Plenum Press.

ASERINSKY, E. & KLEITMAN, N. (1953) Regularly occurring periods of eye motility and concomitant phenomena during sleep. *Science*, 118, 273–274.

AX, A.F. (1953) The physiological differentiation of fear and anger in humans. *Psychosomatic Medicine*, 15, 422–433.

BALASUBRAMAMIAM, V., KANATA, T.S. & RAMAMURTHI, B. (1970) Surgical treatment of hyperkinetic and behaviour disorders. *International Surgery*, 54, 18–23.

BALES, J. (1986) New studies cite drug use dangers. *APA Monitor*, 17 (11), 26.

BANDURA, A. (1984) Recycling misconceptions of perceived self-efficacy. *Cognitive Therapy and Research*, 8, 231–235.

BANYAI, E.I. & HILGARD, E.R. (1976) A comparison of active-alert hypnotic induction with traditional relaxation induction. *Journal of Abnormal Psychology*, 85, 218–224.

BARBER, T.X. (1969) *Hypnosis: A Scientific Approach*. New York: Von Nostrand.

BARBER, T.X. (1970) *LSD, Marijuana, Yoga And Hypnosis*. Chicago: Aldine Press.

BARBER, T.X. (1979) Suggested ('hypnotic') behaviour: The trance paradigm versus an alternative paradigm. In Fromm, E. & Shor, R.E. (Eds.) *Hypnosis: Developments in Research and New Perspectives*. Chicago: Aldine Press.

BARD, P. (1928) Diencephalic mechanism for the expression of rage with special reference to the sympathetic nervous system. *American Journal of Physiology*, 84, 490–515.

BARON, R.A. (1989) *Psychology: The Essential Science*. London: Allyn & Bacon.

BARTUS, R.T., DEAN, R.L., BEER, R. & LIPPA, A.S. (1982) The cholinergic hypothesis of geriatric memory dysfunction. *Science*, 217, 408–417.

BEAUMONT, J.G. (1988) *Understanding Neuropsychology*. Oxford: Blackwell.

BERKMAN, L.F. (1984) Assessing the physical health of social networks and social support. *Annual Review of Public Health*, 5, 413–432.

BERRY, D.T.R. & WEBB, W.B. (1983) State measures and sleep stages. *Psychological Reports*, 52, 807–812.

BIANCHI, A. (1992) Dream chemistry. *Harvard Magazine*, September–October, 21–22.

BLAKEMORE, C. (1988) *The Mind Machine*. London: BBC Publications.

BLOCH, V. (1976) Brain activation and memory consolidation. In Rosenzweig, M.A. & Bennett, E.L. (Eds.) *Neural Mechanisms of Learning and Memory*. Cambridge, MA: MIT Press.

BLUM, K. (1984) *Handbook of Abusable Drugs*. New York: Gardner Press.

BLUNDELL, J.E. & HILL, A.J. (1995) Hunger and appetite. In Parkinson, B. & Colman, A.M. (Eds.) *Emotion and Motivation*. London: Longman.

BOGEN, J.E. (1969) The other side of the brain. *Bulletin of the Los Angeles Neurological Societies*, 34, 3.

BOKERT, E. (1970) The effects of thirst and related auditory stimulation on dream reports. Paper presented to the Association for the Physiological Study of Sleep, Washington DC.

BOLLES, R.C. (1967) *Theory of Motivation*. New York: Harper & Row.

BOLTER, A., HEMINGER, A., MARTIN, G. & FRY, M. (1976) Outpatient clinical experience in a community drug abuse program with phencyclidine. *Clinical Toxicology*, 9, 593–600.

BORBELY, A. (1986) *Secrets of Sleep*. Harmondsworth: Penguin.

BORNSTEIN, M.H. & MARKS, L.E. (1982) Colour revisionism. *Psychology Today*, 16 (1), 64–73.

BOWERS, K.S. (1976) *Hypnosis for the Seriously Curious*. Monterey, CA: Brooks Cole.

BOYCE, P. & PARKER, G. (1988) Seasonal affective disorder in the southern hemisphere. *American Journal of Psychiatry*, 145, 609–615.

BRADY, J.V. & NAUTA, W.J.H. (1953) Subcortical mechanisms in emotional behaviour: Affective changes following septal forebrain lesions in the albino rat.

Journal of Comparative and Physiological Psychology, 46, 339–346.

BREGGIN, P.R. (1973) Psychosurgery (letter to the editor). *Journal of the American Medical Association*, 226, 1121.

BREHM, J.W. (1966) *A Theory of Psychological Reactance*. New York: Academic Press.

BRUCE, V. & GREEN, P.R. (1990) *Visual Perception* (2nd edition). Sussex: Lawrence Erlbaum Associates.

CAHILL, A. & AKIL, L. (1982) Plasma beta-endorphin-like immunoreactivity, self-reported pain perception and anxiety levels in women during pregnancy and labour. *Life Sciences*, 31, 1879–1882.

CAMPFIELD, L.A., BRANDON, P. & SMITH, F.J. (1985) On-line continuous measurement of blood-glucose and meal pattern in free-feeding rats: The role of glucose in meal initiation. *Brain Research Bulletin*, 14, 605–616.

CANNON, W.B. (1927) The James-Lange theory of emotions: A critical reexamination and an alternative theory. *American Journal of Psychology*, 39, 106–124.

CANNON, W.B. (1929) *Bodily Changes in Pain, Hunger, Fear, and Rage*. New York: Appleton.

CANNON, W.B. & WASHBURN, A.L. (1912) An explanation of hunger. *American Journal of Physiology*, 29, 441–454.

CANTIN, M. & GENEST, J. (1986) The heart as an endocrine gland. *Scientific American*, 254, 76–81.

CARLSON, N.R. (1977) *Physiology of Behaviour*. Boston: Allyn & Bacon.

CARLSON, N.R. (1987) *Discovering Psychology*. London: Allyn & Bacon.

CARLSON, N.R. (1988) *Foundations of Physiological Psychology*. Boston: Allyn & Bacon.

CARSON, R. (1989) Personality. *Annual Review of Psychology*, 40, 227–248.

CARTWRIGHT, R.D. (1978) *A Primer on Sleep and Dreaming*. Reading, MA: Addison-Wesley.

CHASE, M. & MORALES, F. (1990) The atonia and myoclonia of active (REM) sleep. *Annual Review of Psychology*, 41, 557–584.

COE, W.C. & YASHINSKI, E. (1985) Volitional experiences associated with breaching post-hypnotic amnesia. *Journal of Personality and Social Psychology*, 48, 716–722.

COHEN, D.B. (1973) Sex role orientation and dream recall. *Journal of Abnormal Psychology*, 82, 246–252.

COLLEE, J. (1993) Symbol minds. *The Observer Life Magazine*, September 26th, 14.

CORNELL-BELL, A.H., FINKBEINER, S.M., COOPER, M.S. & SMITH, S.J. (1990) Glutamate induces calcium waves in cultured astrocytes: Long-range glial signalling. *Science*, 247, 470–473.

COTMAN, C.W. & McGAUGH, J.L. (1980) *Behavioural Neuroscience*. New York: Academic Press.

COUNCIL, J.R., KIRSCH, I. & HAFNER, L.P. (1986) Expectancy versus absorption in the prediction of hypnotic responding. *Journal of Personality and Social Psychology*, 50, 182–189.

CRICK, F. & MITCHISON, G. (1983) The function of dream sleep. *Nature*, 304, 111–114.

CROWNE, D.P. & MARLOWE, D. (1964) *The Approval Motive*. New York: Wiley.

CULLITON, B.J. (1976) Psychosurgery: National commission issues surprisingly favourable report. *Science*, 194, 299–301.

DALTON, K. (1964) *The Premenstrual Syndrome*. Springfield, ILL: Charles C. Thomas.

DAMASIO, A.R. & DAMASIO, H. (1993) Brain and language. In *Mind and Body: Readings from Scientific American*. New York: W.H. Freeman and Company.

DAVIDSON, R.J. (1992) Anterior cerebral asymmetry and the nature of emotion. *Brain and Cognition*, 20, 280–299.

DELGADO, J.M.R. (1969) *Physical Control of the Mind*. New York: Harper & Row.

DEMENT, W.C. (1960) The effects of dream deprivation. *Science*, 131, 1705–1707.

DEMENT, W.C. (1974) *Some Must Watch While Some Must Sleep*. San Francisco: W.H. Freeman.

DEMENT, W.C. & KLEITMAN, N. (1957) Cyclical variations in EEG during sleep and their relation to eye movements, body motility and dreaming. *Electroencephalography and Clinical Neurophysiology*, 9, 673–690.

DEMENT, W.C. & WOLPERT, E. (1958) The relation of eye movements, body motility and external stimuli to dream content. *Journal of Experimental Psychology*, 55, 543–553.

DEPARTMENT OF HEALTH (1994) *Drugs: A Parent's Guide*. Central Print Unit.

DEVALOIS, R.L. & JACOBS, G.H. (1984) Neural mechanisms of colour vision. In Darian-Smith, I. (Ed.) *Handbook of Physiology* (Volume 3). Bethesda, MD: American Physiological Society.

DICARA, L.V. & MILLER, N.E. (1968) Instrumental learning of systolic blood pressure responses by curarized rats. *Psychosomatic Medicine*, 30, 489–494.

DIXON, N.F. (1980) Humour: A cognitive alternative to stress? In Sarason, I.G. & Spielberger, C.D. (Eds.) *Stress and Anxiety*. Washington, DC: Hemisphere.

DIXON, P., REHLING, G. & SHIWACH, R. (1993) Peripheral victims of the Herald of Free Enterprise disaster. *British Journal of Medical Psychology*, 66, 193–202.

DOCKRAY, G.J., GREGORY, R.A. & HUTCHINSON, J.B. (1978) Isolation, structure and biological activity of two cholecystokinin octapeptides from the sheep brain. *Nature*, 274, 711–713.

DONCHIN, E. (1975) On evoked potentials, cognition and memory. *Science*, 190, 1004–1005.

DUTTON, D.G. & ARON, A.P. (1974) Some evidence for heightened sexual attraction under conditions of high anxiety. *Journal of Personality and Social Psychology*, 30, 510–517.

ECCLES, J.C. (1973) The cerebellum as a computer: Patterns in space and time. *Journal of Physiology*, 229, 1–32.

EKMAN, P., FRIESEN, W.V. & SIMONS, R.C. (1985) Is the startle reaction an emotion? *Journal of Personality and Social Psychology*, 49, 1416–1426.

ELLENBERG, L. & SPERRY, R.W. (1980) Lateralised division of attention in the commissurotomised and intact brain. *Neuropsychologia*, 18, 411–418.

ELLISON, G.D. & FLYNN, J.P. (1968) Organised aggressive behaviour in cats after surgical isolation of the hypothalamus. *Archives Italiennes de Biologie*, 106, 1–20.

EMPSON, J.A.C. (1989) *Sleep and Dreaming*. London: Faber and Faber.

EMPSON, J.A.C. & CLARKE, P.R.F. (1970) Rapid eye movements and remembering. *Nature*, 228, 287–288.

ESQUIROL, J. (1845) *Mental Maladies: Treatise on Insanity* (translated by E. Hunt). Philadelphia: Lea and Blanchard.

ESTERLING, B. & RABIN, B. (1987) Stress-induced alteration of T-lymphocyte subsets and humoral immunity in mice. *Behavioural Neuroscience*, 101, 115–119.

EVANS, C. (1984) *Landscapes of the Night: How and Why We Dream*. New York: Viking.

EYSENCK, M.W. & KEANE, M.J. (1990) *Cognitive Psychology*. Sussex: Lawrence Erlbaum Associates.

FESTINGER, L. (1954) A theory of social comparison processes. *Human Relations*, 7, 117–140.

FISCHMAN, J. (1985) Mapping the mind. *Psychology Today*, September, 18–19.

FISHER, S. & GREENBERG, R. (1977) *Scientific Credibility of Freud's Theories*. New York: Basic Books.

FLEMING, R., BAUM, A. & SINGER, J.E. (1984) Towards an integrative approach to the study of stress. *Journal of Personality and Social Psychology*, 46, 939–949.

FOULKES, D. (1971) Longitudinal studies of dreams in children. In Masserman, J. (Ed.) *Science and Psychoanalysis*. New York: Grune & Stratton.

FOULKES, D. (1985) *Dreaming: A Cognitive-Psychological Analysis*. Hillsdale, NJ: Lawrence Erlbaum Associates.

FOX, J.L. (1984) The brain's dynamic way of keeping in touch. *Science*, 225, 82–821.

FRESE, M. (1985) Stress at work and psychosomatic complaints: A causal interpretation. *Journal of Applied Psychology*, 70, 314–328.

FREUD, S. (1900) *The Interpretation of Dreams*. London: Hogarth Press.

FRIEDMAN, M. & ROSENMAN, R.H. (1974) *Type A Behaviour and Your Heart*. New York: Harper Row.

FRIEDMAN, M. & ULMER, D. (1984) *Treating Type A Behaviour and Your Heart*. New York: Fawcett Crest.

FRIEDMAN, M.I. & STRICKER, E.M. (1976) The physiological psychology of hunger: A physiological perspective. *Psychological Review*, 83, 409–431.

GAZZANIGA, M.S. (1967) The split-brain in man. *Scientific American*, 221, 24–29.

GAZZANIGA, M.S. (1983) Right hemisphere language following brain bisection: A 2-year perspective. *American Psychologist*, 38, 525–537.

GEEN, R.G. (1995) Social motivation. In Parkinson, B. & Colman, A.M. (Eds.) *Emotion and Motivation*. London: Longman.

GEISELMAN, P.J. (1983) The role of hexoses in hunger motivation. Unpublished doctoral dissertation, University of California, Los Angeles.

GESCHWIND, N. (1972) Language and the brain. *Scientific American*, 226, 76–83.

GESCHWIND, N. (1979) *The Brain*. San Francisco: Freeman.

GESCHWIND, N., QUADFASEL, F.A. & SEGARRA, J.M. (1968) Isolation of the speech area. *Neuropsychologia*, 6, 327–340.

GILLETT, P.L. & COE, W.C. (1984) The effects of rapid induction analgesia (RIA), hypnotic susceptibility, and the severity of discomfort on the reduction of dental pain. *American Journal of Clinical Hypnosis*, 27, 81–90.

GORDON, R.M. (1978) Emotion labelling and cognition. *Journal for the Theory of Social Behaviour*, 8, 125–135.

GOTTLEIB, G. (1975) Development of species identification in ducklings. III. Maturational rectification of perceptual deficit caused by auditory deprivation. *Journal of Comparative and Physiological Psychology*, 89, 899–912.

GREEN, S. (1980) Physiological studies I and II. In Radford, J. & Govier, E. (Eds.) *A Textbook of Psychology*. London: Sheldon Press.

GREEN, S. (1994) *Principles of Biopsychology*. Sussex: Lawrence Erlbaum Associates.

GREENBERG, R. & PEARLMAN, C. (1967) Delerium tremens and dreaming. *American Journal of Psychiatry*, 124, 133–142.

GREENBERG, R., PILLARD, R. & PEARLMAN, C. (1972) The effect of dream (stage REM) deprivation on adaptation to stress. *Psychosomatic Medicine*, 34, 257–262.

GUR, R.C., SKOLNICK, B.E. & GUR, R.E. (1994) Effects of emotional discrimination tasks on cerebral blood flow: Regional activation and its relation to performance. *Brain and Cognition*, 25, 271–286.

GUR, R. C. et al. (1995) cited in Highfield, R., Brain scans show sexes are not on the same wavelength. *Daily Telegraph*, January 27th, 11.

GWINNER, E.A. (1971) A comparative study of circannual rhythms in warblers. In Menaker, M. (Ed.) *Biochronometry: Proceedings of a Symposium.* Washington: National Academy of Sciences.

HABER, R.N. & HERSHENSON, M. (1980) *The Physiology of Visual Perception.* New York: Holt, Rinehart & Winston.

HALL, C.S. (1966) *The Meaning of Dreams.* New York: McGraw-Hill.

HALL, C. & VAN DE CASTLE, R.L. (1966) *The Content Analysis of Dreams.* E. Norwalk, CT: Appleton-Century-Crofts.

HALLIGAN, P.W. (1995) Drawing attention to neglect: The contribution of line bisection. *The Psychologist,* 8, 257–264.

HARBURG, E., ERFURT, J.C., HAUENSTEIN, L.S., CHAPE, C., SCHULL, W.J. & SCHORK, M.A. (1973) Socioecological stress, suppressed hostility, skin colour, and black-white male blood pressure: Detroit. *Psychosomatic Medicine,* 35, 276–296.

HARTMANN, E.L. (1973) *The Functions of Sleep.* New Haven, CT: Yale University Press.

HASSETT, J. & WHITE, K.M. (1989) *Psychology in Perspective.* London: Harper & Row.

HAURI, P. (1970) Evening activity, sleep mentation, and subjective sleep quality. *Journal of Abnormal Psychology,* 76, 270–275.

HAYES, N.J. (1994) *Foundations of Psychology: An Introductory Text.* London: Routledge.

HERMAN, J. & ROFFWARG, H. (1983) Modifying oculomotor activity in awake subjects increases the amplitude of eye movement during REM sleep. *Science,* 220, 1074–1076.

HETHERINGTON, A.W. & RANSON, S.W. (1942) The relation of various hypothalamic lesions to adiposity in the rat. *Journal of Comparative Neurology,* 76, 475–499.

HEUSER, J.E., REESE, T.S., DENNIS, M.J., JAN, L. & EVANS, L. (1979) Synaptic vesicle membrane during transmitter release at the frog neuromuscular junction. *Journal of Cell Biology,* 81, 275–300.

HICKS, R. & PELLEGRINI, R. (1982) Sleep problems and Type A-B behaviour in college students. *Psychological Reports,* 51, 96.

HILGARD, E.R. (1973) A neodissociation interpretation of pain reduction in hypnosis. *Psychological Review,* 80, 396–411.

HILGARD, E.R. (1977) *Divided Consciousness: Multiple Controls in Human Thought and Action.* New York: Wiley-Interscience.

HILGARD, E.R. (1979) Divided consciousness in hypnosis: The implications of the hidden observer. In Fromm, E. & Shor, R.E. (Eds.) *Hypnosis: Developments in Research and New Perspectives.* New York: Aldine Press.

HILGARD, E.R., ATKINSON, R.L. & ATKINSON, R.C. (1979) *Introduction to Psychology* (7th edition). New York: Harcourt Brace Jovanovich.

HINSHAW, S.P., HENKER, B. & WHALEN, C.K. (1984) Cognitive-behavioural and pharmacological interventions for hyperactive boys: Comparative and combined effects. *Journal of Consulting and Clinical Psychology,* 52, 739–749.

HOBSON, J.A. (1988) *The Dreaming Brain.* New York: Basic Books.

HOBSON, J.A. (1989) Dream theory: A new view of the brain-mind. *The Harvard Medical School Mental Health Letter,* 5, 3–5.

HOBSON, J.A. & McCARLEY, R.W. (1977) The brain as a dream state generator: An activation-synthesis hypothesis of the dream process. *American Journal of Psychiatry,* 134, 1335–1348.

HOHMANN, G.W. (1966) Some effects of spinal cord lesions on experienced emotional feelings. *Psychophysiology,* 3, 143–156.

HORNE, J.A. & OSTERBERG, O. (1976) A self-assessment questionnaire to determine morningness-eveningness in human circadian rhythms. *International Journal of Chronobiology,* 4, 97–190.

HUBEL, D.H. & WIESEL, T.N. (1965) Receptive fields of single neurons in the two non-striate visual areas, 18 and 19 of the cat. *Journal of Neurophysiology,* 28, 229–289.

HUBEL, D.H. & WIESEL, T.N. (1977) Functional architecture of the macaque monkey visual cortex. *Proceedings of the Royal Society of London, Series B,* 198, 1–59.

HÜBER-WEIDMAN, H. (1976) *Sleep, Sleep Disturbances and Sleep Deprivation.* Cologne: Kiepenheuser & Witsch.

IVERSEN, L.L. (1979) The chemistry of the brain. *Scientific American,* 241, 134–149.

JACOB, R.G., KRAEMER, H.C. & AGRAS, W.S. (1977) Relaxation therapy in the treatment of hypertension: A review. *Archives of General Psychiatry,* 34, 1417–1427.

JACOBS, B.L. (1987) How hallucinogenic drugs work. *American Scientist,* 75, 386–392.

JACOBS, T.J. & CHARLES, E. (1980) Life events and the occurrence of cancer in children. *Psychosomatic Medicine,* 42, 11–24.

JACOBSON, E. (1938) *Progressive Relaxation.* Chicago: University of Chicago Press.

JAMES, W. (1890) *The Principles of Psychology.* New York: Henry Holt and Company.

JANOWITZ, H.D. & GROSSMAN, M.I. (1949) Effects of variations in nutritive density on intake of food in dogs and cats. *American Journal of Physiology,* 158, 184–193.

JASNOS, T.M. & HAKMILLER, K.L., (1975) Some effects of lesion level and emotional cues on affective expression in spinal cord patients. *Psychological Reports,* 37, 859–870.

JOHNSON, R.N. (1972) *Aggression in Man and Animals.* Philadelphia: Saunders.

JOUVET, M. (1967) Mechanisms of the states of sleep: A neuropharmacological approach. *Research Publications of the Association for the Research in Nervous and Mental Diseases*, 45, 86–126.

JOUVET, M. (1983) Hypnogenic indolamine-dependent factors and paradoxical sleep rebound. In Monnier, E. & Meulders, A. (Eds.) *Functions of the Nervous System, Volume 4: Psychoneurobiology*. New York: Elsevier.

KALES, A., KALES, J.D. & BIXLER, E.O. (1974) Insomnia: An approach to management and treatment. *Psychiatric Annals*, 4, 28–44.

KEESEY, R.E. & POWLEY, T.L. (1975) Hypothalamic regulation of body weight. *American Scientist*, 63, 558–565.

KERTESZ, A. (1979) Anatomy of jargon. In Brown, J. (Ed.) *Jargonapahasia*. New York: Academic Press.

KEYE, W.R. (1983) Update: Premenstrual syndrome. *Endocrine and Fertility Forum*, 6 (4), 1–3.

KIHLSTROM, J.F. (1985) Hypnosis. *Annual Review of Psychology*, 36, 385–418.

KIMURA, D. (1993) Sex differences in the brain. In *Mind and Brain: Readings from Scientific American*. New York: W.H. Freeman & Company.

KIMZEY, S. (1975) The effects of extended space flight on hematologic and immunologic systems. *Journal of American Women's Association*, 30, 218–232.

KINNUNEN, T., ZAMANSKY, H.S. & BLOCK, M.L. (1995) Is the hypnotised subject lying? *Journal of Abnormal Psychology*, 103, 184–191.

KLUVER, H. & BUCY, P. (1937) 'Psychic blindness' and other symptoms following bilateral temporal lobectomy in Rhesus monkeys. *American Journal of Physiology*, San Diego, CA: Edits.

KOBASA, S.C. (1979) Stressful life events, personality, and health: An inquiry into hardiness. *Journal of Personality and Social Psychology*, 37, 1–11.

KOUKKOU, M. & LEHMAN, D. (1980) Psychophysiologie des Traumens und der Neurosentherapie: Das Zustands-Wechsel Modell, eine Synopsis. *Fortschritte der Neurologie, Psychiatrie unter ihrer Grenzgebeite*, 48, 324–350.

KRANTZ, D. & MANUCK, S. (1984) Acute psychophysiologic reactivity and risk of cardiovascular disease: A review and methodological critique. *Psychological Bulletin*, 96, 435–464.

LAND, E.H. (1977) The retinex theory of colour vision. *Scientific American*, 237, 108–128.

LAURENCE, J.R. & PERRY, C. (1983) Hypnotically created memory among highly hypnotisable subjects. *Science*, 222, 523–524.

LAZARUS, R.S. (1982) Thoughts on the relations between emotion and cognition. *American Psychologist*, 37, 1019–1024.

LAZARUS, R.S. & FOLKMAN, S. (1984) *Stress, Appraisal, and Coping*. New York: Springer.

LEDOUX, J.E. (1989) Cognitive-emotional interactions in the brain. *Cognition and Emotion*, 3, 267–289.

LEVINE, J.D., GORDON, N.C. & FIELDS, H.L. (1979) Naloxone dose dependently produces analgesia and hyperalgesia in post-operative pain. *Nature*, 278, 740–741.

LEVY, J. (1983) Language, cognition and the right hemisphere: A response to Gazzaniga. *American Psychologist*, 38, 538–541.

LEVY, J., TREVARTHEN, C. & SPERRY, R.W. (1972) Perception of bilateral chimeric figures following hemispheric disconnection. *Brain*, 95, 61–78.

LEVY, S. (1983) Death and dying: Behavioural and social factors that contribute to the process. In Burish, T. & Bradley, L. (Eds.) *Coping with Chronic Illness: Research and Application*. New York: Academic Press.

LEY, R.G. & BRYDEN, M.P. (1979) Hemispheric differences in processing emotions and faces. *Brain and Language*, 7, 127–138.

LLOYD, P., MAYES, A., MANSTEAD, A.S.R., MEUDELL, P.R. & WAGNER, H.L. (1984) *Introduction to Psychology: An Integrated Approach*. London: Fontana.

LOOMIS, A.L., HARVEY, E.N. & HOBART, A. (1937) Cerebral states during sleep as studied by human brain potentials. *Journal of Experimental Psychology*, 21, 127–144.

LORD, B.J., KING, M.G. & PFISTER, H.P. (1976) Chemical sympathectomy and two-way escape and avoidance learning in the rat. *Journal of Comparative and Physiological Psychology*, 90, 303–316.

LUCE, G.G. (1971) *Body Time: The Natural Rhythms of the Body*. St. Albans: Paladin.

LUCE, G.G. & SEGAL, J. (1966) *Sleep*. New York: Coward, McCann & Geoghegan.

LUGARESSI, E., MEDORI, R., MONTAGNA, P., BARUZZI, A., CORTELLI, P., LUGARESSI, A., TINUPER, A., ZUCCONI, M. & GAMBETTI, P. (1986) Fatal familial insomnia and dysautonomia in the selective degeneration of thalamic nuclei. *New England Journal of Medicine*, 315, 997–1003.

LURIA, A.R. (1973) *The Working Brain: An Introduction to Neuropsychology* (translated by B. Haigh). New York: Basic Books.

LURIA, A.R. (1980) *Higher Cortical Functions in Man* (2nd edition, revised). New York: Basic Books.

MACLEAN, P.D. (1973) *A Triune Concept of Brain and Behaviour*. Toronto: University of Toronto Press.

MACLEAN, P.D. (1982) On the origin and progressive evolution of the triune brain. In Armstrong, E. & Falk, D. (Eds.) *Primate Brain Evolution*. New York: Plenum Press.

MANDLER, G. (1962) Emotion. In Brown, R. (Ed.) *New Directions in Psychology*. New York: Holt, Rinehart & Winston.

MANNING, A. (1975) *An Introduction to Animal Behaviour*. London: Edward Arnold.

MARANON, G. (1924) Contribution à l'etude de l'action emotive de l'adrenaline. *Revue Française d'Endocrinologie*, 2, 301–325.

MARK, V. & ERVIN, F. (1970) *Violence and the Brain*. New York: Harper & Row.

MARKS, M. & FOLKHARD, S. (1985) Diurnal rhythms in cognitive performance. In Nicholson, J. & Beloff, H. (Eds.) *Psychology Survey 5*. Leicester: British Psychological Society.

MARSHALL, G. & ZIMBARDO, P. (1979) Affective consequences of inadequately explaining physiological arousal. *Journal of Personality and Social Psychology*, 37, 970–988.

MARTIN, J.H. & BRUST, J.C.M. (1985) Imaging the living brain. In Kandel, E.R. & Schwartz, J.H. (Eds.) *Principles of Neural Science*. New York: Elsevier.

MARTIN, R.A. & LEFCOURT, H.M. (1983) Sense of humour as a moderator of the relation between stressors and moods. *Journal of Personality and Social Psychology*, 45, 1313–1324.

MASLACH, C. (1978) Emotional consequences of arousal without reason. In Izard, C.E. (Ed.) *Emotions and Psychopathology*. New York: Plenum Publishing Company.

MASLOW, A. (1954) *Motivation and Personality*. New York: Harper & Row.

MAUNSELL, J.H.R. & NEWSOME, W.T. (1987) Visual processing in monkey extrastriate cortex. *Annual Review of Neuroscience*, 10, 363–401.

MAYER, J. & MARSHALL, N.B. (1956) Specificity of Gold Thioglucose for ventromedial hypothalamic lesions and obesity. *Nature*, 178, 1399–1400.

McCANN, J.J. (1987) Retinex theory and colour constancy. In Gregory, R.L. (Ed.) *Oxford Companion to the Mind*. Oxford: Oxford University Press.

McCANNE, T.R. & ANDERSON, J.A. (1987) Emotional responding following manipulation of facial feedback. *Journal of Personality and Social Psychology*, 52, 759–768.

McCLELLAND, D.C. (1958) Methods of measuring human motivation. In Atkinson, J.W. (Ed.) *Motives in Fantasy Action and Society*. Princeton, NJ: Van Nostrand.

McDOUGALL, W. (1908) *An Introduction to Social Psychology*. London: Methuen.

McWILLIAMS, S.A. & TUTTLE, R.J. (1973) Long-term psychological effects of LSD. *Psychological Bulletin*, 79, 341–351.

MEDDIS, R. (1975) *The Sleep Instinct*. London: Routledge, Kegan and Paul.

MEDDIS, R., PEARSON, A.J.D. & LANFORD, G. (1973) An extreme case of healthy insomnia. *Electroencephalography and Clinical Neurophysiology*, 35, 213–214.

MEICHENBAUM, D.H. (1985) *Stress Inoculation Training*. New York: Pergamon.

MILLER, G.A. (1962) *Psychology: The Science of Mental Life*. Harmondsworth: Penguin.

MILLER, L. (1987) The emotional brain. *Psychology Today*, 22, 35–42.

MILLER, N., GOLD, M. & MILLIMAN, R. (1989) Cocaine. *American Family Physician*, 39, 115–121.

MILLER, R.J., HENNESSY, R.T. & LEIBOWITZ, H.W. (1973) The effect of hypnotic ablation of the background on the magnitude of the Ponzo perspective illusion. *International Journal of Clinical and Experimental Hypnosis*, 21, 18–191.

MILNER, B. (1971) Interhemispheric differences in the localisation of psychological processes in man. *British Medical Bulletin*, 27, 272–277.

MITCHELL, T.R. & LARSON, J.B. Jnr. (1987) *People in Organisations: An Introduction to Organisational Behaviour* (3rd edition). New York: McGraw-Hill.

MONEY, J. & ERHARDT, A. (1972) *Man and Woman, Boy and Girl*. Baltimore, MD: The Johns Hopkins University Press.

MOOS, R.H. (1988) *Coping Response Inventory Manual*. Social Ecology Laboratory, Department of Psychiatry, Stanford University and Veterans Administration Medical Centers. Palo Alto, California.

MORGAN, A.H. & HILGARD, E.R. (1973) Age differences in susceptibility to hypnosis. *International Journal of Clinical and Experimental Hypnosis*, 21, 78–85.

MORRIS, C.G. (1988) *Psychology: An Introduction* (Sixth edition). London: Prentice-Hall.

MORRIS, J.N. (1953) Coronary heart disease and physical activity of work. *The Lancet*, 2, 1053–1057.

MORUZZI, G. & MAGOUN, H.W. (1949) Reticular formation and activation of the EEG. *Electroencephalography and Clinical Neurophysiology*, 1, 455–473.

MURRAY, H.A. (1938) *Explorations in Personality*. New York: Oxford University Press.

NATHANS, J. (1989) The genes for colour vision. *Scientific American*, 226, 42–49.

NEBES, R.D. (1974) Hemispheric specialisation in commissurotomised man. *Psychological Bulletin*, 81, 1–14.

NEILL, J. (1987) 'More than medical significance': LSD and American psychiatry 1953 to 1966. *Journal of Psychoactive Drugs*, 19, 39–45.

NISBETT, R.E. (1972) Hunger, obesity and the ventromedial hypothalamus. *Psychological Review*, 79, 433–453.

NORMAN, R., PEARLMAN, I., KOLB, H., JONES, J. & DALEY, S. (1984) Direct excitatory interactions between cones of different spectral types in the turtle retina. *Science*, 224, 625–627.

OHTSUKA, T. (1985) Relation of spectral types to oil droplets in cones of turtle retina. *Science*, 229, 874–877.

OLDS, J. & MILNER, P. (1954) Positive reinforcement produced by electrical stimulation of the septal area and other regions of the rat brain. *Journal of Comparative and Physiological Psychology*, 47, 419–427.

ORNE, M.T. & EVANS, F.J. (1965) Social control in the psychological experiment: Anti-social behaviour and hypnosis. *Journal of Personality and Social Psychology*, 1, 189–200.

ORNE, M.T., SHEEHAN, P.W. & EVANS, F.J. (1968) Occurrence of posthypnotic behaviour outside the experimental setting. *Journal of Personality and Social Psychology*, 9, 189–196.

ORNSTEIN, R. (1986) *The Psychology of Consciousness* (2nd edition, revised). Harmondsworth: Penguin.

OSWALD, I. (1966) *Sleep*. Harmondsworth: Penguin.

PAIGE, K.E. (1973) Women learn to sing the menstrual blues. *Psychology Today*, 7, 41.

PAPEZ, J.W. (1937) A proposed mechanism of emotion. *Archives of Neurology and Psychiatry*, 38, 725–743.

PARFIT, D. (1987) Divided minds and the nature of persons. In Blakemore, C. & Greenfield, S. (Eds.) *Mindwaves*. Oxford: Blackwell.

PARROTT, A. & YEOMANS, M. (1995) Wobble, rave, inhale or crave. *The Psychologist*, 8, 305.

PASSINGHAM, R.E. (1985) Memory of monkeys (Macaca mulatta) with lesions in prefrontal cortex. *Behavioural Neuroscience*, 99, 3–21.

PATRICK, G.T.W. & GILBERT, J.A. (1898) On the effects of loss of sleep. *The Psychological Review*, 3, 469–483.

PATTIE, F.A. (1937) The genuineness of hypnotically produced anaesthesia of the skin. *American Journal of Psychology*, 49, 435–443.

PENFIELD, W. (1947) Some observations on the cerebral cortex of man. *Proceedings of the Royal Society*, 134, 349.

PENFIELD, W. & ROBERTS, L. (1959) *Speech and Brain Mechanisms*. Princeton: Princeton University Press.

PENGELLEY, E.T. & FISHER, K.C. (1957) Onset and cessation of hibernation under constant temperature and light in the golden-mantled ground squirrel, Citellus Lateralis. *Nature*, 180, 1371–1372.

PENNEBAKER, J.W. & SKELTON, J.A. (1981) Selective monitoring of physical sensations. *Journal of Personality and Social Psychology*, 41, 213–223.

PERT, C.B. & SNYDER, S.H. (1973) Opiate receptor: Demonstration in the nervous tissue. *Science*, 179, 1011–1014.

PINEL, J.P.J. (1993) *Biopsychology* (2nd edition). Boston: Allyn & Bacon.

PINES, A. (1984) Ma Bell and the Hardy Boys. *Across the Board*, July/August, 37–42.

PUCETTI, R. (1977) Sperry on consciousness: A critical appreciation. *Journal of Medicine and Physiology*, 2, 127–146.

RAGLAND, D.R. & BRAND, R.J. (1988) Type A behaviour and mortality from coronary heart disease. *New England Journal of Medicine*, 318, 65–69.

RAPPORT, M.D. (1984) Hyperactivity and stimulant treatment: Abusus non tollit usum. *The Behaviour Therapist*, 7, 133–134.

RATHUS, S.A. (1987) *Psychology*. New York: Holt, Rinehart & Winston.

REBER, A.S. (1984) *The Penguin Dictionary of Psychology*. Harmondsworth: Penguin.

RECHTSCHAFFEN, A. & KALES, A. (1968) A manual of standardised terminology, techniques, and scoring system for sleep stages of human subjects. *National Institute of Health Publication 204*. Washington, DC: US Government Printing Office.

RECHTSCHAFFEN, A., GILLILAND, M., BERGMANN, B. & WINTER, J. (1983) Physiological correlates of prolonged sleep deprivation in rats. *Science*, 221, 182–184.

REINBERG, A. (1967) Eclairement et cycle menstruel de la femme. Rapport au Colloque International du CRNS, la photoregulation de la reproduction chez les oiseaux et les mammifères, Montpelier.

REISENZEIN, R. (1983) The Schachter theory of emotion: Two decades later. *Psychological Bulletin*, 94, 239–264.

REISER, M. & NIELSON, M. (1980) Investigative hypnosis: A developing speciality. *American Journal of Clinical Hypnosis*, 23, 75–83.

RESTAK, R. (1975) Jose Delgado: Exploring inner space. *Saturday Review*, August 9th.

RESTAK, R. (1984) *The Brain*. New York: Bantam Books.

ROBERTSON, J. (1995) Recovery of brain function: People and nets. *The Psychologist*, 8, 253.

ROCHFORD, G. (1974) Are jargon aphasics dysphasic? *British Journal of Disorders of Communication*, 9, 35.

RODIN, F. & SLOCHOWER, J. (1976) Externality in the non-obese: Effects of environmental responsiveness on weight. *Journal of Personality and Social Psychology*, 33, 338–344.

ROGERS, M., DUBEY, D. & REICH, P. (1979) The influence of the psyche and the brain on disease immunity and disease susceptibility: A critical review. *Psychosomatic Medicine*, 41, 147–164.

ROLLS, B.J., WOOD, R.J. & ROLLS, E.T. (1980) The initiation, maintenance and termination of drinking. In Sprague, J.M. & Epstein, A.N. (Eds.) *Progress in Psychobiology and Physiological Psychology* (Volume 9). New York: Academic Press.

ROSENKILDE, C.E. & DIVAC, I. (1976) Time-discrimination performance in cats with lesions in prefrontal cortex and caudate nucleus. *Journal of Comparative and Physiological Psychology*, 90, 343–352.

ROSS, E.D. (1981) The aprosodias: Functional-anatomic organisation of the affective components of language in the right hemisphere. *Archives of Neurology*, 38, 561–569.

ROSSI, E.I. (1973) The dream protein hypothesis. *American Journal of Psychiatry*, 130, 1094–1097.

ROTTER, J.B. (1966) Generalised expectancies for internal versus external control of reinforcement. *Psychological Monographs*, 30 (1), 1–26.

ROUTTENBERG, A. (1968) The two arousal hypothesis: Reticular formation and limbic system. *Psychological Review*, 75, 51–80.

RUBIN, F. (Ed.) (1968) *Current Research in Hypnopaedia.* New York: Elsevier.

RUSSEK, M. (1971) Hepatic receptors and the neurophysiological mechanisms in controlling feeding behaviour. In Ehrenpreis, S. (Ed.) *Neurosciences Research* (Volume 4). New York: Academic Press.

RYBACK, R.S. & LEWIS, O.F. (1971) Effects of prolonged bed rest on EEG sleep patterns in young, healthy volunteers. *Electroencephalography and Clinical Neurophysiology*, 31, 395–399.

SABBAGH, K. & BARNARD, C. (1984) *The Living Body.* London: Macdonald.

SACKHEIM, H.A. (1982) Hemispheric asymmetry in the expression of positive and negative emotions. *Archives of Neurology*, 39, 210–218.

SACKS, O. (1985) *The Man who Mistook his Wife for a Hat and Other Clinical Tales.* New York: Summit Books.

SATZ, P. (1979) A test of some models of hemispheric speech organisation in the left- and right-handed. *Science*, 203, 1131–1133.

SCHACHTER, S. (1959) *The Psychology of Affiliation.* Stanford, CA: Stanford University Press.

SCHACHTER, S. & SINGER, J.E. (1962) Cognitive, social and physiological determinants of emotional state. *Psychological Review*, 69, 379–399.

SCHWARTZ, G.E., WEINBERGER, D.A. & SINGER, J.A. (1981) Cardiovascular differentiation of happiness, sadness, anger, and fear following imagery and exercise. *Psychosomatic Medicine*, 43, 343–364.

SELIGMAN, M.E.P. (1975) *Helplessness: On Depression, Development and Death.* San Francisco: Freeman.

SELYE, H. (1976) *The Stress of Life* (revised edition). New York: McGraw-Hill.

SELYE, H. (1980) The stress concept today. In Kutash, I.L. (Ed.) *Handbook on Stress and Anxiety.* San Francisco: Jossey-Bass.

SEM-JACOBSEN, C.W. (1968) *Depth-Electrographic Stimulation of the Human Brain and Behaviour.* Springfield, ILL: Charles C. Thomas.

SHAPIRO, C.M., BORTZ, R., MITCHELL, D., BARTEL, P. & JOOSTE, P. (1981) Slow-wave sleep: A recovery period after exercise. *Science*, 214, 1253–1254.

SHEFFIELD, F.D. & ROBY, T.B. (1950) Reward value of a non-nutritive sweet taste. *Journal of Comparative and Physiological Psychology*, 43, 471–481.

SIEGEL, R.K. (1982) Quoted by Hooper, J. in 'Mind tripping'. *Omni*, October, 155.

SMITH, A. & SUGAR, O. (1975) Development of above normal language and intelligence 21 years after left hemispherectomy. *Neurology*, 25, 813–818.

SMITH, D.E., WESSON, D.R., BUXTON, M.E., SEYMOUR, R. & KRAMER, H.M. (1978) The diagnosis and treatment of the PCP abuse syndrome. In Peterson, R.C. & Stillman, R.C. (Eds.) *Phencyclidine (PCP) Abuse: An Appraisal.* NIDA Research Monograph No. 21, DHEW Publication No. ADM 78–728. Washington, DC: US Government Printing Office.

SNYDER, S.H. (1977) Opiate receptors and internal opiates. *Scientific American*, 236, 44–56.

SNYDER, S.H. (1984) Drug and neurotransmitter receptors in the brain. *Science*, 224, 22–31.

SOLOMON, R. & CORBIT, J. (1974) An opponent-process theory of motivation. *Psychological Review*, 81, 119–145.

SONSTROEM, R.J. (1984) Exercise and self-esteem. *Exercise and Sport Sciences Review*, 12, 123–155.

SPANOS, N.P. (1986) Hypnotic behaviour: A social-psychological interpretation of amnesia, analgesia, and 'trance logic'. *The Behavioural and Brain Sciences*, 9, 499–502.

SPANOS, N.P., JONES, B. & MALFARA, A. (1982) Hypnotic deafness: Now you hear it – now you still hear it. *Journal of Abnormal Psychology*, 91, 75–77.

SPANOS, N.P., GWYNN, M.I. & STAM, H.J. (1983) Instructional demands and ratings of overt and hidden pain during hypnotic analgesia. *Journal of Abnormal Psychology*, 92, 479–488.

SPERRY, R.W. (1964) The great cerebral commissure. *Scientific American*, 210, 42–52.

SPERRY, R.W. (1974) Lateral specialisation in the surgically separated hemispheres. In Schmitt, F.O. & Worden, F.G. (Eds.) *The Neurosciences: Third Study Program.* Cambridge, MA: MIT Press.

SPERRY, R.W. (1982) Some effects of disconnecting the cerebral hemispheres. *Science*, 217, 1223–1226.

SWEENEY, K. (1995) Stay calm and heal better. *The Times*, 21 December, 5.

SWEET, W.H., ERVIN, F. & MARK, V.H. (1969) The relationship of violent behaviour to focal cerebral disease. In Garattini, S. & Sigg, E.B. (Eds.) *Aggressive Behaviour.* New York: Wiley.

TACHE, J., SELYE, H. & DAY, S. (1979) *Cancer, Stress, and Death.* New York: Plenum Press.

TALLMAN, J.F. & GALLAGHER, D.W. (1985) The GABA-ergic system: A locus of benzodiazepine action. *Annual Review of Neuroscience*, 8, 21–44.

TAYLOR, S. (1990) Health psychology: The science and

the field. *American Psychologist*, 45, 40–50.

TEITELBAUM, P.H. (1955) Sensory control of hypothalamic hyperphagia. *Journal of Comparative and Physiological Psychology*, 48, 156–163.

TEITELBAUM, P.H. & EPSTEIN, A.N. (1962) The lateral hypothalamic syndrome: Recovery of feeding and drinking after hypothalamic lesions. *Psychological Review*, 67, 74–90.

TILLEY, A.J. & EMPSON, J.A.C. (1978) REM sleep and memory consolidation. *Biological Psychology*, 6, 293–300.

TIMONEN, S., FRANZAS, B. & WISCHMANN, K. (1964) Photosensibility of the human pituitary. *Annales Chirurgiae et Gynaecologiae Feminae*, 53, 156–172.

TINBERGEN, N. (1951) *The Study of Instinct*. Oxford: Clarendon Press.

TOLMAN, E.C. (1923) The nature of instinct. *Psychological Bulletin*, 20, 200–216.

TOMARKEN, A.J. & DAVIDSON, R.J. (1994) Frontal brain activation in repressors and non-repressors. *Journal of Abnormal Psychology*, 103, 334–349.

TOMKINS, S.S. (1962) *Affect, Imagery, and Consciousness. Volume 1: The Positive Affects*. New York: Springer-Verlag.

TRIESCHMANN, R.B. (1980) *Spinal Cord Injuries*. New York: Pergamon Press.

VALENSTEIN, E.S. (1973) *Brain Control*. New York: John Wiley and Sons.

VALENSTEIN, E.S. (1977) The brain and behaviour control. In *Master Lectures on Behaviour Control*. Washington, DC: American Psychological Association.

VAN ESSEN, D.C. (1985) Functional organisation of primate visual cortex. In Peters, A. & Jones, E.G. (Eds.) *Cerebral Cortex, Volume 2 – Visual Cortex*. New York: Plenum Press.

VISINTAINER, M., SELIGMAN, M. & VOLPICELLI, J. (1983) Helplessness, chronic stress and tumor development. *Psychosomatic Medicine*, 45, 75–76.

WAHBA, N. & BRIDWELL, L. (1976) Maslow reconsidered: A review of research on the need hierarchy theory. *Organisation Behaviour and Human Performance*, 15, 212–240.

WALKER, S. (1984) *Learning Theory and Behaviour Modification*. London: Methuen.

WALLACE, B. & FISHER, L.E. (1987) *Consciousness and Behaviour* (second edition). Boston: Allyn & Bacon.

WEBB, W.B. (1975) *Sleep: The Gentle Tyrant*. Englewood Cliffs, NJ: Prentice-Hall.

WEBB, W.B. (1982) Sleep and biological rhythms. In Webb, W.B. (Ed.) *Biological Rhythms, Sleep and Performance*. Chichester: John Wiley & Sons.

WEBB, W.B. & CAMPBELL, S. (1983) Relationships in sleep characteristics of identical and fraternal twins. *Archives of General Psychiatry*, 40, 1093–1095.

WEBB, W.B. & CARTWRIGHT, R.D. (1978) Sleep and dreams. *Annual Review of Psychology*, 29, 223–252.

WEHR, T. & ROSENTHAL, N. (1989) Seasonability and affective illness. *American Journal of Psychiatry*, 146, 201–204.

WEIL, A. & ROSEN, W. (1983) *Chocolate to Morphine: Understanding Mind-Active Drugs*. Boston: Houghton Mifflin.

WEIL, A. & ZINBERG, N.E. (1969) Acute effects of marijuana on speech. *Nature*, 222, 434–437.

WEISKRANTZ, L. (1986) *Blindsight: A Case Study and Implications*. Oxford: Oxford University Press.

WILLIAMS, M. (1981) *Brain Damage, Behaviour and the Mind*. Chichester: John Wiley & Sons.

WOLF, S. & WOLFF, H.G. (1947) *Human Gastric Function*. New York: Oxford University Press.

WOLF, S. & BRUHN, J. (1993) *The Power of the Clan: The Influence of Human Relationships on Heart Disease*. New York: Transaction.

WOODWORTH, R.S. (1918) *Dynamic Psychology*. New York: Columbia University Press.

WRIGHT, L. (1988) The Type A behaviour pattern and coronary artery disease: Quest for the active ingredients and the elusive mechanism. *American Psychologist*, 43, 2–14.

ZAIDEL, E. (1983) A response to Gazzaniga. *American Psychologist*, 38, 542–546.

ZAJONC, R.B. (1984) On the primacy of affect. *American Psychologist*, 39, 117–123.

ZEKI, S. (1993) The visual image in mind and brain. In *Mind and Brain: Readings from Scientific American*. New York: W.H. Freeman and Company.

ZUCKERMAN, M. (1979) *Sensation Seeking: Beyond the Optimum Level of Arousal*. Hillsdale, NJ: Erlbaum.

INDEX

Please note that page numbers in **bold** refer to definitions and main explanations of particular concepts.

ablation studies, **34**
absolute refractory period (ARP), **8**
accidental damage to the brain, 33–4
accommodation, 72
acetylcholine (ACh), 10–11, 100, 107, 108
acetylcholinesterase (AChE), 10
ACh (*see* acetylcholine)
AChE (*see* acetylcholinesterase)
achromatic colour, **73**
achromatic light, 70
acromegaly, 28
ACTH (*see* adrenocorticotrophic hormone)
action potential, 7
activation synthesis theory of dreams, **107–8**
Adam, K., 97
Adam, M.N., 89
additive colour mixing, 76–7
ADH (*see* antidiuretic hormone)
adipocytes, 133
adipose tissue, 133
adrenal cortex, 29
adrenal glands, 28, 30, 170
adrenaline, 160, 170
adrenocorticotrophic hormone (ACTH), 28, 83, 170
adrenogenital syndrome (AGS), **30**
Aesculapius, 106, 111
afferent neurons (*see* sensory neurons)
age
    regression, 117
    and sleep, 88, 98
aggregate field, 74
aggression (*see* emotion)
agraphia, **55**
AGS (*see* adrenogenital syndrome)
Akil, L., 12
alarm reaction, 170
alcohol, 121
    and sleep, 98
Alcoholics Anonymous, 121
Alden, P., 118
all-or-none rule, **8**
Allen, Woody, 95
alpha waves, **38**, 85
Alzheimer's disease, 11, 42

amacrine cells, 73
amnesic aphasia (*see* anomic aphasia)
amotivational syndrome (and cannabis), 127
amphetamine psychosis, 123
amphetamines, 11, 122–4
amplitude (and electrical activity of the brain), 38
amygdala, 20, 21, 136, 151, 152
analgesic property (of opiates), 120, 124
analyser (left hemisphere as), 65–6
Anand, B.K., 135
Anderson, J.A., 161
androgens, 29, 30
ANF (*see* atrial natriuretic factor)
angiotensin, 136
angular gyrus, 57, 58
anomic aphasia (amnesic aphasia), **56–7**
anterior commissure, 20
anterior hypothalamus, 153
anterior pituitary gland, 28
antibodies, **171**
antidiuretic hormone (ADH), 28, 136
antigens, 171
anxiety, 11, 29, 98
aphagia, **133**
aphasia
    anomic, 56–7
    Boston classification of, 55
    Broca's, 55
    conduction, 57
    isolation, 57
    transcortical, 57–8
    Wernicke's, 55–6
aqueous humour, 72
arcuate fasciculus, 57
aromatic solvents, 122
Aron, A.P., 164
ARP (*see* absolute refractory period)
Aschoff, J., 82, 90
Aserinsky, Eugene, 85, 103
assertiveness training, **177**
association areas, **21**, 47–50
association neurons (connector neurons), **6**
ataxic aphasia (*see* Broca's aphasia)
atrial natriuretic factor (ANF), 30
auditory association areas, 49–50

auditory information, 46, 66
autonomic nervous system, **17**, 24–6, 72, 112, 121, 169–70
    and emotion, 160
    parasympathetic branch, **26**, 170
    and stress, 170
    sympathetic branch, **25**, 170
Ax, A.F., 159
axons, 6, 7

B-endorphin, 11–12
Balsubramamiam, V., 152
Bales, J., 123
Bandura, A., 176
Banyai, E.I., 117
Barber, T.X., 115, 116, 117, 118
barbiturates, 122
Bard, Philip, 150, 161–2
Barnard, C., 84
Baron, R.A., 114, 118
baroreceptors, **136**
Bartus, R.T., 11
basal ganglia, 20
Beaumont, J.G., 55, 57, 73
behaviour
    and ablation studies, 34
    and brain damage, 33–4
    influences on, 24
    and lesions, 34–5
    and the limbic system, 20
    species-typical, 20
    and stress, 177–8
    Type A personalities, 173–4, 178
    Type B personalities, 173–4
    see also emotion; motivation
behavioural inertia, 50
Berger, Hans, 38
Berkman, L.F., 177
Berry, D.T.R., 97
beta waves, **38**, 85
Bianchi, A., 108
bilateral representation, 59
bilateral stereotactic amygdalectomy, 162
binocular fields, 74
biofeedback, **26**, 175
bipolar cells, 72
Blakemore, C., 96

blind people and dreams, 104
blindsight, **74**
blind spot, 73
Bloch, V., 98
blood
 glucose levels, 132, 133
 and the immune system, 172
 sugar levels, 29
Blum, K., 123
Blundell, J.E., 134
bodily rhythms, **82**
 circadian rhythms, 82–3
 circannual rhythms, 89–90
 diurnal rhythms, 89
 infradian rhythms, 83–4
 menstrual cycle, 29–30, 83–4, 90
 Seasonal Affective Disorder (SAD), 90
 sleep-waking cycle, 83
 ultradian rhythms, 84–8
Bogen, Joseph, 61
Bokert, E., 104
Bolles, R.C., 141
Bolter, A., 126
Borberly, A., 93, 97, 109
Bornstein, M.H., 77
Boston classification of aphasias, 55
botulinum toxin, 10
Bowers, K.S., 114
Boyce, P., 90
Brady, J.V., 152
Braid, James, 111
brain
 ablation studies, **34**
 accidental damage to, 33–4
 chemical stimulation of, 37
 development, 16–17
 electrical self-stimulation of (ES-SB), 144–5
 electrical stimulation of (ESB), 35–7
 and emotion, 150–7
 and facial muscles, 161
 forebrain, 16, 19–21
 and gender, 155–6
 hindbrain, 16, 17–19
 hippocampus, 11, 20, 41, 153
 and language, 58–9
 see also aphasia
 lesion production, 34–5
 measurement of electrical activity, 38
 micro-electrode recording, 37
 midbrain, 16–19
 and motivation, 131–9
 pain centres, 36
 recording electrical activity of, 37–9
 scanning and imaging devices, 39–42
 triune model, **15**
 see also cerebral cortex
Brand, R.J., 174
Breggin, P.R., 152

Brehm, J.W., 141
Breuer, J., 117
Bridwell, L., 148
brightness, 70
Brobeck, J.R., 135
Broca, Paul, 33–4, 54, 155
Broca's aphasia, **55**
Broca's area, **54**, 58
Bruce, V., 74
Bruhn, J., 177
Brust, J.C.M., 41
Bucy, Paul, 151, 152
bundle theory, 67
Bush, George, 56

caffeine, 122
Cahill, A., 12
Cajal, Santiago Ramon y, 8
Campbell, S., 97
Campfield, L.A., 133
cancer, 172–3
cannabis, **127**
Cannon, Walter, 25, 131–2, 143, 158–9, 161, 162, 170
Cannon-Bard thalamic theory of emotion, **161–2**
Cantin, M., 30
carbachol, 100
carbohydrates, 136
cardiovascular disorders, 173–4
Carlson, N.R., 39, 48, 51, 57–8, 118, 120, 124, 125, 126, 133, 136, 152
Carson, R., 174
Cartwright, Rosalind, 106
CAT (*see* Computerised Axial Tomography)
catastrophic reaction, 154
catatonia (and PCP), 126
Caton, Richard, 38
CCK (*see* cholecystokinin)
cell body (cell soma), 6
cell soma (*see* cell body)
cellular dehydration, 136
central aphasia (*see* conduction aphasia)
central core (reptilian brain), 15
central fissure (fissure of Rolando), 21
central nervous system, 5, 15, 24, 169
cerebellum, 17–18
cerebral asymmetries
 and the intact brain, 66–7
 and the split-brain, 61–6, 67
cerebral cortex (new mammalian brain), 15, 19, 20, 21
 auditory association area, 49–50
 electrical stimulation of, 36
 and emotion, 150, 154–5
 frontal lobe damage, 50–1, 54
 fusiform gyrus (V4 area), 79
 holistic theory and, 51
 motor association areas, 47–8

primary auditory area, 46
primary motor area, 44–5
primary sensory areas, 45
primary somatosensory areas, 45–6
primary visual area, 46–7, 74–5
and psychological functions, 50
sensory association areas, 58–60
somatosensory association area, 48–9
temporal lobe damage, 51
theory of localisation, 44, 59
visual association area, 49
see also brain
cerebrospinal fluid (CSF), 17
cerebrovascular accidents (strokes), 33
cerebrum, 19, 21
Charcot, J.M., 117
Charles, E., 172
Chase, M., 100
chemical stimulation of the brain, **37**
chimerics, 65
cholecystokinin (CCK), 132, 136
choline, 11
choroid coat, 72
chromatic colour, **73**
chromatic light, 70
ciliary muscles, 72
cingulate gyrus, 20, 153, 155, 156
circadian rhythms, **82–3**
circannual rhythms, **89–90**
Clarke, P.R.F., 99
clinical and anatomical methods of investigating the brain, 33–4
CNS (*see* central nervous system)
Coca-Cola, 123
cocaine (cocaine hydrochloride), 122, 123–4
cocaine psychosis, 123
codeine, 124
Coe, W.C., 114, 115
cognitive appraisal (in emotion), **162**
Cohen, D.B., 104, 105
Cold Pressor Test (CPT), 115, 116
Collee, J., 106, 109
colour vision, 75–9
 colour blindness, 77
 colour constancy, **78–9**
 colour Mondrians, 78
 and the colour wheel, 76–7
 and complementary colours, 76
 and light wavelengths, 70
 negative after-images, 77–8
 opponent process theory of, 77–8
 and rods, 73
 Young-Helmholtz theory of, 77
 see also visual perception
coma (and PCP), 126
combativeness (and PCP), 126
commissurotomy, **61**, 62, 66
complex cell, 74

Computerised Axial Tomography (CAT), **39–40**
computerised electroencephalography, **39**
conduction aphasia, **57**
connector neurons (*see* association neurons)
cones, 72
contralateral connection, **17**, 45
controlled drinking (treatment of alcoholism), 122
convulsions (and PCP), 126
coping strategies, 176–7
Corbit, J., 146
cornea, 72
Cornell-Bell, A.H., 6
corpus callosum, 21, 61, 62, 67, 154
cortex (*see* cerebral cortex)
cortical steroids (*see* corticosteroids)
corticospinal decussation, **45**
corticosteroids, 28, 170
corticotrophin-releasing hormone, 28, 170
Cotman, C.W., 50
Council, J.R., 114
countershock phase (of alarm reaction), 170
CPT (*see* Cold Pressor Test)
crack cocaine, 124
cranial nerves, 24
cretinism, 29
Crick, Francis, 108–9
cross-modal matching, **49**
Crowne, D.P., 142
CSF (*see* cerebrospinal fluid)
Cullition, B.J., 152
curare, 10

Dalton, K., 84
Damasio, A.R., 58
Damasio, H., 58
Davidson, R.J., 154, 155
Darwin, C., 142
de-activation, **10**
decortication (and emotion), **150**
Delgado, Jose, 35, 44–5, 153
delirium tremens, 121
delta waves, **38**, 86
delta-9-tetrahydrocannabinol (THC), 127
Dement, William, 85, 93, 97, 98, 103, 104
dendrites, 6, 9
Department of Health, 124
depersonalisation (and LSD), 126
depressant drugs, **120–2**
depression, 90
Devalois, R.L., 78
diabetes mellitus, 29
Dicara, L.V., 26
dichotic listening tasks, **67**
dichromatic vision, 77
disease model of alcoholism, **121**
diseases of adaptation, 170

diurnal rhythms, **89**
diurnal types, 89
Divac, I., 50
divided field technique, **63**
Dixon, N.F., 174
Dixon, P., 177
Dockray, G.J., 132
dominant hemisphere (*see* major hemisphere)
Donchin, E., 39
dopamine, 11, 20, 124, 126, 144
dorsal hypothalamus, 150
dorsal root, 15
double brain theory, **67**
dreams, 39, 85, 103–10
    activation synthesis theory of, 107–8
    Freud's theory of, 104–6
    lucid dreaming, 104
    problem-solving theories of, 106
    reprogramming theories of, 106–7
    research findings concerning, 103–4
    reverse learning theory of, 108–9
    and sleep stages, 103
    and sleepwalking, 104
    see also sleep
drinking, 136–7
drive reduction theory of motivation, **143–5**
drugs, 120–30
    addiction, **120**, 146
    cannabis, 127
    depressants (sedatives), 120–2
    hallucinogens, 125–6
    opiates, 124–5
    psychological dependence, **120**
    psychotherapeutic, 174–5
    stimulants, 122–4
    tolerance, **120**
    withdrawal (abstinence syndrome), **120**
dry mouth theory of thirst, **136**
dual hypothalamic control theory of eating, **135**
Dutton, D.G., 164
dysphasia, 54

eating, 131–6
Eccles, J.C., 118
ecstasy (MDMA), 122, 124
EEG (*see* electroencephalogram)
EEG imaging, 39
efferent neurons (*see* motor neurons)
ego theory, 67
Ekman, P., 166
electrical self-stimulation of the brain (ES-SB), **144–5**
electrical stimulation of the brain (ESB), **35–7**
electroencephalogram (EEG), **38–40**, 66, 84–5, 87, 111

electromyogram (EMG), **38**, 85, 87
electrooculogram (EOG), **38**, 85, 87
Ellenberg, L., 66
Ellison, G.D., 150
emergent cycle of sleep, 86
EMG (*see* electromyogram)
emotion
    and the brain, 150–7
    Cannon-Bard thalamic theory of, 161–2
    and the cerebral cortex, 150, 154–5
    facial expression of, 160–1
    facial feedback theory, 161
    and gender, 155–6
    and the hypothalamus, 150–2, 162
    James-Lange theory of, 158–61
    Lazarus' theory of, 165–6
    and the limbic system, 151–3, 162
    and misattribution therapy, 165
    Schachter and Singer's (two-factor) theory of, 162–5
    theories of, 158–68
emotion-focused coping strategies, **176**
Empson, J.A.C., 97, 99
encephalin, 12
endogenous cues (and bodily rhythms), 83
endocrine system, 5, 24, 25, 26–30, 170
    adrenal glands, 28
    gonads, 29–30
    heart, 30
    pancreas, 29
    parathyroid glands, 229
    pituitary gland, 19, 27, 28, 84
    thyroid glands, 28–9
endogenous opioid peptides (endorphins), **11–12**, 115, 125, 174
endorphins (*see* endogenous opioid peptides)
entorhinal cortex, 153
EOG (*see* electrooculogram)
Epidaurus, 106
epilepsy, 61, 66
epinephrine, 28, 122, 163–4
Epstein, A.N., 135
Epstein-Barr virus, 172
Erhardt, A., 30
eros, 148
Ervin, F., 152
Eskdale, James, 111
Esquirol, J., 90
Esterling, B., 172
estrogen, 29, 30
ethologists, 142
eustress, **169**, 171
Evans, C., 96, 106, 114
Evans, F.J., 114
evoked potential, **39**
evolutionary theories of sleep, **95–6**
exercise, 97, 175–6
exocrine glands, 26

exogenous cues (and bodily rhythms), **83**
expectancy theory of motivation, **145–6**
expressive aphasia (*see* Broca's aphasia)
extracellular body compartments, 137
extroverts, 89
eye, 71–4
    see also colour vision; visual perception
Eysenck, M.W., 166

facial expressions of emotion, 160–1
facial feedback theory of emotion, **161**
facial muscles, 161
False Memory Syndrome, **118**
fats, 132, 133, 135
Fechner, Gustav, 36
Festinger, L., 142
fight-or-flight response, 25, 161, 170
Fink, George, 42
Fischman, J., 39
Fisher, K.C., 89
Fisher, L.E., 175
Fisher, S., 89, 105, 175
fissure of Rolando (*see* central fissure)
fissure of Sylvius (*see* lateral fissure)
fixation point, 62
fixed action pattern, 142
Fleming, R., 177
Flourens, Pierre, 34
fluent aphasia (*see* Wernicke's aphasia)
Flynn, J.P., 150
foetal alcohol syndrome, 121
Folkhard, S., 169, 176
Folkman, S., 169, 176
follicle stimulating hormone, 29
forebrain, 16, 19–21
formication (and cocaine), 123
fornix, 20
Foulkes, D., 105, 106–7, 108
fovea, 73
Fox, J.L., 45
free basing, 124
frequency (and electrical activity of the brain), 38
Freud, Sigmund, 56, 104–5, 117, 123
    theory of dreams, 104–6, 107
    theory of motivation, 148
Frese, M., 171
Friedman, Meyer, 173, 178
Friedman, M.I., 135
Frolich, Alfred, 134
frontal lobe, 21, 50
frontal lobotomy, 51
functional architecture, 74
functional reorganisation, 59
fusiform gyrus (V4 area), 79

GABA (*see* Gamma-Amino-Butyric Acid)
Galen, 33
Gall, Franz Joseph, 44, 54

Gallagher, D.W., 11
Gamma-Amino-Butyric Acid (GABA), 11, 121
ganglia, 25, 26
ganglion cells, 73
Gardner, Randy, 93, 94
GAS (*see* general adaptation syndrome)
Gazzaniga, Michael, 61, 62, 64
Geen, R.G., 131
Geiselman, P.J., 133
general adaptation syndrome (GAS), **169–71**, 172
Genest, J., 30
geniculostriate path, **74**
Geschwind, Norman, 55, 56, 57, 58
giant cells, 107
Gilbert, J.A., 93
Gillett, P.L., 115
glands, 26, 90
    see also endocrine system
glial cells, 5–6
glucagon, 29
glucoreceptors, 133, 134
glucose/blood levels, 132, 133
glucostat, **133**
glucostatic theory, **133**
gold thioglucose, 133
gonads, 28, 29–30
Gordon, R.M., 12, 165
Gottleib, G., 143
graded potential, **8**
Green, P.R., 74
Green, S., 74, 135, 143, 145, 175
Greenberg, R., 89, 98, 105, 175
Grossman, M.I., 132
growth hormone (*see* somatotrophin)
Gunter, Barry, 93, 94
Gur, Robin, 41, 155, 156
Gwinner, E.A., 89

Haber, R.N., 78
Hakmiller, K.L., 160
Hall, Calvin, 104, 105
Halligan, P.W., 48
hallucinations (positive and negative), 112
hallucinogens (psychedelics), **125–6**
Harburg, E., 174
hardiness (and stress), **176**
Hartmann, E.L., 97, 106
hash (*see* hashish)
hashish (hash), 127
Hassett, J., 117
hat phenomenon (in sleep deprivation), 94
Hauri, P., 103
Hayes, N.J., 118
hearing, 46, 66
heart, 30
    cardiovascular disorders, 173–4
    reduction in heart rate, 26

Hering, Edward, 77–8
Herman, J., 106
heroin, 124–5
Hershenson, M., 78
Hetherington, A.W., 134
Heuser, J.E., 9
hibernation theory of sleep, **96**
Hicks, R., 173–4
hidden observer phenomenon, **115**, 116
hierarchy of needs, 146–8
Hilgard, Ernest, 113, 114–15, 117, 165
Hill, A.J., 134
hindbrain, 16, 17–19
Hinshaw, S.P., 122
hippocampus, 11, 20, 41, 136, 153
Hitzig, Eduard, 36
Hobson, J. Allan, 107–8
Hohmann, G.W., 159
holistic theory, 51, 59
homeostasis, **20**, 26, 131
homeostatic drive theory, **143**
horizontal cells, 73
hormones, 11, 25, 26–7
    and circadian rhythms, 82, 83
    and drinking, 136
    and eating behaviour, 132
    and emotion, 163–4
    and Seasonal Affective Disorder (SAD), 90
    and stress, 170
    types of, 28–30
Horne, J.A., 89
Hubel, David, 37, 73, 74
Hüber-Weidman, H., 94
hue, 70, 76
hunger, 131–6
Huntingdon's Chorea, 11
5-hydroxytryptophan, 100
hypercolumns, 74
hypercomplex cell, 74
hyperglycaemia, 29
hypermnesia, 116–17
hyperorality, 151
hyperphagia, 134
hyperphagic syndrome (dynamic and static phases), **134–5**
hypersexuality, 151
hypertension, 174
hyperthyroidism, 29
hypnagogic state, 85
hypnopaedia, 99
hypnopompic images, 86
hypnosis, 111–19
    and absorption, 113
    age regression, 113, 117
    as an analgesic, 111, 115–16
    animal magnetism, 111
    and behaviour control, 118
    characteristics of, **112–13**

hypnosis – *cont.*
  in criminal investigations, 116–18
  and fantasy proneness, 113
  genuineness of, 114
  history of, 111
  Hollywood theory of, 118
  individual susceptibility, 113–14
  inducing hypnotic states, 111–12
  neo-dissociation theory of, **114–15**
  non-state theory of, **116**
  and psychoanalytic theory, 117–18
  resistance to, 113
  and social role, 116
  state theory of, **114–16**
  and television technique, 117
hypnotherapist, 113
hypoglycaemia, 29
hypothalamus, 19–20, 27
  and drinking, 136–7
  and eating, 20, 34, 133, 134–6
  and electrical self-stimulation of the
    brain (ES-SB), 144–5
  and emotion, 150–2, 162
  and heat control, 20
  and pain, 36
  and 'pleasure', 20, 36
  and sex drive, 20
  and stress, 170
  and water balance, 20
  suprachiasmatic nuclei (SN), 83, 99
hypothyroidism, 29

Ibuprofen, 30
illusions, 75
immune system, 170, 171–2
immunoglobulin A, 172
incentive theory of motivation, **145–6**
indifference reaction, 154
infradian rhythms, 30, **83–4**
infundibulum (pituitary stalk), 28
instinct theories of motivation, **142–3**
insulin, 29
interleukin b, 172
intracellular body compartments, 137
introverts, 89
invasive methods (of investigating the
  brain), 33, 34–7
iodopsin, 73
ipsilateral connection, **17**, 45
iris, 72
isolation aphasia, **57**
Iversen, L.L., 9

Jackson, John Hughlings, 56
Jacobs, B.L., 126
Jacobs, G.H., 78
Jacobs, R.G., 175
Jacobs, T.J., 172
Jacobson, W., 175

James, William, 142, 158–61, 162, 164
James-Lange theory of emotion, **158–61**
Janiger, Oscar, 84
Janowitz, H.P., 132
jargon (*see* neologisms)
Jasnos, T.M., 160
jet lag, 83
Johnson, R.N., 151
Jouvet, M., 99–100, 109

K-complexes, 85
Kales, A., 97
Keane, M.J., 166
Keesey, R.E., 133, 135
Kekule, August, 108
Kertesz, A., 55, 56
Keye, W.R., 84
Kihlstrom, J.F., 113
Kimura, D., 59, 155
Kimzey, S., 172
Kinnunen, T., 114
Kluver, Heinrich, 151, 152
Kluver-Bucy syndrome, 151
Kobasa, S.C., 176
Korsakoff's psychosis, 42
Koukkou, M., 107
Krantz, D., 174

L-dopa, 11
lactogenic hormone (*see* prolactin)
Land, Edwin, 78–9
Lange, Carl, 158, 159, 160, 161, 162, 164
language, 48, 58–9
  lateralisation of, 59
  and split-brain patients, 62–4
  and the theory of localisation, 44, 59
  see also aphasia
Larson, J.B. Jnr., 145
Lashley, Karl, 51, 59, 61
latent content (of dreams), **105**
lateral fissure, 21
lateral geniculate body, 19
lateral geniculate nucleus (LGN), 74
lateral hypothalamus (LH), 133, 134–6,
  150
lateral preoptic area (of hypothalamus)
  (LPH), 136
lateralisation, **59**, 61
Laurence, J.R., 117
law of equipotentiality, **59**
law of mass action, **51**
Lazarus, Richard, 165–6, 169, 176
Lazarus' theory of emotion, **165–6**
learned helplessness, **141**
learning and drive reduction theory, 143–5
Leary, Timothy, 126
LeDoux, J.E., 153, 166
Lefcourt, H.M., 174
left visual field, 47, 62, 63, 64, 66

Lehman, D., 107
lens, 72
lesion production, 34–5
leucocytes, 171, 172
Leviant, Isia, 75
Levine, J.D., 12
Levy, J., 64, 65
Levy, S., 173
Lewis, O.F., 97
Ley, R.G., 154
LGN (*see* lateral geniculate nucleus)
LH (*see* lateral hypothalamus)
librium, 175
light, 70
  and the menstrual cycle, 84
limbic system (old mammalian brain), 15,
  20, 35, 162
  and emotion, 151–3
lipids, 132, 133
lipogenesis, 135
lipolysis, 135
lipostatic theory, **133**
liver, 132
Lloyd, P., 9
lobotomy (*see* frontal lobotomy)
localisation, **44**, 51, 59
locus coeruleus, 100
locus of control, **141**, 176
Long, Crawford, 111
longitudinal fissure, 21
long-sightedness, 72
Loomis, A.L., 84
Lord, B.J., 25
LPH (*see* lateral preoptic area)
LSD (*see* lysergic acid diethylamide)
Luce, G.G., 83, 84
lucid dreaming, **104**
Lugaressi, E., 95
Luriea, A.R., 50, 55
lysergic acid diethylamide (LSD), 125–6
luteinising hormone, 29

MacLean, Paul, 15, 17, 153
macula lutea, 73
magic mushrooms, 125
Magnetic Resonance Imaging (MRI), **40**
magnetoencephalograms (MEG), **39**
Magoun, H.W., 99
mamillary body, 20
Mandler, G., 159
major (dominant) hemisphere, 63
manifest content (of dreams), **105**
Manning, A., 89
mantra, 175
Manuck, S., 174
Maranon, G., 159
marijuana, 127
Mark, V., 152
Marks, L.E., 77

Marks, M., 82, 89
Marlowe, D., 142
Marshall, G., 165
Marshall, N.B., 133, 134
Martin, J.H., 41
Martin, R.A., 174
Maslach, C., 165
Maslow, A., 146–8
Maslow's theory of motivation, **146–8**
master clock, 83
Maunsell, J.H.R., 74
Mayer, J., 133, 134
McCann, J.J., 78
McCanne, T.R., 161
McCarley, Robert, 107–8
McClelland, D.C., 141
McDougall, W., 142
McGaugh, J.L., 50
McWilliams, S.A., 126
MDMA (*see* ecstasy)
measurement of brain waves, 38
Meddis, R., 83, 95
medial geniculate body, 19
medicine preference effect, 134
meditation, 175
medulla oblongata, 17–18, 45
median forebrain bundle (MFB), 144
MEG (*see* magnetoencephalograms)
Meichenbaum, D.H., 176
melatonin, 30, 90, 99
memory consolidation theory of sleep, **99**
menarche, 84, 90
meninges, 17
menstrual cycle, 29–30, 83–4, 90
mescaline, 125
Mesmer, Franz Anton, 111
mesmerism, 111
methadone, 125
methylenedioxymethamphetamine (*see* MDMA)
methylphenidate (Ritalin), 122
MFB (*see* median forebrain bundle)
micro-electrodes, 37
micro-electrode recordings, **37**
microspectrophotometry research, 78
midbrain, 16, 19
Miller, G.A., 131
Miller, L., 155
Miller, N., 123
Miller, N.E., 26
Miller, R.J., 112
Milner, B., 54
Milner, Peter, 36, 144
minor (subordinate) hemisphere, 63
misattribution therapy, **165**
Mitchell, T.R., 145
Mitchison, Graeme, 108–9
mixed transcortical aphasia (MTA), 57
Money, J., 30

Moniz, Egas, 59
monoamine, 99
monoamine hypothesis of sleep, **100**
monoamine neurotransmitters, 99–100
monochromatic vision, 77
Moos, R.H., 177
Morales, F., 100
Morgan, A.H., 114
Morris, C.G., 39
Morris, J.N., 175
Moruzzi, G., 99
motivation
    biologically based motives, 140
    and the brain, 131–9
    complex psychosocial motives, **140**, 141–2
    deficiency or D-motives, **147**
    and drinking, 136–7
    drive reduction theory, 143–5
    expectancy theory of, 145–6
    Freud's theory of, 148
    growth or being (B-motives), **147**
    and hunger, 131–6
    incentive theory of, 145–6
    instinct theories of, 142–3
    intrinsic and extrinsic reward, **146**
    Maslow's humanistic theory of, 146–8
    opponent process theory of, 146
    optimum level of arousal (OLA) theory of, 145
    sensation-seeking, 140–1, 145
    social motives, **141–2**
    theories of, 140–9
    work motivation, 145–6
motor aphasia (*see* Broca's aphasia)
motor areas, 21, 47–8
motor association areas, 47–8
motor neurons (efferent neurons), **6**, 24
motor strip (*see* primary motor area)
MRI (*see* Magnetic Resonance Imaging)
MTA (*see* mixed transcortical amnesia)
multiple sclerosis, 7
Murray, H.A., 141
muscular memory, 18
myelin sheath, 6, 7–8
Myers, Reginald, 61

nAch (*see* need for achievement)
nAff (*see* need for affiliation)
nApp (*see* need for approval)
naloxone, 12, 125
narcolepsy, 122
Nathans, J., 77
Nauta, W.J.H., 152
Nebes, R.D., 63
need for achievement (nAch), **141**
need for affiliation (nAff), **141**
need for approval (nApp), **141**
need for power (nPower), **141**

negative after-images, 77–8
negative feedback loop, 27
Neill, J., 125
neologisms, 56
nerves, 6–7
    cranial, 24
    optic, 72
    roots, 15
    spinal, 24
    vagus, 131, 132
    nervous system (NS), 5
    central nervous system, 5, 24
    see also peripheral nervous system
neural tube, 16
neuroendocrine reflex, 28
neuromodulators, 5, **11**, 12
neurons, 5
    damage to, 24
    development of, 16
    in the eye, 73
    function of, 7–10
    resting state, 7
    structure of, 6–7
    types of, 6
neurotoxin, 133
neurotransmitters, 5, 8, 9, **10–12**, 25, 37–8
    de-activation, 10
    and emotion, 161
    and hormones, 27
    monoamine, 88–100
    re-uptake, 10
    and REM sleep, 100
    types of, 9
new mammalian brain (*see* cerebral cortex)
Newsome, W.T., 74
Newton, Sir Isaac, 70, 75–6
nicotine, 122
Nielson, M., 117
Nisbett, R.E., 133
nodes of Ranvier, 7, 8
nominal aphasia (*see* anomic aphasia)
non-fluent aphasia (*see* Broca's aphasia)
non-invasive methods (of investigating the brain), 33, **37–42**, 163
non-rapid eye movement sleep (NREM sleep), **85**
noradrenaline (*see* norepinephrine)
norepinephrine, 11, 27, 28, 100, 124, 136, 161, 170
Norman, R., 78
nPower (*see* need for power)
NREM sleep (*see* non-rapid eye movement sleep)
novel stimulation, 140
nucleus acubens, 144

obesity, 134
occipital lobe, 21

oculomotor system maintenance theory of sleep, **99**
ocular dominance, 74
Ohtsuka, T., 77
OLA theory (*see* optimum level of arousal theory of motivation)
old mammalian brain (*see* limbic system)
Olds, James, 36, 144
olfaction, 19, 20
olfactory bulb, 19, 20
opiate receptors, 125
opiates, **124–5**
opium poppy, 124
opponent-process theory of colour vision, 77–8
opponent-process theory of motivation, **146**
optic chiasma, 47
optic disc, 73
optic nerve, 72
optimum level of arousal (OLA) theory of motivation, **145**
orienting reflex, **19**
Orne, Martin, 114, 116
Ornstein, R., 67, 71
osmoreceptors, **136**
osmosis, 136
osmotic thirst, **136**
Osterberg, O., 89
Oswald, Ian, 96, 97, 98
oxytocin, 28
ovaries, 29

Paige, Karen, 30
pain centres, 36, 144
pancreas, 29
Papez, J.W., 153
Papez circuit, **153**
Papez-MacLean limbic model of emotion, 153
parachlorophenylalanine (PCPA), 100
paranoid delusions (and amphetamines), 122
paranoid schizophrenia (and amphetamines), 123
parathormone, 29
parathyroid glands, 29
paraventricular nucleus (PVN), 136
Parfit, D., 67
parietal lobe, 21
Parker, G., 90
Parkinson's disease, 11, 20
Parrott, A., 124
Passingham, R.E., 50
Patrick, G.T.W., 93
Pattie, F.A., 115
PCP (*see* phencyclidine)
PCPA (*see* parachlorophenylalanine)
peak experiences, **147**

Pearlman, C., 98
Pellegrini, R., 173–4
Penfield, Wilder, 36, 44–5, 46, 51, 57
Pengelley, E.T., 89
Pennebaker, J.W., 112
peripheral nervous system (PNS), 5, 16, 18, 24–6
  autonomic nervous system, 17, 24–6, 112
  and emotion, 160
  parasympathetic branch, 26, 170
  and stress, 170
  somatic nervous system, 24
  sympathetic branch, 25
Perry, C., 117
perseveration, **50**
Pert, C.B., 11
PET (*see* Positron Emission Tomography)
phencyclidine (PCP), 125, 126
phenothiazines, 11
phonemic paraphrasias, 55
photochemical reaction, 73
photons, 70, 73
photopic vision, **73**
photopigment, 77
photoreceptors (*see* photosensitive cells)
photosensitive cells, 72–3
phototherapy, 90
phrenology, 44, 54
pineal gland, 30, 90, 99
Pinel, J.P.J., 122, 132, 134, 136
Pines, A., 176
pituitary gland, 19, 27, 28, 84, 97, 170
pituitary stalk (*see* infundibulum)
pituitary-adrenal stress syndrome (*see* general adaptation syndrome)
placebo effect, **12**, 111
plasticity (of the brain), **59**
PMS (*see* pre-menstrual syndrome)
pleasure centres (in the brain), 144
polygraph, 38
pons, 17, 18, 100, 107
Ponzo illusion, 112
Positron, Emission Tomography (PET), **40–1**, 58, 153, 155
post-hypnotic amnesia, **112**, 113, 114
post-hypnotic suggestion, **113**
post-synaptic membrane, 9
posterior pituitary gland, 28
Powley, T.L., 133, 135
pre-menstrual syndrome (PMS), 30, 84
pre-synaptic membrane, 9
precognitive emotional responses, 153
primary and secondary appraisal (of stressors), **171**
primary auditory area, 46
primary motor area, 44–5
primary sensory areas, 45–7
primary sex characteristics, 29

primary somatosensory area, 45–6
primary visual area, 46–7, 74
primitive evaluative perception, 166
problem-solving theories of dreaming, **106**
progesterone, 29, 30
progressive relaxation, 175
prolactin, 28, 82
prostoglandins, 12, 30
protein synthesis, 98
psilocybe mexicana (*see* psilocybin)
psilocybin (psilocybe mexicana), 125
psychedelics (*see* hallucinogens)
psychoactive drugs (*see* drugs)
psychological dependence on drugs, 120
psychological reactance, **141**
psychoneuroimmunology, **172**
psychosurgery, 51, 152
psychotherapeutic drugs, 174–5
Pucetti, R., 67
pupil, 72
Purkinje cells, 18
PVN (*see* paraventricular nucleus)

quiet biting attack, 150

Rabin, B., 172
Ragland, D.R., 174
Raichle, Marcus, 58
Ranson, S.W., 134
raphe nuclei, 100
rapid eye movement sleep (REM sleep), **85**, 86, 87, 97–9, 106, 107–8
Rapport, M.D., 122
RAS (*see* reticular activating system)
Rathus, S.A., 117
receptive aphasia (*see* Wernicke's aphasia)
receptive field, **73**
receptor sites, 9
Rechtschaffen, Allan, 85, 94
reflex
  arc, 6
  neuroendocrine, 28
  orienting, 19
  spinal, 15
regression, 117
Reinberg, A., 84, 90
Reisenzein, R., 164
Reiser, M., 117
relative absorptions, 79
relative refractory period (RRP), **8**
relaxation, 175
releasing hormones, 28
REM Behaviour Disorder, 100
REM rebound effect, **97–8**
REM sleep (*see* rapid eye movement sleep)
REM starvation, **97**
repression, 117
reprogramming theory of dreaming, **106**
reptilian brain (*see* central core)

reserpine, 11
Restak, R., 36, 41
resting state, 7
restoration theories of sleep, **96–7**, 98
reticular activating system, 19, 99, 107
reticular formation, 19
  see also reticular activating system
re-uptake, **10**
retina, 47, 62, 63, 72
retinex theory of colour constancy, **78**
reverse learning theory of dreams, **108–9**
reverse tolerance (and cannabis), 127
rhodopsin, 73
right visual field, 47, 62, 64, 66
Ritalin (*see* methylphenidate)
Roberts, L., 57
Robertson, J., 45, 59
Roby, T.B., 144
Rochford, G., 55, 56
Rodin, F., 134
rods, 72
Roffwarg, H., 106
Rogers, M., 173
Rolls, B.J., 137
Rosen, W., 120
Rosenkilde, C.E., 50
Rosenman, Ray, 173
Rosenthal, N., 90
Ross, E.D., 155
Rossi, E.I., 98
Rotter, J.B., 141, 146, 176
Routtenberg, A., 145
RRP (*see* relative refractory period)
Rubin, F., 99
Russek, M., 132
Ryback, R.S., 97

Sabbagh, K., 84
Sackheim, H.A., 155
Sacks, Oliver, 49
SAD (*see* Seasonal Affective Disorder)
saltatory conduction, **8**
Sanctorius, 83
satiety, **132**, 133, 134
saturation, **70**
Satz, P., 59
scanning and imaging devices, 39–42
Schachter, Stanley, 141, 162–5
Schachter and Singer's (two-factor theory)
  of emotion, **162–5**
schizophrenia, 11
scopolamine, 100
scotopic vision, 73
Schwann cells, 7
Schwartz, G.E., 159
sclera, 71
SCR (*see* Skin Conductance Reaction)
Seasonal Affective Disorder (SAD), 90
secondary sex characteristics, 29

sedatives (*see* depressants)
Segal, J., 83
self-actualisation, 147
self-efficacy expectations, **176**
Seligman, M.E.P., 141
Selye, Hans, 169, 170, 171
Sem-Jacobsen, C.W., 150
semantic paraphrasias, 56
sensory aphasia (*see* Wernicke's area)
sensory areas, 21
sensory deprivation studies, 140
sensory isolation, 140
sensory neglect, **48–9**
sensory neurons (afferent neurons), **6**, 24
sensory specific satiety, **134**
sentinel theory of sleep, **99**
septum pellucidum, 20, 152
serotonin, 11, 99, 124, 126, 136, 161
set point (and body weight), **133**
settling point (and body weight), **133**
sexual glands, 29–30
sexual responses, 25, 151, 164
sexual symbols in dreams, 105
sham rage, 150
Shapiro, G.M., 96
Sheffield, F.D., 144
shock phase (of alarm reaction), 170
short-sightedness, 72
Siegel, R.K., 126
Siffre, Michel, 82
sign stimulus, 142
simple cell, 74
Singer, Jerome, 159, 162–5
Single Positron Emission Tomography
  (SPET), 41
Skelton, J.A., 112
Skin Conductance Reaction (SCR), 114
sleep, 39, 93–102
  and age, 88, 98
  and alcohol, 98
  and anxiety, 98
  deprivation psychosis, 94
  emergent cycle of, 86
  evolutionary theories of, 95–6
  and exercise, 97
  hibernation theory of, 96
  hypnagogic state, 85
  memory consolidation theory of, 99
  monoamine hypothesis, 100
  non-rapid eye movement (NREM)
    sleep, 85
  oculomotor system maintenance theory
    of, 99
  and personality, 89
  paradoxical, **86**
  physiology of, 99–100
  and psychological problems, 97
  rapid eye movement (REM) sleep, 85,
    86, 87–8, 97–9, 106, 107–8

REM Behaviour Disorder, 100
  restoration theories of, 96–7, 98
  sentinel theory of, 99
  spindles, 85
  staircase, **86**
  Stage 1, 85, 86
  Stage 2, 85–6
  Stage 3, 86
  Stage 4, 86, 88, 97
  studies of sleep deprivation, 93–5, 97–8
  see also dreams
sleep-waking cycle, 83
Slochower, J., 134
Smith, A., 59
Smith, D.E., 126
SN (*see* suprachiasmatic nuclei)
Snyder, Fred, 99
Snyder, S.H., 11, 125
social desirability scale, 142
social model of alcoholism, **122**
social motives, 141–2
social support networks, 172, 177–8
sociobiologists, **143**
sodium potassium pumps, 7
Solomon, R., 146
somatic nervous system, **24**
somatotrophin, 28
Sonstroem, R.J., 176
Spanos, N.P., 114, 116
species-typical behaviour, **20**
speech (*see* language)
Sperry, Robert, 61, 62, 65, 66, 67
SPET (*see* Single Positron Emission
  Tomography)
spinal cord, 15, 16
  emotion and damage to, 160
spinal nerves, 15, 24
spinal reflex, 15
spinal vertebrae, 15
split-brain operations, **34**
split-brain patients, 34, 61–6, 67, 154
SQUID (*see* Superconducting Quantum
  Imaging Device)
Stanford Hypnotic Susceptibility Scale,
  113
stereotaxic apparatus, **34**, 35, 37
steroids, 28, 172
stimulants, **122–4**
stomach loading, **132**
stress, 169–80
  alarm reaction (of GAS), **170**
  and cancer, 172–3
  and cardiovascular disorders, 173–4
  coping strategies, 176–7
  definition of, **169**
  effects on the body, 169–71
  and exercise, 175–6
  exhaustion stage (of GAS), **170**
  and hypertension, 174

stress – *cont.*
    and the immune system, 170, 171–2
    inoculation, 176
    management programmes, 176
    psychological responses to, 171
    reducing
        by changing behaviour, 177–8
        by changing cognitions, 176–7
        physiological responses, 174–6
    resistance stage (of GAS), **170**
Stricker, E.M., 135
strokes (*see* cerebrovascular accidents)
subordinate hemisphere (*see* minor
    hemisphere)
subtractive colour mixing, 76
Sugar, O., 59
summation, **10**
Superconducting Quantum Imaging
    Device (SQUID), 41
superperson syndrome, 177
suprachiasmatic nuclei (SN), 83, 99
suspension of planning (in hypnosis), **112**
suspension of self-control (in hypnosis),
    116
Sweeney, K., 172
Sweet, W.H., 151
symbols (in dreams), 105
synaesthesia (and LSD), 126
synapse (*see* synaptic cleft)
synaptic cleft (synapse), 8
synaptic transmission, 8–10
    and chemical stimulation of the brain,
        37
synaptic vesicles, 8
synthesiser (right hemisphere as), 65–6

Tache, J., 172
Tallma, J.F., 11
TAT (*see* Thematic Apperception Test)
Taylor, S., 171
Teitelbaum, P.H., 135
temporal lobe, 21, 51
temporal-limbic system, **155–6**
terminal buttons, 7, 8–9
testes, 29
testosterone, 29
thalamus, 19, 20, 74, 100, 156, 162
thanatos, 148
THC (*see* delta-9-tetrahydrocannabinol)
Thematic Apperception Test (TAT), 141
theory of localisation, 44, 59
theta waves, **38**, 85
threshold of response, **8**

thyrotrophic hormones, 28–9
thyroid gland, 28–9
thyroxin, 29
Tilley, A.J., 99
time management training, 177
Timonen, S., 84
Tinbergen, N., 142
tissue need, 143
Tolman, E.C., 142
Tomarken, A.J., 155
Tomkins, Sylvia, 160
TMA (*see* transcortical motor aphasia)
tracts, 6
trance logic, **114**
transcortical motor aphasia (TMA), 57
transcortical sensory aphasia (TSA), 57
transient cell, 73
trichromatic theory of colour vision (*see*
    Young-Helmholtz theory of colour
    vision)
trichromatic vision, 77
Trieschmann, R.B., 160
Tripp, Peter, 93, 94
triune model (of the brain), **15**
TSA (*see* transcortical sensory aphasia)
Tuttle, R.J., 126
Type A personalities, **173**–4, 178
Type B personalities, **173**–4

Ulmer, D., 178
ultradian rhythms, **84–8**

V4 area (*see* fusiform gyrus)
vagus nerve, 131, 132
Valenstein, E.S., 37, 153
valium, 11, 122, 175
van de Castle, R.L., 104
van Essen, D.C., 75
ventral root, 15
ventricles, 17
ventrobasal complex, 19
ventromedial hypothalamus (VMH)
    as satiety centre, 133, 134–6
    and emotion, 160
virtual paralysis, 86
viscera, 24
Visintainer, M., 172
visual agnosia, 49, 151
visual association area, 49–50
visual capture, 70
visual perception, 47, 70–81
    and the eye, 71–4
    illusions, 75

and light, 70
    primary visual area, 46–7, 74–5
    and split-brain patients, 62, 63, 64
    see also colour vision
vitreous humour, 72
VMH (*see* ventromedial hypothalamus)
Vogel, Philip, 61
volumetric thirst, **136**
von Helmholtz, H., 77, 78

Wada, Julian, 66
Wada test, **66**
Wahba, N., 148
Walker, S., 26
Wallace, B., 175
Ward, W.S., 111
Washburn, A.L., 131
wavelength, 70
Webb, W.B., 94, 95, 96, 97, 98, 106
Wehr, T., 90
Weil, A., 120, 127
Weiskrantz, L., 74
Wernicke, Carl, 33–4, 54, 58
Wernicke's aphasia, **55–6**
Wernicke's area, **54**, 58
Wernicke-Geschwind theory of language,
    58
Wever, R., 82, 90
White, K.M., 117
Whitman, Charles, 151
Wiesel, Torsten, 37, 73, 74
Williams, M., 56
Wolf, S., 159, 177
Wolff, H.G., 159
Wolpert, E., 104
Woodworth, R.S., 143
work motivation, 145–6
Wright, L., 174

Yashinski, E., 114
Yeomans, M., 124
Young, Thomas, 77, 78
Young-Helmholtz theory of colour vision
    (trichromatic theory of colour vision),
    77

Zaidel, Eran, 64
Zajonc, R.B., 165–6
Zeitgebers, **82**
Zeki, Semir, 75, 79
Zimbardo, P., 165
Zinberg, N.E., 127
Zuckerman, M., 145

PICTURE CREDITS

The authors and publisher would like to thank the following copyright holders for their permission to reproduce illustrative materials in this book:

Dr D. Cohen for Figure 9.2 (p. 87); **Harcourt, Brace and Company** for Figure 14.2 (p. 135); **Harper & Row, Publishers, Inc.** for Figure 3.1 (p. 25), reprinted with permission of HarperCollins Publishers, Inc; **Holt, Rinehart and Winston** for Figures 8.5 (p. 76) and 11.1 (p. 105) from *Psychology, Fourth Edition* by Spencer A. Rathus, copyright © 1990, reproduced by permission of the publisher and for Figures 10.1 (p. 95) and 14.1 (p. 132) from *Psychology: Science, Behavior, and Life, Second Edition* by Robert, L. Crooks and Jean Stein, copyright © 1991, reproduced by permission of the publisher; **Oxford University Press** for Figure 4.3 (p.36); **Isia Leviant** for Figure 8.4 (p. 75); **Prentice-Hall** for Figures 1.2 (p. 8) and 7.1 (p. 63); **The Science Photo Library** for Figures, 2.4 (p. 21), 6.1 (p. 54) and 6.2 (p. 57).

Every effort has been made to obtain necessary permission with reference to copyright material. The publishers apologise if inadvertently any sources remain unacknowledged and will be glad to make the necessary arrangements at the earliest opportunity.